Human Rights Law an Terrorism Strategies

In 2006, the United Nations urged Member States to ensure that counter terrorism policies guaranteed respect for human rights and the rule of law. This book demonstrates that, in many cases, counter terrorism policies relating to preventive detention, targeted killing and measures relating to returning foreign terrorist fighters have failed to respect human rights, and this encourages vulnerable people to be drawn towards supporting or committing acts of terrorism. Furthermore, in recent years, jurisprudence and public opinion in some countries have shifted from being at one stage more protective of human rights, to an acquiescence that some particularly draconian counter terrorism methods are necessary and acceptable. This book analyzes why this has happened, with a focus on the United States, United Kingdom, and Israel, and offers suggestions to address this issue. The work will be essential reading for students, academics and policy-makers working in the areas of human rights, humanitarian law, and counter terrorism.

Diane Webber is a British Solicitor who earned her doctorate at Georgetown University Law Center in Washington D.C. after working in private practice in London focusing on criminal law, and employment and discrimination law. She lives in Washington, D.C., writing on national security law and human rights issues.

Routledge Research in Terrorism and the Law

Available titles in this series include

Domestic Counter-Terrorism in a Global World
Post-9/11 Institutional Structures and Cultures in Canada and the UK
Daniel Alati

Anti-Terrorism Law and Foreign Terrorist Fighters
Edited By Jessie Blackbourn, Deniz Kayis, and Nicola McGarrity

Digital Privacy, Terrorism and Law Enforcement
The UK's Response to Terrorist Communication
Simon Hale-Ross

National Security, Personal Privacy and the Law
Surveying Electronic Surveillance and Data Acquisition
Sybil Sharpe

Law, Politics and Countering Violent Extremism
Mustafa Amin Farooq

Tackling Terrorism in Britain
Threats, Responses, and Challenges Twenty Years After 9/11
Steven Greer

Human Rights Law and Counter Terrorism Strategies
Dead, Detained or Stateless
Diane Webber

For more information about this series, please visit: www.routledge.com/Routledge-Research-in-Terrorism-and-the-Law/book-series/TERRORISMLAW

Human Rights Law and Counter Terrorism Strategies

Dead, Detained or Stateless

Diane Webber

First published 2022
by Routledge
4 Park Square, Milton Park, Abingdon, Oxon OX14 4RN

and by Routledge
605 Third Avenue, New York, NY 10158

Routledge is an imprint of the Taylor & Francis Group, an informa business

British Library Cataloguing-in-Publication Data
A catalogue record for this book is available from the British Library

Library of Congress Cataloging-in-Publication Data
A catalog record for this book has been requested

ISBN: 978-0-367-42001-7 (hbk)
ISBN: 978-0-367-42035-2 (pbk)
ISBN: 978-0-367-81727-5 (ebk)

DOI: 10.4324/9780367817275

Typeset in Galliard
by Apex CoVantage, LLC

Contents

Acknowledgements

This book could not have been written without the encouragement and support of many people, particularly my wonderful family, John, Daniel, Katie, Jonathan, and Leora.

I especially want to thank Jonathan Hall Q.C., David Koplow, Gary Solis, and David Stewart for their comments and suggestions along the way.

Tables

Table of cases

Africa

African Commission on Human and Peoples' Rights v. Libya, Appl. No. 002/2013, Judgment, African Court on Human and Peoples' Rights, (Jun. 3, 2016)

European Court of Human Rights

A. and Others v. United Kingdom, Appl. No. 3455/05, ECtHR (Feb. 19, 2009)
Al-Jedda v. United Kingdom, Appl. No. 27021/08, ECtHR (Jul. 7, 2011)
Al-Saadoon & Mufhdi v. United Kingdom, Appl. No. 61498/08, ECtHR (Jun. 30, 2009)
Al- Skeini v. United Kingdom. Appl. No. 55721/07, ECtHR (Jul. 7, 2011)
Bankovic v. Belgium, Appl. No. 52207/99, ECtHR (Dec. 12, 2001)
Benzer v. Turkey, Appl. No. 23502/06, ECtHR (Mar. 24, 2014)
Brannigan and McBride v. United Kingdom, Appl. No. 5/1992/350/423-4, ECtHR (Apr. 22, 1993).
Brogan v. United Kingdom, Appl. No. 11209/94;11234/84; 112266/84; 11386/85/, ECtHR (Nov. 29, 1988)
Brusco v. France, Appl. No. 1466/07, ECtHR (Oct. 14, 2010)
Cuilla v. Italy, Appl. No. 11152/84, ECtHR (Feb. 22, 1989)
Dayanan v. Turkey, Appl. No. 7377/03, ECtHR (Jan. 13, 2010)
De Tommaso v. Italy, Appl. No. 43395/09. ECtHR (Feb. 23, 2017)
Finogenov & Ors. v. Russia., Appl. Nos. 18299/03, 27311/03, Final Judgment, ECtHR, (Jun. 4, 2012)
Fox, Hartley and Campbell v. United Kingdom, Appl. Nos. 12244/86, 12245/86, 12383/86, ECtHR (Aug. 30, 1990)
Gasyak v. Turkey, Appl. No. 27872/03, ECtHR (Jan. 13, 2010)
Ghoumid and Others v. France, Appl. No. 52273/16, ECtHR (Jun. 25, 2020)
Grubic v. Croatia, Appl. No. 5384/11, ECtHR (Oct. 30, 2012)
Grubnyk v. Ukraine, Appl. No. 58444/15, ECtHR (Sep. 17, 2020)
Guzzardi v. Italy, Appl. No. 7367/76, ECtHR (Jun. 7, 1980)
Hassan v. United Kingdom, Appl. No. 29750/09, ECtHR (Sep. 16, 2014)

France

Inter-American Court of Human Rights (IACtHR) and Inter-American Commission on Human Rights (IACHR)

Ameziane, Djamel, v. United States of America, IACHR, Case No. 12.865, Report No. 29/20, OEA/Ser.L/V/II, Doc. 39 (Apr. 22, 2020)

Baldeon-Garcia v. Peru, IACtHR (Series C) No. 147, Judgment (2006)

Calderon, Acosta, IACtHR (Series C) No. 129, Judgment, (Jun. 24, 2005) (Ecuador)

Habeas Corpus in Emergency Situations, (Arts. 27(2) and 7(6) of the American Convention on Human Rights), Advisory Opinion OC-8/87, IACtHR. (Ser. A) No. 8 (Jan. 30, 1987)

IACHR Guantanamo Bay Precautionary Measures (No. 259/02) (Mar. 12, 2002)

IACHR Extension of Guantanamo Bay Precautionary Measures (No. 259/02) (Oct. 28, 2005)

IACHR Extension of Guantanamo Bay Precautionary Measures (No. 259/02) (Jul. 23, 2013)

IACHR Precautionary Measure 8/06, Omar Khadr, United States (Mar. 21, 2006)

IACHR Precautionary Measure 211/08, Djamel Ameziane, United States, (Aug. 20, 2008)

IACHR Precautionary Measure 422/14, Mustafa Adam Al-Hasawi, United States, (Mar. 21, 2015)

Jiminez, Dayra Maria Levoyer, Case No. 11.922, Report No. 66/01 IACHR, (Jun. 14, 2001) (Ecuador)

Judicial Guarantees in States of Emergency (Arts. 27(2), 25 and 8 of the American Convention on Human Rights), Advisory Opinion OC-9/87, IACtHR (Ser. A) No. 9 (Oct. 6, 1987)

Leiva, Barrieto v. Venezuela, 19 IHRR 810 (Nov. 17, 2009)

Lopez-Alvarez, Case No. 12.387, Report No. 124/01 IACtHR, Judgment of Feb. 1, 2006 (Honduras)

Montero Aranguren (Detention Center of Calia) v. Venezuela, IACtHR Series C No. 150 (2006)

Panday, Gangaram, IACtHR (Ser. C), No. 16, Judgment of Jan. 21, 1994 (Suriname)

Saldano v. Argentina, Report No. 38/99, IACHR, Mar. 11, 1999 (Annual Report, 1998)

Santo Domingo Massacre v. Colombia, IACtHR Judgment (Preliminary objections, Merits and Reparations) Series C No. 159 (Nov. 30, 2012).

Valencia and Llanos, IACHR, Report no. 79/11 Case No. 10.916 (Jul. 21, 2011) (Colombia)

Villagran-Morales v. Guatemala, IACtHR Series C No. 63 (Nov. 19, 1999)

Zambrano Velez v. Ecuador, IACtHR Series C No. 166, (Jul. 4, 2007)

International Court of Justice

Armed Activities on the Territory of the Congo (Democratic Republic of the Congo v. Uganda) Judgment, I.C.J. Reports 168 (2005)

Case Concerning Gabcikovo-Nagymaros Project, International Court of Justice, (Hungary/Slovakia) Judgment of 25 Sep. 1997, I.C.J. Reports (1997)

Case Concerning Oil Platforms, (Iran v. United States), [2003] I.C.J. Rep. 161

Legal Consequences of the Construction of a Wall in the Occupied Palestinian Territory, Advisory Opinion, I.C.J. Reports 136 (2004)

Legality of the Threat or Use of Nuclear Weapons, Advisory Opinion, I.C.J. Rep. 226 (1996)

Military and Paramilitary Activities in and against Nicaragua, Nicaragua v. United States of America, I.C.J. Reports (1986)

International Criminal Tribunal for Rwanda

Prosecutor v. Musema (Appeals Judgment) ICTR- 96–13-A (Nov. 16, 2001)

International Criminal Tribunal for the former Yugoslavia

Prosecutor v. Kupreskic, IT-95–16-T (Jan. 14, 2000)

Prosecutor v. Tadic, IT-94–1, Appeals Decision on Jurisdiction (Oct. 2, 1995)

Prosecutor v. Tadic, (Decision on the Defense Motion for Interlocutory Appeal on Jurisdiction) ICTY-94–1, (Oct. 2, 1995).

Israel

A v. State of Israel, CrimA 6659/06 62(4) PD 329 (Jun. 11, 2008)

Adalah Legal Center for Arab Minority Rights in Israel v. General Officer Commanding Central Command 60(3) PD 67 (2005)

Anonymous Persons v. Minister of Defense, CrimA 7048/97, 54(1) PD 721 (Apr. 12, 2002)

B'Tselem v. Judge Advocate General, HCJ 9594/03 (Aug. 21, 2011)

Physicians for Human Rights v. Israel Defense Force Commander in the Gaza Strip, HCJ 4764/04, 58(5) PD 385 (2004)

Public Committee Against Torture (PCAT) v. Government of Israel, HCJ 5100/94, (May 26, 1999)

Public Committee against Torture ("PCAT") v. Government of Israel, HCJ 769/02, (unreported judgment of Dec. 14, 2006).

Public Committee Against Torture v. The Government of Israel, HCJ 5100/94, 4054/95, 518/96, (Jul. 6, 2009)

United Kingdom

A (F.C.) and Others (F.C.) v. Secretary of State for the Home Department, [2004] UKHL 56 (Dec. 16, 2004)

Abu Hamza v. Secretary of State for the Home Department, Special Immigration Appeals Commission, Appeal No. SC/23/2003 (Nov. 5, 2010)

United Nations Human Rights Committee

United Nations Committee on the Rights of the Child

United States

Husayn v. Mitchell, 938 F.3d 1123 (Sep. 18, 2019)
In re: Guantanamo Bay Detainee Litigation, Misc. No. 08–442 (TFH) (D.D.C. Mar. 13, 2009)
Kareem v. Haspel, 412 F. Supp. 3d 52, (Sep. 24, 2019)
Kareem v. Haspel, 2021 U.S. App. LEXIX 1128 10. (Jan. 15, 2021)
Kentucky v. King, 31 S. Ct. 1849 (2011)
Maqaleh v. Gates, 605 F.3d 84 (May 21, 2010)
Muthana v. Pompeo, 2019 U.S. Distr. LEXIS 218098, Civil Action No. 19–445 (RBW), 4, D.D.C. (Dec. 17, 2019)
Muthana v. Pompeo, 985 F.3d 893, 899 (Jan. 19, 2021)
Payton v. New York, 445 U.S. 573 (1980)
Rasul v. Bush, 542 U.S. 466 (2004)
Turkmen v. Ashcroft, No. 02 Civ. 2307, 2006 WL 1662663 (E.D.N.Y. Jun. 14, 2006)
Turkmen v. Ashcroft, 589 F.3d 542, 550 (2d Cir. 2009)
Turkmen v. Ashcroft, 915 F. Sup. 2d 314 (E.D.N.Y. 2013)
Turkmen v. Ashcroft, 2018 U.S. Dist. LEXIS 137492 (Aug. 13, 2018)
Turkmen v. Hasty, 789 F.3d 18 (Jun. 17, 2015)
United States v. Ahmed, 2019 U.S. Dist. LEXIS 175388, Case No. 18-cv-4598 (Sep. 20, 2019)
United States v. Abu Khatallah, 151 F. Supp. 3d (D.D.C. 2015)
United States v. Paracha, No. 03-cr-1197, 2004 WL 1900336 (S.D.N.Y. 2004)
United States v. Watson, 423 U.S. 411 (1976)
USA v. Al Nashiri, Military Commissions Trial, Judiciary Guantanamo Bay, AE 353AA Ruling (May 18, 2021)
USA v. Majid Khan, Military Commissions Trial, Judiciary Guantanamo Bay, AE 033K Ruling (Jun. 4, 2020)
Zadvydas v. Davis, 533 U.S. 678 (2001)
Zaidan v. Trump, 317 F. Supp. 3d 8 (Jun. 13, 2018)
Ziglar v. Abbasi, 137 S. Ct 1843 (Jun. 19, 2017)

Table of legislation

Australia

Australian Citizenship Act 2007
Australian Citizenship Amendment (Allegiance to Australia) Act 2015, No. 166, 2015
Australian Passports Act 2005, No. 5
Terrorism (Temporary Exclusion Orders) Act 2019, No. 53, 2019
Criminal Code (Cwlth)
National Security Information (Criminal and Civil Proceedings) Act 2004 (Cwth)

Belgium

Code de la Nationalité Belge
Constitution of Belgium
Pre-trial Detention Act of 1990
Loi portant des dispositions des dispositions diverses en matière de lutte contre le terrorisme, 2016–08–03/15

Canada

Canadian Passport Order, SI81–86, as amended on May 29, 2019
Citizenship Act 1977
Strengthening Canadian Citizenship Act 2014 c.24

Denmark

The Constitution of Denmark 1953

France

Art No. 96–647 of Jul. 22 1996
Art. L228(1–7) Law of Internal Security, introduced by Art. 3 of Law No. 2017–1510 (Oct. 30, 2017)

Code Civile
Code de Procédure Pénale
Loi No. 2014–1353, Art. L224–1 (Nov. 13, 2014)

Germany

Nationality Act of 22 July 1913, as amended in June 2019.

Israel

Basic Law (5752–1992): Human Dignity and Liberty
Criminal Procedure Law (Powers of Enforcement – Arrest) 1996
Defence (Emergency) Regulations 1945, Palestine Gazette No. 1442, Supp. No. 2
Emergency Powers (Detention) Law, 5739–1979, S.H. 76, 33 L.S.I. 89–92 (1979)
Incarceration of Unlawful Combatants Law, 5762–2002
Nationality (Amendment No. 13) Law 5777–2017
Penal Law 5737/1977

Kazakhstan

Law of the Republic of Kazakhstan on Citizenship of the Republic of Kazakhstan 1991, KAZ-1991-L-43968, adopted on Dec. 20, 1991 as amended by KAZ-2011-L-90204 on Jul. 22, 2011, KAZ-2014-L-97825 on Jul. 4, 2014, and KAZ-2015-L-102040 on Nov. 24, 2015.

The Netherlands

Code of Criminal Procedure
Dutch Nationality Act

United Kingdom

Anti-Terrorism, Crime and Security Act 2001, c.24
British Nationality Act 1981, c.61
British Nationality (General) Regulations, SI 2018/851
Counter-Terrorism and Security Act 2015, c.6
Human Rights Act 1998, c.42
Immigration Act 2014, c.222
Immigration, Asylum and Nationality Act 2006 (c. 13)
Justice and Security Act 2013, c.18
Overseas Operations (Service Personnel and Veterans) Act 2021, c.23
Prevention of Terrorism Act 2005, c.2
Serious Crime Act 2007, c. 27
Special Immigration Appeals Commission Act 1997, c.68

Terrorism Act 2000, c.11
Terrorism Prevention Measures and Investigation Act 2011, c.23

United States

8 United States Code §1226
8 United States Code §1451
8 United States Code §1481
8 United States Code §1504
10 United States Code §127e
10 United States Code §130f
18 United States Code § 2339A
18 United States Code §2339B
18 United States Code §3144
50 United States Code §3093
Administrative Procedure Act 5 U.S.C. §551
Authorization for the Use of Military Force, Pub. L. No. 107–40, 115 Stat. 224 (2001)
Detainee Treatment Act of 2005, Pub. L. 109–148, 119 Stat. 2739 (2005)
Executive Order 13491, Ensuring Lawful Interrogations, (Jan. 22, 2009)
Executive Order 13567, Periodic Review of Individuals Detained at Guantanamo Bay Naval Station Pursuant to the Authorization for Use of Military Force (Mar. 7, 2011)
Executive Order No. 13732 of Jul. 1, 2016, 81 U.S. Fed. Reg. 130
Executive Order No. 13862 of Mar. 6, 2019, Revocation of Reporting Requirement, §2, 84 FR 8789
Freedom of Information Act, 5 U.S.C. §552
Military Commissions Act of 2007, Pub. L. 109–366, 120 Stat. 2600 (2006)
National Defense Authorization Act of 2012, Pub. L. 112–88
National Defense Authorization Act of 2013, Pub. L. 112–239
National Defense Authorization Act for Fiscal Year 2016, Public Law 114–92 (Nov. 25, 2015)
United States Constitution
United States Constitution Amendment XIV

Table of treaties and other sources

Treaties

African (Banjul) Charter on Human and Peoples' Rights, O.A.U. Doc. CAB/LEG/67/3 rev. 5, 21 I.L.M. 58, (1982), entered into force Oct. 21, 1986)

American Convention on Human Rights, O.A.S. Treaty Series No. 36, 1144 U.N.T.S. 123 (entered into force Jul. 18, 1978)

American Declaration on the Rights and Duties of Man, (adopted by the Ninth International Conference of American States, Bogotá, Colombia, 1948

Arab Charter on Human Rights, reprinted in 12 Int'l Hum. Rts. Rep. 893 (2005), entered into force Mar. 15, 2008

Convention Against Torture and Other Cruel, Inhuman or Degrading Treatment or Punishment, G.A. Res. 39/46, annex, 39 U.N. GAOR Supp. (No. 51) at 107 U.N. Doc. A/39/51 (1984), entered into force Jun. 26, 1987

Convention on the Reduction of Statelessness, U.N.T.S., Vol. 989, p. 175, adopted Aug. 30, 1961, entry into force Dec. 13, 1975

Convention on the Rights of the Child, G.A. Res. 44/25, annex, 44 U.N. GAOR Supp. (No. 49) at 167 U.N. Doc. A/44/49 (1989), entered into force Sep. 2, 1990

Convention relating to the Status of Stateless Persons, Art. 1, U.N.T.S. Vol. 360, p. 117, adopted Sep. 28, 1954, entry into force Jun. 6, 1960

European Convention on Nationality, ETS 166, adopted Nov. 6, 1997, entry into force Nov. 6, 2000

European Convention for the Protection of Human Rights and Fundamental Freedoms, 213 U.N.T.S. 222, entered into force Sep. 3, 1953

International Covenant on Civil and Political Rights, G.A. Res. 2200A (XXI), 21 U.N. GAOR Supp. (No. 16) at 52 U.N. Doc. A/6316 (1966), 999 U.N.T.S. 171, entered into force Mar. 23, 1976

International Covenant on Economic, Social and Cultural Rights, U.N.T.S. Vol. 993, 3 entered into force Jan. 3, 1976

International Convention for Protection of All Persons from Enforced Disappearances, G.A. Res. 61/177, U.N. Doc. A/RES/61/177 (2006), adopted Dec. 20, 2006

Geneva Convention for the Amelioration of the Condition of the Wounded and Sick in Armed Forces in the Field, (Aug. 12, 1949), 6 U.S.T. 3114, 75 U.N.T.S. 31

Geneva Convention for the Amelioration of the Condition of the Wounded, Sick and Shipwrecked Members of Armed Forces at Sea, (Aug. 12, 1949). 6 U.S.T. 3217, 75 U.N.T.S. 85

Geneva Convention Relative to the Treatment of Prisoners of War, (Aug. 12, 1949), 6 U.S.T. 3316, 75 U.N.T.S. 135

Geneva Convention Relative to the Protection of Civilian Persons in Time of War, (Aug. 12, 1949), 6 U.S.T. 3516, 75 U.N.T.S. 287

Hague Convention II with respect to the Laws and Customs of War on Land, 187 CTS Jul. 29, 1899, entered into force Sep. 1900

Hague Convention IV with respect to the Laws and Customs of War on Land and its annexed regulations, Oct. 18, 1907, entered into force Jan. 26, 1910

Optional Protocol to the International Covenant on Civil and Political Rights, Adopted and opened for signature, ratification and accession by General Assembly resolution 2200A (XXI) of Dec. 16, 1966, entry into force Mar. 23, 1976, in accordance with Article 9.

Protocol Additional to the Geneva Conventions of August 12, 1949 and Relating to the Protection of Victims of International Armed Conflicts, (Jun. 8, 1977), 1125 U.N.T.S. 3

Protocol Additional to the Geneva Conventions of August 12, 1949 and Relating to the Protection of Victims of Non-International Armed Conflicts, (Jun. 8, 1977), U.N.T.S. 609

Protocol to the African Charter on Human and Peoples' Rights on the Establishment of an African Court on Human and Peoples' Rights, Jun. 10, 1988, Organization of African Unity (entered into force on Jun. 25, 2004)

Protocol No. 4 to the European Convention for the Protection of Human Rights and Fundamental Freedoms, ETS 46, Sep. 16, 1963

Second Hague Peace Conference Convention Regarding the Laws and Customs of Land Warfare (Oct. 18, 1907), pmbl., 36 Stat. 2277, 3 Martens (3d) 362, reprinted in 2 Am. J. Int'l L. 90, 91–92 (Supp. 1908)

Universal Declaration of Human Rights, adopted by the U.N. General Assembly in Res. 217 A (III), U.N. Doc. A/RES/217 (111), December 10, 1948

Vienna Convention on the Law of Treaties, U.N.T.S. vol. 1155, 331 dated May 23, 1969, entered into force Jan. 27, 1980)

Other sources

Africa

African Commission on Human and Peoples' Rights, General Comment No. 3 on the African Charter on Human and Peoples' Rights: The Right to Life (Article 4), (adopted during the 57th Ordinary Session of the African

Commission on Human and Peoples' Rights held from Nov. 4 to 18 in Banjul, The Gambia, 2015)

Europe

Council of Europe, European Commission on Human Rights, Preparatory Work on Article 5 of the European Convention on Human Rights, 6–8, DH (56) 10, A.28.646 TD 979/AEG/WM, Aug. 8, 1956

Directive 2013/48/EU of the European Parliament and of the Council of Oct. 22, 2013

Europol, European Union Terrorism Situation and Trend Report 2020

Organization for Security and Co-operation in Europe (OSCE) and Office for Democratic Institutions and Human Rights (ODIHR), Guidelines for Addressing the Threats and Challenges of "Foreign Terrorist Fighters" Within a Human Rights Framework, 2018

Organization of American States

Organization of American States (OAS), Inter-American Commission on Human Rights, Resolution1/08, Principles and Best Practices on the Protection of Persons Deprived of Liberty in the Americas, Mar. 31, 2008

Inter-American Commission on Human Rights, Ten Years of Activities 1971–1981, OAS, 1982

Inter-American Commission on Human Rights Report on the Situation of Human Rights of a Segment of Miskito Origin, Pt. II, subdiv. E, OEA/Ser.L/V.II.62 doc.10, rev.3 Nov. 29, 1983

Inter-American Commission on Human Rights, Recommendations for the Protection of Human Rights by OAS Members in the Fight Against Terrorism, OEA/Ser.G. CP/doc.4117/06, May 9, 2006

Inter-American Commission on Human Rights, Annual Report 2019, OEA/Ser.L/V/II, Doc. 9, (Feb. 24, 2020).

Inter-American Commission on Human Rights, Annual Report 2020, OEA/Ser.L/V/II, Doc.28, (Mar. 30, 2021).

United Nations

Agnes Callimard and Fionnuala Ni Aolain, Special Rapporteurs, United Nations Human Rights Special Procedures, Extra-territorial Jurisdiction of States over Children and their Guardians in Camps, Prisons or elsewhere in the northern Syrian Arab Republic, (2020).

United Nations (UN) Assistance Mission in Afghanistan, Afghanistan: Protection of Civilians in Armed Conflict, Annual Report 2018, Feb. 2019

U.N. Body of Principles for the Protection of All Persons under Any Form of Detention or Imprisonment, A/RES/ 43/173, Dec. 9, 1988

UN Department of Economic and Social Affairs, Study of the Right of Everyone to be Free From Arbitrary Arrest, Detention and Exile, E/CN.4/826 Rev. 1, 1964

UN Economic and Social Council, Commission on Human Rights, The Siracusa Principles on the Limitation and Derogation Provisions in the International Covenant on Civil and Political Rights, E/CN.4/1985/4, Sep. 28, 1984

United Nations General Assembly (UNGA) Resolution adopted by the General Assembly (UNGA Res.) 51/210 Dec. 17, 1996

UNGA Res. 57/219, Feb. 27, 2003

UNGA Res., Sep. 8, 2006, 60/288, The United Nations Global Counter-Terrorism Strategy, U.N. Doc. A/RES/60/288, Sep. 20, 2006

UNGA Fifth Review Global Terrorism Strategy, A/70/L.55, Jul. 1, 2016

United Nations Human Rights Committee (UN HRC) General Comment No. 8 (General Comments) (Right to Liberty and Security of Persons) (Article 9) (Sixteenth Session 1982) U.N. Doc. HRI/GEN/1/Rev.1, Jun. 30, 1982

UN HRC CCPR General Comment (GC) No. 27: Article 12 (Freedom of Movement), Adopted at the Sixty-seventh session of the HRC on 2 Nov. 1999, CCPR/C/21/Rev.1/Add.9

UN HRC, CCPR General Comment No. 29. States of Emergency (Article 4), U.N. Doc. CCPR/C/21/Rev.1/Add.11, Aug. 31, 2001

UN HRC General Comment No. 31, Nature of the General Legal Obligations Imposed on States Parties to the Covenant, CCPR/C/21/Rev.1/Add.13 (General Comments), May 26, 2004

UN HRC General Comment No. 35, CCPR/C/GC/35, Dec. 16, 2014

UN HRC General Comment No. 36 (2018) on Article 6 of the International Covenant on Civil and Political Rights, on the right to life, CCPR/C/GC/36, (Oct. 30, 2018)

UNGA, Human Rights Council, Report of the Special Rapporteur on the promotion and protection of human rights and fundamental freedoms while countering terrorism, U.N. Doc. A/65/258, Aug. 6, 2010

U.N.G.A. Human Rights Council, Report of the Working Group on Arbitrary Detention, A/HRC/22/44, 16 IIIA, Dec. 24, 2012

U.N.G.A. Human Rights Council, Report of the Working Group on Arbitrary Detention, A/HRC/39/45, Jul. 2, 2018

UNGA Human Rights Council, The Working Group on Arbitrary Detention, Revised Fact Sheet No. 26, Feb. 8, 2019

UNGA Human Rights Council, Report of the Independent Commission of Inquiry established pursuant to Human Rights Council resolution S-21/1, U.N.G.A. A/HRC/29/52, (Jun. 24, 2015)

UNGA Human Rights Council, Report of the Special Rapporteur on the promotion and protection of human rights and fundamental freedoms while countering terrorism, A/68/389, (Sep. 18, 2013).

UNGA Human Rights Council, Report of the Special Rapporteur on the promotion and protection of human rights and fundamental freedoms while countering terrorism, U.N. Doc. A/HRC/34/61, Feb. 21, 2017

UNGA Human Rights Council, Report of the Special Rapporteur on the promotion of human rights and fundamental freedoms while countering terrorism on the human rights challenge of states of emergency in the context of countering terrorism, A/HRC/37/52, Mar. 1, 2018

UNGA, Human Rights Council, Report of the Special Rapporteur on the promotion and protection of human rights and fundamental freedoms while countering terrorism, U.N. Doc. A/73/361, Sep. 3, 2018

UNGA, Human Rights Council, Report of the Special Rapporteur on the promotion and protection of human rights and fundamental freedoms while countering terrorism, U.N. Doc. A/76/261, Aug. 3, 2021.

UNGA, Human Rights Council, Report of the Special Rapporteur on extrajudicial, summary or arbitrary executions, Philip Alston, Addendum, Study on targeted killings, A/HRC/14/24/Add.6 May 28, 2010.

UNGA Human Rights Council, Report of the Special Rapporteur on extrajudicial, summary or arbitrary executions, U.N. Doc. A/68/382, (Sep. 13, 2013).

U.N. Human Rights Council, Report of the Special Rapporteur on extrajudicial, summary or arbitrary executions, A/HRC/44/38, (Jun. 29, 2020).

U.N. Office of Counter-Terrorism, Statement by Mr. Vladimir Voronkov, Under-Secretary-General of the United Nations Office of Counter-Terrorism, Twelfth Report of the Secretary-General on the threat posed by ISIL (Da'esh) to international peace and security and the range of United Nations efforts in support of Member States in countering the threat, (Feb. 10, 2021),

United Nations Office on Drugs and Crime Investigation, Prosecution and Adjudication of Foreign Terrorist Fighter Cases for South and South-East Asia, 2018

United Nations Security Council (UNSC) U.N. Doc. S/RES/1373, Sep. 28, 2001

UNSC S/RES/1456, Jan. 20, 2003

UNSC S/RES1546 Jun. 8, 2004

UNSC S/RES/2178, Sep. 24, 2014

UNSC S/RES/2396 (2017).

UNSC Counter-Terrorism Committee, Madrid Guiding Principles, S/2015/939, (Dec. 23, 2015).

UNSC Counter-Terrorism Committee, Annex to the letter dated Dec. 28, 2018 from the Chair of the Security Council Committee established pursuant to resolution 1373 (2001) concerning counter-terrorism addressed to the President of the Security Council, 2018 Addendum to the 2015 Madrid Guiding Principles. S/2018/1177

U.N. Office of Counter-Terrorism, Handbook, Children affected by the foreign-fighter phenomenon: Ensuring a child rights-based approach, (Sep. 2018)

Foreword

Terrorists are criminals, but liberal democracies have found criminal law inadequate on the preventive issue. The public safety imperative leads to bespoke responses, three of which are surveyed in this book: preventive detention, targeted killing, and removing citizenship from Foreign Terrorism Fighters. Each of these responses, jarring as they do against familiar standards of fair process and individual accountability, require unflinching treatment. Dr. Diane Webber's thorough analysis of the international human rights and humanitarian norms, coupling a deep dive into jurisprudential authorities with an examination of public attitudes, achieves this.

As Professor Alan Dershowitz has established, criminal justice based on evidence of past deeds has never been the only response to future threat in common law jurisdictions; nor is it in civil law jurisdictions, notably Germany whose body of police law operates against *Gefährder* (potentially dangerous persons).

The inadequacy of criminal law as a response to future harm rests on two factors. Firstly, the need to gather evidence means that authorities find it difficult to achieve the perfect balance between early intervention, when the evidential landscape is thin, and establishing that an individual has committed a serious offence meriting long-term incapacitation. This is despite the development of a specialist corpus of criminal law, as in the United Kingdom, based on precursor offences that shift the point of liability ever further back from deed towards thought and intention.

The second inadequacy arises where threatening activity occurs outside the jurisdiction. Overseas battlefields have not in practice proven a rich source of evidence for prosecuting jihadis; and criminal justice measures cannot neutralize a threat where the threat actor remains overseas. Information in this sphere is most likely to be based on information obtained from military, intelligence, and diplomatic channels, bringing the problem of proof into even sharper perspective.

The first topic, preventive detention, demonstrates that some states have found preventive measures easier to achieve abroad than on home soil. As Diane Webber notes, the United Kingdom's experience of full preventive detention was a brief one, limited to foreign national terrorists who could not be deported because of a risk of torture or death if deported, and ultimately struck down by the courts as discriminatory.

Notwithstanding the terrorist threat from its own nationals, in the period since 9/11 the United Kingdom held back from implementing type of regime that is present elsewhere in the world, most notably in Israel where, as Diane Webber shows, an accommodation of sorts has been achieved between judicial oversight and stringent domestic detention measures.

As for overseas preventive detention, no easy accommodation is to be found. Like other states, the U.K. has sought, with varying degrees of success, to limit judicial scrutiny of military detention on the basis that there are no justiciable standards. Other states have gone further to insulate detention from judicial inquiry: at the extremity, though use of secret sites.

But at least preventive detention is reversible. Targeted killing overseas carries a risk of error and collateral impact but it has proven irresistible to states with the technological and military capacity to do so. Despite the connotations of warfare and sovereignty, it is necessary to confront the topic and seek to frame it within legal standards. This book does so.

The problem of foreign fighters leads back to fears about the adequacy of the criminal law, principally that poverty of evidence of overseas terrorist activity will lead to little or no jail time. Uncertainty about securing a change of heart from returning jihadis and their families, and the risks presented by prolonged and often violent alienation from the home state, results in a general reluctance on the part of states to secure their return. Hence the preventive measure, widely adopted by European states, that can best be described in negative terms: the stripping of citizenship meaning the right for states *not* to play any further part in managing risk.

It is appealing to believe that preventive measures could ultimately be measured by common standards, including where the risk crosses international boundaries; that the competence of judicial bodies could be established without caveat; and that the public could be persuaded that what is done in their name can be discussed meaningfully, as Diane Webber does, without reverting to clichés about warfare.

But the legitimacy of preventive measures turns on so many factors that no general formula can be constructed to evaluate individual decisions. This is especially true set against a changing domestic threat landscape which includes a decline in the role of organized terrorist groups and the rise of the online self-initiator; new and evolving motivating ideologies; and an ever-younger cohort of radicalized individuals.

This book brings to light practices that, whatever one's preferences, are established aspects of counter-terrorism practice. Diane Webber patiently spells out the international humanitarian law and international human rights law standards by which these practices can be judged through a thorough analysis of the practices of individual countries.

She draws attention to the role played by the courts and the illustrates the complexities at work when judges are asked to show deference to state actions taken under the preventive imperative.

It is therefore a great privilege to have been asked to provide the introduction to a book that gives preventive state actions the unflinching treatment they deserve.

Jonathan Hall Q.C.
United Kingdom Independent Reviewer of Terrorism Legislation
October 2021.

Part I

Introduction

1 Introduction

The issue

In 2006 the United Nations urged Member States to ensure that counter-terrorism policies guaranteed respect for human rights and the rule of law.[1] This book demonstrates that in many cases, counter-terrorism policies have failed to respect human rights. This failure encourages vulnerable people to be drawn towards supporting or committing acts of terrorism. Furthermore, in recent years, jurisprudence and public opinion in some countries have shifted from being at one stage more protective of human rights, to an acquiescence that some particularly draconian counter-terrorism methods are necessary and acceptable. The book analyzes why this has happened and offers suggestions to address these issues.

The mention of the name "Beatles" usually conjures up the memory of the much-loved music of the "fab four" from Liverpool. In 2014 four British members of ISIS were given the nickname "Beatles" by their hostages because of their British accents – Shafee El Sheikh "George," Alexanda Kotey "Ringo," Aine Davis "Paul," and Mohammed Emwazi "John." These four individuals were allegedly responsible for the brutal killings and treatment of many people in Syria, including the beheading of British aid workers Alan Henning and David Haines, and United States journalists Steven Sotloff and James Foley.

The actions of people like the "Beatles" are a reason why some people may believe that the harshest counter-terrorism measures are necessary to prevent terror attacks. After the heinous activities that the "Beatles" were alleged to have committed took place, Emwazi was killed by a targeted United States drone strike in November 2015.[2] Davis was convicted in Turkey of terrorism charges in 2017 and was jailed for seven and a half years.[3] El Sheikh and Kotey were detained by Syrian Democratic Forces in January 2018. They were taken into United States custody in October 2019,[4] and they were detained at the Al Asa air base in Iraq for almost two years.[5] The United Kingdom government stripped them of their British citizenship in December 2014.[6]

The example of El Sheikh and Kotey demonstrates a number of legal issues that highlight the difficulties of dealing with suspected terrorists and how human rights are interwoven in almost every case. It is a story that is replicated with variations throughout this book. When British authorities determined in 2018

DOI: 10.4324/9780367817275-2

that they had insufficient evidence to prosecute El Sheikh and Kotey, the United Kingdom and United States authorities discussed the feasibility of prosecution in the United States. Complex human rights issues emerged because the British acknowledged that the provision of certain information by way of mutual legal assistance without assurances meant that if convicted in the United States, El Sheikh and Kotey could face the death penalty, which had been abolished in the United Kingdom in 1969. The United Kingdom supplied many witness statements to the United States authorities without those assurances. El Sheikh's mother instituted court proceedings in the United Kingdom, claiming that the supply of this information would facilitate the imposition of the death penalty and violated the law. In a landmark 2020 case, a majority of the United Kingdom Supreme Court ruled that individuals do not have a common law right not to have a trial in a foreign jurisdiction if there is a risk that the trial might result in the execution of that individual. However, the Supreme Court unanimously held that in the particular circumstances of this case, the transmission of the information was unlawful because it violated data protection laws.[7] In July 2020 the United States Attorney General indicated his willingness to drop the United States' insistence on the death penalty, paving the way for the prosecution of El Sheikh and Kotey in the United States.[8] In August 2020 the United Kingdom Supreme Court lifted a stay that barred the sharing of information with United States prosecutors,[9] and in October 2020 El Sheikh and Kotey were transferred to the United States to face trial in a federal court on charges of hostage taking resulting in death, conspiracy charges relating to the hostage taking, and for providing material support to a foreign terrorist organization.[10] Kotey pleaded guilty to eight counts on September 2, 2021, with the expectation of spending the rest of his life in prison.[11] El Sheikh still awaits trial.

The three counter-terrorism tools of targeted killing, preventive detention, and the stripping of citizenship used by the United Kingdom and United States against these four individuals and others like them, and the resulting jurisprudence in which international human rights feature heavily, are analyzed in this book.

Counter-terrorism strategies and human rights law do not sit comfortably together. They are often presented as the contents of two scale pans, each being weighed against the other as countries struggle to craft ways to prevent terror attacks whilst protecting individual freedoms to a lesser or greater extent.[12] Are the pans equally balanced or does one side of the balance have primacy over the other all of the time, or some of the time? Do their positions shift and if they do, what prompts the change?

The background

Human rights did not immediately feature in the international response to the devastating terrorist attacks in the United States on September 11, 2001 ("9/11"), which were the trigger for many countries to re-evaluate their counter-terrorism strategies. United Nations (U.N.) Security Council Resolution 1373[13] established new binding rules of international law,[14] but it did not mention human rights, which appeared to have been relegated to a "second zone,"[15] or define terrorism.

In early 2003, both the Security Council and the General Assembly referred to human rights for the first time in their resolutions;[16] a trend that continued going forward. In 2006, the U.N. declared that human rights were to be one of four central pillars of its Global Counter-Terrorism Strategy and set out "Measures to ensure respect for human rights for all and the rule of law as the fundamental basis of the fight against terrorism" – which recognized that "effective counter-terrorism measures and the protection of human rights are not conflicting goals, but complementary and mutually reinforcing."[17] States were urged *inter alia* to "ensure that any measures taken to combat terrorism comply with their obligations under international law, in particular human rights law, refugee law, and international humanitarian law."[18] In 2016 UNGA reviewed the U.N. Global Counter-Terrorism strategy, during which it recognized the importance of "preventing violent extremism as conducive to terrorism."[19] The review was the catalyst for creating a new Office of Counter-Terrorism.[20]

Since 9/11 the U.N. involvement in counter-terrorism matters has become extremely wide ranging, involving a massive structure with multiple groups and committees that frequently overlap and duplicate each other's activities.[21] This is not without its own problems. The International Federation for Human Rights (FIDH)'s 2017 report expressed a number of concerns, including that the U.N. were faced with the risk that authoritarian states that have a strong position in the existing U.N. structure may have "non-human rights compliant counter-terrorist policies, already applied in their own territories, endorsed by the international community and replicated widely."[22] FIDH also expressed the hope that the creation of the new Office of Counter-Terrorism would lead to reforming their procedures for the benefit of both human rights and counter-terrorism activities.[23]

FIDH commented that protecting human rights had not been a prominent feature of U.N. counter-terrorism work,[24] and three U.N. Special Rapporteurs on human rights and counter-terrorism have voiced concerns that this U.N. legislative activity has actually undermined the protection of human rights.[25]

At the Second High Level Conference of Heads of Counter-Terrorism Agencies of Member States that took place in June 2021, the U.N. Secretary General Antonio Guterres acknowledged that "the fight against terrorism has itself caused damage" and expressed the need for "consistent, coordinated and comprehensive efforts across countries, sectors and disciplines, anchored in human rights and the rule of law."[26] He prioritized the building of resilience: strong, just, and accountable institutions for inclusive access to justice, to deny terrorists the space to operate, bring them to justice, and provide security to the people. He also called for a

> human rights reset for counter-terrorism. . . . We know that when counter-terrorism is used to infringe upon the rights and freedoms of people, the result is more alienation within communities and stronger terrorist narratives . . . [which] must be addressed by protecting and promoting human rights, including gender equality.[27]

Why are we still talking about counter-terrorism strategies and human rights 20 years after 9/11? Although worldwide deaths from terrorism are reported in the 2020 Global Terrorist Index (GTI) to have fallen in the last five years due to the decline of ISIS in Iraq and Syria, 63 countries experienced at least one death from terrorism in 2019, and 17 countries recorded over 100 deaths from terrorism.[28] This is the second highest number of countries reporting one or more terrorist deaths in the last 20 years.[29] In 2020 the threat of global terrorism remained high, irrespective of the fact that fewer attacks had taken place in the first half of 2020 during the COVID-19 pandemic.[30]

The return of the Taliban in August 2021 as the governing power in Afghanistan is very likely to be a catalyst for a resurgence of terror attacks in the West.[31] In addition to Islamist terrorism, the threat of far-right political terrorism has surged in North America, Western Europe, and Oceania by 250% since 2014.[32] This means that countries cannot reduce their vigilance, or relax their efforts to combat terrorism, and they must still take appropriate steps to keep their citizens safe within the international human rights and humanitarian legal frameworks and in accordance with the rule of law; something that few, if any, countries have got totally right during the last 20 years.

In the years that followed 9/11, a number of countries developed and used a variety of stringent security-focused counter-terrorism tools such as collecting intelligence by methods that sometimes included the use of torture, preventive detention, placing restrictions on freedom of movement and targeted killing, to protect their citizens and residents. Yet draconian counter-terrorism measures that render people dead, detained or stateless have not succeeded in eradicating or reducing that threat to any significant extent. This book's analysis of these practices viewed through the lens of the international law frameworks, will show that many States still do not sufficiently comply with their obligations to respect human and humanitarian rights whilst combating terrorism. This scant regard to human rights in counter-terrorism measures at worst foments, or at best does not reduce, the threat and acts of terrorism.

Terminology

International Human Rights Law (IHRL)

IHRL is found in international treaties and declarations, as well as customary international law, which are norms that arise because they are already used in practice by countries that believe that such law exists.[33] These all build on the foundation or principles enshrined in the Universal Declaration of Human Rights.[34] A number of treaties are devoted specifically to general human rights, and they deal for example with the rights to life, liberty and fair treatment: the International Covenant on Civil and Political Rights (ICCPR);[35] the International Covenant on Economic, Social and Cultural Rights (ICESCR);[36] the European Convention for the Protection of Human Rights and Fundamental Freedoms (ECHR);[37] the American Convention on Human Rights (ACHR);[38] the African Charter on

Human and Peoples' Rights;[39] and the Arab Charter on Human Rights.[40] Many other treaties are in place to deal with specific human rights situations. These include treaties relating to stamping out torture,[41] enforced disappearances,[42] and protecting the rights of children.[43] However, treaties are only applicable to the countries that have ratified them, and there is little by way of effective enforcement mechanisms to deal with violations. U.N. declarations do not create legally binding obligations, but are recommendations made to member States.[44]

However in recent years, a number of U.N. resolutions have been issued that are more legislative in content, requiring States to enact legislation.[45] Martin Scheinin, a former U.N. Special Rapporteur on human rights and counter-terrorism, comments that this function of the U.N. in respect of Resolution 1373 is *ultra vires*.[46] He describes these resolutions as "legislative . . . with teeth,"[47] but in fact these measures do not have "teeth" because no effective mechanisms exist to sanction States who do not adopt measures that adequately protect human rights.

Many countries have enacted domestic legislation that reflects their obligation to protect and promote human rights through all their domestic laws, including counter-terrorism measures. However, the position relating to respecting human rights whilst conducting counter-terrorism operations overseas is more complex. Some States are parties to more than one general human rights treaty. For example, most European countries are parties to the ECHR and also the ICCPR. One problematic area concerns the territorial reach of the treaties. This is particularly relevant for the practice of using counter-terrorism measures such as targeted killings and detention, overseas. This will be discussed more fully in the following sections.

International Humanitarian Law (IHL): a brief overview of key concepts

IHL, also known as the law of armed conflict (LOAC), is a huge and complex topic, most of which is outside the scope of this book.[48] The book, which focuses on counter-terrorism strategies seen through a human rights lens, offers a brief overview of IHL in this section and in Part III so that the reader can gain an understanding of the differences in each legal framework, and the extent to which the frameworks fit together or complement each other.

IHL derives from two sources: customary international law and international treaties.[49] Conflicts arising between two or more State parties to the four Geneva Conventions (GCs) are known as international armed conflicts (IACs), and all the rules of the GCs together with Additional Protocol (AP) I apply. If IAC combatants are captured during an armed conflict, they are entitled to prisoner of war (POW) status, with the rights and protections as set out in GC III.

Conflicts between a State party and a non-State armed group are characterized as non-international armed conflicts (NIACs),[50] to which only Common Article 3 of the GCs applies, (so described because the same wording appears as Article 3 in all four GCs), together with AP II and applicable customary international law. Common Article 3 merely prescribes humane treatment and lists a number of prohibited acts, such as murder, mutilation, torture, cruel, humiliating and degrading treatment, the taking of hostages, and unfair trial. The purpose of the GCs is to protect the sick and wounded, prisoners of war and civilians from the effects of armed conflict.

Several complex issues derive from the question of how counter-terrorism fits into the armed conflict, and thus the IHL paradigm. Can terrorists be considered a party to a NIAC? Can there exist a single NIAC or global or transnational NIACs between a State and one or several non-State armed groups that operate out of a number of different territories – thus linking the applicability of IHL to the person (and their belonging to a group) rather than to the territory?[51]

According to the International Committee for the Red Cross (ICRC), for a NIAC to exist two conditions must be fulfilled: "(1) the fighting must occur between governmental armed forces and the forces of one or more non-State armed groups having a certain level of organization, or between such armed groups; and (2) the armed confrontation must have reached a certain threshold of intensity."[52]

In a NIAC, all persons who are not members of State armed forces or organized armed groups of a party to the conflict are civilians and thus entitled to protection against direct attack unless and for such time as they take a direct part in hostilities.[53] Directly participating in hostilities means (i) carrying out an act that either is likely to adversely affect the military operations or capacity of the other party or to kill or injure persons, or destroy objects that would protect against direct attack; (ii) there must be a direct causal link between the act and the harm likely to result; and (iii) the act must be specifically designed to directly cause the required level of harm in support of the perpetrator's armed group and to the detriment of another.[54] Preparatory acts before direct participation fall within the three criteria.[55]

The decisive criterion for membership in an organized armed group is whether the civilian individual assumes a continuous combat function involving direct participation in hostilities.[56] Continuous combat function is a term that was created to deal with the problem arising from Additional Protocol I, Article 51.3[57] whereby a civilian could be protected when not directly participating but would lose the protection when he was directly participating: in other words, on/off conduct. An occasional hostile act by a person not involved in an organized group, does not amount to membership in an organized armed group or constitute continuous combat function.[58]

The legal frameworks governing armed conflict and terrorism are different: "armed conflict is a situation in which certain acts of violence are allowed (lawful) and others prohibited (unlawful), while *any* act of violence designated as terrorist is always unlawful."[59] A civilian who directly participates in hostilities, also referred to as an unlawful combatant, would not have the right to POW status if captured.[60]

As to whether terrorist groups that state they have global reach, such as al Qaeda and ISIS (also referred to as ISIL or Da'esh), can be considered organized armed groups for the purposes of participation in a NIAC, various positions have been taken: the ICRC has repeatedly asserted that it does not consider that an armed conflict of global dimensions is or has been taking place;[61] the United Kingdom has stated that it was in a NIAC with ISIS in Iraq and Syria; and since 9/11 the United States adopted the controversial stance that it was first in a global war on terror, then in a war against al Qaeda and now its armed conflict with ISIS, all of which formed part of a single global non-international armed conflict.[62] It is now therefore increasingly recognized that it is at least theoretically possible to have a transnational or global NIAC with non-State armed groups.[63]

Over recent years, some States have resorted to using targeted killing as a counter-terrorism tool against groups such as ISIS. This will be dealt with more fully in Part III. The use of such counter-terrorism tools has "significantly contributed to a blurring of the lines between armed conflict and terrorism, with potentially adverse effects on IHL."[64]

Under IHL, in armed conflicts there are four inextricably linked core principles: distinction; military necessity; proportionality; and unnecessary suffering. The use of force is therefore lawful provided that it is used proportionately, i.e. where incidental loss of civilian life, civilian injuries, or damage to civilian objects is not excessive in relation to the anticipated concrete and direct military advantage. Force may only be used against lawful combatants who must be distinguished from civilians, and against military rather than civilian objectives, in situations of military necessity, i.e. where the use of measures that are not forbidden by international law are justified as indispensable for securing the complete submission of the enemy as soon as possible; but without inflicting unnecessary suffering.[65] In NIACs these criteria are equally applicable through customary international humanitarian law.[66] The reason that a State party might wish to assert that it is in a NIAC with a terrorist group is because the rules of IHL are more permissive than those of international human rights law.

Another contentious issue relates to whether and when IHRL applies in armed conflicts. Europeans, the International Committee of the Red Cross, International Court of Justice, and the European Court of Human Rights maintain that IHRL always applies, in tandem with IHL. The United States and Israel insist that IHL applies in situations of armed conflict overseas. However, the United States *does* consider itself bound by the extra-territorial application of human rights law found in customary international law, but not by the extra-territorial reach of the ICCPR.[67]

Terrorism

Hundreds of variations or "definitions" of the term "terrorism" can be found.[68] In 1996 the U.N. General Assembly established an Ad Hoc Committee *inter alia* to develop a comprehensive legal framework of conventions dealing with international terrorism,[69] but international agreement has still not yet been achieved as to the definition of "terrorism."[70] One issue contributing to the stalled discussions is about whether and how acts committed in armed conflict should be excluded from the scope of the convention.[71]

The lack of an agreed definition has significant consequences. As states can unilaterally decide what amounts to terrorism, this can lead,[72] and has led,[73] to arbitrary and excessive responses with vaguely and broadly defined crimes of terrorism. The definition of terrorism directly adversely affects human rights, in some cases where States could "breach fundamental rights all while seemingly complying with Security Council obligations."[74]

For example, in the United Kingdom, in a 2013 case concerning the dissemination of terrorist publications, the Supreme Court considered the meaning of "terrorism" in the context of attacks by a non-State group against State armed forces in a NIAC. The Court concluded that the definition of terrorism in United Kingdom terrorism legislation was very far-reaching,[75] and was intended for good reasons to be very wide.[76] The legislation was considered broad enough for five persons who went to Syria to fight with the Kurdish group YPG *against* ISIS to be prosecuted. However, these cases were discontinued in 2019 for no clearly stated reasons: perhaps one reason was that YPG was not a proscribed terrorist organization.[77]

For the purposes of this book, the following working definition of "terrorism" is adopted:

> *the unlawful use, or threat, of violence by non-state actors against persons, property, critical infrastructures or key resources, intended to intimidate or coerce a government, or all or part of the general public, in furtherance of political, religious, or ideological objectives.*[78]

As will be seen from the analysis that follows in the book, the lack of an agreed definition of terrorism has had a significant adverse impact on each of the counter-terrorism tools that are discussed in depth: preventive detention; targeted killing by drone strike; and restrictions of movement and citizenship of foreign fighters.

The counter-terrorism strategies

Preventive detention

Preventive detention is a term that is frequently used in by commentators and countries in different terminology and contexts.[79] It is a problematic concept, because its goal is to prevent future conduct; something that is impossible to predict, and therefore it is a tool that carries a huge risk of abuse. Yet preventive detention is used in at least forty countries around the world,[80] in the context of law enforcement, administrative measures such as immigration, dealing with persons perceived to be dangerous in health, law enforcement and counter-terrorism situations, and armed conflict.

In the counter-terrorism context it is used to disrupt terrorist plots and incapacitate suspects based on a certain level of suspicion or belief that a terror attack may be imminent. There is of course a huge risk that innocent people might be detained as future conduct is impossible to predict with complete accuracy.

For the purpose of this book, "preventive detention" refers to *detention before or without charge for the purpose of preventing a terrorist act.* This means detention in three types of situation:

(1) when a person is arrested on suspicion of being about to commit a terrorist offense. For example, he is suspected of having carried out some early steps of terrorist activity but has not done any sufficiently overt act to enable police to make an immediate charge. The person may be detained for incapacitation and/or investigation purposes;
(2) when a person is detained under immigration law for security reasons; and
(3) when a person who cannot be criminally prosecuted because of issues such as the danger of compromising sources, is detained for security reasons.[81]

Part II will highlight areas where the substantive and procedural aspects of detention in both international and domestic laws that govern how and when preventive detention may be used are defective to a lesser or greater extent, and how this can adversely affect the fundamental right to liberty.

In addition to an analysis of the substantive and procedural aspects of detention, Part II will also cover the treatment of detainees, with a focus on interrogation measures, and the difficulties associated with obtaining adequate redress for violations. Part IV also covers some aspects of detention that relate to the treatment of returning foreign fighters.

Targeted killing

Targeted killing by drone strikes is tackled in Part III. It typically describes an intentional pre-planned killing by a State of a specific enemy individual,[82] whereby individuals may be tracked and killed with great precision by small, light unmanned weapons, that do not pose any risk to the lives of the forces that operate them, and that are much cheaper than traditional manned aircraft.[83] This is not a legal category, but a form of killing, and during war, the targeted killing of an enemy fighter can be legal,[84] provided the action falls within with the relevant international law framework. A relatively small number of countries are known to have used armed drones in combat with the intention of killing suspected or known terrorists: the United States; the United Kingdom; Israel; Pakistan; Nigeria; Iraq; Iran; and Turkey.[85] Other countries that are members of the United States Coalition[86] may have done so too. For example, Airwars reports that France may have killed a number of civilians in Iraq and Syria.[87]

It is hard to discover exactly how many strikes, fatalities, and casualties there have been, because the subject appears to be shrouded in a certain amount of secrecy, with huge differences in the numbers published in the official government reports and in those compiled by NGOs. For example, CENTCOM's 2019 report states "The Coalition conducted 34,464 strikes in Iraq and Syria between August 2014 and the end of March 2019. During this period, based on information available, CJTF-OIR assesses at least 1,291 civilians have been unintentionally killed by Coalition strikes since the beginning of Operation Inherent Resolve."[88] The CENTCOM report for 2020 states that "approximately 23 civilians were killed and approximately 10 civilians were injured" in Afghanistan, Iraq, Somalia, Syria, Yemen, and Nigeria in 2020 as a result of U.S. military operations.[89] That report notes that between 2014 and 2020, NGOs had conveyed 2,531 reports of civilian casualties in "Operation Inherent Resolve" in Iraq and Syria. The DoD stated that it had reviewed all the reports and had assessed that civilian casualties had occurred in respect of 351 of those reports.[90] One civilian was confirmed as having been killed unintentionally in Iraq in 2020.[91]

Regarding the conflict in Afghanistan, the U.N. documented 632 civilian casualties (393 deaths and 239 injured) from 107 aerial operations carried out by international military forces during 2018.[92] The Department of Defense assessed the damage in Afghanistan in 2018 as 76 civilians killed and 58 injured,[93] with 108 civilians killed and 75 civilians injured in 2019,[94] and 20 civilians were confirmed killed and five injured in 2020.[95]

Yet the figures produced by a number of NGOs paint a totally different story.[96] For example, Airwars reported in July 2021 that over the last six years the United States has confirmed 1,410 civilian deaths and 349 civilians wounded in Iraq and Syria alone, but Airwars has assessed the numbers as between 19,279 and 29,643 civilian deaths and between 5,819 and 9,034 civilians injured. The Bureau of Investigative Journalism estimated that in Afghanistan between 2018 and 2020 between 880 and 5,604 were killed, with between 158 and 1072 injured.[97]

Measures relating to returning foreign fighters

The concept of foreign fighters going overseas to participate in conflicts dates back at least 250 years.[98] However, what was a new phenomenon was that more than 40,000 foreign fighters from at least 110 countries traveled to Iraq, Syria, Afghanistan, Yemen, Libya, Pakistan, and Somalia to join ISIS and al-Qaeda and its affiliates for the purposes of fighting with or offering support to those groups.[99]

One report dated October 2017, estimates that 5,600 individuals from 33 countries had returned home.[100] Another report at that time suggests that 6,957 foreign fighters had been killed on the battlefield, and at least 14,910 had left the Levant, of which 5,395 were in prison, 6,837 had returned home without entering into the criminal justice system, and 2,678 were unaccounted for.[101] As of October 31, 2017, returning foreign fighters were responsible for 51 attacks outside of Syria and Iraq, and 87 attacks by foreign fighters who had gone elsewhere, but not "back home."[102] The U.N. Office of Counter Terrorism observed that not many foreign fighters went to Syria with the intention of training to be a domestic terrorist back home, nor did all go there with the objective of becoming fighters.[103]

In March 2021 after the fall of the ISIS caliphate, some 2,000 foreign fighters with 10,000 associated family members, including about 60,000 children were being held in Syrian Democratic Forces camps in execrable conditions. Because those children "have been exposed to fairly horrific conditions" for a considerable period of time, there were concerns that "down the road they could end up being able to go to other places and potentially do bad things."[104]

It is difficult to extrapolate trends from data relating to different categories of returnees, with different levels of indoctrination and ideology, but some evidence supports the contention that the majority of attacks attempted, generated, or carried out by returnees took place within the first year of returning, often within the first four months.[105] Because of these concerns, the fear of the threat posed by the returnees has been the impetus for far-reaching counter-terrorism legislation and policies.

Scheme of the book

The book will examine by analysis of topical international and domestic jurisprudence, the extent to which States are complying with their international human rights and humanitarian law obligations whilst implementing counter-terrorist strategies. Court rulings will be examined to identify judicial trends in terms of whether rulings in both international and domestic cases involving counter-terrorism measures are perceived to be driven by a human rights approach or tend to be deferential to government policy, whether these trends have changed in the last 20 years, and if so, will suggest reasons why. The book also analyzes how the press portray counter-terrorism stories and examines trends in public opinion about counter-terrorism and related human rights issues.

In the domestic law sections on preventive detention in Part II and targeted killing in Part III, the focus is on the laws and practices in three countries: the United States; the United Kingdom; and Israel. These countries have been chosen for a number of reasons. All of them have a history of fighting terrorism and have built up bodies of jurisprudence in the English language that reflect different approaches to dealing with the similar problem of countering terrorism. All three countries are parties to the ICCPR, and additionally, the United Kingdom is a party to the ECHR, and each country has a different approach in the way they apply and comply with IHRL.

The United States has mainly dealt with terrorist activity through its domestic criminal law, despite the fact that no federal crime of terrorism *per se* exists. After the catastrophic events of 9/11, the Bush Administration deemed the criminal law inadequate and decided that an IHL model was more appropriate to deal with the Taliban, al-Qaeda, and later ISIS terrorists. Although right-wing terrorism began to rise steadily from about 2009,[106] and now accounts for 75% of terrorist attacks in the United States,[107] until 2021 every National Security Strategy focused entirely on the risks from Islamist terrorism.[108]

In June 2021 the Biden Administration issued the first ever and essential National Strategy for Countering Domestic Terrorism.[109] It focuses entirely on domestic right-wing terrorism but does not mention Islamist terrorism or the issue of returning foreign fighters. Perhaps a second strategy dealing with those issues will be published in the future. The domestic National Strategy is reminiscent of the United Kingdom's CONTEST structure mentioned below, in that this strategy is organized around four "pillars": understanding domestic terrorism and sharing the fruits of the research with appropriate federal entities; preventing domestic terrorism recruitment and mobilization to violence; disrupting and deterring domestic terrorism activity; and confronting long-term contributors to domestic terrorism.[110]

The United Kingdom has had to deal with terrorism both at home and in former colonies for decades, and enacted legislation specifically designed to deal with terrorism within its domestic criminal law. The United Kingdom first crafted its CONTEST counter-terrorism strategy in 2009 to deal with international terrorism. It has been a model for other countries, such as Australia. It has four strands: Pursue – to stop terror attacks; Prevent – to stop people becoming terrorists or supporting violent extremism; Protect – to strengthen protection against terrorist attacks; and Prepare – where an attack cannot be stopped, to mitigate its impact.[111] The most recent version of CONTEST was published in June 2018, and it noted the shift in the threat caused by the rise of right-wing terrorism.[112] It also set out the policies relating to returning foreign fighters, and introduced its Desistance and Disengagement Programs, which are discussed in Part IV.[113] In October 2020 the Director General of MI5, which is the British intelligence and counter-terrorism agency dealing with domestic threats, noted that the biggest threat to the United Kingdom still derived from Islamist extremists, but right-wing terrorism was on the rise, together with a continuing threat of terrorism from Northern Ireland.[114]

The principal terrorist threat in Israel emanates from Palestinian armed groups such as Hamas that operate in Palestinian territories, and from Hezbollah in Lebanon. Israel has been in a permanent state of emergency since the inception of the State in 1948. Although Israel will prosecute terrorists under its domestic criminal law, it also detains persons under administrative law if they cannot be prosecuted. No formal counter-terrorism strategy exists, and Israel tends to apply a unique mix of IHL applicable to an international armed conflict together with the fundamental principles of its own Basic Law.[115]

A different approach has been taken in Part IV which deals with returning foreign fighters. Apart from the United Kingdom, other countries have not yet amassed sufficiently large bodies of case law that challenge the strategies from which useful conclusions can be extracted. Therefore, twelve countries (United Kingdom, Australia, Belgium, Canada, Denmark, France, Germany, Israel, Italy, Kazakhstan, the Netherlands, and the United States) are surveyed in order to get a picture of how these different countries with data in English have responded to the problems posed by returning foreign fighters.

Part V sets out the conclusions drawn from analyzing the judicial trends and examines the response of the public to the counter-terrorism measures of preventive detention, targeted killing and methods of dealing with returning foreign fighters that have been reviewed. It concludes that the judicial approach has shifted to being predominantly deferential to government policy, and that a significant number of the public is largely disinterested in any human rights implications arising out of these counter-terrorism measures.

The book does not advocate that the judiciary should not defer to government policy, but stresses the relevance and importance of having policies that take into account human rights issues and the rule of law. It discusses the implications of the judicial and public trends. It argues that the failure to respect human and humanitarian rights adequately may provide some explanation as to why the threat of terrorist activity has not decreased in response to current counter-terrorism strategies, and that some of these strategies may even encourage individuals to resort to use terrorist violence. The book concludes with some suggestions to resolve the deficiencies caused by current policies.

Notes

1 United Nations (U.N.) General Assembly (UNGA), Resolution adopted by the General Assembly on Sep. 8, 2006, 60/288, U.N. Global Counter-Terrorism Strategy, U.N. Doc. A/RES/60/288 (Sep. 20, 2006).

2 Dana Ford and Steve Almasy, *ISIS Confirms Death of 'Jihadi John'*, CNN, (Jan. 20, 2016), www.cnn.com/2016/01/19/middleeast/jihadi-john-dead/index.html.

3 Martin Chulov and Jamie Grierson, *British Jihadi Aine Davis Convicted in Turkey on Terror Charges*, The Guardian, (May 9, 2017), www.theguardian.com/world/2017/may/09/british-jihadist-aine-davis-convicted-in-turkey-on-terror-charges.

4 Bethan McKernan and Dan Sabbagh, *US Takes Custody of British ISIS Pair*, The Guardian, (Oct. 10, 2019), www.theguardian.com/world/2019/oct/10/us-reportedly-takes-custody-of-two-british-isis-beatles.

5 Ellen Nakashima, Rachel Weiner, Souad Mekhennet and Missy Ryan, *AG Barr Willing to Consider Forgoing Death Penalty to Secure Prosecution of ISIS Detainees Allegedly Involved in Beheadings of American Hostages*, Washington Post, (Jul. 31, 2020), www.washingtonpost.com/national-security/ag-barr-willing-to-consider-forgoing-death-penalty-to-secure-prosecution-of-isis-detainees-allegedly-involved-in-beheadings-of-american-hostages/2020/07/31/71e475f0-cdd4-11ea-91f1-28aca4d833a0_story.html.

6 *Islamic State 'Beatles' Duo Complain about Losing UK Citizenship*, BBC News, (Mar. 31, 2018), www.bbc.com/news/uk-43601925.

7 Elgizouli v. Secretary of State for the Home Department (SSHD), [2020] UKSC 10, (Mar. 25, 2020).

8 David Charter, *ISIS Pair Face Trial in the UN as Death Penalty Threat Lifted*, The Times, (Aug. 1, 2020), www.thetimes.co.uk/article/isis-beatles-face-trial-in-us-as-death-penalty-threat-lifted-v89z9fhrn.

9 Danica Kirka, *UK Supreme Court Lifts info Share Block on IS 'Beatles Case*, Washington Post, (Aug. 26, 2020), www.washingtonpost.com/world/the_americas/uk-supreme-court-lifts-info-share-block-on-is-beatles-case/2020/08/26/e821a9fe-e7c9-11ea-bf44-0d31c85838a5_story.html.

10 U.S. Dept. of Justice, Office of Public Affairs, *ISIS Militants Charged with Deaths of Americans in Syria*, (Oct. 7, 2020), www.justice.gov/opa/pr/isis-militants-charged-deaths-americans-syria.

11 Rachel Weiner and Tom Jackman, *ISIS Militant Admits Involvement in Torture, Killings of American Hostages*, Washington Post, (Sep. 2, 2021), www.washingtonpost.com/local/legal-issues/islamic-state-hostage-plea/2021/09/02/669d2b2c-0b56-11ec-9781-07796ffb56fe_story.html.

12 *See e.g.* Ancieto Masferrer, *The Fragility of Fundamental Rights in the Origins of Modern Constitutionalism*, 37–40, *in* Counter-Terrorism, Human Rights

and the Rule of Law, (Ancieto Masferrer and Clive Walker, eds., Edward Elgar, 2013).

13 U.N. Security Council (UNSC), U.N. Doc. S/RES/1373 (Sep. 28, 2001), which calls inter alia on member states to "take the necessary steps to prevent the commission of terrorist acts."

14 Martin Scheinin, *Impact of Post-9/11 Counter-Terrorism Measures on All Human Rights*, 93–4, *in* Using Human Rights to Counter Terrorism, (Manfred Nowak and Anne Chabord, eds., Edward Elgar, 2018). Scheinin also refers to his comment in *Report of the Special Rapporteur on the Promotion and Protection of Human Rights and Fundamental Freedoms While Countering Terrorism*, U.N. Doc. A/65/258, ¶69 (Aug. 6, 2010), that in adopting this Resolution the Security Council was acting ultra vires, exceeding the powers granted to it under the U.N. Charter.

15 Manfred Nowak and Anne Chabord, *Key Trends in the Fight against Terrorism and Key Aspects of International Human Rights Law*, 20, *in* Using Human Rights to Counter Terrorism.

16 U.N. Doc. S/RES/1456 (Jan. 20, 2003) and U.N.G.A. 57/219 (Feb. 27, 2003).

17 U.N. Doc. A/RES/60/288 (Sep. 20, 2006), ¶IV.

18 *Id.*, ¶IV.2.

19 International Federation for Human Rights, (FIDH) The United Nations Counter-Terrorism Complex, 73, (Sep. 2017), www.fidh.org/IMG/pdf/9.25_fidh_final_compressed-2.pdf, *citing* UNGA Fifth Review Global Terrorism Strategy, A/70/L.55, (last accessed 2016).

20 *Id.*, 74.

21 *Id.*, 52.

22 *Id.*, 5, 57, mentioning Russia, China, Egypt, and Saudi Arabia in this context, and the United States and France as countries who call for the practice of human rights, but "do not show a genuine commitment in protecting fundamental freedoms and human rights in their counter-terrorism measures."

23 *Id.*, 172.

24 *Id.*, 15.

25 Scheinin, *Impact of Post-9/11 Counter-Terrorism Measures on All Human Rights*, 96, commenting on the problems caused by the U.N. imposing obligations on States in the absence of an agreed definition of terrorism; U.N. Doc. A/HRC/34/61, *Report of Special Rapporteur* [Ben Emmerson Q.C.] *on the Promotion and Protection of Human Rights and Fundamental Freedoms While Countering Terrorism*, ¶63 (Feb. 21, 2017), "the absence of a systematic and substantial human rights element in the Security Council's implementation machinery and the relative weight placed on human rights as against counter-terrorism and security policy are issues that raise real concern . . . there is simply insufficient emphasis on human rights protection in the United nations counter-terrorism acquis;" U.N. Doc. A/73/361, *Report of Special Rapporteur* [Fionnuala Ni Aolain] *on the Promotion and Protection of Human Rights and Fundamental Freedoms While Countering Terrorism*, ¶10, (Sep. 3, 2018), while U.N. treaty making has long been and remains important today, "it has been overtaken by the assertive role taken by the Security Council in regulating State responses to terrorism through the adoption of resolutions. This shift in regulatory approach" [together with several other factors] "have had a distinctly negative effect on the overall advancement of meaningful protection for human rights within the counter-terrorism sphere. Moreover, the Special Rapporteur articulates her grave concern that the well-entrenched constitutional and domestic protections for human rights embedded in national legal systems in many countries are being rendered irrelevant or powerless in the new regulatory landscape;"

26 U.N. Secretary-General's remarks at the Second High-Level Conference of Heads of Counter-Terrorism Agencies of Member States, [as delivered], (Jun. 28, 2021), www.un.org/sg/en/content/sg/statement/2021-06-28/secretary-generals-remarks-the-second-high-level-conference-of-heads-of-counter-terrorism-agencies-of-member-states-delivered

27 *Id.*

28 Institute for Economics and Peace and National Consortium for the Study of Terrorism and Responses to Terrorism, Global Terrorism Index 2020, 2 ("GTI 2020"), (summarizing data from the beginning of 1998 to November 2020), (Nov. 2020), www.visionofhumanity.org/wp-content/uploads/2020/11/GTI-2020-web-1.pdf.

29 *Id.*

30 UNSC Counter-Terrorism Committee Executive Directorate (CTED), The Impact of the COVID-19 Pandemic on Terrorism, Counter-Terrorism and Countering Violent Extremism, (Jun. 2020); Jessica Davis, *Terrorism during a Pandemic: Assessing the Threat and Balancing the Hype*, Just Security, (Apr. 28, 2020), www.justsecurity.org/69895/terrorism-during-a-pandemic-assessing-the-threat-and-balancing-the-hype/.

31 Hugh Tomlinson, *Return of Taliban in Afghanistan Will Boost Jihadists in Europe and America*, The Times, (Aug. 17, 2021), www.thetimes.co.uk/article/return-of-taliban-in-afghanistan-will-boost-jihadists-in-europe-and-america-827fds0f6; Daniel Byman, *Will Afghanistan Become a Terrorist Safe Haven Again?*, Foreign Affairs, (Aug. 18, 2021), www.foreignaffairs.com/articles/afghanistan/2021-08-18/afghanistan-become-safe-haven-again-taliban?utm_medium…FA%20Today20-%20112017; Chris Smyth, Alistair Dawber and Charlie Faulkner, *Terror Threat 'Worst in Years,'* The Times, (Aug. 30, 2021), https://epaper.thetimes.co.uk/the-times/20210830/281483574479194.

32 GTI 2020, 3.

33 Brian D. Lepard, *Why Customary International Law Matters in Protecting Human Rights*, Voelkerrechtsblog, (Feb. 25, 2019), https://voelkerrechtsblog.org/why-customary-international-law-matters-in-protecting-human-rights/.

34 Universal Declaration of Human Rights, U.N. Doc. A/RES/217(111), (adopted by U.N.G.A., Dec. 10, 1948), (UDHR).

35 International Covenant on Civil and Political Rights, G.A. Res. 2200A (XXI), 21 U.N. GAOR Supp. (No. 16) at 52 U.N. Doc. A/6316, (1966), 999 U.N.T.S. 171 (entered into force Mar. 23, 1976), (ICCPR).

36 International Covenant on Economic, Social and Cultural Rights, U.N.T.S. Vol. 993, 3 (entered into force Jan. 3, 1976), (ICESCR).

37 European Convention for the Protection of Human Rights and Fundamental Freedoms, 213 U.N.T.S. 222 (entered into force Sep. 3, 1953), (ECHR).

38 American Convention on Human Rights, O.A.S. Treaty Series No. 36, 1144 U.N.T.S. 123 (entered into force Jul. 18, 1978), (ACHR).

39 African (Banjul) Charter on Human and Peoples' Rights, O.A.U. Doc. CAB/LEG/67/3 rev. 5, 21 I.L.M. 58, (1982), entered into force Oct. 21, 1986), (AfC).

40 Arab Charter on Human Rights, reprinted in 12 Int'l Hum. Rts. Rep. 893, (2005), entered into force Mar. 15, 2008, (ArC).

41 Convention Against Torture and Other Cruel, Inhuman or Degrading Treatment or Punishment, G.A. Res. 39/46, annex, 39 GAOR Supp. (No. 51) at 107, U.N. Doc. A/39/51 1984, entered into force Jun. 26 1987, (CAT).

42 International Convention for Protection of All Persons from Enforced Disappearances, G.A. Res. 61/177, U.N. Doc. A/RES/61/177, (2006), adopted Dec. 20, 2006.

43 Convention on the Rights of the Child, G.A. Res.44/25, annex, 44 U.N. GAOR Supp. (No. 49) at 167, U.N. Doc. A/44/49, (1989), entered into force Sep. 2, 1990), (CRC).

44 *Id.*
45 *E.g.* U.N. SCR 1373; U.N. SCR 2178, (Sep. 24, 2014).
46 Scheinin, *Impact of Post-9/11 Counter-Terrorism Measures on All Human Rights*, 94. This "exceeded the powers" granted to the Security Council under the U.N. Charter.
47 *Id.*, 95.
48 For a more thorough understanding of IHL *see e.g.* Gary D. Solis, The Law of Armed Conflict, (Cambridge University Press, 2nd ed., 2016); Laurie Blank and Gregory P. Noone, International Law and Armed Conflict: Fundamental Principles and Contemporary Challenges in the Law of War, (Wolters Kluwer, 2018); Yoram Dinstein, The Conduct of Hostilities Under the Law of Armed Conflict, (Cambridge University Press, 2016).
49 Second Hague Peace Conference Convention Regarding the Laws and Customs of Land Warfare, (Oct. 18, 1907), pmbl., 36 Stat. 2277, 3 Martens (3d) 362, reprinted in 2 Am. J. Int'l L. 90, 91–92 (Supp. 1908), (Hague Regulations); Geneva Convention for the Amelioration of the Condition of the Wounded and Sick in Armed Forces in the Field, (Aug. 12, 1949), 6 U.S.T. 3114, 75 U.N.T.S. 31 (GC I); Geneva Convention for the Amelioration of the Condition of the Wounded, Sick and Shipwrecked Members of Armed Forces at Sea, (Aug. 12, 1949). 6 U.S.T. 3217, 75 U.N.T.S. 85 (GC II); Geneva Convention Relative to the Treatment of Prisoners of War, (Aug. 12, 1949), 6 U.S.T. 3316, 75 U.N.T.S. 135 (GC III); Geneva Convention Relative to the Protection of Civilian Persons in Time of War, (Aug. 12, 1949), 6 U.S.T. 3516, 75 U.N.T.S. 287 (GC IV); Protocol Additional to the Geneva Conventions of August 12, 1949 and Relating to the Protection of Victims of International Armed Conflicts, (Jun. 8, 1977), 1125 U.N.T.S. 3 (API); Protocol Additional to the Geneva Conventions of August 12, 1949 and Relating to the Protection of Victims of Non-International Armed Conflicts, (Jun. 8, 1977), U.N.T.S. 609 (APII).
50 Prosecutor v. Tadic, IT-94–1, Appeals Chamber Decision on Jurisdiction, International Criminal Tribunal for the Former Yugoslavia, Oct. 2, 1995), ¶70: "an armed conflict exists whenever there is a resort to armed force between States, or protracted armed violence between governmental authorities and organized armed groups within a State."
51 Nowak and Chabord, *Key Trends in the Fight against Terrorism and Key Aspects of International Human Rights Law*, 30–1.
52 International Committee of the Red Cross (ICRC), International Humanitarian Law (IHL) and the Challenges of Contemporary Armed Conflicts, 8, 32IC/15/11, (Geneva, Oct. 2015); Prosecutor v. Tadic, (Decision on the Defense Motion for Interlocutory Appeal on Jurisdiction) ICTY-94–1, ¶70, (Oct. 2, 1995).
53 ICRC, IHL and the Challenges of Contemporary Armed Conflicts, 43, 31IC/11/5.1.2, (Geneva, Oct. 2011). AP II Art. 13(2) & (3); Jean-Marie Henkaerts and Louise Doswwald-Beck, ICRC., Customary International Humanitarian Law, Vol. I: Rules, Rule 6, (Cambridge University Press, 2009).
54 ICRC, IHL and the Challenges of Contemporary Armed Conflicts, 42–3.
55 Solis, The Law of Armed Conflict, 219.
56 *Id.*, 220; ICRC, IHL and the Challenges of Contemporary Armed Conflicts, 43.
57 API Art. 51.3: Civilians shall enjoy the protection afforded by this section, unless and for such time as they take a direct part in hostilities.
58 Solis, The Law of Armed Conflict, 221.
59 ICRC, IHL and the Challenges of Contemporary Armed Conflicts, 48.
60 Solis, The Law of Armed Conflict, 216.
61 *Id.*, ICRC, IHL and the Challenges of Contemporary Armed Conflicts, 18 (2015).

62 Christine Gray, *Targeting Killing Outside Armed Conflict: A New Departure for the UK?*, 3(2) Journal of the Use of Force and International Law 198, 204, (Dec. 21, 2016).
63 Nowak and Chabord, *Key Trends in the Fight against Terrorism and Key Aspects of International Human Rights Law*, 31.
64 ICRC, IHL and the Challenges of Contemporary Armed Conflicts, 17, (2015).
65 AP I, Arts. 35, 48, 51 for IACs. AP II 13(2), proportionality has been deemed a component of Common Art. 3, and AP II Art. 13(2) is the closest to minimizing damage. *See* Solis, The Law of Armed Conflict, 268–310 for a thorough analysis of these core principles.
66 Henkaerts and Doswwald-Beck, ICRC., Customary International Humanitarian Law, Vol. I, Rule 1 (distinction); Rule 8 (military necessity); Rule 14 (proportionality); and Rule 15 minimizing damage and injury.
67 Ryan Goodman, *Human Rights Law and U.S. Military Operations in Foreign Countries: The Prohibition on Arbitrary Deprivation of Life*, Just Security, (Feb. 19, 2019), www.justsecurity.org/62630/international-human-rights-law-u-s-military-oerations-foreign-countries-prohibition-arbitrary-life/. *Also see* Part II on the subject of jurisdiction.
68 *See e.g.* Alex P. Schmid, *The Definition of Terrorism*, 39, *in* The Routledge Handbook of Terrorism Research, (A.P. Schmid, A. Jongman and E. Price, eds., Routledge, 2011).
69 UNGA Res. 51/210 (Dec. 17, 1996).
70 See e.g. Al-Sirri v. SSHD (United Nations High Commissioner for Refugees intervening), [2013] 1 A.C. 745 (U.K.), ¶37 "there is as yet no internationally agreed definition of terrorism [and] no comprehensive international Convention binding member States to take action against it."
71 Nowak and Chabord, *Key Trends in the Fight against Terrorism and Key Aspects of International Human Rights Law*, 28.
72 Ben Saul, Defining Terrorism in International Law, 5, (Oxford University Press, 2006).
73 Scheinin, *Impact of Post-9/11 Counter-Terrorism Measures on All Human Rights*, 96–7.
74 R. v. Gul, [2013] UKSC 64, ¶29, (Oct. 23, 2013).
75 *Id.*
76 *Id.*, ¶38.
77 Jonathan Hall Q.C., The Terrorism Acts in 2019, Report of Independent Reviewer of the Terrorism Legislation on the Operation of the Terrorism Acts 2000 and 2006, ¶¶7.27–7.60, (Mar. 2021), where he analyzed the YPG prosecutions in detail, highlighting the breadth of the definition of terrorism and the extent and importance of prosecutorial discretion.
78 Diane Webber, Preventive Detention of Terror Suspects: A New Legal Framework, 5, (Routledge, 2016).
79 *E.g.* administrative detention, investigative detention, security detention and immigration detention. *See* Diane Webber, *Preventive and Administrative Detention*, in Elgar Encyclopedia of Human Rights, (Edward Elgar Publishing, forthcoming).
80 Webber, Preventive Detention of Terror Suspects: A New Legal Framework, Appendix 1, (data as in 2016).
81 *Id.*, 4.
82 Sarah Knuckley (ed.), Drones and Targeted Killings: Ethics, Law, Politics, 4, (IDebate Press, 2015); H.L. Pohlman, U.S. National Security Law: An International Perspective, 209, (Rowman & Littlefield, 2019).
83 International Bar Association Human Rights Institute (IBAHRI), The Legality of Armed Drones Under International Law, 7, (Jul. 2017).

84 Knuckley, Drones and Targeted Killings, 5.
85 *World of Drones*, New America, www.newamerica.org/in-depth/world-of-drones/2-who-has-what-countries-drones-used-combat/, (last accessed May 6, 2019).
86 The Coalition Comprises Armed Forces of the U.S., with 33 other nations, see www.centcom.mil/AREA-OF-RESPONSIBILITY/CENTCOM-COALITION/.
87 Marie Forestier, *France's War without Accountability*, AIRWARS, (May 1, 2019), https://airwars.org/news-and-investigations/french-non-accountability-for-civilian-harm/.
88 U.S. Central Command, Combined Joint Task Force – Operation Inherent Resolve Monthly Civilian Casualty Report, Release No. 19–025, (Apr. 25, 2019), www.centcom.mil/MEDIA/PRESS-RELEASES/Press-Release-View/Article/1824000/combined-joint-task-force-operation-inherent-resolve-monthly-civilian-casualty. (The Coalition comprises armed forces of the U.S., with 33 other nations, see www.centcom.mil/AREA-OF-RESPONSIBILITY/CENTCOM-COALITION/).
89 U.S. Dept. of Defense (DoD) Annual Report on Civilian Casualties in Connection with United States Military Operations in 2020, 6, (Apr. 29, 2021), https://media.defense.gov/2021/Jun/02/2002732834/-1/-1/0/ANNUAL-REPORT-ON-CIVILIAN-CASUALTIES-IN-CONNECTION-WITH-UNITED-STATES-MILITARY-OPERATIONS-IN-2020.PDF.
90 *Id.*
91 *Id.*, 7.
92 UN Assistance Mission in Afghanistan, Afghanistan: Protection of Civilians in Armed Conflict, Annual Report 2018, 35, (Feb. 2019), https://unama.unmissions.org/sites/default/files/unama_annual_protection_of_civilians_report_2018_-_23_feb_2019_-_english.pdf.
93 U.S. DoD, Annual Report on Civilian Casualties in Connection with United States Military Operations in 2018, 13, (Apr. 29, 2019), https://media.defense.gov/2019/May/02/2002126767/-1/-1/1/ANNUAL-REPORT-CIVILIAN-CASUALTIES-IN-CONNECTION-WITH-US-MILITARY-OPERATIONS.PDF.
94 U.S. DoD, Annual Report on Civilian Casualties in Connection with United States Military Operations in 2019, 12, (Apr. 22, 2020), https://media.defense.gov/2020/May/06/2002295555/-1/-1/1/SEC-1057-CIVILIAN-CASUALTIES-MAY-1-2020.PDF.
95 *Id.*, 10.
96 *Drone Wars: The Full Data*, Bureau of Investigative Journalism, (BIJ), www.thebureauinvestigates.com/stories/2017-01-01/drone-wars-the-full-data, (last accessed May 7, 2019); *Pentagon Report: 120 Civilians Killed in Operations Abroad*, BIJ, (May 2, 2019), www.thebureauinvestigates.com/stories/2019-05-02/pentagon-report-more-transparent-on-civilian-casualties; *Revealed: Britain has Flown 301 Reaper Drone Missions against ISIS in Iraq, Firing at Least 102 Missiles*, BIJ, (May 15, 2015), www.thebureauinvestigates.com/stories/2015-05-15/revealed-britain-has-flown-301-reaper-drone-mis sions-against-isis-in-iraq-firing-at-least-102-missiles; *U.S. Strikes in the Long War*, Long War Journal, (Foundation for Defense of Democracies), www.longwarjournal.org/us-airstrikes-in-the-long-war, (last accessed May 7, 2019); *Drone Warfare*, BIJ, www.thebureauinvestigates.com/projects/drone-war, (last accessed Jul. 17, 2020).
97 *Strikes in Afghanistan 2018–2020*, BIJ, www.thebureauinvestigates.com/projects/drone-war/charts?show_casualties=1&show_injuries=1&show_strikes=1&locat ion=afghanistan&from=2018-1-1&to=now, (last accessed Jul. 16, 2021).

98 UN Office on Drugs and Crime (UNODC), *Investigation, Prosecution and Adjudication of Foreign Terrorist Fighter Cases for South and South-East Asia*, 1, (2018). The phenomenon probably dates back centuries to the Crusades.

99 Organization for Security and Co-operation in Europe (OSCE), Office for Democratic Institutions and Human Rights (ODIHR), Guidelines for Addressing the Threats and Challenges of "Foreign Terrorist Fighters" Within a Human Rights Framework, 11, (2018). These figures were as estimated in November 2017.

100 Richard Barrett, Beyond the Caliphate: Foreign Fighters and the Threat of Returnees, 5, (The Soufan Group, Oct. 2017).

101 Kim Cragin, *Foreign Fighter 'Hot Potato,'* Lawfare, (Nov. 26, 2017), www.lawfareblog.com/foreign-fighter-hot-potato.

102 *Id.*

103 OSCE, Guidelines for Addressing the Threats and Challenges of "Foreign Terrorist Fighters" Within a Human Rights Framework, 16, *citing* UN Office of Counter Terrorism, Enhancing the Understanding of the Foreign Terrorist Fighter Phenomenon in Syria, 5, and n. 27, (Jul. 2017).

104 U.S. Dept. of State, Office of the Spokesperson, Briefing with Acting Special Envoy for the Global Coalition to Defeat ISIS, John Godfrey on U.S. Participation in the Upcoming D-ISIS Ministerial, Special Briefing, via Teleconference, (Mar. 29, 2021).

105 David Malet and Rachel Hayes, *Foreign Fighter Returnees: An Indefinite Threat?*, 32(8) Terrorism and Political Violence 1617, (2020).

106 *See e.g.* Seth G. Jones and Catrina Doxsee, *The Escalating Terrorism Problem in the United States*, Center for Strategic and International Studies, (Jun. 17, 2020), www.csis.org/analysis/escalating-terrorism-problem-united-states; Vera Bergengruen and W.J. Hennigan, *'We Are Being Eaten From Within.' Why America Is Losing the Battle Against White Nationalist Terrorism*, Time, (Aug. 8, 2019), https://time.com/5647304/white-nationalist-terrorism-united-states/; Mirren Gidda, *Most Terrorists in the U.S. Are Right Wing, Not Muslim: A Report*, Newsweek, (Jun. 22, 2017), www.newsweek.com/right-wing-extremism-islamist-terrorism-donald-trump-steve-bannon-628381; Scott Shane, *Homegrown Extremists Tied to Deadlier Toll Than Jihadists in U.S. since 9/11*, New York Times, (Jun. 24, 2015), www.nytimes.com/2015/06/25/us/tally-of-attacks-in-us-challenges-perceptions-of-top-terror-threat.html.

107 Robert O' Harrow Jr., Andrew Ba Tran and Derek Hawkins, *The Rise of Domestic Extremism in America*, Washington Post, (Apr. 12, 2021), www.washingtonpost.com/investigations/interactive/2021/domestic-terrorism-data/.

108 *See e.g.* The White House, National Security Strategy, 19–22, (May 2010), https://obamawhitehouse.archives.gov/sites/default/files/rss_viewer/national_security_strategy.pdf; The White House, National Security Strategy, 9–10, (Feb. 2015), https://obamawhitehouse.archives.gov/sites/default/files/docs/2015_national_security_strategy_2.pdf; The White House, National Security Strategy of the United States of America, 10–11, (Dec. 2017), https://trumpwhitehouse.archives.gov/wp-content/uploads/2017/12/NSS-Final-12-18-2017-0905.pdf.

109 The White House, National Strategy for Countering Domestic Terrorism, (Jun. 2021), www.whitehouse.gov/wp-content/uploads/2021/06/National-Strategy-for-Countering-Domestic-Terrorism.pdf.

110 *Id.*

111 Pursue, Prevent, Protect, Prepare: The United Kingdom's Strategy for Countering International Terrorism, Home Office, CM 7547, ¶0.19, (Mar. 2009).

112 Contest: The United Kingdom's Strategy for Countering Terrorism, Home Office, CM 9608, (Jun. 2018), ¶¶26, 53, 61.
113 *Id.*, ¶¶129–30, 140, 166–72.
114 MI5, News and Speeches, Director General Ken McCallum Makes First Public Address,(Oct.14,2020),www.mi5.gov.uk/news/director-general-ken-mccallum-makes-first-public-address.
115 Webber, Preventive Detention of Terror Suspects: A New Legal Framework, 15, 142.

Part II

Preventive detention

2 The international law framework for preventive detention

International human rights law (IHRL) provides the framework that underpins preventive detention.[1] Because there is still no internationally agreed definition of "terrorism,"[2] states each have the right to decide what criminal activity amounts to terrorism, and this can result in vague broadly defined crimes that have adverse effects on human rights. Five general human rights treaties contain similar but slightly different provisions dealing with liberty.[3]

International Covenant on Civil and Political Rights (ICCPR)

Right to liberty

Table 2.1 The right to liberty in the ICCPR

Liberty	Art. 9(1) Everyone has the right to liberty and security of the person. No one shall be subjected to arbitrary arrest or detention. No one shall be deprived of his liberty except on such grounds and in accordance with such procedures as are established by law.
Treatment	Art. 10(1) All persons deprived of their liberty shall be treated with humanity and with respect for the inherent dignity of the human person.
Procedure	Art. 9(2) Anyone who is arrested shall be informed, at the time of arrest, of the reasons for his arrest and shall be promptly informed of any charges against him. Art. 9(3) Anyone arrested or detained on a criminal charge shall be brought promptly before a judge or other officer authorized by law to exercise judicial power and shall be entitled to trial within a reasonable time or to release. It shall not be the general rule that persons awaiting trial shall be detained in custody, but release may be subject to guarantees to appear for trial, at any other stage of the judicial proceedings, and, should occasion arise, for execution of the judgment. Art. 9(4) Anyone who is deprived of his liberty shall be entitled to take proceedings before a court, in order that that court may decide without delay on the lawfulness of his detention and order his release if the detention is not lawful.

(*Continued*)

DOI: 10.4324/9780367817275-4

Table 2.1 (Continued)

Redress	Art. 9(5) Anyone who has been the victim of unlawful arrest or detention shall have an enforceable right to compensation.
Jurisdiction	Art. 2 Each State party to the present Covenant undertakes to respect and to ensure to all individuals within in its territory and subject to its jurisdiction the rights recognized in the present Covenant.
Derogation	Art. 4 In time of public emergency which threatens the life of the nation and the existence of which is officially proclaimed, the States Parties to the present Covenant may take measures derogating from their obligations under the present Covenant to the extent strictly required by the exigencies of the situation, provided that such measures are not inconsistent with their other obligations under international law and do not involve discrimination solely on the ground of race, color, sex, language.

Arbitrary detention is not defined in the ICCPR but its meaning, particularly in the context of preventive detention, has evolved over the years through guidance,[4] but mainly in the jurisprudence. However, serious abuses continue: the most recent report of U.N. Working Group on Arbitrary Detention in 2018 dealt with hundreds of allegations of arbitrary detention in 2017 alone.[5]

The most recent Human Rights Committee[6] (HRC) guidance, General Comment (GC) No. 35, was issued in December 2014. Although it referred to preventive detention, it only discussed its use in very general terms and added little in the way of new guidance in interpreting the meaning of "arbitrary."[7] The HR Council's Working Group on Arbitrary Detention which was established in 1991 has a mandate *inter alia* to investigate cases where it is alleged that the deprivation of liberty has been imposed arbitrarily.[8] Its approach has been to conclude that the deprivation of liberty will be arbitrary if it violates the UN Body of Principles[9] and other international standards, and the Working Group has categorized deprivation of liberty into five groups.[10] This does not greatly assist in understanding the meaning of arbitrary.

However, the HRC jurisprudence in key cases, such as *Hugo van Alphen v. The Netherlands, A v. Australia, C v. Australia* and the more recent decisions of *Ribeiro v. Mexico, Formonov v. Uzbekistan* and *Khadzhiyev v. Turkmenistan*, is more nuanced in that these cases identify nine core elements that are required to ensure that detention is not arbitrary.[11] Detention must be appropriate, just, predictable, reasonable, necessary, proportionate, it should not continue longer than can be justified, it should not be used if a less invasive method would be just as effective, and it must be on grounds and in accordance with procedures established by law.[12] This approach for assessing whether or not detention is arbitrary has been applied consistently by the HRC Committee for many years.

Fair treatment

Some states pay scant heed to their international law obligations relating to treatment. For example, in *Formonov v. Uzbekistan*, a human rights activist was arrested arbitrarily, was held incommunicado for one week and tortured in order to elicit a false confession. He was eventually allowed access to a lawyer, who did not act independently. He was not permitted a lawyer of his choice at his trial and no evidence was submitted on his behalf. After conviction he was sentenced to nine years imprisonment. During his sentence he was repeatedly tortured. The Human Rights Committee determined that his treatment violated multiple provisions of the ICCPR, including Article 9(i) and Article 3.[13]

Right to access to justice

Article 9 contains a number of provisions dealing with due process. HRC guidance suggests that sufficient factual information should be given about the substance of the complaint to enable the detainee to challenge the detention.[14] The ICCPR does not make any reference to what evidence would be required to justify detention,[15] but the Working Group on Arbitrary Detention has recommended that detention should not be justified by evidence to which the detainee is not able to respond.[16]

Article 9(4) is pertinent to cases of detention without or before charge. Although a court is obliged to make a decision without delay, neither Article 9(4) nor the guidance stipulate how soon after arrest a court appearance should take place. The ICCPR does not mention any entitlement to legal representation, but in 2014 this omission was addressed in HRC guidance: "To facilitate effective review, detainees should be afforded prompt and regular access to counsel."[17]

Redress

Optional Protocol to the ICCPR permits the HRC to receive and consider communications from individuals claiming to be victims of ICCPR violations provided they are subject to the jurisdiction of State parties.[18] In practical terms these provisions do not deter States from violating the ICCPR. The Human Rights Council monitors and investigates arbitrary detention and the Human Rights Committee investigates and adjudicates complaints, but only after domestic remedies have been exhausted. Often a significant number of years will have elapsed between the violating actions and the hearing of the complaint. The best an aggrieved complainant can hope for is a direction from the Human Rights Committee that the offending State provides "adequate or appropriate" compensation in an unspecified amount. No mechanism exists to compel compliance.[19]

Jurisdiction

The issue of jurisdiction is relevant in the analysis of how States detain terrorism suspects overseas. The words in Article 2 ICCPR guaranteeing rights to "all individuals within in its territory ***and*** subject to its jurisdiction" have been the subject of controversial judicial and scholarly debate. The United States and Israel interpret the "and" in the emphasized words conjunctively, with the effect that those states maintain that the guarantees of the ICCPR do not apply to persons detained by the United States in Guantanamo Bay in Cuba and other places of detention around the world, or by Israel in the Occupied Territories. Conversely, the view of the HRC,[20] as confirmed by the International Court of Justice (ICJ),[21] is that the ICCPR *travaux préparatoires* (documents that recorded the treaty negotiations) corroborate the stance that a disjunctive approach (replacing "and" with "or") was the correct interpretation. The effect of this is that most states and organizations believe that the ICCPR can apply to protect human rights overseas if they have domestic laws that apply outside the home territory.[22]

Derogation

In some situations of public emergency States party to the ICCPR may be released from certain treaty guarantees,[23] including the right to liberty in Article 9, but States must still comply with all their obligations under IHRL, IHL, and refugee law. States are never permitted to derogate from guaranteeing the rights to life, judicial review, freedom of thought, conscience or religion, recognition of a person before the law or the rights that prohibit slavery, punishment without law, or torture and inhumane treatment.[24] Acts of terrorism can, but may not always, prompt the need for emergency powers.[25]

The use of such powers under both international and the national laws of a State must always be subject to the requirements of legality, proportionality, and non-discrimination.[26] ICCPR guidance mandates that (i) the state of emergency must threaten the life of the whole nation and relate to an actual or imminent danger; (ii) the State must officially proclaim a state of emergency; (iii) the derogating measures must be necessary and proportionate; and the measures must be exceptional and temporary.[27] It appears to be an unspoken rule that each state should be given some latitude in deciding when to derogate and what measures are appropriate. The guidance does not mention the margin of appreciation[28] afforded by the European Court of Human Rights ("ECtHR") which is discussed below. In 2018 the Special Rapporteur for Human Rights expressed a concern that international law obligations relating to emergency powers were being used as a justification for the failure of certain states to comply with their domestic human rights standards.[29] She emphasized that states have "specific and concrete human rights obligations when emergency powers are triggered by counter-terrorism law and practice."[30] The Special Rapporteur also raised many concerns about the indefinite use of emergency powers through counter-terrorism legislation,[31] and concluded that states of emergency "remain a pernicious and under-supervised source of human rights violations globally."[32] These remarks apply to derogation from the human rights guarantees in all the treaties discussed in this chapter.

European Convention on Human Rights (ECHR)

Right to liberty

Table 2.2 The right to liberty in the ECHR

Liberty	Art. 5(1) **Everyone has the right to liberty and security of the person. No one shall be deprived of his liberty save in the following cases and in accordance with a procedure prescribed by law**: (a) the lawful detention of a person after conviction by a competent court; (b) the lawful arrest or detention for non-compliance with the lawful order of a court or in order to secure the fulfilment of any obligation prescribed by law; (c) **the lawful arrest or detention of a person effected for the purpose of binging him before the competent legal authority on reasonable suspicion of having committed an offence, or when it is reasonably considered necessary to prevent his committing an offence, or fleeing after having done so**; (d) the detention of a minor by lawful order of educational supervision or his lawful detention for the purpose of bringing before the competent legal authority; (e) the lawful detention of persons for the prevention of the spreading of infectious diseases, of persons of unsound mind, alcoholics, or drug addicts or vagrants; (f) the lawful arrest or detention of a person to prevent his effecting an unauthorized entry into the country or of a person against whom action is being taken with a view to deportation or extradition.
Treatment	Art. 3 No one shall be subjected to torture or to inhuman or degrading treatment or punishment.
Procedure	Art. 5(2) Everyone who is arrested shall be informed promptly, in a language which he understands, of the reasons for his arrest and any charge against him. (3) Everyone arrested or detained in accordance with the provisions of paragraph (1)(c) of this article shall be brought promptly before a judge or other officer authorized by law to exercise judicial power and shall be entitled to trial within a reasonable time or to release pending trial. (4) Everyone who is deprived of his liberty by arrest or detention shall be entitled to take proceedings by which the lawfulness of his detention shall be decided speedily and his release ordered if the detention is not lawful.
Redress	Art. 5(5) Everyone who has been the victim of arrest or detention in contravention of the provisions of this article shall have an enforceable right to compensation. Art. 13 Everyone whose rights and freedoms as set forth in the Convention are violated shall have an effective remedy before a national authority notwithstanding that the violation has been committed by persons acting in an official capacity.

(*Continued*)

Table 2.2 (Continued)

Jurisdiction	Art. 1 The High Contracting Parties shall secure to everyone within their jurisdiction the rights and freedoms defined in Section 1 of this Convention.
Derogation	Art. 15(1) In time of war or other public emergency threatening the life of the nation any Contracting Party may take measures derogating from its obligations under this Convention to the extent strictly required by the exigencies of the situation, provided that such measures are not inconsistent with its other obligations under international law.

The drafters of the ECHR considered that the way the ICCPR dealt with restrictions on liberty was imprecise.[33] Consequently, they decided on a different formula. This has generated a vast body of case law that has debated the interpretation of Article 5(1) ECHR which lists six grounds where detention will be permitted in accordance with a procedure prescribed by law.[34] *Grubnyk v. Ukraine* is an example of arrest and detention that was not in accordance with a procedure prescribed by law, where a suspected terrorist was arrested without a prior required court decision authorizing the arrest, and the arrest report was not drawn up within the prescribed period.[35]

The ECHR contains no reference to "arbitrary" detention but the concept and the importance of protecting persons from arbitrary detention is mentioned consistently in ECtHR jurisprudence.[36] Key principles as to what might constitute arbitrary detention have been developed on a case by case basis, and the topic was addressed in detail in *Saadi v. United Kingdom*, which identified requirements that the detention must be necessary to achieve the stated aim, proportionate, should not continue for an unreasonable time, and should be a measure of last resort where other less serious measures have been considered.[37]

Article 5(1)(c) is the clause most pertinent to preventive detention of terror suspects. The interpretation of this clause in the context of detention to prevent the commission of an offense has been the subject of much jurisprudential and scholarly discussion, mainly because 5(1)(c) appears to set out three separate situations in which a person might be detained on reasonable suspicion: (1) after an offense has been committed (first limb); (2) when it is reasonably considered necessary to prevent the commission of an offense (second limb); or (3) if someone flees after having committed an offense (third limb).[38]

ECtHR interpretative opinion about the meaning of preventive detention pursuant to Article 5(1)(c) has moved over the years from one end of the spectrum to the other, and in many cases the analysis returned to the preparatory work or *travaux préparatoires*[39] of the ECHR, which suggests that the drafters had contemplated the idea of detention to prevent the commission of a crime.[40] The first seminal case was that of *Lawless v. Ireland*.[41] Lawless, who admitted that he was a member of the IRA, was detained without trial in a military camp between July 13 and December 11 1957. The Court interpreted the meaning of Article 5(1)(c) in the following terms:

> Whereas the wording of Article 5, paragraph 1 (c), is sufficiently clear to give an answer to this question; whereas it is evident that the expression "effected for the purpose of bringing him before the competent legal authority" qualifies every category of cases of arrest or detention referred to in that sub-paragraph; whereas it follows that the said clause permits deprivation of liberty only when such deprivation is effected for the purpose of bringing the person arrested or detained before the competent judicial authority, irrespective of whether such person is a person who is reasonably suspected of having committed an offence, or a person whom it is reasonably considered necessary to restrain from committing an offence, or a person whom it reasonably considered necessary to restrain from absconding after having committed an offence;
>
> Whereas . . . paragraph 1 (c) of Article 5 can be construed only if read in conjunction with paragraph 3 of the same Article, with which it forms a whole; whereas paragraph 3 stipulates categorically that "everyone arrested or detained in accordance with the provisions of paragraph 1 (c) of this Article shall be brought promptly before a judge" and "shall be entitled to trial within a reasonable time"; whereas it plainly entails the obligation to bring everyone arrested or detained in any of the circumstances contemplated by the provisions of paragraph 1 (c) before a judge *for the purpose of examining the question of deprivation of liberty or for the purpose of deciding on the merits*; whereas such is the plain and natural meaning of the wording of both paragraph 1 (c) and paragraph 3 of Article 5.[42]

The ECtHR unanimously held that despite the lack of any foundation in law to detain Lawless without trial pursuant to Article 5(1)(c), Ireland was justified to derogate from Article 5 and the detention did not breach the ECHR. The Court interpreted the words of Article 5 and the *travaux preparatoires* very literally.[43] Thus detention only authorized lawful arrest or detention for the purpose of bringing a person before a lawful authority. Detention without trial was not for that purpose and was not authorized under Article 5.[44]

In *Guzzardi v. Italy*, the meaning of Article 5 (1)(c) was discussed and dismissed as not relevant to the case under consideration. However, the words in the judgment are useful as regards interpreting the meaning of the prevention element of Article 5(1)(c), which:

> is not adapted to a policy of general prevention directed against an individual or a category of individuals who, like mafiosi, present a danger on account of their continuing propensity to crime; it does not do more than afford the Contracting States a means of preventing a concrete and specific offence.[45]

The "concrete and specific" requirement has been repeated in many cases.[46] In *Schwabe v. Germany*, the ECtHR repeated the *Lawless* formula: "detention to prevent a person from committing an offence, must in addition [to being a specific and concrete offence], be 'effected for the purpose of bringing him before the competent legal authority,' a requirement which qualifies every category of detention referred to in Article 5(1)(c)."[47]

In *Ostendorf v. Germany*, whilst finding no violation of Articles 5(1)(b) or 5(1)(c), in addition to reiterating the *Lawless* formula, the ECtHR went further regarding the interpretation, commenting that the second limb set out in Article 5(1)(c) "only governs pre-trial detention and not custody for preventive purposes without the person concerned being suspected of having already committed a criminal offence,"[48] such as a preparatory offence. However, two judges in a concurring opinion moved towards a more preventive approach. They noted (with emphasis added) that whilst ECtHR case law confirmed that

> a preventive detention is possible "only in the context of criminal proceedings, for the purpose of bringing (a person) before the competent legal authority on suspicion of his having committed an offence." . . . In our view this case law has gone too far in holding that the requirement in Article 5 §1(c) of bringing the arrested or detained person "before the competent legal authority" means, in all of the situations set out in that provision, that the intention should be to bring "criminal proceedings" against that person. *We think that in situations where there is a vital public interest in preventing someone from committing an offence, a limited possibility does exist for the law enforcing authorities to detain that person for a short period, even if he has not yet committed a crime and therefore without the possibility that criminal proceedings will be opened against him.*[49]

The judges opined that the case law had derogated from what it had said in *Lawless* in that it has "unduly restricted the purpose of bringing the detainee before a judge to 'deciding on the merits', and done away with the possible purpose of 'examining the question of deprivation of liberty.'"[50] They considered that a return to the true *Lawless* formula did "more justice to prevention as a possible justification for a deprivation of liberty than does the current interpretation."[51]

In order to protect the rights of a detainee, the possibilities for such preventive detentions should be limited, and one such existing guarantee is that a detainee is to be brought promptly before a judge, pursuant to Article 5(3).[52] The ECHR has held that the fact that a detained person is not charged or brought before a court does not necessarily violate Article 5(3). If a person has been released before it would have been feasible to have appeared in a court, no violation of Article 5(3) will have occurred.[53] The judges concluded:

> An early, "prompt" release, without any appearance before a judge or judicial officer, may occur frequently in cases of "administrative" detention for preventive purposes. Even so, in such a situation it will be enough for the purpose of guaranteeing the rights inherent in Article 5 of the Convention if the lawfulness of the detention can subsequently be challenged and decided by a court.[54]

Ostendorf did not refer to remarks in *Al-Jedda v. United Kingdom* where an Iraqi national had been detained in Iraq by British forces allegedly on the grounds of imperative reasons of security. The ECtHR commented that it has "long been established that the list of grounds of permissible detention in Article 5(1) does not include internment or preventive detention where there is no intention to bring criminal charges within a reasonable time."[55] Could those words be interpreted to mean that arresting authorities might be able to detain preventively within the scope of Article 5(1)(c) and 5(3) before they are able to decide that they do not intend to bring criminal charges, provided that the detainee is brought promptly before a court to challenge detention?[56] That interpretation seems to be what the concurring judges in *Ostendorf* were advocating for.

A further shift of ECtHR opinion regarding the interpretation of preventive detention under Article 5(1) was discerned in 2018 when it commented that there was a need to revisit and further clarify the case law because "modern societal problems of the kind at issue in the case" needed to be addressed "more appropriately."[57] The case *of S, V and A v. Denmark* concerned the detention of three alleged football hooligans, who travelled to Copenhagen to watch a football match between Denmark and Sweden. They were detained for periods of just over seven hours pursuant to a statute that permitted detention for up to six hours if other less intrusive measures were inadequate to avert the risk of disturbance of public order and any danger to the safety of individuals and public security.[58]

The ECtHR revisited the *travaux preparatoires* and noted that the drafters of the ECHR did contemplate that it "might be necessary in certain circumstances to arrest an individual in order to prevent his committing a crime, even if the facts which show his intention to commit the crime do not of themselves constitute a penal offence."[59]

The Court specifically addressed whether Article 5(1)(c) could be applicable to preventive detention outside criminal proceedings, whilst noting that the Court in *Ostendorf* had already rejected this possibility.[60] The crucial question for the Court was whether the second limb of Article 5(1)(c) ought to be seen as a distinct ground for deprivation of liberty, independently of the first limb.[61] The Court reviewed *Lawless* and subsequent cases and determined that the judgment considered that each of the three limbs of Article 5(1)(c) referred to three distinct grounds for detention, and in each case there was an obligation to bring the detainee before a judge either to evaluate the detention or to decide on the merits of a criminal charge.[62] There were numerous permissible examples of preventive detention that had occurred outside of the context of criminal proceedings such as in *Ireland v. United Kingdom:*

> Irrespective of whether extrajudicial deprivation of liberty was or was not founded in the majority of cases on suspicions of a kind that would render detention on remand justifiable under the Convention, such detention is permissible under Article 5 para. 1 (c) only if it is "effected for the purpose of bringing [the detainee] before the competent legal authority."[63]

It appears that the ECtHR followed this approach for 27 years, only to depart from it without any explanation, or reference to inconsistency in cases such as *Cuilla v. Italy* and *Jecius v. Lithuania*.[64] In parallel to the cases that followed the *Cuilla* line, down to *Ostendorf*, is an inconsistent trio of cases which seem to contemplate that preventive detention under the second limb of Article 5(1)(c) can be lawful in certain distinct situations.[65] Those cases, read together with the *travaux preparatoires* led the Court in *S, V and A* to conclude that the second limb of Article 5(1)(c) should be considered as a "distinct ground, notably separate from the first limb,"[66] provided that the detained person is protected from arbitrariness.[67]

The Court went on to consider whether the purpose requirement might pose an obstacle to preventive detention. It noted that this has been interpreted and applied with some flexibility when the intention to bring the detainee before a court has not materialized for some reason. For example, in *Brogan v. United Kingdom*, where four applicants had been arrested and detained for almost six days on suspicion of being concerned in the commission, preparation or instigation of terrorist acts, the detention had violated Article 5(3) because they had not been released promptly, but there had been no violation of Article 5(1)(c). In that case the Court separated the existence of the purpose for bringing a person to court, from actually being able to do so:

> the existence of such a purpose must be considered independently of its achievement and Article 5(1)(c) does not presuppose that the police should have obtained sufficient evidence to bring charges, either at the point of arrest or while the applicants were in custody.[68]

The *S, V, and A* Court commended this flexible approach as being compatible with the spirit of Article 5, and noted that

> Article 5 cannot be interpreted in such a way as to make it impracticable for the police to fulfil their duties of maintaining order and protecting the public, provided that they comply with the underlying principle of the provision, which is to protect the individual from arbitrariness[69] . . . and the other safeguards embodied in Article 5(1).[70]

This means that that the deprivation of liberty must be lawful, not arbitrary, that the offence be concrete and specific, that the authorities must supply facts from which an objective observer would deduce that the detainee would in all likelihood have been involved in the concrete and specific offence if the commission of the act had not been prevented by the detention, and that the detention was reasonably considered as necessary.[71] The Court concluded that subject to the availability of safeguards pursuant to Articles 5(3) and (5), the purpose requirement should not pose an obstacle to short-term preventive detention.[72]

The Court offered useful guidance on the question of how to assess whether detention is necessary:

less severe measures have to be considered and found to be insufficient to safeguard the individual or public interest which might require that the person concerned be detained. Preventive detention cannot reasonably be considered necessary unless a proper balance is struck between the importance in a democratic society of preventing an imminent risk of an offence being committed and the importance of the right to liberty. In order to be proportionate to such a serious measure as deprivation of liberty, the concrete and specific "offence" referred to under the second limb of Article 5 § 1 (c) must also be of a serious nature, entailing danger to life and limb or significant material damage. It follows in addition that the detention should cease as soon as the risk has passed, which requires monitoring, the duration of the detention being also a relevant factor.[73]

Fair treatment

Many violations of Article 3 continue in the context of detention irrespective of the reason for such detention. Over a number of years, the ECtHR has refined the meaning of inhuman or degrading treatment to cover poor conditions in detention facilities[74] and lack of, or inadequate medical treatment.[75] In the counter-terrorism context, the ECtHR was petitioned to adjudicate on the two consolidated cases brought against Poland by Husayn (aka Abu Zubayda) and al Nashiri.[76] The applicants each claimed that Poland had enabled the CIA to detain them secretly and incommunicado, and to subject them to torture, mental and physical abuse, in breach of Articles 3, 5, and 8 (respect for family life) ECHR.

The ECtHR reiterated that "even in the most difficult circumstances, such as the fight against terrorism and organized crime, the Convention prohibits in absolute terms torture and inhuman or degrading treatment."[77] The Court concluded that the treatment amounted to torture within the meaning of Article 3.[78] It also concluded that Poland knew of the nature and purpose of the CIA's activities on its territory and that it had co-operated in the rendition, secret detention and interrogation of the terrorist suspect, and ought to have known and must have known that the detention exposed the applicants to a serious risk of treatment that would violate Article 3.[79] The ECtHR therefore held that because of its facilitation of, and complicity, acquiescence, and connivance in the CIA activities, Poland must be regarded as responsible for the violation of the applicants' rights. Poland had also failed in its Article 1 duty to take measures to protect those in its jurisdiction from torture and inhuman treatment.[80]

Right to access to justice

The primary goal of Article 5(2) has been said to be to "provide a safeguard against arbitrary deprivation of liberty and allow the applicant to obtain an effective review of the lawfulness of his detention, which would not be possible without knowing the reasons for it."[81] Thus all detainees must be told the "essential legal and factual grounds" for their arrest, but not necessarily at the moment of arrest.[82]

All persons, including those detained on preventive grounds must be brought promptly before a court so that the lawfulness of the detention may be assessed.[83] As to the meaning of "promptly," this determination has to be made in the light of the object and purpose of Article 5,[84] and in accordance with the special features of each case, the strict time constraint leaves little room for any flexibility in interpretation, "otherwise there would be a serious weakening of a procedural guarantee to the detriment of the individual and a risk of impairing the very essence of the right protected by this provision."[85] In *Brannigan v. McBride v. United Kingdom*, detention without charge and judicial control for a period of less than seven days was considered acceptable.[86] However, in *S, V, and A v. Denmark*, preventive detention for more than four days was deemed *prima facie* too long.[87]

Although Article 6 ensures that persons who have been charged may have legal representation, there is nothing in Article 5 that affords this right to detainees held without charge. The first move towards addressing this lacuna seems to derive from ECtHR comments in *Salduz v. Turkey*, which suggested that "access to a lawyer should be provided from the first interrogation of a suspect by the police, unless it is demonstrated in the light of the particular circumstances of each case that there are compelling reasons to restrict this right."[88] In *Dayanan v. Turkey*, the ECtHR commented:

> In accordance with the generally recognized international norms, which the Court accepts and which form the framework for its case-law, an accused person is entitled, as soon as he or she is taken into custody, to be assisted by a lawyer, and not only while being questioned.[89]

All EU Member States were required to transpose into their national laws the 2013 EU Directive that *inter alia* gave persons the right of access to a lawyer without undue delay after deprivation of liberty,[90] by November 27, 2016.[91] The 2013 Directive also gave individuals the right to have a third party informed of the deprivation of liberty without undue delay and to communicate with a third party and consular authorities, except where there is an urgent need to avert serious adverse consequences affecting a person, or to prevent jeopardizing criminal proceedings.[92] As of September 2019, it appeared that almost all Member States had complied with the transposition that would give detainees access to a lawyer, but a number of Member States had not complied fully with the transposition that would have a third party informed of the detention.[93]

Redress

Victims must initially seek redress at national level. A complaint may only be initiated at the international level when all attempts to obtain relief at the domestic level have been exhausted. As of August 31, 2020, 64,200 applications were pending in the ECtHR.[94] In 2019, 25% of the 790 violations (the largest percentage per violation) related to Article 5.[95] Between 1955 and 2019, 20.9% of the 18,977 violations were of Article 5.[96] The ECtHR is empowered to order the payment of a specified amount of damages to an applicant. The Committee of Ministers of the Council of Europe supervise the activities of a Member State and monitor the payments of damages, the majority of which tend not to be paid promptly, or at all.[97] In addition the ECtHR operates a system of non-contentious proceedings which encourages the achievement of friendly settlements, which have averaged around 1,400 a year for the last seven years.[98]

Jurisdiction

The interpretation of extraterritorial application of the ECHR, particularly in relation to acts committed by a State's armed forces overseas, has also been a subject generating much discussion and debate. Through a series of rulings,[99] the ECtHR extended the interpretation of "within the jurisdiction" in what it called exceptional circumstances, to cover acts anywhere overseas where the State exercised authority and control over individuals.[100]

For example, in *Al-Jedda v. United Kingdom* the applicant was Iraqi-born but acquired British nationality in 2000. In 2004 he travelled to Iraq and was arrested by U.S. soldiers in Baghdad who were acting on British intelligence. He was taken to Basra on a British military aircraft and interned on the grounds that his detention was necessary for imperative reasons of security in a British run detention center until December 30, 2007. The first question for the ECtHR to consider was the issue of jurisdiction. It held that as the internment took place within a detention facility in Basra City controlled exclusively by British forces, the applicant was within the authority and control of the United Kingdom throughout, and therefore within the jurisdiction of the United Kingdom.[101]

Derogation

State parties may derogate from the right to liberty in Article 5 provided all the stated criteria for a state of emergency are met.[102] Rights can only be lawfully derogated if there is a public emergency. This has been defined as "a situation of exceptional and imminent danger or crisis affecting the general public as distinct from particular groups and constituting a threat to the organized life of the community which composes the state in question."[103] The European Commission identified four characteristics of a public emergency: it must be actual or imminent; its effects must involve the whole nation; the continuance of the organized life of the community must be threatened; and the crisis must be exceptional in that normal measures are plainly inadequate.[104] ECtHR jurisprudence has confirmed that terrorism may amount to a situation of emergency.[105] In such cases of public emergency, derogating measures are only permitted to the extent strictly required by the exigencies of the situation: they must be "proportionate to strict necessity."[106] The ECtHR has recognized a margin of appreciation when it has assessed the need for and scope of derogating measures,[107] and has generally tended to defer to the decisions that governments have made in response to emergencies.[108]

No temporal limits are placed on states of emergency in the ECHR. ECtHR jurisprudence which operates on a case-by-case basis, has implicitly accepted long and entrenched states of emergency in Northern Ireland and Turkey,[109] but the margin of appreciation afforded to States may be less deferential when evaluating the proportionality of derogating measures,[110] including the duration of detention.

American Convention on Human Rights (ACHR)

Table 2.3 The right to liberty in the ACHR

Liberty	Art. 7(1) Every person has the right to personal liberty and security. (2) No one shall be deprived of his personal liberty except for the reasons and under the conditions established beforehand by the constitution of the State party concerned or by a law established thereto. (3) No one shall be subject to arbitrary arrest or imprisonment.
Treatment	Art. 5(2) No one shall be subjected to torture or to cruel, inhuman, or degrading punishment or treatment. All persons deprived of their liberty shall be treated with respect for the inherent dignity of the human person.
Procedure	Art. 7(4) Anyone who is detained shall be informed of the reasons for his detention and shall be promptly notified of the charges against him. (5) Any person detained shall be brought promptly before a judge or other officer authorized by law to exercise judicial power and shall be entitled to trial within a reasonable time or to be released without prejudice to the continuation of the proceedings. His release may be subject to guarantees to assure his appearance for trial. (6) Anyone who is deprived of his liberty shall be entitled to recourse to a competent court, in order that the court may decide without delay on the lawfulness of his arrest or detention and order his release if the arrest or detention is unlawful. In States Parties whose laws provide that anyone who believes himself to be threatened with deprivation of his liberty is entitled to recourse to a competent court in order that it may decide on the lawfulness of such a threat, this remedy may not be restricted or abolished. The interested party or another person on his behalf is entitled to seek these remedies.
Redress	Art. 25(1) Everyone has the right to simple and prompt recourse, or any other effective recourse, to a competent court or tribunal for protection against acts that violate his fundamental rights recognized by the constitution or laws of the state concerned or by this Convention, even though such violation may have been committed by persons acting in the course of their official duties.
Jurisdiction	Art. 1 The States' parties to this Convention undertake to respect the rights and freedoms recognized herein and to ensure to all persons subject to their jurisdiction the free and full exercise of those right and freedoms, without any discrimination for reasons of race, color, sex, language, religion, political or other opinion, national or social origin, economic status, birth, or any other social condition.

Derogation	Art. 27(1) In time of war, public danger, or other emergency that threatens the independence or security of a State Party, it may take measures derogating from its obligations under the present Convention to the extent and for the period strictly required by the exigencies of the situation, provided that such measures are not inconsistent with its other obligations under international law and do not involve discrimination on the ground of race, color, sex, language, religion, or social origin. (Under 27(2) no derogation is permitted from Article 5 (*inter alia*) at any time).

Right to liberty

Inter-American jurisprudence and guidance has elaborated on the meaning of arbitrary arrest, citing requirements of reasonableness, foreseeability, proportionality, necessity, legality, and lack of arbitrariness:[111]

> No person may be deprived of his or her personal freedom except for reasons, cases or circumstances expressly defined by law (material aspect) and, furthermore, subject to strict adherence to the procedures objectively set forth in that law (formal aspect). . . . No-one may be subjected to arrest or imprisonment for reasons and by methods which, although classified as legal, could be deemed to be incompatible with the respect for the fundamental rights of the individual because, among other things, they are unreasonable, unforeseeable or lacking in proportionality.[112]

As to preventive detention:

> The preventive detention is limited by the principles of legality, the presumption of innocence, need, and proportionality, all of which are strictly necessary in a democratic society. . . . The legitimacy of the preventive detention does not arise only from the fact that the law allows its application under certain general hypotheses. The adoption of this precautionary measure requires a judgment of proportionality between said measure, the evidence to issue it, and the facts under investigation. If the proportionality does not exist, the measure will be arbitrary.[113]

In March 2008 the Inter-American Commission for Human Rights (IACHR) resolved to approve Principles and Best Practices on the Protection of Persons Deprived of Liberty in the Americas ("IACHR Principles").[114] This guidance reiterates the requirements of legality, necessity, and proportionality. Furthermore, detention is seen as an exceptional measure to be applied for the minimum necessary period.[115]

Fair treatment

The IACHR Principles mandate humane treatment with "unconditional respect for their inherent dignity" for all persons. The wording continues in a somewhat limiting way by stating that all detainees "shall be afforded minimum conditions compatible with their dignity."[116] Despite the jurisprudence and guidance, many violations continue unabated. One example of this is *Jimenez*, who was detained without judicial order and held for 51 days without appearing before a judicial authority. During that time she was held incommunicado for 39 days, and subjected to psychological torture.[117]

Right to access to justice

Article 7 mandates that every detainee shall be told the reason for detention and promptly notified of the charges against him.[118] This wording could suggest that there is no requirement to give the reason for detention promptly. Detained persons must be brought before a judge promptly and are entitled to a trial within a reasonable time.[119] All persons detained are entitled to recourse to a competent court, in order that the court can decide if the detention is lawful.[120]

In 2006 the IACHR issued guidance for detention in the context of counter-terrorism strategies which listed requirements for measures to comply with prescribed minimum standards. These included placing limits on the duration of detention and ensuring that detainees had prompt access to legal counsel, family, medical attention, and consular assistance.[121]

Redress

The ACHR guarantees the right to seek a remedy for violation of fundamental rights. In the first instance, once domestic remedies have been exhausted or are inaccessible, a person may petition the IACHR for redress.[122] In 2019 the IACHR received 3,034 petitions, the highest number in its history.[123] For a number of years there had been a large backlog, but by the end of 2019, the IACHR had published 123 reports on admissibility, 23 reports on inadmissibility, and two reports on merits.[124] They held hearings on four cases.[125] In 2020 the IACHR decided to proceed with only 17% of the 1,990 petitions that it processed,[126] and approved 45 reports on admissibility.[127]

Much of the IACHR's work is related to following up on its recommendations. This is a slow and lengthy process. In 2020, out of 113 cases, only ten had been closed, and at best, partial compliance had been achieved in the majority of cases, some of which were years old, such as the 2001 case of *Jimenez*.[128] The IACHR submitted 32 contentious cases to the Inter-American Court for Human Rights (IACtHR) in 2019[129] and 23 in 2020.[130] These included claims relating to detention and forced disappearance of an alleged rebel in Ecuador,[131] and arbitrary detention in Venezuela.[132] Like the ECtHR, the IACHR also operates a system of friendly settlements, and it "made progress" with 45 matters and settled 10 in 2020.[133]

Jurisdiction

The scope of extraterritorial jurisdiction in the ACHR covers "all persons subject to their jurisdiction."[134] The IACHR opined that in certain circumstances a

State Party might be responsible for the acts and omissions of its agents which produces effects or are undertaken outside that State's territory.[135] The United States has not ratified the ACHR, but considers itself bound by the earlier American Declaration on the Rights and Duties of Man,[136] which is silent as to jurisdictional scope.

In 2002 the IACHR authorized precautionary measures in favor of unnamed detainees at Guantanamo Bay, Cuba. They requested information from the United States. Some information was provided, but the United States disputed the IACHR's jurisdiction to adopt precautionary measures. Further information was requested but none was received. The scope of these precautionary measures was extended in 2005, requiring the United States to investigate and prosecute all instances of torture, and in 2013, requiring the United States to close Guantanamo.[137] Precautionary measures were also adopted for Omar Khadr,[138] Djamel Ameziane,[139] and Mustafa Adam Al-Hawsawi.[140] Ameziane also petitioned the IACHR for relief in August 2008. The 2020 report relating to Ameziane is discussed below in the section on the United States.

Derogation

The American Declaration contains a clause limiting the effect and application of its provisions in a very minor way.[141] Some guidance relating to the interpretation of Article 27 ACHR, which does not permit derogation from the prohibition on inhuman treatment,[142] can be found in comments by the IACHR[143] and the IACtHR.[144] However there is little evidence of a clear analysis of the requirement of proportionality in derogation.[145] The right to *habeas* corpus can never be suspended.[146] Although Article 27 contains a temporal limitation, a number of States have not complied.[147]

African Charter on Human and Peoples' Rights (African Charter)

Table 2.4 The right to liberty in the African Charter

Liberty	Art. 6 Every individual shall have the right to liberty and to the security of his person. No one may be deprived of his freedom except for reason and conditions previously laid down by law. In particular, no one may be arbitrarily arrested or detained.
Treatment	Art. 5 Every individual shall have the right to the respect of the dignity inherent in a human being and to the recognition of his status. All forms of exploitation and degradation of man, particularly slavery, slave trade, torture, cruel, inhuman, or degrading punishment and treatment shall be prohibited.
Procedure	Art. 7(1) Every individual shall have the right to have his cause heard.

(*Continued*)

Table 2.4 (Continued)

Redress	Art. 7(1) Every individual shall have the right to have his cause heard. This comprises: 1. The right to an appeal to competent national organs against acts of violating his fundamental rights as recognized and guaranteed by conventions, laws, regulations, and customs in force.
Jurisdiction	Art. 2 Every individual shall be entitled to the enjoyment of the rights and freedoms recognized and guaranteed in the present Charter without distinction of any kind such as race, ethnic group, color, sex, language, religion, political, or any other opinion, national and social origin, fortune, birth, or any status.
Derogation	None

Right to liberty

The only completed case before the African Court on Human and Peoples' Rights relating to detention appears to have been *African Commission on Human and Peoples' Rights v. Libya.*[148] This concerned the detention of Saif Al-Islam Kadhafi by a "revolutionary brigade" in a secret location without access to family, friends, or a lawyer and with no opportunity to challenge the detention for over two years, despite the existence of rights to complain about detention under the Libyan Criminal Procedure Code. Furthermore, he was sentenced to death *in absentia* in July 2015. Libya had ignored all of the African Court's Orders for Provisional Measures.

In its opinion, the Court referred to two other IHRL treaties, commenting that "every deprivation of liberty must meet a number of minimum guarantees commonly enshrined in international human rights instruments, in particular in Article 9 of the ICCPR which is also applicable in the instant case."[149] It also referred to the ECtHR decisions of *Brusco v. France*[150] and *Dayanan v. Turkey*[151] to highlight the importance of and the failings in this case regarding access to and representation by a lawyer. It ruled that the incommunicado detention in isolation violated Article 6 and 7 of the African Charter. Ultimately the ruling merely ordered Libya to guarantee and protect Kadhafi's legal rights, rendering it a judgment without teeth.

Fair treatment

This is guaranteed in the Charter, which specifically mentions slavery in addition to the other forms of mistreatment.

Right to access to justice

Article 7 merely guarantees a right to have one's cause heard. Procedural guarantees are therefore non-existent, as nothing specifically deals with challenging detention, either promptly or at all, or access to counsel, or notifying anyone of the fact of arrest.[152]

Redress

Article 7 guarantees a right to appeal against acts violating fundamental rights. In terms of treaty violations, The African Court on Human and Peoples' Rights was established in 2004[153] and started operations in 2006. Individuals can only petition the Court if their home State has ratified the Protocol establishing the Court. As of July 2020, only nine out of 30 States have ratified. 287 applications have been made to the Court, of which 268 were brought by individuals. 181 cases are still pending.[154] Judgments are binding but the Court may also issue non-binding advisory opinions.

Jurisdiction

Reference to jurisdiction in the African Charter is limited to a statement that every individual shall be entitled to enjoy the rights and freedoms set out in the Charter.[155] One unique aspect of this Court is that it has jurisdiction to decide cases about violations of human rights from treaties other than the African Charter by states that have ratified such other human rights instrument.[156] However, in practice, although other treaties have been considered in a number of cases, the Court appears to be reluctant to adjudicate on alleged violations of other human rights treaties, and it is not clear why.[157]

Allegations of violations of the ICCPR as well as the African Charter were considered in *African Commission on Human and Peoples' Rights v. Libya*.[158] The Court mentioned the ICCPR in its judgment but did not rule as to whether the ICCPR had been violated.

Derogation

Derogation is not possible from any of the guarantees of the African Charter.

Arab Charter on Human Rights (Arab Charter)

Table 2.5 The right to liberty in the Arab Charter

Liberty	Art. 14(1) Everyone has the right to liberty and security of person. No one shall be subjected to arbitrary arrest, search or detention without a legal warrant. (2) No one shall be deprived of his liberty except on such grounds and in such circumstances as are determined by law and in accordance with such procedure as is established thereby.
Treatment	Art. 8 No one shall be subjected to physical or psychological torture or to cruel, degrading, humiliating, or inhuman treatment. Art. 20 (1) All persons deprived of their liberty shall be treated with humanity and with respect for the inherent dignity of the person.

(*Continued*)

Table 2.5 (Continued)

Procedure	Art. 14 (3) Anyone who is arrested shall be informed, at the time of arrest, in a language that he understands, of the reasons for his arrest and shall be promptly informed of any charges against him. He shall be entitled to contact his family members. (4) Anyone who is deprived of his liberty by arrest or detention shall have the right to a medical examination and must be informed of that right. (6) Anyone who is deprived of his liberty by arrest or detention shall be entitled to petition a competent court in order that it may decide without delay on the lawfulness of his arrest or detention and order his release if the arrest or detention is unlawful.
Redress	Art. 14 (7) Anyone who has been the victim of arbitrary or unlawful arrest shall be entitled to compensation. Article 23 Each State Party to the present Charter undertakes to ensure that any person whose rights or freedoms as herein recognized are violated shall have an effective remedy, notwithstanding that the violation has been committed by persons acting in an official capacity.
Jurisdiction	Art. 3 (1) Each State party to the present Charter undertakes to ensure to all individuals subject to its jurisdiction the right to enjoy the rights and freedoms set forth herein, without distinction on grounds of race, color, sex, language, religious belief, opinion, thought, national or social origin, wealth, birth, or physical or mental disability.
Derogation	Art. 4 (1) In exceptional situations of emergency which threaten the life of the nation and the existence of which is officially proclaimed, the States parties to the present Charter may take measures derogating from their obligations under the present Charter, to the extent strictly required by the exigencies of the situation, provided that such measures are not inconsistent with their other obligations under international law and do not involve discrimination solely on the grounds of race, color, sex, language, religion, or social origin. (2) No derogation may be made from Article 14.

Right to liberty

The relevant rights are set out in Article 14. No other guidance exists.

Fair treatment

The Charter prohibits physical or mental torture and cruel, inhuman, or degrading treatment or punishment.[159]

Right to access to justice

No case law exists in respect of alleged violation of any of the Charter, which does not contain a complaints mechanism. On September 7, 2014, the League of Arab States approved the Statute of the Arab Court of Human Rights,[160] which does not give individuals access to a court to seek redress.[161] The Statute has been criticized for falling short of international standards.[162] As of September 2021 no States had ratified it.

Jurisdiction

The Arab Charter guarantees its rights to all individuals subject to its jurisdiction.[163]

Derogation

Article 4 permits derogation from the right to liberty in times of public emergencies, but not from the right to challenge detention during emergencies.

Detention in International Humanitarian Law (IHL)

Very few detention provisions in exist in IHL. Those that do are found within the context of IACs and relate to the duration of hostilities.[164] The basis for and standards of detention are found to a limited extent in Common Article 3 (CA3), AP I, AP II, and customary international law.[165]

Table 2.6 Detention provision found in IHL

Geneva Conventions (GC)

Common Article 3
In NIACS the following minimum standards shall apply:

1 (1) Persons taking no active part in hostilities, including members of armed forces who have laid down their arms and those placed hors de combat by . . . detention shall in all circumstances be treated humanely, without any adverse distinction founded on race, color, religion nor faith, sex, birth or wealth, or any other similar criteria. To this end the following acts are and shall remain prohibited at any time and in any place whatsoever with respect to the above-mentioned persons:
   (a) violence to life and person, in particular murder of all kinds, mutilation, cruel treatment and torture;
   (b) taking of hostages;
   (c) outrages upon personal dignity, in particular humiliating and degrading treatment . . .

GC III – Prisoners of war
Art. 21 Prisoners of war may not be held in close confinement except where necessary to safeguard their health and then only during the continuation of the circumstances which make such confinement necessary.
Art. 118 Prisoners of war shall be released and repatriated without delay after the cessation of hostilities.

GC IV – Civilians (protected persons)
Art. 42 The internment or placing in assigned residences of protected persons may be ordered only if the security of the Detaining Power makes it absolutely necessary.

(*Continued*)

Table 2.6 (Continued)

Art. 78 If the Occupying Power considers it necessary, for imperative reasons of security, to take safety measures concerning protected persons, it may, at the most, subject them to assigned residence or internment. Decisions regarding such assigned residence or internment shall be made according to a regular procedure prescribed by the Occupying Power in accordance with the provisions of the present Convention. This procedure shall include the right of appeal for the parties concerned. Appeals shall be decided with the least possible delay. In the event of the decision being upheld, it shall be subject to periodical review, if possible every six months, by a competent body set up by the said Power.

Additional Protocol (AP) I[166] (relating to IACs)

Art. 75 (1) Persons in the power of a Party to the conflict shall be treated humanely in all circumstances and shall enjoy, as a minimum, the protection provided by this Article without any adverse distinction based upon race, color, sex, language, religion or belief, political or other opinion, national or social origin, wealth, birth or other status, or on any other similar criteria. Each party shall respect the person, honor, convictions, and religious practices of all such persons.

(2) the following acts are and shall remain prohibited at any time and in any place whatsoever, whether committed by military or civilian agents:

- (a) violence to the life, health, or physical or mental well-being of persons, in particular:
  - (i) murder;
  - (ii) torture of all kinds, whether physical or mental;
  - (iii) corporal punishment; and
  - (iv) mutilation;
- (b) outrages upon personal dignity, in particular humiliating and degrading treatment, enforced prostitution, and any form of indecent assault;
- (c) the taking of hostages;
- (d) collective punishments; and
- (e) threats to commit any of the foregoing acts.

(3) Any person arrested, detained or interned for actions related to the armed conflict shall be informed promptly, in a language he understands, of the reasons why these measures have been taken. Except in cases of arrest or detention for penal offenses, such person shall be released with the minimum delay possible and in any event as soon as the circumstances justifying the arrest, detention or internment have ceased to exist.

APII – relating to NIACs

Art. 4(1) All persons who do not take a direct part or who have ceased to take part in hostilities, whether or not their liberty has been restricted, are entitled to respect for their person, honor, and convictions and religious practices. They shall in all circumstances be treated humanely, without any adverse distinction.

(2) . . . the following acts against the persons referred to in paragraph (1) are and shall remain prohibited at any time and in any place whatsoever.

- (a) violence to life, health and physical or mental well-being of persons, in particular murder, as well as cruel treatment such as torture, mutilation or any form of corporal punishment.:
- (b) collective punishments;
- (c) taking of hostages;
- (d) acts of terrorism;

(e) outrages upon personal dignity, in particular humiliating and degrading treatment, rape, enforced prostitution and any form of indecent assault;
(f) slavery and the salve trade in all their forms;
(g) pillage;
(h) threats to commit any of the foregoing acts.

As very little material exists within either IHL or IHRL to give guidance on detention in NIACs, and because CA3 does not set out specific rules to protect detainees, a number of states attempted to hold discussions with a view to crafting some guiding principles. It soon became apparent that one of the most contentious issues concerned the relationship between IHL and IHRL. Regrettably, even the huge amount of good faith among the participating states "could not overcome States' differing interpretations of their legal and political obligations."[167] One commentator notes that while there was a growing acknowledgement within IHRL jurisprudence[168] that IHRL binds non-state armed groups in certain circumstances (e.g. where they control territory), the source of such obligations currently appeared limited to custom. As in the case of those detained by states that are not party to a human rights treaty, therefore, those held by non-state armed groups are similarly protected at most by only customary IHRL and the basic IHL rules.[169]

In 2012, a number of states concluded the Copenhagen Process, which resulted in a set of non-binding principles and guidance relating to detention in NIAC.[170] Some IHRL concepts have been incorporated, such as that detentions must be lawful, and not arbitrary. This is interpreted as reasonable and necessary in all the circumstances, with a lawful and continuing objective.[171]

Simultaneously, since 2011 the ICRC have been consulting with various bodies and experts to find a way to strengthen IHL, particularly in connection with the detention of persons that take place in NIACs, in view of the fact that IHL in NIAC is still not "elaborate and clear with regard to persons deprived of their liberty."[172] The ICRC seems to have encountered difficulties in producing concrete and implementable guidance owing to lack of agreement between participants.[173] Guarantees for fair and humane treatment under IHL are found in CA3 of the Geneva Conventions, in AP II[174] (which is not widely ratified) and in customary IHL.

Summary

Many substantive elements of IHRL relating to preventive detention have been clarified and refined through the cases that have been adjudicated, as well as in guidance issued by the various treaty judicial bodies. Some of this material has addressed a number of procedural shortcomings, such as ensuring that all detainees have access to legal representation, and that the relatives of detainees are informed about any detention. However, despite these substantive and procedural improvements, many states continue to violate the human rights of persons arrested and detained. Sanctions for violations are virtually non-existent, and those that do exist are to all intents and purposes meaningless and do not provide any meaningful deterrent.

Notes

1 *See generally* Diane Webber, Preventive Detention of Terror Suspects, a New Legal Framework, (Routledge, 2016); Diane Webber, *Preventive and Administrative Detention*, *in* Elgar Encyclopedia of Human Rights, (Edward Elgar Publishing, forthcoming 2022).

2 *See e.g.* Al-Sirri v. Secretary of State for the Home Department (SSHD), (United Nations High Commissioner for Refugees intervening), [2013] 1 AC 745 (U.K.), ¶37 "there is as yet no internationally agreed definition of terrorism [and] no comprehensive international Convention binding Member States to take action against it."

3 International Covenant on Civil and Political Rights, G.A. Res. 2200A (XXI), 21 U.N. GAOR Supp. (No. 16) at 52 U.N. Doc. A/6316, (1966), 999 U.N.T.S. 171 (entered into force Mar. 23, 1976), (ICCPR); European Convention for the Protection of Human Rights and Fundamental Freedoms, 213 U.N.T.S. 222 (entered into force Sep. 3, 1953), (ECHR); American Convention on Human Rights, O.A.S. Treaty Series No. 36, 1144 U.N.T.S. 123 (entered into force Jul. 18, 1978), (ACHR); African (Banjul) Charter on Human and Peoples' Rights, O.A.U. Doc. CAB/LEG/67/3 rev. 5, 21 I.L.M. 58, (1982), entered into force Oct. 21, 1986), ("AfC"); Arab Charter on Human Rights, reprinted in 12 Int'l Hum. Rts. Rep. 893 (2005), entered into force Mar. 15, 2008, ("ArC").

4 *E.g.* U.N. Dept. of Economic and Social Affairs, Study of the Right of Everyone to be Free from Arbitrary Arrest, Detention and Exile, E/CN.4/826 Rev. 1, (1964); U.N. Body of Principles for the Protection of all Persons under any Form of Detention or Imprisonment, A/RES/ 43/173 (Body of Principles), (Dec. 9, 1988); U.N.G.A. Human Rights Council (UNGA HR Council), Report of the Working Group on Arbitrary Detention, A/HRC/22/44, 16 IIIA, (2012); U.N. Human Rights Committee General Comment (UN HRC GC) No. 8 (General Comments) (Right to Liberty and Security of Persons) (Art. 9) (Sixteenth Session. 1982) U.N. Doc. HRI/GEN/1/Rev.1.

5 UNGA HR Council, Report of the Working Group on Arbitrary Detention, A/ HRC/39/45, (Jul. 2, 2018).

6 The Human Rights Committee (HRC) is a treaty-based body comprising a group of independent experts that monitor the implementation of core human rights treaties and adjudicate complaints. The Human Rights Council (HR Council) is a U.N. Charter body. Its remit through special rapporteurs, working groups or independent experts is to address either specific country situations or thematic issues around the world. See United Nations Human Rights, www.ohchr.org/EN/HRBodies/Pages/HumanRightsBodies.aspx, (last accessed Aug. 25, 2020).

7 Webber, Preventive Detention of Terror Suspects, 50–1, *citing* U.N. HRC General Comment No. 35, CCPR/C/GC/35 (Dec. 16, 2014)

8 HR Council, The Working Group on Arbitrary Detention, Revised Fact Sheet No. 26, 3 ("Working Group Fact Sheet 2019"), (Feb. 8, 2019).

9 Body of Principles.

10 Working Group Fact Sheet 2019, 5–7, (Category I – where the detention has no basis in law; Category II – where detention is used in response to the legitimate exercise of human rights of e/g/ freedom of expression, assembly and preventing refugees to seek asylum; Category III -where the right to a fair trial has been

partially or totally violated, particularly; Category IV – where asylum seekers, immigrants or refugees are detained without the possibility of administrative review; and Category V – where the detention involves discrimination based on birth, national, ethnic or social origin, political or other opinions, gender, sexual orientation, or other status).

11 Webber, Preventive Detention of Terror Suspects, 50–2, *citing* Hugo van Alphen v. The Netherlands, HRC Communication No. 305/1988, CCPR/C/39/D/305/1988, ¶5.8, (Aug. 15, 1990); A v. Australia, HRC Communication No. 560/1993 CCPR/C/59/D/560/1993, ¶9.2, (Apr. 30, 1997); C v. Australia, HRC Communication No. 900/1999 CCPR/C/76/D/900/1999, ¶8.2, (Nov. 13, 2002); Ribeiro v. Mexico, HRC, Views adopted by the Committee under Art. 5(4) of the Optional Protocol, concerning Communication No. 2767/2016, CCPR/C/123/D/2767/2016, ¶10.10, (Aug. 29, 2018); Formonov v. Uzbekistan, HRC, Views adopted by the Committee under Art. 5(4) of the Optional Protocol, concerning Communication No. 2577/2015CCPR/C/122/D/2577/2015, ¶9.3, (Jun. 2, 2018); Khadzhiyev v. Turkmenistan, HRC Views adopted by the Committee under Art. 5(4) of the Optional Protocol, concerning Communication No. 2252/2013, CCPR/C/122/2252/2013, ¶7.7, (May 24, 2018).

12 Webber, Preventive Detention of Terror Suspects, 52, *citing* Claire Macken, Counter-Terrorism and the Detention of Suspected Terrorists, 50, (Routledge, 2011).

13 Formonov v. Uzbekistan, ¶9.3.

14 HRC General Comment No. 35, ¶25.

15 Webber, Preventive Detention of Terror Suspects, 81.

16 *Id.*, *citing* UNGA HR Council, Report of the Working Group on Arbitrary Detention, ¶72.

17 *Id.*, 81, *citing* HRC General Comment No. 35, ¶46.

18 Optional Protocol to the ICCPR, Adopted and opened for signature, ratification and accession by General Assembly resolution 2200A (XXI) of Dec. 16, 1966, entry into force Mar. 23, 1976, in accordance with Art. 9. 116 countries have ratified it: among those that have not, are the United Kingdom, the United States and Israel, *see* https://indicators.ohchr.org, (last accessed Aug. 26, 2020).

19 Webber, *Preventive and Administrative Detention.*

20 *See e.g.* Lopez Burgos v. Uruguay, HRC Communication No. R.12/52, UN Doc. Supp. No. 40, 176, (Jul. 29, 1981); HRC GC No. 31 [80], Nature of the General Legal Obligations Imposed on States Parties to the Covenant, CCPR/C/21/Rev.1/Add.13 (General Comments), (May 26, 2004), ¶10.

21 Legal Consequences of the Construction of a Wall in the Occupied Palestinian Territory, Advisory Opinion, I.C.J. Reports 136 2004, 179, ¶109; Armed Activities on the Territory of the Congo (Democratic Republic of the Congo v. Uganda) Judgment, I.C.J. Reports 2005, 168, 242–3, ¶216.

22 Webber, Preventive Detention of Terror Suspects, 32–4.

23 ICCPR, Art. 4.

24 *Id.*

25 UNGA HR Council, *Report of the Special Rapporteur on the Promotion of Human Rights and Fundamental Freedoms While Countering Terrorism on the Human Rights Challenge of States of Emergency in the Context of Countering Terrorism*, A/HRC/37/52, 3, ¶3, (Mar. 1, 2018), ("Special Rapporteur Derogation Report 2018").

26 *Id.*

27 U.N. Economic and Social Council, Commission on Human Rights, the Siracusa Principles on the Limitation and Derogation Provisions in the International Covenant on Civil and Political Rights, (Sep. 28, 1984), E/CN.4/1985/4,

("Siracusa Principles"); Richard B. Lillich, *The Paris Minimum Standards of Human Rights Norms in a State of Emergency*, 79 AM. J. INT'L L. 1072 (1985), ("Paris Minimum Standards"); HRC, CCPR GC No. 29. States of Emergency (Art. 4), U.N. Doc. CCPR/C/21/Rev.1/Add.11, (2001).

28 Webber, Preventive Detention of Terror Suspects, 67, *citing e.g.* Andrew Legg, The Margin of Appreciation in International Human Rights Law, 5–6, (Oxford University Press, 2012); Christopher Michaelson, *Permanent Legal Emergencies and the Derogation Clause in International Human Rights Treaties: A Contradiction?*, *in* Post 9/11 and the State of Permanent Legal Emergency, 297, (Ancieto Masferrer, ed., Springer, 2012).

29 Special Rapporteur Derogation Report 2018, 7, ¶20.

30 *Id.*, 11, ¶39.

31 *Id.*, 15, ¶¶57–60.

32 *Id.*, 18, ¶72.

33 Council of Europe, European Commission on Human Rights, Preparatory Work on Art. 5 of the European Convention on Human Rights, 6–8, DH (56) 10, A.28.646 TD 979/AEG/WM, (Aug. 8, 1956).

34 *See generally*, Webber, Preventive Detention of Terror Suspects, 52–6; Macken, Counter-Terrorism and the Detention of Suspected Terrorists, 52–6.

35 Grubnyk v. Ukraine, Appl. No. 58444/15 ECtHR, ¶¶69–86, (Sep. 17, 2020).

36 *See e.g.* Fox, Hartley and Campbell v. United Kingdom, Appl. Nos. 12244/86, 12245/86, 12383/86, ECtHR, ¶32, (Aug. 30, 1990): "the reasonableness of the suspicion on which an arrest must be based forms an essential part of the safeguard against arbitrary arrest and detention;" Grubic v. Croatia, Appl. No. 5384/11 ECtHR, ¶38, (Oct. 30, 2012) any deprivation of liberty should "be in keeping with the purpose of protecting the individual from arbitrariness." The same words were used in Triflovic v. Croatia, Appl. No. 36653/09, Judgment (Merits and Just Satisfaction) ECtHR (First Section), ¶93, (Nov. 6, 2012).

37 Saadi v. United Kingdom, Appl. No. 13229/03 ECtHR, ¶¶67–74 (Jan. 29, 2008), *See also, for a discussion on proportionality*, Yukata Arai-Takahashi, The Margin of Appreciation and the Principle of Proportionality in the Jurisprudence of the ECHR, 14, (Intersentia, 2002).

38 Webber, Preventive Detention of Terror Suspects, 53; Macken, Counter-Terrorism and the Detention of Suspected Terrorists, 56.

39 The preparatory materials may be referred to in cases of ambiguity in treaty texts in order to aid interpretation, see Vienna Convention on the Law of Treaties, U.N.T.S. vol. 1155, 331 dated May 23, 1969, (entered into force Jan. 27, 1980), Art. 32.

40 Webber, Preventive Detention of Terror Suspects, 54, *citing* Committee of Experts, Collected Edition of the 'Travaux Preparatoires', Vol. IV, 260 (Jun. 8–17, 1950).

41 The merits of this case were finally ruled upon in Lawless v. Ireland (No. 3), Appl. No. 332.57, Judgment (Merits) ECtHR (Jul. 1, 1961). For the history of this case, see Brian Doolan, Lawless v. Ireland (1957–1961): The First Case Before the European Court of Human Rights, (Routledge, 2001).

42 Lawless v. Ireland (No. 3), ¶14.

43 Brian Doolan, Lawless v. Ireland, 201–2.

44 Lawless v. Ireland (No. 3), ¶14.

45 Guzzardi v. Italy, Appl. No. 7367/76, ECtHR, ¶102 (Jun. 7, 1980).

46 *See e.g.* M v. Germany, App. No. 19359/04, ECtHR, ¶89, (Dec. 17, 2009); Schwabe v. Germany, Appl. Nos. 8080/08 and 8577/08 ECtHR, ¶70, (Mar. 1, 2012); Ostendorf v. Germany, Appl. No. 15598, ECtHR, ¶66, (Jun. 7, 2013).

47 Schwabe v. Germany, ¶71.

48 Ostendorf v. Germany, ¶82.

49 *Id.*, Concurring Opinion of Judges Lemmens & Jaderblom, ¶4, *citing* Jecius v. Lithuania, Appl. No. 34578/97, ECtHR, ¶50, (Jul. 31, 2000).
50 Concurring Opinion, ¶4.
51 *Id.*
52 *Id.*, ¶5.
53 *Id.*, *citing* Brogan v. United Kingdom, Appl. No. 11209/94;11234/84; 112266/84; 11386/85/ ECtHR, ¶58, (Nov. 29, 1988); Ikincisoy v. Turkey, Appl. No. 26144/95, ECtHR, ¶103, (Jul. 27, 2004).
54 *Id.*
55 Al-Jedda v. United Kingdom, Appl. No. 27021/08, ECtHR, ¶100, (Jul. 7, 2011).
56 Webber, Preventive Detention of Terror Suspects, 56.
57 S, V and A v. Denmark, Appl. Nos. 35553/12, 36678/12, 36711/12 ECtHR, ¶103, (Oct. 22, 2018).
58 *Id.*, ¶¶9–35.
59 *Id.*, ¶99, *citing* Report of the Conference of Senior Officials on Human Rights to the Committee of Ministers on Art. 5(1)(c) and (3) of the second draft of the ECHR, 32.
60 *Id.*, ¶93, *citing* Ostendorf v. Germany, ¶¶77–89.
61 *Id.*, ¶96.
62 *Id.*, ¶105.
63 *Id.*, ¶107, *citing* Ireland v. United Kingdom, Appl. No. 5310/71, ECtHR, (Dec. 13, 1977).
64 *Id.*, ¶108, *citing* Cuilla v. Italy, Appl. No. 11152/84 ECtHR, ¶38, (Feb. 22, 1989) *and* Jecius v. Lithuania, Appl. No. 34578/97 ECtHR, ¶50, (Jul. 31, 2000).
65 *Id.*, ¶¶109–13, *citing* Steel v. United Kingdom, Appl. No. 67/1997/851/1058, ECtHR, (Sep. 23, 1998); Nicol & Selvanayagam, Appl. No. 32213/96 ECtHR, (Jan. 11, 2001); McBride v. United Kingdom, Appl. No. 27786/95 ECtHR, (Jul. 5, 2001).
66 *Id.*, ¶114.
67 *Id.*, ¶116.
68 *Id.*, ¶118, *citing* Brogan v. United Kingdom, ¶53; O'Hara v. United Kingdom, Appl. No. 37555/97 ECtHR, ¶¶35, 36, (Jan. 16, 2002).
69 *Id.*, ¶¶120–3.
70 *Id.*, ¶127.
71 *Id.*
72 *Id.*, ¶137.
73 *Id.*, ¶161.
74 Rezmives & others v. Romania, Appl. Nos. 61467/12, 39516/13, 48213/13, 68191/13, ECtHR, (Apr. 25, 2017), (inadequate sanitary facilities, poor hygiene, overcrowding, presence of rats and insects in cells, poor quality food).
75 Rooman v. Belgium, Appl. No. 18052/11 ECtHR, (Jan. 31, 2019) (lack of psychiatric medical treatment).
76 Husayn (Abu Zubaydah) v. Poland, Appl. No 7511/13, 28761/11, ECtHR, (Feb. 16, 2015), and see within the United States section of Domestic Perspectives below.
77 *Id.*, ¶499.
78 *Id.*, ¶511.
79 *Id.*, ¶¶444, 512.
80 *Id.*, ¶512,
81 Grubnyk v. Ukraine, ¶97.
82 Fox, Hartley and Campbell v. United Kingdom, ¶40.
83 Lawless v. Ireland, ¶14.
84 Brogan v. United Kingdom, ¶58.

85 S, V and A v. Denmark, ¶130.
86 Brannigan and McBride v. United Kingdom, Appl. No. 5/1992/350/423–424 ECtHR, ¶60, (Apr. 22, 1993).
87 S, V and A v. Denmark, ¶133.
88 Salduz v. Turkey, Appl. No. 36391/02, ECtHR, ¶55, (Nov. 27, 2009).
89 Dayanan v. Turkey, Appl. No. 7377/03, ECtHR, ¶32, (Jan. 13, 2010).
90 Directive 2013/48/EU of the European Parliament and of the Council of 22 October 2013 on the right of access to a lawyer in criminal proceedings and in European arrest warrant proceedings, and the right to have a third party informed upon deprivation of liberty and to communicate with third persons and with consular authorities while deprived of liberty, 2013, O.J. (L.294/1), Art. 3.2(c).
91 *Id.*, Art. 15.
92 *Id.*, Arts. 5, 6, and 7.
93 Report from the Commission to the European Parliament and the Council, on the implementation of Directive 2013/48/EU of the European Parliament and of the Council of October 22, 2013 on the right of access to a lawyer in criminal proceedings and in European arrest warrant proceedings, and the right to have a third party informed upon deprivation of liberty and to communicate with third persons and with consular authorities while deprived of liberty, at 7,12, COM (2019) 560 final (Sep. 26, 2019).
94 European Court of Human Rights (ECtHR), Pending Applications Allocated to a Judicial Formation 31/08/2020, www.echr.coe.int/Documents/Stats_pending_month_2020_BIL.PDF, (last accessed Sep. 22, 2020).
95 ECtHR, Violations by Article and State 2019, www.echr.coe.int/Documents/Stats_violation_2019_ENG.pdf, (last accessed Sep. 22, 2020).
96 ECtHR, Violations by Article and State, 1959–2019, www.echr.coe.int/Documents/Stats_violation_1959_2019_ENG.pdf, (last accessed Sep. 22, 2020).
97 Walter Kalin and Jorg Kunzli, The Law of International Human Rights Protection, 223, (Oxford University Press, 2019).
98 ECtHR, Analysis of Statistics 2020, Chart 10 (Jan. 2020).
99 *See e.g.* Bankovic v. Belgium, Appl. No. 52207/99 ECtHR, 2001, (Dec. 12, 2001); Ilascu v. Moldova & Russia, Appl. No. 48787/99 ECtHR, 2004-VII, (Jul. 2004); Al-Saadoon & Mufhdi v. United Kingdom, Appl. No. 61498/08, ECtHR, (Jun. 30, 2009). *Also see* Webber, Preventive Detention of Terror Suspects, 34–7.
100 Al- Skeini v. United Kingdom. Appl. No. 55721/07, ECtHR, (Jul. 7, 2011); Al-Jeddah v. United Kingdom, Appl. No. 27021/08, ECtHR, (Jul. 7, 2011); Hassan v. United Kingdom, Appl. No. 29750/09, ECtHR, (Sep. 16, 2014); Jaloud v. The Netherlands, Appl. No. 47708/08, ECtHR, (Nov. 20, 2014); Webber, Preventive Detention of Terror Suspects, 34–7.
101 Al-Jeddah v. United Kingdom, ¶85.
102 ECHR, Art. 15(1). The rights to life, freedom from torture, freedom from slavery are non-derogable, ***and see*** Webber, Preventive Detention of Terror Suspects, 69–71.
103 Lawless v. Ireland, Report of the European Commission (Adopted on Dec. 19, 1959), Appl. No. 332/57 (Commission) 1 ECtHR (Ser. B), ¶90.
104 The Greek Case, Report of the European Commission, (Nov. 5, 1969) 12 Ybk (the Greek Case).
105 *See e.g.* Al-Jeddah v. United Kingdom.
106 Arai-Takahashi, The Margin of Appreciation and the Principle of Proportionality in the Jurisprudence of the ECHR, 177, *citing* Brannigan & McBride v. United Kingdom, ¶43.
107 *Id.*, 178.

108 Oren Gross, *'Once More Unto the Breach': The Systemic Failure of Applying the European Convention on Human Rights to Entrenched Emergencies*, 23 Yale J. Int. L, 437, 463, (1998).
109 Webber, Preventive Detention of Terror Suspects, 71, *citing* Lawless v. Ireland, *and* the Greek Case.
110 *Id.*, *citing* Stefan Sottiaux, Terrorism and the Limitation of Rights, 259, (Hart Publishing, 2008).
111 *See e.g.* Webber, Preventive Detention of Terror Suspects, 56–7, *citing* Sergio Garcia Ramirez, *The Inter-American Court of Human Rights' Perspective on Terrorism*, 805, *in* Counter-Terrorism, International Law and Practice, (Ana Maria Salinade Frias, Katja L.H. Samuel, Nigel D. White, eds., Oxford University Press, 2012).
112 *Id.*, *citing* Case of Gangaram Panday, IACtHR (Ser. C), No. 16, Judgment of Jan. 21, 1994, ¶47 (Suriname). *See also* Case of Acosta Calderon, IACtHR (Ser. C) No. 129, Judgment of Jun. 24 2005, ¶57 (Ecuador).
113 Case of Lopez-Alvarez IACtHR, Judgment of Feb. 1, 2006, ¶¶67, 68 (Honduras). *See also* Barrieto Leiva v. Venezuela, ¶¶111, 122, 19 IHRR 810, (Nov. 17, 2009).
114 Organization of American States (OAS), Inter-American Commission on Human Rights (IACHR), Resolution 1/08, Principles and Best Practices on the Protection of Persons Deprived of Liberty in the Americas, (Mar. 31, 2008).
115 *Id.*
116 *Id.*, Principle I.
117 *See e.g.* Case of Dayra Maria Levoyer Jimenez (Ecuador), Case 11.922, Report No. 66/01 IACHR, (Jun. 14, 2001).
118 ACHR Art 7(4). *See also* Webber, Preventive Detention of Terror Suspects, 83–4.
119 *Id.*, Art. 7(5).
120 *Id.*, Art. 7(6).
121 IACHR, Recommendations for the Protection of Human Rights by OAS Members in the Fight against Terrorism, OEA/Ser.G. CP/doc.4117/06, (May 9, 2006) §B 1. *See also* Case of Valencia and Llanos, IACHR, Report no. 79/11 Case No. 10.916, (Jul. 21, 2011) (Colombia), 126.
122 IACHR, Recommendations for the Protection of Human Rights, Arts. 48–51 deal with the procedure for obtaining redress.
123 IACHR, Annual Report 2019, Chapter II, The Petitions, Cases and Precautionary Measures System, Statistics, 62, 63, OEA/Ser.L/V/II, Doc. 9, (Feb. 24, 2020).
124 *Id.*, 82.
125 *Id.*, 99.
126 IACHR, Annual Report 2020, Chapter II, The System of Petitions and Cases, Friendly Settlements, and Precautionary Measures, 25, ¶14, OEA/Ser.L/V/II, Doc.28, (Mar. 30, 2021).
127 *Id.*, 26, ¶21.
128 IACHR, Annual Report 2019, 106; Case of Dayra Maria Levoyer Jimenez.
129 *Id.*, 113.
130 IACHR, Annual Report 2020, 39, ¶44.
131 IACHR, Annual Report 2019, 125, *citing* Cesar Garzon Guzman v. Ecuador, (Jul. 26, 2019).
132 *Id.*, 128, *citing* Olimpiades Gonzalez et al. v. Venezuela, (Aug. 16, 2019).
133 IACHR, Annual Report 2020, 58–9, ¶¶71, 73.
134 ACHR, Art. 1(1).
135 Saldano v. Argentina, Report No. 38/99, IACHR, Mar. 11, 1999, (Annual Report, 1998).

136 American Declaration on the Rights and Duties of Man, (adopted by the Ninth International Conference of American States, Bogotá, Colombia, 1948, ("American Declaration").
137 IACHR Guantanamo Bay Precautionary Measures (No. 259/02), (Mar. 12, 2002); IACHR Extension of Guantanamo Bay Precautionary Measures (No. 259/02), (Oct. 28, 2005); IACHR Extension of Guantanamo Bay Precautionary Measures (No. 259/02), (Jul. 23, 2013).
138 IACHR Precautionary Measure 8/06, Omar Khadr, United States, (Mar. 21, 2006).
139 IACHR Precautionary Measure 211/08, Djamel Ameziane, United States, (Aug. 20, 2008).
140 IACHR Precautionary Measure 422/14, Mustafa Adam Al-Hasawi, United States, (Mar. 21, 2015).
141 American Declaration, Art. XXVIII: "The rights of man are limited by the rights of others, by the security of all, and by the just demands of the general welfare and the advancement of democracy."
142 ACHR Art. 27(2).
143 *See e.g.* IACHR, Ten Years of Activities 1971–1981, 337–8, (OAS, 1982); IACHR on Human Rights Report on the Situation of Human Rights of a Segment of Miskito Origin, at Pt. II, subdiv. E, ¶¶6–8, OEA/Ser.L/V.II.62 doc.10, rev.3, (Nov. 29, 1983).
144 *See e.g.* Habeas Corpus in Emergency Situations, (Arts. 27(2) and 7(6) of the American Convention on Human Rights), Advisory Opinion OC-8/87, January 30, 1987, Inter-Am. Ct. H.R. (Ser. A) No. 8 (1987), ¶19; Judicial Guarantees in States of Emergency (Arts. 27(2), 25 and 8 of the American Convention on Human Rights), Advisory Opinion OC-9/87, October 6, 1987, Inter-Am Ct. H.R. (Ser. A) No. 9 (1987), 21.
145 Webber, Preventive Detention of Terror Suspects, 74, *citing* Jaime Oraa, Human Rights in States of Emergency in International Law, 161–8, (Clarendon Press Oxford, 1992).
146 *Id.*
147 *Id.*, 73, *citing* Oraa, Human Rights in States of Emergency in International Law, 30; Edel Hughes, *Entrenched Emergencies and the 'War on Terror': Time to Reform the Derogation Procedure in International Law?*, 20 N.Y. INT'L L. REV. 1, 43, (2007).
148 African Commission on Human and Peoples' Rights v. Libya, Appl. No. 002/2013, Judgment, African Court on Human and Peoples' Rights, (Jun. 3, 2016).
149 *Id.*, ¶82.
150 Brusco v. France, Appl. No. 1466/07, ECtHR, (Oct. 14, 2010).
151 Dayanan v. Turkey.
152 *Id.*, Art. 7.
153 Protocol to the AfC on the Establishment of an African Court on Human and Peoples' Rights, June 10, 1988, Org. of African Unity (OAU) (entered into force on Jun. 25, 2004.
154 African Court on Human and Peoples' Rights, www.african-court.org/en/ (last accessed Aug. 18, 2020).
155 AfC, Art. 2.
156 Nani Yakare-Oule, Jansen Reventlow and Rosa Curling, *The Unique Jurisdiction of the African Court on Human and Peoples' Rights: Protection of Human Rights Beyond the African Charter*, 33 EMORY INT'L L. REV. 203, 204, (2019).
157 *Id.*, 209–22.
158 African Commission on Human and Peoples' Rights v. Libya, ¶¶83–5.
159 *Id.*, Art. 8.

160 Arab Center for International Humanitarian Law and Human Rights Education, English Version of the Statute of the Arab Court of Human Rights, The Council of the League of Arab States, Ministers of Foreign Affairs, adopted during the (142) session and by resolution No. 7790, E.A. (142) C 3, 07/09, 2014, the Statute of the Arab Court of Human Rights, ("Statute of the Arab HR Court"), https://acihl.org/texts.htm?article_id=44&lang=ar-SA, (last accessed Aug. 19, 2020).

161 *Id.*, Art. 19.

162 International Commission of Jurists, The Arab Court of Human Rights: A Flawed Statute for an Ineffective Court, (2015).

163 ArC, Art. 3.

164 Webber, Preventive Detention of Terror Suspects, 58–9, 85.

165 Jelena Pejic, *Procedural Principles and Safeguards for Internment/Administrative Detention in Armed Conflict and Other Situations of Violence*, 87 Int'l Rev. Red Cross 375, 377, (2005).

166 Although the United States has not ratified API, it does acknowledge that much of it has become part of customary international law, including art. 75. *See* Gary D. Solis, The Law of Armed Conflict, 143–6 (Cambridge University Press, 2nd ed., 2016), *citing* Mike Matheson, *Additional Protocol I as Expressions of Customary International Law*, 2(2) American Journal of International Law and Policy 415, 425, (Fall, 1987), and noting the stance towards API taken by the Obama Administration, which did not accept that Art. 75 API was customary international law but did not deny its customary status.

167 Thomas Winkler, *The Copenhagen Process and the Copenhagen Process Principles and Guidelines on the Handling of Detainees in International Military Operations: Challenges, Criticism and the Way Ahead*, 5 Journal of International Humanitarian Legal Studies, 258, 263, (2014).

168 *See e.g.* discussion about Hassan v. United Kingdom, below.

169 Lawrence Hill-Cawthorne, Detention in Non-International Armed Conflict, 226, (Oxford University Press, 2016).

170 Bruce Oswald and Thomas Winkler, *The Copenhagen Process on the Handling of Detainees in International Military Operations*, Oct. 19, 2012, 16(39) American Society of International Law, Insights, (Dec. 26, 2012), www.asil.org/insights/volume/16/issue/39/copenhagen-process-principles-and-guidelines-handling-detainees. The participating countries were Argentina, Australia, Belgium, Canada, China, Denmark, Finland, France, Germany, India, Malaysia, New Zealand. Nigeria, Norway, Pakistan, Russia, South Africa, Sweden, Tanzania, the Netherlands, Turkey, Uganda, United Kingdom, and the United States.

171 *Id.*, Guidelines, ¶4.4.

172 Tilman Rodenhauser, *Strengthening IHL Protecting Persons Deprived of Their Liberty: Main Aspects of the Consultations and Discussions since 2011*, 98(3) International Review of the Red Cross 941, 944, (2018).

173 *Id.*, 959.

174 AP II builds on CA3, but only defines general rules about food and drinking water, hygiene and medical care. It does not apply if the non-State group does not control any territory.

3 Domestic perspectives on preventive detention

After 9/11, many countries tightened existing, or enacted new counter-terrorism legislation, some of which was draconian. Some of that legislation generated litigation in different countries, with a common complaint: that the counter-terrorism litigation infringed human rights. Initially judicial opinion tended to be deferential to governments, but slowly a more human rights friendly approach emerged. However, in recent years, a shift back towards deference to governments can be perceived in the jurisprudential approach to weighing the liberty/security balance in preventive detention of terror suspects in a number of countries. This section analyzes these trends and focuses on how the United Kingdom, the United States, and Israel have contended with the IHRL/IHL issue in their counter-terrorism detention policies in very different ways over the years since 9/11. The discussion will include the detention of two of the "Beatles," Alexanda Kotey and El Shafee Elsheikh.

United States

In October 2020, a Department of Homeland Security report predicted that the primary terrorist threat within the United States would increase in an "elevated threat environment" until early 2021 at least and would stem from "lone offenders and small cells of individuals, including Domestic Violent Extremists (DVE) and foreign terrorist-inspired Homegrown Violent Extremists. Among the DVEs, the most "persistent and lethal threat" would emanate from racially and ethnically motivated violent extremists, specifically white supremacists."[1] Between January 1 and August 3, 2020, far-right extremists were responsible for 67% of terror attacks, 20% of the attacks were committed by far-left, Salafi-jihadists committed 7% of attacks and the remainder were committed by persons with other motivations.[2]

On January 6, 2021, a right-wing mob of pro-Trump supporters assaulted and breached the security of the Capitol in Washington D.C. The nation and much of the world watched the terror unfolding in real time, as the mob entered the building, terrorizing everyone inside. Five people were killed, and many were injured.[3] Consequently, immediately after President Biden took office, he ordered a review

DOI: 10.4324/9780367817275-5

of the threat of domestic violent extremism,[4] and issued a National Strategy for Countering Domestic Terrorism in June 2021.[5]

After an analysis of the domestic trends, this section will examine the detention of persons pursuant to the law of armed conflict (LOAC) in Guantanamo Bay, Cuba, Afghanistan, and Iraq, and the detention of the two "Beatles," Alexanda Kotey and El Shafee Elsheikh.

Preventive detention in domestic law

Preventive detention of terror suspects is not in itself permitted in U.S. domestic law, although it has been achieved via the use of certain legal devices.[6] For example, some situations exist for an arrest without a warrant if there is probable cause for that arrest, but a suspect must be brought promptly before a magistrate, meaning within 48 hours, to confirm that probable cause existed.[7] Thus technically, suspects can be held preventively for 48 hours.

In the U.S. no federal crime of domestic terrorism *per se* exists.[8] Suspected terrorists have been frequently indicted at an early stage for inchoate offenses, such as conspiracy.[9]

Detention in cases of material support

Many suspects of terrorist activity are charged with homicide, injuring persons or property, hate crimes, or under the very wide-ranging material support statutes.[10] These statutes enable arrests and detentions to be made if there is probable cause of early pre-crime activity, "by shifting the point of potential prosecutorial intervention further back along the continuum between thought and deed."[11] These types of charges have frequently been challenged on the grounds that the charges violated the right to freedom of speech and expression, violating the First Amendment,[12] or of vagueness or over-breadth, which would make the statute unconstitutional under the Due Process Clause of the Fifth Amendment.

For example, Abu Khatallah was charged with violating and conspiring to violate the §2339A material support statute, as well as 16 counts relating to the attack on the U.S. Embassy in Benghazi and murder of the U.S. Ambassador in 2012.[13] Khatallah claimed that the material support charges were unconstitutionally vague and overbroad. He argued that §2339A only punished conduct that constituted terrorism and that the statute is not sufficiently definite as to what constitutes terrorism to give fair notice of what type of conduct is prohibited. He also claimed that as §2339A punishes a substantial and excessive amount of protected speech, it is overbroad and violated the First Amendment.[14] The court rejected both arguments: the first because §2339A does not include terrorist conduct as an element of criminal liability;[15] and the second because the defendant did not provide any supporting evidence, and in any event because the prosecution's evidence in support of the charges bolstered his motive to solicit and procure illegal attacks and constituted speech integral to criminal conduct.[16]

Detention under material witness laws

After 9/11 the United States Department of Justice (DOJ) used the federal material witness statute[17] in international terrorism investigations. This permitted the arrest and detention of persons believed to be a material witness to a crime, if a judicial officer can show probable cause that the person may have information relevant to an investigation but would flee to avoid testifying at a trial or grand jury proceedings. Misuse of this draconian power as a detention tool was widely criticized.[18] An Office of the Inspector General (OIG) report in 2014 identified and conducted an "in-depth review" of ten investigations involving the detention of 12 persons out of 112 material witnesses between 2000 and 2012 that required further review, (ten of these, including one U.S. citizen, were not named in the report) and reported that there was insufficient evidence to conclude that the DOJ "misused the statute in international terrorism investigations."[19] The OIG stated that no material witnesses were detained in international terrorism cases from 2004–2012.[20] The report did not disclose how many had been detained in respect of domestic terrorism cases.

Of the remaining two persons discussed in the OIG report, the case of U.S. citizen Abdullah Al-Kidd came into the public domain after he issued proceedings claiming damages[21] for his arrest at Dulles Airport outside Washington D.C., where he was about to depart to Saudi Arabia, and for 16 days detention as a material witness. This was followed by 14 months supervised release until the trial of a suspected terrorist. He was never called to give evidence. His case went all the way to the Supreme Court.[22] He had alleged that the then Attorney General John Ashcroft had created a practice enabling the material witness statute to be used unlawfully to investigate or preemptively detain him for suspected terrorist activities when there was insufficient evidence to charge him with a crime, in violation of the Fourth Amendment.[23] The District Court had denied the Attorney General's motion to dismiss, but the Supreme Court issued a ruling deferential to the Government that avoided addressing whether the material witness statute was being used pretextually. The Court concluded that Al-Kidd's Fourth Amendment rights had not been violated because his arrest was objectively reasonable following the issuance of an arrest warrant by a neutral magistrate based on the FBI's suspicion that Al-Kidd was a material witness who would soon disappear.[24]

The second named material witness in the OIG report was Pakistani citizen and U.S. permanent resident Uzair Paracha, who lived in New York. A confidential informant named Paracha as being involved in an Al Qaeda plot in the U.S. in March 2003. He was arrested as a material witness in connection with that plot and detained for more than for four months until he was charged and convicted of materially supporting that plot.[25] The evidence relied upon in the OIG Report indicates that Paracha had consented, on the advice of counsel, to the continuation of his material witness status until the time he was charged and had not challenged the use of the material witness warrant at any time. That warrant had been issued on the basis of an affidavit stating that his role in potential terrorist activity, his lack of ties to the United States and possible fear of losing permanent residence status were incentives for him to flee.[26] However, the reasons set out in that affidavit were so broad that they could equally support a complaint about pretextual use of the material witness statute.

Immigration detention

As non-U.S. citizens and non-U.S. residents (referred to as "aliens") may be detained without charge, with or without a showing of probable cause of any crime, merely to determine immigration status,[27] immigration law has been used, and criticized, as a pretext to detain suspected terrorists, with most court rulings showing deference to government policy.[28] Although such detentions may not be indefinite,[29] some have lasted more than 90 days.[30]

The case of Ibrahim Turkmen and seven other non-U.S. citizens, six of whom were Muslim and two were Hindu, is an example of pretextual immigration detention. The men were detained for periods between three to eight months, pursuant to the FBI's "hold-until-cleared" policy which mandated that individuals arrested in the wake of 9/11 would not be released from custody until the FBI cleared them of terrorist ties. The defendants claimed that the alleged immigration violations were used as an excuse to investigate whether they were involved in terrorist activity and that this violated their Fourth and Fifth Amendment rights. The District Court rejected their claims.[31] The Second Circuit upheld that ruling, commenting that the government had shown an "objectively reasonable belief that the detentions were authorized."[32] However, the defendants were permitted to proceed with their complaints as a "*Bivens* claim"[33] against eight federal official defendants, both executive officials and wardens, relating to excessively harsh and restrictive conditions and mistreatment they had endured whilst detained in high security sections of prisons.[34] The District Court dismissed the claims against the executive officers but allowed it to proceed against the wardens. The Second Circuit appeals court affirmed the decision relating to the wardens and reinstated the case against the executive officials,[35] but the Supreme Court took a different approach which was very deferential to the Government.[36]

Justice Kennedy highlighted the limited reach of *Bivens*, which related to the Fourth Amendment prohibition against unreasonable searches and seizures, and two other situations where *Bivens* remedies were allowed: in a Fifth Amendment gender discrimination case;[37] and an Eighth Amendment cruel and unusual punishment case.[38] Since those cases the Court had adopted a "far more cautious course" by looking at "statutory intent" before deciding if an implied cause of action should be recognized, and expanding the range of *Bivens* was considered a "disfavored" judicial activity.[39] Justice Kennedy opined that the Court of Appeals should have ruled that this claim presented a new *Bivens* context, and should have conducted a special factors inquiry.[40] He held that after considering the special factors, which in this case concerned a high level executive policy created in the wake of 9/11, the decision whether a damages action should be allowed was one that Congress should make, rather than the courts.[41] He explained the reasons why courts defer to the Executive Branch in cases of national security.[42] He suggested that a more appropriate remedy could have been sought via injunctive relief or *habeas corpus* petitions.[43] However, the Court vacated the judgment relating to the claim against a warden (Hasty) of prisoner abuse and remanded it to the Court of Appeals to conduct a special factors analysis.[44]

Justice Breyer's dissent highlighted the safeguards that exist against undue interference by the judiciary in times of war or national security emergencies, noted the inappropriateness of suggesting injunctive or habeas remedies so long after the event, and stated that the Court's abolition of or limitation of *Bivens* actions went too far: "If you are cold, put on a sweater, perhaps an overcoat, perhaps also turn up the heat, but do not set fire to the house."[45] The case was ultimately remanded by the to the District Court, where the warden's motion to dismiss was granted on the grounds that the plaintiff had not produced any factual evidence to support the claims.[46]

LOAC detention

After 9/11, the Bush Administration decided that U.S. criminal law was not up to the task of dealing with terrorist activity and turned to the law of armed conflict (LOAC), also known as international humanitarian law (IHL). The Authorization for the Use of Military Force (AUMF), passed by Congress on September 18, 2001, provided the initial authority to detain suspected terrorists, even U.S. citizens,[47] although the text does not actually mention detention. The President was permitted to

> use all necessary and appropriate force against those nations, organizations or persons he determines planned, authorized, committed or aided the terrorist attacks that occurred on September 11, 2001, or harbored such organizations or persons, in order to prevent any future acts of international terrorism against the United States by such nations, organizations or persons.[48]

At first, the Bush Administration maintained that IHL, specifically the Geneva Conventions (GC), did not apply to al-Qaeda or the Taliban. This stance shifted to that of regarding the conflict as an international armed conflict (IAC), which would have given the United States the right to hold terror suspects until the cessation of hostilities, pursuant to GC III, Article 118. However, in 2006 the Supreme Court ruled in *Hamdan* that GC Common Article 3 applied to the conflict with al-Qaeda. This reference to GC Common Article 3 alone suggests that the Court regarded the conflict as a non-international armed conflict (NIAC), with its limited set of protections.[49] Despite this, in terms of duration of detention, a large body of case law has reiterated that the authority of the United States to detain an enemy combatant – i.e. a terror suspect – depends on the continuation of hostilities.[50] The hostilities continue to the present day, as confirmed in Al-Alwi v. Trump in 2018.[51]

Detention in Guantanamo Bay, Cuba

780 people have been detained at Guantanamo.[52] As of July 19, 2021, 39 men remained, of which 11 have been charged with war crimes. 28 are held in indefinite LOAC detention, 18 of whom have not been recommended for transfer.[53] In May 2021, an Afghan detainee regarded as "low value" petitioned the D.C. federal court seeking release, on the basis that the announcement relating to the withdrawal of U.S. troops from Afghanistan amounted to a declaration that the U.S. war in Afghanistan was ending and that this should mean that all prisoners of war should be released.[54] On May 17, three were approved for release,[55] and a detainee who had been approved for release in 2016 was finally repatriated to Morocco in July 2021.[56] Another detainee, Majid Khan, agreed to a deal intended to lead to his release in the next few years in return for relinquishing his right to question the C.I.A. in court about its torture program.[57] This is discussed further below in the section on treatment of detainees.

Most detention provisions derive from the National Defense Authorization Act (NDAA) of 2012[58] as amended, and are still relevant and effective. It provides for the periodic review of detainees, with the aim of ascertaining whether a detainee posed a continuing threat to the security of the United States.[59] Detainees were entitled to be represented by military counsel in status determination hearings before a military judge.[60] The NDAA of 2013 prohibited the indefinite detention of U.S. citizens and lawful permanent residents.[61] The scope of detainees was expanded in 2009 to add persons "who were part of, or substantially supported, Taliban or al-Qaeda forces or associated forces."[62] In 2014 the focus moved from al-Qaeda to ISIS, also referred to as ISIL or Da'esh. In 2015 the Administration contended that as the predecessor of ISIS merged with al-Qaeda, ISIS fell within the scope of the existing AUMF.[63]

Detainees in Guantanamo did not have the right to challenge their detention until the Supreme Court extended statutory *habeas corpus* in *Rasul v. Bush* to non-U.S. citizen detainees at Guantanamo in 2004.[64] Then the Detainee Treatment Act of 2005 (DTA) appeared to proscribe jurisdiction to deal with claims from Guantanamo detainees,[65] but the *Hamdan* court ruled that nothing in the DTA prevented federal courts from hearing *habeas* petitions that were pending after the DTA was passed.[66] More obstacles to challenging detention were put into the Military Commissions Act (MCA) of 2006,[67] but in *Boumediene v. Bush* the Supreme Court ruled that the procedures set out in Section 7 MCA were neither an adequate nor effective substitute for *habeas corpus*, thus opening the door for Guantanamo detainees to have a "meaningful opportunity" guaranteed by the Suspension Clause to claim the constitutional privilege of *habeas corpus* in a federal court.[68] The Court concluded that "at least three factors" were relevant in determining the reach of the Suspension Clause:

> (1) the citizenship and status of the detainee and the adequacy of the process through which that status determination was made; (2) the nature of the sites where apprehension and then detention took place; and (3) the

practical obstacles inherent in resolving the prisoner's entitlement to the writ.[69]

In 2011, President Obama issued an Executive Order revising the process of periodic review of detainees.[70] The policy reflected in this document reflected a move towards IHRL, in that the review procedures offered greater human rights protections than the very limited provisions of GC IV, Article 78 (displayed in Table 2.6 above), with the right to provide the detainee with a summary of factors that would be considered by the Periodic Review Board, together with access to a personal representative.[71]

The extent to which the Fifth Amendment's Due Process clause applied to Guantanamo detentions has been the subject of much judicial discussion. For example, in the case of Algerian citizen Abdul Razak Ali, who has been detained since 2002, the D.C. Court of Appeals, (composed of Circuit Judges Rogers and Millett and Senior Circuit Judge Randolph) commented in 2020 that "whether and which particular aspects of the Due Process Clause apply to detainees at Guantanamo Bay largely remain open questions in this circuit. So too does the question of what procedural protections the Suspension Clause requires."[72] The District Court had denied Ali's first application for *habeas corpus* in 2011, finding that on a preponderance of the evidence he was a member of a force associated with al-Qaeda.[73] He petitioned the District Court again in 2018. They also rejected his claim, holding that the detainees at Guantanamo were not entitled to the protections of the Due Process Clause, but even if that Clause applied, Ali's rights were not violated because circuit precedents "foreclosed Ali's procedural arguments." His substantive arguments that his continuing detention no longer served its ostensible purpose and that the detention exceeded the scope of the AUMF were also dismissed.[74]

On appeal, the D.C. Court of Appeals stated that the District Court's decision that the Due Process Clause was "categorically inapplicable" to the Guantanamo detainees was "misplaced."[75] The Court highlighted that in *Boumediene* the Supreme Court had identified two constitutional protections available to detainees: *habeas corpus* from the Suspension Clause; and the Due Process Clause.[76] However, "circuit precedent has not yet comprehensively resolved which 'constitutional procedural protections apply to the adjudication of detainee habeas corpus petitions,' and whether those 'rights are housed' in the Due Process Clause, the Suspension Clause, or both."[77]

In this case Ali did not rely on the Suspension Clause but argued that both the substantive and procedural requirements of the Due Process Clause applied "wholesale, without any qualifications, to habeas corpus applications filed by all Guantanamo detainees."[78] The Court considered that this went too far, and that all that could be gleaned from precedent is that the issue of which constitutional protections govern Guantanamo habeas petitions must be analyzed "on an issue to issue basis, applying *Boumediene's* functional approach" that takes into account the "unique context and balancing of interests" required when reviewing the detention of foreign nationals captured during ongoing hostilities.[79]

Furthermore, in any event the Due Process Clause would offer no aid in resolving his complaint about having been detained for more than seventeen years.[80] Even though the substantive element of the Due Process Clause barred "certain arbitrary, wrongful government actions regardless of the procedures used to implement them,"[81] arbitrary has been defined as action that is "so egregious, so outrageous, that it may fairly be said to shock the contemporary conscience."[82] The Court commented that Ali's detention was long because the armed conflict out of which his detention arose continues until the present day.[83] The Periodic Review Board had reviewed Ali's detention eight times, and concluded each time that he still posed a significant threat to the security of the United States.[84] Although posing a threat was a factor, the authority to detain was dependent on the continuing hostilities.[85]

In December 2020 Ali petitioned the Supreme Court by filing a Writ of Certiorari for leave to appeal the Court of Appeals decision, seeking a determination as to whether the Due Process Clause applied in any respect to the Guantanamo detainees. The question presented to the Court was "whether the court of appeals correctly rejected the petitioner's claim that his detention at Guantanamo Bay, Cuba, violates the Due Process Clause of the Fifth Amendment."[86] On May 17, 2021, the Supreme Court denied the Writ of Certiorari.[87]

The question of whether the constitutional right to claim *habeas corpus* in a federal court included constitutional due process rights also arose in the case of Yemeni citizen Abdulsalam Ali Abdulrahman Al Hela. He was suspected of maintaining contact with al-Qaeda affiliates and other terrorist groups. He disappeared during a business trip to Egypt in 2002 but the United States obtained custody of him and has detained him at Guantanamo since 2004.

The case management order required the government to provide certain evidence including exculpatory information and provide additional discovery on request. There was a protocol that governed the extent to which Al Hela was permitted to see classified information. Over the years Al Hela filed a number of requests for additional discovery, all of which were denied because the filings described the underlying sensitive classified information. The D.C. District Court, hearing this case at around the same time as *Ali*, denied Al Hela's *habeas* petition on a number of grounds relating to the evidence, and they again held that the Due Process Clause did not apply to Guantanamo detainees.[88]

On appeal, the three-judge Court (Circuit Judges Griffith and Rao, and Senior Circuit Judge Randolph) upheld the findings of fact that Al-Hela had substantially supported al-Qaeda and associated forces and that at August 2020 the hostilities had not ended.[89] The judgment reiterated that the standard of proof to show that detention was lawful was a showing "on the preponderance of the evidence" that the detainee was "part of or substantially supported" enemy forces.[90] The Court also rejected Al Hela's claim that the "meaningful opportunity" guaranteed by the Suspension Clause included personal access to classified information, and noted the ways the court sought to permit reasonable alternatives.[91] Judge Rao noted, "In the wake of *Boumediene*, Guantanamo detainees are entitled to a 'meaningful opportunity' to challenge the basis for their detention, not a perfect one."[92] Finally, the court rejected Al Hela's claim to extend the due process protections, whether substantive or procedural, of the Fifth Amendment to non-citizen detainees at Guantanamo, on the basis that according to U.S. constitutional law, subject to very limited exceptions, "foreign citizens outside U.S. territory do not possess rights under the U.S. Constitution."[93] The full Court of Appeals vacated the panel ruling in April 2021 and decided to rehear the case.[94] The Justice[95] Department's brief filed under seal (because it contained classified information) in early July 2021 is said to have taken "no position on the question of whether Guantanamo detainees have any due process rights."[96] On the first day of the rehearing, there was a sense that the court was reluctant to decide that the detainees had due process rights.

Detention in Afghanistan

Detainees in jurisdictions outside of Guantanamo have not been so fortunate as regards rights. The *Al Maqaleh* litigation concerned the detention of Yemeni and Tunisian citizens at a U.S. military base in Afghanistan, which at the time was a theater of active military combat. The D.C. Court of Appeals ruled that the courts' jurisdiction to hear *habeas* petitions did not extend to detainees held in military detention in Bagram Air Force Base in Afghanistan.[97] The Court referred to the three factors in *Boumediene* mentioned above, commenting that the Supreme Court would not have needed to spell them out had the Court intended to restrict its understanding of the reach of the Suspension Clause to territories where the United States exercised *de facto* sovereignty.[98] The Court rejected the contention that the United States control of Bagram under a lease of the military base was sufficient to trigger the extraterritorial application of the Suspension Clause, on the basis that such an interpretation "would seem to create the potential for the extraterritorial extension of the Suspension Clause to noncitizens held in any United States military facility in the world, and perhaps to an indeterminate number of other United States leased facilities as well."[99]

Detention in Iraq

Similarly, there is no jurisdiction for a U.S. court to hear the *habeas* petitions of non-U.S. citizens detained in Iraq. However, in December 2017 the American Civil Liberties Union Foundation (ACLU) filed a *habeas* petition on behalf of an anonymous U.S. citizen, who was also a citizen of Saudi Arabia, who claimed he had been unlawfully detained since September 2017 in a military facility in Iraq for allegedly being an ISIS fighter in Syria. He had initially been detained in secret without access to a court or to counsel. In December 2017 the D.C. District Court denied the U.S. Defense Department's motion to dismiss and ordered that the detainee be given access to the ACLU (as "nothing in *Boumediene*" prevented the Court from ordered immediate access) to ascertain whether he wished the *habeas* proceedings to continue.[100]

In January 2018 the District Court was asked to address the detainee's concern that the U.S. Defense Department might transfer him to another country before the Court could decide the outcome of the *habeas* petition. The Court ordered the Department of Defense to provide the Court and the detainee's attorney 72 hours notice prior to transfer so that an emergency motion to contest the transfer could be filed.[101] This order was affirmed on appeal.[102] The *habeas* petition was listed for hearing on June 20, 2018, but on June 6 the Government announced their intention to release the detainee into Syria. After negotiations with the ACLU, the Government released the detainee under the terms of a confidential agreement to an unnamed country in October 2018.[103]

The "Beatles"

In February 2018 two of the "Beatles" Alexanda Kotey and El Shafee Elsheikh were captured in Syria by Kurdish fighters from the Syrian Democratic Forces. In October 2019 the U.S. military took custody of them and transferred them to a secure military location in Iraq, where they remained until October 2020 when they were flown to the United States and arraigned in a federal court in Alexandria, Virginia on charges of hostage taking resulting in death and conspiracy charges relating to both hostage taking and providing material support to a foreign terrorist organization.[104] During their detention in Iraq, there was no shortage of legal actions launched on their behalf, but these all related to an attempt to block the United Kingdom from supplying evidence to the United States that would assist in a U.S. prosecution.[105] No attempts appear to have been made to challenge their detention in Iraq. On the basis of the *Maqaleh* ruling, any such claim would have failed due to the lack of jurisdiction.

Treatment of detainees

After 9/11 many draconian strategies were employed by the United States in their attempt to keep the country safe. They considered that the routine criminal law was inadequate, and that LOAC was more suitable to the task in hand. However, as mentioned above, the Administration decided that the Geneva Conventions were not applicable to the conflict against al-Qaeda and the Taliban.[106] Thus "the gloves were off."[107]

Although President Bush insisted that torture was not in the tool chest, he did authorize the CIA to use something euphemistically called "enhanced interrogation techniques."[108] The 12 measures the CIA proposed were the attention grasp, "walling," facial hold, facial slap, cramped confinement, wall standing, stress positions, sleep deprivation, waterboarding, use of diapers, use of insects, and mock burials.[109] News that such techniques were being used first came into the public domain in April 2004, with the photographs of the torture and mistreatment of detainees in Abu Ghraib prison in Iraq.[110]

The Bush Administration had commissioned a number of opinions between 2002 and 2005 from the Office of Legal Counsel, about the legality of these techniques. David Cole comments on these and sets out redacted versions of the now infamous "torture memos." He concludes:

> What became increasingly clear . . . and is confirmed by the memos . . . is that the Bush Administration "adhered" to the law only by twisting its meaning in extraordinary ways. Once the lawyers were done, laws designed to prohibit absolutely all forms of torture and cruel, inhuman and degrading treatment were read instead to *permit* exactly that.[111]

In October 2005 one of the OLC personnel had publicly stated that the policy of the United States Government was to comply with the "substantive constitutional standard incorporated into Article 16 [of the Convention Against Torture]" (CAT)[112] under which a State Party is required to prevent officially instigated torture.[113] The United States had ratified the Convention, subject to a Declaration that its obligation under Article 16 only applied to the extent that "cruel, inhuman or degrading treatment or punishment" means the cruel, unusual and inhumane treatment or punishment prohibited by the Fifth, Eighth, and/or Fourteenth Amendments to the Constitution of the United States.[114] However the May 2005 OLC opinion had concluded that the CIA techniques would not be prohibited by those Amendments.[115]

In December 2005, the Detainee Treatment Act was passed which did nothing to stop the torture because it contained the same legal standards as the U.S. Declaration to the CAT and as set out in the 2005 OLC Opinion. However, in 2006, the Supreme Court held that Common Article 3 applied to the conflict with al-Qaeda. This meant that detainees were entitled to be treated humanely, and outrages on personal dignity, humiliating and degrading treatment, cruel treatment, and torture were prohibited.[116] Yet it was not until President Obama's second day in office in January 2009 that torture and detainee abuse were denounced as absolutely prohibited under both domestic and international law, and he signed an executive order banning the "enhanced interrogation" techniques involving torture or cruel, or inhuman or degrading treatment.[117] This was codified into the National Defense Authorization Act of 2016.[118]

Guantanamo detainee Abu Zubayda (whose 2015 ECtHR case was discussed above) had been subjected to torture in a secret CIA black site in Poland in 2002. In 2017 he sought an order to subpoena two independent contractors who had devised and supervised the infamous "enhanced interrogation" techniques for the CIA, to provide depositions for use in the criminal investigation in Poland. His district court application had been initially granted, but then was quashed after the United States asserted state secrets privilege. In 2019 the Ninth Circuit Appeal Court reversed. Although it agreed that state secrets privilege applied to some of the information, it also concurred with the initial District Court finding that "certain information requested [wa]s not privileged because it is not a state secret that would pose an exceptionally grave risk to national security."[119] In the first Supreme Court Guantanamo case to be adjudicated since 2008, oral argument of Zubayda's case was heard in October 2021, on the government's question:

> Whether the court of appeals erred when it rejected the United States' assertion of the state-secrets privilege based on the court's own assessment of potential harms to the national security, and required discovery to proceed further under 28 U.S.C. 1782(a) against former Central Intelligence Agency (CIA) contractors on matters concerning alleged clandestine CIA activities.[120]

Feedback from the hearing suggests that the issue of considering whether information that has been widely reported could be subject to the state secrets privilege, could be side-stepped by the question posed by several justices as to whether Zubaydah could himself be permitted to provide testimony to the Polish criminal investigators.[121]

In 2020 in the Military Commission case of *Majid Khan*, Military Judge Watkins opined on the extent to which international law governs the treatment of detainees.[122] He noted that the "universal right to be free of torture is a *jus cogens* norm of international law" and is binding customary international law. He opined crucially that IHRL applies in NIACs and that IHRL is not displaced by LOAC which is so sparse in these conflicts.[123] He commented that that if Khan's allegations were true, the CIA mistreatment would amount to torture and "violated the right to the *jus cogens* universal right to be free of torture under U.S. and international law."[124] Yet he did not accept that it was the responsibility of the Commission to hold others accountable for their actions.[125]

In 2021 the subject of detainee torture appears to merit different treatment with double standards, depending on the context in which the issue crops up. David Luban has highlighted how the U.S. government appears reluctant even to have court records that acknowledge that torture of detainees had taken place,[126] but permits evidence obtained through torture to be admissible in certain court proceedings.[127]

Redress

In 2013 a defense contractor whose subsidiary was accused of conspiring to torture detainees at Abu Ghraib, paid a total of $5.28 million to 71 former inmates at held Abu Ghraib and other U.S. run detention sites between 2003 and 2007.[128] A number of persons detained under LOAC by the United States have also sought redress via human rights institutions. One example is the case of Djamel Ameziane. His *habeas* petition to the D.C. courts was stayed after he had been cleared for release in 2009, but he was not transferred to Algeria until 2013. He was never able to challenge the conditions of his detention. He claimed the return of his life savings that had been taken from him on his arrest within his *habeas action,* but the Court rejected this claim, saying that it had no jurisdiction to hear it. The Court acknowledged that although the law may leave the petitioner without a legal remedy, that did not make the law unconstitutional, "not every violation of a right yields a remedy, even when the right is constitutional."[129]

Ameziane petitioned the IACHR in 2008, but this did not result in a hearing until 2017. He sought redress for violations of numerous human rights including arbitrary detention for almost 12 years at Kandahar airbase and Guantanamo, conditions of detention, mistreatment including torture, due process, as well as violation of his right to property because the United States had confiscated and refused to return his possessions, including his life savings, at the time of his forced transfer to Algeria.[130] The United States maintained throughout this litigation that the IACHR had no jurisdiction to consider the case because IHL applied, rather than IHRL.[131] The IACHR reiterated that in situations of armed conflict IHRL is not displaced by IHL, and IHRL applies unless it is displaced in appropriate situations by derogations, which were not relevant to this case.[132]

The IACHR concluded that Ameziane's detention was arbitrary "by any measure" of IHRL or IHL,[133] that the complaints regarding his treatment were substantiated,[134] as were the complaints relating to due process,[135] and lack of an effective civil remedy.[136] Accordingly the IACHR reiterated that the United States should return the confiscated money to Ameziane and make "adequate material and moral reparations" for the human rights violations including both economic compensation and measures of satisfaction for the years of detention and torture, as well as provide for Ameziane's rehabilitative care needs and conduct criminal investigations for the torture.[137] Unfortunately there is no mechanism to compel any of this, not least because the United States does not accept that the IACHR has any jurisdiction over the matter.

United Kingdom

In the year ending September 30, 2020, 215 persons were arrested on suspicion of terrorist-related activity, 48 fewer than in the previous twelve-month period. Of the 215, 62 arrests resulted in a charge, of which 55 were for terrorism-related offenses. 33 of the arrests involved detention. Although the majority of the arrests were in relation to Islamist extremism, arrests for far-right extremism increased.[138]

Preventive detention

Under current U.K. law, persons reasonably suspected to be terrorists (those who are, or have been concerned in the commission, preparation or instigation of acts of terrorism), may be arrested without a warrant.[139] A number of human rights protections are enshrined in domestic law. Suspects may be detained without charge for an initial period of 48 hours, during which time the detention must be reviewed at regular intervals. If further detention is deemed necessary by the police, a senior police officer must apply to a judicial authority for a warrant to extend the detention for a further five days. After seven days in custody, application must be made for a further extension of detention without charge for up to another seven days. If after 14 days in custody, no charges are preferred, the suspect must be released.[140] At every stage the detainee has the right to challenge the detention.[141] The detainee has the right to have one person informed of the detention.[142] Access to counsel is permitted but can be delayed in certain circumstances.[143]

Treatment of detainees

The United Kingdom has been fighting terrorism emanating from Northern Ireland for decades. In August 1971 the Northern Ireland government introduced extra-judicial measures of detention and internment of suspected terrorists.[144] In November 1972 the British Government assumed direct rule, and in August 1973 enacted the Emergency Provisions Act, which permitted arrest for interrogation, detention for further interrogation, and preventive detention.[145] They also declared a state of emergency and issued notices of derogation from the ECHR.[146]

At that time five particular techniques of interrogation were used, either singly or as a package. These were:

> (1) wall-standing: putting detainees in a stress position spreadeagled against a wall, making them stand on their toes, placing the most weight on fingers held above the head; (2) hooding at all times except during interrogation; (3) continuous subjection to loud noise; (4) sleep deprivation; and (5) deprivation of food and drink.[147]

The Irish government initially complained to the European Commission on Human Rights in in December 1971. The Commission produced a report stating that the treatment amounted to torture and inhuman treatment.[148] The Irish government then petitioned the European Court of Human Rights (ECtHR). A majority (13 out of 17) of the ECtHR judges held that the treatment in question did not amount to torture. The Court reached this decision by analyzing what it perceived to be the difference between torture and inhuman treatment. It commented that

> this distinction derives principally from a difference in the intensity of the suffering inflicted. . . . Although the five techniques, as applied in combination, undoubtedly amounted to inhuman and degrading treatment, although their object was the extraction of confessions, the naming of others and/or information and although they were used systematically, they did not occasion suffering of the particular intensity and cruelty implied by the word torture as so understood.[149]

A larger majority (all but one judge) believed that the treatment did constitute inhuman and degrading treatment that violated Article 3 ECHR.[150]

For 50 years, nine out of 14 men who had been tortured while interned in Northern Ireland have been calling for an independent investigation into the interrogation measures. In June 2021 the Supreme Court heard an appeal by the police service of Northern Ireland against the 2019 ruling by the Belfast Court of Appeal that an investigation of the treatment of the men should proceed.[151] As of September 2021 the judgment had not yet been delivered.

Issues surrounding the reasons for arrest: the Sher cases

The requirement that suspects must be told the reason for their arrest[152] has generated litigation. Sultan Sher and two other men were arrested without a warrant on suspicion of terrorism and were detained for 13 days. Each man was told that the reason for the arrest was that he was currently, or had been involved in the commission, preparation, or instigation of acts of terrorism, and that the arrest was necessary to allow the prompt and effective investigation of the offence. When the police requested further warrants of detention, owing to the sensitivity of the material that the police wished to adduce in court, the special advocate (SIAC) procedure[153] was used to deal with this sensitive, or classified information in a closed hearing, i.e. a hearing not open to the general public.

Sher complained about both issues. The court stated that no other information was required at the time of arrest and commented that "a general statement of that sort will not usually amount to a breach of Article 5(2) [ECHR], *provided of course* that thereafter, further information as to how and why such suspicions are held is promptly given to the suspect."[154]

Sher's petition to the ECtHR regarding the Article 5(2) complaint was ruled inadmissible because domestic remedies had not been exhausted.[155] As to the question of whether the authorization by a court of extended detention on the basis of evidence offered in a closed setting was fair, the ECtHR noted that terrorist crime fell into a special category, that the procedure in this case was not unfair, and did not violate Article 5(4).

> Article 5 § 1 (c) of the Convention should not be applied in such a manner as to put disproportionate difficulties in the way of the police authorities in taking effective measures to counter organized terrorism in discharge of their duty under the Convention to protect the right to life and the right to bodily security of members of the public. Contracting States cannot be asked to establish the reasonableness of the suspicion grounding the arrest of a suspected terrorist by disclosing the confidential sources of supporting information or even facts which would be susceptible of indicating such sources or their identity (see *Fox, Campbell and Hartley v. the United Kingdom*, 30 August 1990, §§ 32–34, Series A no. 182). It follows that Article 5 § 4 cannot require disclosure of such material or preclude the holding of a closed hearing to allow a court to consider confidential material.[156]

However, the Court made it clear that the authorities must disclose adequate information to enable the applicant to know the nature of the allegations against him and have the opportunity to adduce evidence to refute them. The authorities must also ensure that the applicant or his legal advisers are able to participate effectively in court proceedings concerning continued detention.[157]

The issue of disclosing adequate information is especially pertinent to the many cases involving closed hearings with SIAC special advocates. In 2009, in a case concerning the now abolished U.K. control orders,[158] the ECtHR endorsed the special advocate system, commenting that SIAC was best placed to ensure that no material was unnecessarily withheld, but the controlee – and a detainee – must be given sufficient evidence to enable him to give effective instructions to the special advocate.[159] Some months later the then named House of Lords acknowledged the requirement to permit a controlee – and a detainee – to know "the essence of the case" against him.[160]

Compatibility with Article 5 ECHR: the Hicks cases

In 2017, the U.K. Supreme Court analyzed the complaints of a group of four men who claimed that their detention breached Article 5 ECHR.[161] They had been arrested to prevent an imminent breach of the peace by anti-monarchists on the 2011 wedding day of the Duke and Duchess of Cambridge and were detained for between two and a half and five and a half hours. The initial tribunal (the Administrative Court) interpreted that in Article 5(1)(c), the phrase "effected for the purpose of bringing him before the competent legal authority" was limited in its application to the words immediately following it, i.e. "for the purpose of bringing the person concerned before the court on reasonable suspicion of having committed an offence." The Administrative Court thought that the section did not apply when the purpose of the arrest was to prevent an offence, even though this appeared to be a more natural reading of Article 5(1)(c), but that "Strasbourg case law on the point was inconclusive."[162]

The Court of Appeal agreed with the decision of the Administrative Court, but not the reasoning. Its view was that "effected for the purpose of bringing him before the competent legal authority" governed all the limbs of 5(1)(c). It chose not to follow the majority view set out in *Ostendorf*[163] (as described above) that Article 5(1)(c) "was incapable of authorizing purely preventive detention, despite the existence of grounds to believe that an offence was imminent and that the suspect must be suspected of already having committed an offence."[164]

The Supreme Court reviewed the relevant ECtHR jurisprudence and commented that on the facts of this case, the decisions to arrest and detain were not arbitrary, were taken in good faith and were proportionate to the situation.[165] However, the Court perceived that this was "a difficult question of law as to how such preventive power can be accommodated within Article 5. The Strasbourg law on this point is not clear and settled."[166] The Court concluded that it would "read the qualification on the power of arrest or detention under Article 5(1)(c) contained in the words 'for the purpose of bringing him before the competent legal authority' as implicitly dependent on the cause for detention continuing long enough for the person to be brought before the court."[167]

The comments in *Hicks* were referred to in *S, V and A v. Denmark* as discussed above in its analysis of the unsettled state of Article 5 interpretation.[168]

Detention and mistreatment of detainees by British forces

The next set of cases deal with complaints about detention or mistreatment by British troops during conflicts in Iraq and Afghanistan, often with a co-mingling of IHRL and IHL issues.

In 2007 the case of *Al-Jedda* reached the then-called House of Lords.[169] Al-Jeddah was born in Iraq, was granted British nationality in 2000, but was stripped of British citizenship in 2007. In 2004 he traveled to Iraq where he was suspected of being a member of a terrorist group involved with a number of activities, and of involvement in a number of terrorist activities. He was arrested and detained in Iraq for over three years without charge, on the grounds that his internment was determined necessary for imperative reasons of security in Iraq. Al-Jeddah claimed that his detention breached Article 5 ECHR.

In 2003 the United Kingdom and the United States had become recognized by the United Nations as occupying powers in Iraq, but in June 2004 the Iraqi interim government was in charge. The Multinational Force that included British forces remained in Iraq pursuant to Iraqi government requests and UN Security Council (UNSC) resolutions and authorizations. A number of questions arose: who was responsible for the detention of Al-Jedda, was it the United Nations or the United Kingdom; did the UNSCR 1546[170] displace Article 5 ECHR; did U.K. or Iraqi law apply to the detention, and if it was British law, was there a legal basis for the detention?

A majority of the House of Lords ruled that the U.K. and U.S. forces were not under the effective command and control of the United Nations. This meant that the United Kingdom were responsible for the detention.[171] As to the second question, the Court unanimously ruled that the United Kingdom

> may lawfully, where it is necessary for imperative reasons of security, exercise the power to detain authorized by UNSCR 1456 and successive resolutions, but must ensure that the detainee's rights under Article 5 are not infringed to any greater extent than is inherent in such detention.[172]

On the third question, the Court unanimously ruled that Iraqi common law applied to the detention.[173]

Al-Jedda then complained to the ECtHR that his internment in Iraq for over three years violated Article 5 ECHR.[174] Despite the House of Lords ruling, the U.K. Government continued to contend that the internment was attributable to the United Nations and not the United Kingdom, and alternatively argued that the detention was carried out under UNSCR 1546 which overrode Article 5. The ECtHR agreed with the House of Lords that the internment was attributable to the United Kingdom, and that the detention fell within the jurisdiction of the United Kingdom, and therefore the ECHR.[175]

The ECtHR concluded that while paragraph 10 of UNSCR 1546 authorized the United Kingdom to take measures that would assist in maintaining security and stability in Iraq, none of the relevant international Resolutions "explicitly or implicitly" required the United Kingdom to place an individual considered to be a risk to the security of Iraq in indefinite detention without charge. As there was no binding obligation to use internment, no conflict existed between the United Kingdom's U.N. and ECHR obligations. Article 5(1) applied, and as the detention did not fall within any of its categories, Al-Jedda's detention violated Article 5(1). This case was criticized for requiring the authority to detain to be placed in UNSC Resolutions instead of IHL and for casting "a chilling shadow on the current and future lawfulness of detention operations carries out by ECHR state abroad," leaving the ability of such states to engage with other non-ECHR states in multinational forces in a detention mandate, uncertain at best.[176]

Conversely, in *Hassan v. United Kingdom*, the ECtHR did not find a violation of Article 5.[177] The applicant's brother was arrested Iraq in April 2003 by British forces and detained in Camp Bucca which was administered by the British, although U.S. interrogators also worked there. Pursuant to the requirements of the Article 122, GC III, details of detainees were supposed to be collated promptly and given to the International Committee of the Red Cross Central Tracing Agency. Hassan's details were not notified to that Agency for three months until July owing to computer issues. It appears that he was released at some time in May, but his body was found with bullet wounds in the countryside in September 2003. The issues relating to his treatment and death are discussed in Part III.

In considering the Article 5 complaint, although the facts occurred in a period of active hostilities, the ECtHR decided that because Hassan was within the physical power and control of British forces, he fell within U.K. jurisdiction.[178] The Court referred to the long line of cases that established that the list of permissible grounds of detention set out in Article 5(1) did not include internment, or preventive detention when there is no intention to bring criminal charges within a reasonable time. (This case was heard and decided before the shift in opinion in *S, V. and Av. Denmark* referred to above occurred).

The Court also noted the differences of context and purpose between arrest and detention in peace time, and when that occurred in the course of an armed conflict. So, what did Article 5 mean in the context of armed conflict? The Court commented that there was no congruence between detention as envisaged in Geneva Convention (GC) III or GCIV and Article 5(1)(c), and no correlation between security internment and suspicion of having committed, or risk of committing a criminal offence. Similarly, detention of combatants as prisoners of war does not fall within Article 5(1)(c).[179] The Court pointed out that whilst the Contracting Parties to the ECHR have not reached any agreement as to the interpretation of Article 5 in situations of armed conflict, the practice of the parties is not to derogate from their Article 5 obligations in order to detain persons pursuant to GCIII and GCIV during international armed conflicts (IACs).[180] The Court referred to International Court of Justice (ICJ) jurisprudence in Article 2

ECHR cases where that Article was to be interpreted as far as possible in the light of the general principles in international law, including IHL. The ECtHR noted that the ICJ has held that "the protection offered by human rights conventions and that offered by international humanitarian law co-exist in situations of armed conflict."[181] The ECtHR opined that the same principles should apply to Article 5 cases, and held that even in situations of IACs, the safeguards of the ECHR continue to apply,

> albeit interpreted against the background of the provisions of international humanitarian law. By reason of the co-existence of the safeguards provided by international humanitarian law and by the Convention in time of armed conflict, the grounds of permitted deprivation of liberty set out in subparagraphs (a) to (f) of that provision should be accommodated, as far as possible, with the taking of prisoners of war and the detention of civilians who pose a risk to security under the Third and Fourth Geneva Conventions.[182]

Furthermore, deprivation of liberty under IHL must be "lawful" to preclude a violation of Article 5 ECHR, i.e. any detention must comply with the rules of IHL and "most importantly . . . it should be in keeping with the fundamental purpose of Article 5(1), which is to protect the individual from arbitrariness."[183] The applicant had also complained that the detention had violated Articles 5(2) and (4), and the Court confirmed that those procedural safeguards should be interpreted "in a manner which takes into account the context and applicable rules" of IHL.[184]

On the particular facts of *Hassan*, the ECtHR ruled that his detention was not arbitrary and that there was no violation of Article 5.[185] However, these remarks in *Hassan* were made in the context of an IAC for which some protections are set out in the GCs. In non-international conflicts (NIACs) there is a low IHL bar to cross because only GC Common Article 3 applies, and the question for the United Kingdom of whether IHRL was applicable in a NIAC did not have a definitive answer until 2017.

As of January 2017 the United Kingdom government were being sued for damages in hundreds of cases by detainees alleging unlawful detention, maltreatment, and some cases of unlawful killing by British forces in Afghanistan and Iraq,[186] and had paid out approximately £14 million in 2012 to hundreds of Iraqis who had claimed that they had been illegally detained and tortured.[187] British troops were in those countries as part of a multi-national force in accordance with UNSC resolutions. In each country they were participating in NIACs because they were required to deal with exceptional levels of violence by organized armed groups.[188] The key issue in all of these cases was to establish the extent to which Article 5 ECHR applied to military detention in the territory of a non-Convention state during NIAC operations in support of its government in accordance with UNSC mandates.[189]

In 2017 the Supreme Court adjudicated a number of inter-related cases. One such action in this mosaic of cases was brought by Abd Ali Hameed Ali Al-Waheed and Serdar Mohammed. Al-Waheed was detained in February 2007 during a search at his wife's home in Iraq, where allegedly, components for improvised explosive devices were found. He was held at a British detention center for six and a half weeks before being released without charge.[190] The question before the Supreme Court was whether the British forces had the power to detain him.[191]

Mohamed was captured in Afghanistan in April 2010 by British forces in the course of a planned operation during a firefight. He was detained for three and a half months by British forces despite the then prevailing UNSC resolutions that required the handing over of detainees to Afghan authorities after no more than 96 hours of detention. After the eventual transfer to Afghan authorities Mohammed was convicted by an Afghan court and sentenced to ten years imprisonment.[192]

The question before the Supreme Court was whether British forces had the power to detain Mohammed in excess of 96 hours pursuant to relevant UNSC resolutions and IHL in a non-international law (NIAC) context, and if so whether Article 5(1) should be read to accommodate, as permissible grounds, detention pursuant to such a power under a UNSC Resolution and/or IHL. The Court also had to consider whether Mohammed's detention was compatible with Articles 5(1) and 5(4) ECHR.[193]

In the Supreme Court, Lord Sumption (with whom the majority of the Court agreed wholly or in part), discussed the legal basis for detention in a NIAC and said it depended on customary international law and/or the authority of the UNSC.[194] Two things are required to establish customary international law (CIL): the almost uniform practice by states adhering to a particular rule; and that the rule must be followed as if it were required by law. At that time, despite the long-standing practice of states to capture and detain members of an opposing armed force, that detention was not sanctioned by CIL in a NIAC.[195] He concluded that the relevant UNSC resolutions in principle "constituted authority in international law for the detention of members of the opposing armed forces whenever it was required for imperative reasons of security."[196]

In Afghanistan the UNSC authorized the establishment of an International Security Assistance Force, (ISAF), of which the United Kingdom was part. ISAF policy limited detention to 96 hours, but several countries within the ISAF (the United Kingdom, United States, Canada, and the Netherlands) considered this inadequate because of the high level of violence in the area. Accordingly, the United Kingdom decided to adopt its own detention policy, which was not limited to 96 hours, and this was accepted by NATO and ISAF.[197]

Lord Sumption concluded that the United Kingdom was entitled to adopt its own detention policy, provided that it was consistent with the UNSC Resolutions, in that detention could only be authorized when it was necessary for imperative reasons of security.[198] In his analysis of the application of Article 5 ECHR, he pointed out that human rights cannot be protected in a war zone in the same way as they are in peace time, and as UNSC Resolutions are addressed to every country in the world, they cannot be construed by reference to a particular national or regional code of human rights protection. The applicable code of human rights is the international law body of principles relevant to armed conflict.[199] Lord Sumption concluded that although IHL does not specifically authorize detention in a NIAC, the UNSC Resolutions did, and those Resolutions "conferred an authority in international law to detain in circumstances where this was necessary for imperative reasons of security."[200]

He also considered that the principle decided in *Hassan*, that the six grounds listed in Article 5(1) were not necessarily to be treated as exhaustive in the context of an armed conflict, did not depend on the character of the armed conflict, nor did the principle exclusively apply to IACs, but was equally applicable to NIACs.[201] Lord Sumption concluded that the effect of *Hassan* was that where the armed forces of a Convention state act under a UNSC mandate to use all necessary measures, Article 5(1) cannot be construed to prevent them from detaining persons for imperative reasons of security, but the procedural provisions in Article 5(4) could technically be adapted to apply if necessary in an armed conflict context, provided that minimum standards of protection exist to ensure that detention is not imposed arbitrarily, with an initial review of whether the detention was appropriate and regular reviews thereafter in accordance with a fair procedure.[202]

In the case of Mohamed, Lord Sumption concluded that British forces had the legal power to detain him in excess of 96 hours pursuant to the UNSC Resolutions because this was necessary for imperative reasons of security.[203] His detention did not fall within either Articles 5(1)(c) or (f).[204] However, although Mohamed was able to challenge the lawfulness of the detention, the procedures did not satisfy the *Hassan* test of providing sufficient guarantees of impartiality and fairness to protect against arbitrariness.[205] In the case of Al-Waheed, British forces had the legal power to detain him pursuant to UNSC Resolutions where this was necessary for imperative reasons of security.[206] The question of whether the facts supported that requirement are discussed below in the context of another separate claim by Al-Waheed within the inter-related cases.

Mohammed also claimed that his detention was unlawful pursuant to the Afghan law of tort. That claim was heard together with the tort claim brought by Yunus Rahmatullah, and the Supreme Court delivered their judgments on the same day.[207] Rahmatullah, a Pakistani citizen, had been detained on February 28, 2004, by British forces in Iraq on suspicion of being a terrorist during an IAC when the United Kingdom and the United States were the occupying forces. A few days later he was transferred to the custody of U.S. forces. By the end of March 2004, Rahmatullah was transferred to Bagram airbase in Afghanistan, where he was detained for over ten years without charge or trial. In 2010 a Detainee Review Board had found Ramatullah's continued detention unnecessary.

As the country that initially detained him had been the United Kingdom, Ramatullah applied for a writ of *habeas corpus* in the United Kingdom. This was granted in 2011 by the Court of Appeal which required the United Kingdom to seek the return of Ramatullah or demonstrate why it could not. In a letter, the United States asserted the legality of the detention and suggested that Pakistan had requested repatriation. In February 2012 a second Court of Appeal judgement ruled that the United States letter had demonstrated why the release could not be secured. However, in October 2012, the Supreme Court ruled that Ramatullah qualified as a protected person under Article 45 of GC IV,[208] and that the United Kingdom had a clear obligation to correct any violation of Article 45, or request the return of Ramatullah.[209] Despite this, he remained in Bagram until he was released in 2014. He claimed that he had suffered severe mistreatment in both the British and the American detention, and that the British were complicit in his unlawful detention and treatment by American forces.[210]

The British Government raised the doctrine of Crown act of state as a defense to the tort claims. What does this term mean? As a general rule, if a wrongful act has been committed against a person or his property, the wrongdoer cannot escape liability by claiming that the wrongful act was done at the command of the Crown. The only exception relates to cases where acts have been committed abroad against a foreigner, in which case the wrongdoer can raise as a defense to a claim in a British court, that the wrongful act was done on the orders of the British Government.[211] As Lord Sumption explained it: "The rule of law relating to Crown acts of state defines the limits which, as a matter of policy, the law sets upon certain categories of rights and liabilities, on the ground that they would otherwise be inconsistent with the exercise by the executive of the proper functions of the state."[212]

In this case the U.K. Government asked the Court to adopt a deferential approach, claiming (1) that the case was not justiciable on the grounds that "certain acts committed by a sovereign state are, by their very nature, not susceptible to adjudication in the courts," and (2) that a foreigner cannot sue the Government, or its servants or agents, in the British courts "in respect of certain acts committed abroad pursuant to deliberate United Kingdom policy in the conduct of its foreign affairs."[213] The Court agreed that the detention by British forces and their transfer to United States and Afghan custody were Crown acts of state which were

> not justiciable or open to question in domestic proceedings for common law damages as the present. They were, on the actual or presently assumed facts, steps taken pursuant to or in implementation of deliberately formed policy against persons (none owing any allegiance to the Crown) reasonably suspected to be insurgents or terrorists in the context of and furtherance of foreign military operations during a time of armed conflict.[214]

Belhaj and Rahmatullah (No 1) dealt with unlawful detention, rendition, and torture, which are outside the scope of a defense of Crown act of state.[215] In addition to Rahmatullah's claim as described above, this case also concerned Libyan national Belhaj and his Moroccan national wife, who tried to take a commercial flight from Beijing to London in early 2004, but Chinese authorities deported them to Kuala Lumpur. They claimed that the British security service MI6 knew of the detention and alerted Libyan intelligence authorities. The complainants alleged that they were unlawfully detained by Malaysian officials in Kuala

Lumpur, then by Thai and United States agents in Bangkok, and were then sent on a United States plane to Libya where Belhaj was detained for six years and his wife was detained for over three months. They claimed that they were tortured by the United States agents in Bangkok and on the plane, and by Libyan officials in Libya. They also alleged that the United Kingdom "by common design arranged, assisted and encouraged [their] unlawful rendition . . . to Libya."[216]

In this action the British Government were seeking to establish that the claims were inadmissible or non-justiciable due to the principles relating to state immunity and/or foreign act of state. Although the British Government had accepted that the defense of state immunity was not available to them, nonetheless they invoked it because the issues in the case engaged the interests of Malaysia, Thailand, Libya, and the United States. The Supreme Court unanimously ruled that the defense of state immunity failed. This was best explained by Lord Sumption:

> No decision in the present cases would affect any rights or liabilities of the four foreign states in whose alleged misdeeds the United Kingdom is said to have been complicit. The foreign states are not parties. Their property is not at risk. The court's decision on the issues raised would not bind them. The relief sought, namely declarations and damages against the United Kingdom, would have no impact on their legal rights, whether in form or substance, and would in no way constrict the exercise of those rights. It follows that the claim to state immunity fails.[217]

On the issue of foreign act of state, Lord Sumption stated that its purpose was "to preclude challenges to the legality or validity of the sovereign acts of foreign states. It is not to protect English parties from liability for their role in it."[218] He held that English public policy did not permit the application of the foreign act of state doctrine to prevent the court from adjudicating on allegations or torture or conniving in torture, as in this case.[219] Similarly, Lord Sumption considered that the irreducible core of the international obligation to guarantee liberty of the person, is that detention is unlawful without any legal basis, or without recourse to the courts, and this core prohibition corresponds to a fundamental principle of English public policy.[220] He ruled that the foreign act of state doctrine cannot be applied to the detention that the complainants allege they endured at the hands of Libyan and United States officials.[221] The ruling in this case was the catalyst for progress in hundreds of cases in which compensation was claimed in respect of detention, ill-treatment and killing by British armed forces in Iraq.

One such case involved Ali Al-Waheed whose other case was discussed above.[222] The claims involving four complainants were treated as a lead case in the High Court for over 600 claims that were active at the date of that trial.[223] As discussed above, the Supreme Court had ruled that U.K. forces were permitted to detain Al-Waheed if this was necessary for imperative reasons of security.[224] In the High Court the claims were made in tort – in this case, as the events had occurred in Iraq, the Iraqi law of tort applied. As discussed above, according to the Supreme Court ruling in *Al-Waheed and Mohammed v. MOD*, Crown act of state doctrine precluded the High Court from adjudicating in connection with a tort arising out of an act done with the authority of the British government during a military operation abroad.[225] However, the claimants could bring proceedings pursuant to the Human Rights Act 1998,[226] which enabled victims of ECHR violations to claim compensation in damages.

The High Court judge determined (i) that although Al-Waheed's tort claims were time-barred, he could proceed under the Human Rights Act; (ii) that he had endured inhuman and degrading treatment on arrest and during detention in contravention of the ECHR; and (iii) although the first 21 days of his detention were deemed necessary for imperative reasons of security, the next 33 days were not, and that second period of detention was unlawful. Accordingly, he was awarded damages of £15,000 in respect of the beating he received after arrest, £15,000 in respect of the additional mistreatment and £3,300 in respect of his unlawful detention of 33 days.[227] Al-Waheed should consider himself fortunate to have received even that award, because in April 2021, the United Kingdom Parliament enacted legislation which placed a number of restrictions on historical prosecutions of military personnel in respect of claims in respect of death or injuries connected with operations overseas.[228]

In this complicated mosaic of cases, the Supreme Court had applied a legal *pot-pourri*: the more permissive rules of IHL detention where it could, such as in *Mohamed*; it applied Article 5 ECHR in cases where it was clear that the United Kingdom had jurisdiction, such as in *Al-Jedda* and to some extent in *Al-Waheed*; it attempted to view the procedural aspects of detention in *Mohamed* through a human rights lens; and the Court was deferential to the government in the foreign tort cases where the government had raised defenses of act of state or Crown act of state such as in *Belhaj* and *Rahmatullah*.

Israel

Since the founding of the State of Israel in 1948, it has been "almost continuously engaged in some sort of violent military confrontation with one or more of its neighbors,"[229] and has been in a permanent state of emergency.[230] Between September 2015, which heralded the start of a particularly intensive wave of terrorist attacks[231] to the end of June 2021, Israel had endured 14,737 terror attacks resulting in 99 fatalities and 653 casualties.[232] The May 2021 Guardian of the Walls conflict with Hamas emanating from Gaza, is discussed in Part III. The main terrorist threat in Israel emanates from Palestinian armed groups from the Palestinian territories in the West Bank and Gaza, and from Hezbollah from Lebanon. The type of terror attack ranges from stone throwing to firebombing, stabbing, grenades, small arms fire, arson, vehicular and rocket attacks.

Israel uses a mixture of detention models.[233] Under the general criminal law, if there are reasonable grounds to suspect that an offense has been committed in Israel, pre-trial detention is permitted in cases where a prosecution is envisaged. This is controlled by judicial review at regular intervals up to a maximum of 75 days.[234]

However, the focus of this section is on administrative detention, which is a preventive regime that operates on a completely separate track in addition to the regular domestic criminal law. It is not intended to replace the criminal law, but is a tool to prevent terrorist activity, and may only be used if prosecution is not an option and if administrative detention is the only tool available to detain a terror suspect.[235]

Emergency Powers Detention Law

The first piece of legislation has its roots in British colonial law, the Defense (Emergency) Regulations, enacted during the British Mandate.[236] In 1979 the Emergency Powers (Detention) Law ("EPDL") replaced that law. It is only applicable in a state of emergency,[237] and gives the authority to issue detention orders to the civilian Minister of Defense.[238] A "particular person" may be detained for up to six months if the Defense Minister has "reasonable cause to believe that reasons of state security or public security" require it.[239] These terms are not defined in the legislation, but Saar and Wahlhaus opine that the Israel Supreme Court has interpreted this legislation in a restrictive manner.[240] Detention is to be a measure of last resort[241] and is regarded as a "tool intended solely to negate an actual danger" and in reality the EPDL is not used very often.[242] However the law permits the detention orders to be renewed unlimited times.[243]

The EPDL has some procedural safeguards, but from the IHRL perspective there are many flaws. Within 48 hours of arrest, the detainee must be taken to the District Court so that the detention may be judicially reviewed by the President of that Court. The detention order will be set aside if it has been "proved . . . that the reasons for which it was made were not objective reasons of state security or public security or that it was made in bad faith or from irrelevant considerations."[244] A confirmed detention order must be reviewed again not later than three months after confirmation[245] and detention decisions may be appealed to the Supreme Court.[246] Detainees have the right of access to counsel "as soon as possible,"[247] but this can be delayed in designated circumstances for up to ten days by the arresting authorities.[248] Even this delay can be extended by the President of the District Court for up to 21 days in total.[249] Hearings are *in camera*[250] and detainees have the right to be present at each hearing,[251] yet the law also states that orders may be made in the absence of the detainee.[252] Detainees and their representatives may be precluded from seeing the evidence against them if the President of the District Court is satisfied that "the disclosure of evidence to either of them may impair state security or public security."[253] Israel has created a practice known as the "judicial management model" whereby the judge alone will see and review all the evidence, examining it in a critical fashion, even from the detainee's viewpoint. However, the State must disclose the basic allegations to the detainee and make full disclosure to the Court.[254] One scholar has examined 322 cases that were adjudicated between 2000 and 2010, which revealed that not one case resulted in a release order, and the secret evidence was never openly rejected by the Court.[255]

The scope of the EPDL was challenged in 2000 by a number of Lebanese men who had been held in detention since 1991 after serving prison sentences for security offenses even though they were not at that time considered to pose a danger to national security. They were being used as "bargaining chips" for negotiations that were taking place for the release of prisoners and missing persons held by Israel.[256] In the lower court, the then Judge Barak held that in these circumstances the prisoners could be held as "bargaining chips."[257] However, on appeal President Barak had second thoughts and reflected that a "balance is required – a delicate and difficult balance – between the liberty and the dignity of the individual and national security and public safety."[258] A majority of the Court ruled that that it was unlawful to detain a person who did not pose a danger to national security but was simply a "bargaining chip."[259] President Barak stated that the purpose of the legislation was that detention was permissible of a person who himself posed a danger to security,[260] and that in any event administrative detention could not continue endlessly: "the more the period of detention that has passed lengthens, so too are weightier considerations needed to justify an additional extension of detention. With the passage of time, the means of administrative detention is no longer proportional."[261]

Unlawful Combatants Law

The second law was crafted to deal with trans-boundary hostile acts against Israel by non-State actors, or unlawful fighters. In other contexts, one might expect this situation to be classified as a NIAC, governed by IHL in general and Common Article 3 specifically, together with IHRL. However, this is a mixed model, as it is situated in the domestic (and not military) law of Israel and uses elements of IHL relating to an IAC as well as IHRL. The Incarceration of Unlawful Combatants Law ("UCL") was enacted in 2002, with the object of regulating "the incarceration of unlawful combatants not entitled to prisoner-of-war status, in a manner conforming with the obligations of the State of Israel under the provisions of international humanitarian law."[262] An unlawful combatant is defined as a person who has "participated either directly or indirectly in hostile acts against the State of Israel or is a member of a force perpetrating hostile acts against the State of Israel," where the conditions prescribed in GC III, Article 4 with respect to prisoners-of-war and granting prisoner-of-war status in IHL do not apply to that person.[263]

Under the UCL, foreign nationals as defined above can be interned for the purpose of removing them from the cycle of hostilities.[264] If the Chief of General Staff "has reasonable cause to believe that a person held by the State authorities is an unlawful combatant and that his release will harm State security" he can order the internment of that person, in the absence of that person.[265] The law does not specify the duration of the detention. The UCL contains several elements of procedural safeguards. The District Court must review the detention order within fourteen days in the presence of the detainee. Once every six months the detainee must be brought to the District Court for further review. Each decision of the District Court may be appealed to the Supreme Court within thirty days.[266] Detainees have the right to meet with a lawyer at the "earliest possible date on which such a meeting may be held without harming State security requirements" but no later than seven days before the first judicial review.[267] The UCL contains provisions similar to the EPDL that restrict the evidence that may be seen by the detainee and his representative, and provides that all hearings are to be *in camera*.[268]

The constitutionality of the UCL was scrutinized extensively in a seminal case where two persons from Gaza who were alleged to be major activists in Hezbollah were placed in administrative detention pursuant to military law in 2002 in the case of the first detainee, and from 2003 in the case of the second.[269] They questioned whether their internment under UCL from 2005 after military rule had ended in Gaza complied with IHL, and whether UCL measured up to the constitutional standards of Israel's Basic Law: Human Dignity and Liberty.[270]

The Supreme Court (sitting as the Court of Criminal Appeals) confirmed that the UCL only applied to persons who participate in the cycle of hostilities, or who belong to forces that carry out hostilities against Israel, but not to innocent civilians or to citizens and residents of Israel who endanger state security.[271] The Court noted that

> the detention powers provided in the law significantly and seriously violate the personal liberty of the detainee. This violation is justified in appropriate circumstances in order to protect state security. Notwithstanding, in view of the extent of the violation of personal liberty and in view of the exceptional nature of the measure of detention that is provided in the law, an interpretive effort should be made in order to minimize the violation of the right to liberty as much as possible so that it is proportionate to the need to achieve the security purpose and does not go beyond this.[272]

The Court also stated that consideration of whether the UCL complied with IHL was dependent on the premise that an IAC was prevailing between the State of Israel and the terrorist organizations operating outside Israel.[273] The detainees had complained that the definition of unlawful combatant was not recognized in IHL, but the Court noted that the issue had been addressed previously in Israeli law in *Public Committee against Torture in Israel (PCAT) v. Government in Israel* which held that

> the term "unlawful combatants" does not constitute a separate category but is a sub- category of "civilians" recognized by international law. This conclusion is based on the approach of customary international law, according to which the category of "civilians" includes everyone who is not a "combatant."[274]

However, the Court considered that the UCL definition of unlawful combatant was broader than that discussed in the PCAT case. It based this conclusion on the basis that the PCAT case was dealing with the legality of a military operation intended to kill an unlawful combatant whilst he was directly participating in hostilities, whereas the UCL addressed internment. Where detention was concerned, an unlawful combatant need not be directly participating in hostilities, nor is it essential that the detention should take place during the time that he is participating in hostilities. All that is required is that the conditions of the UCL definition of unlawful combatant are satisfied.[275]

Thus the unlawful combatant would be subject to GC IV which would permit him to be detained if he represented a threat to state security, although an unlawful combatant would not be entitled to the same level of protection as GC IV offers to an innocent civilian.[276] UCL does not therefore create a new category of person for the purposes of IHL, but "merely determines special provisions for the detention of 'civilians' according [to the IHL term] who are 'unlawful combatants.'"[277] It seems to resemble the continuous combat function in IHL, discussed in Part III. Furthermore, the UCL did not create a third category of detention which is something other than detention pursuant to the criminal law and administrative detention: the internment under this law was administrative detention and was not inconsistent with GC IV.[278]

The Court opined that IHL required that the detainee must pose an individual threat to state security,[279] and that the UCL reflects this, and therefore (introducing an element of IHRL) does not permit anyone to be detained arbitrarily.[280]

Treatment of detainees: interrogation methods

Regarding the treatment of detainees suspected of terrorism, Israel too, used certain unacceptable methods of interrogation until this was outlawed by the courts. In 1999, following a Commission of Inquiry,[281] the Supreme Court sitting at the High Court was petitioned to adjudicate on the legality of certain interrogation techniques of terrorism suspects used by the General Security Service (GSS) which were deemed as "immediately necessary for saving human lives." These included, shaking a person, holding a person in the "Shabach" position, forcing a person into a frog crouch for five minutes at a time, the use of tight handcuffs, and sleep deprivation.[282]

The judgment of the Court was delivered by President Barak. He commented that

> First, a reasonable investigation is necessarily free of torture, free of cruel, inhuman treatment of the subject and free of any degrading handling whatsoever. . . . Second, a reasonable investigation is likely to cause discomfort; it may result in insufficient sleep. The conditions under which it is conducted risk being unpleasant, indeed, it is possible to conduct an effective investigation without resorting to violence. Within the confines of the law, it is permitted to resort to various machinations and specific sophisticated investigations – accepted in the most progressive of societies – that can be effective in achieving their goals. In the end result, the legality of

> the investigation is deduced from the propriety of its purpose and from its methods.[283]

President Barak turned to the interrogation methods in the complaint and decreed that shaking should not be used in ordinary investigations, or outside the bounds of the "necessity" defense.[284] Frog crouching was deemed a prohibited method.[285] Every element of the "Shabach" position was prohibited.[286]

Next President Barak addressed the "necessity" defense.[287] He said

> we are prepared to accept that the "necessity" exception is likely to arise in instances of "ticking time bombs" and that the immediate need ("necessary in an immediate manner" for the preservation of human life) refers to the imminent nature of the act rather than that of the danger . . . in other words, there exists a concrete level of imminent danger.[288]

President Barak stated that a general authority to use physical means during a GSS interrogation could not be implied from the "necessity" defense.[289] He noted that the Commission of Inquiry Report had commented that "if an investigator finds himself in a situation of 'necessity,' constraining him to choose the 'lesser evil' – harming the suspect for the purpose of saving human lives – the 'necessity' defense shall be available to him."[290] The Court decided that neither the government not the security services had the authority to authorize the use of physical interrogation methods, and that a legal statutory authority was required in order to authorize the government to permit the use particular physical tactics beyond what is allowed in ordinary investigations. The "necessity" defense was not a basis for that authority.[291] The Court therefore did not rule directly on this point, leaving it as a matter for the legislature.[292]

In 2009 the Supreme Court sitting as the High Court rejected a petition claiming that the 1999 ruling had been violated in many cases and that the Government should be held in contempt. The Court stated that the arguments were not suitable for a contempt hearing but may have been appropriate in a different type of proceedings, and that "ticking bomb" cases were isolated and rare.[293] However, human rights organizations have long complained about Israel's treatment of detainees.[294]

Summary

Under United States domestic law, while there is no such thing as preventive detention of terror suspects *per se*, preventive detention can result from arrests made at early stages of conspiracy and material support cases, and where there is probable cause of immigration violations. The majority of preventive detention occurs in the LOAC context overseas, i.e. in Guantanamo, Afghanistan and Iraq. Other than a brief shift between 2004 and 2008 to a more human rights direction in cases such as *Hamdi, Hamdan, Rasul, and Boumediene*, nearly all cases have deferred to the policy of the prevailing Administration.

In the United Kingdom, immediately after 9/11 one of the government's policies was to detain suspected international terrorists indefinitely, although suspected British terrorists could only be detained without charge for up to fourteen days. In 2004 the Supreme Court (then called the House of Lords) held that the discrimination between U.K. citizens and non-citizen detention was incompatible with Article 5.[295] Many cases until about 2015 were more human rights protective, particularly cases involving the rights to liberty and to a fair trial.[296] A definite shift back towards deference to the government can be discerned since at least 2017.

In Israel, certainly in the period that Aharon Barak was the Presiding Judge of the Supreme Court from 1995 to 2006, and for some years thereafter, the Court positioned itself to highlight how Israel adhered to the Rule of Law and issued judgments that emphasized cognizance of and respect for human rights. A shift towards deference to the Government since about 2014 has been perceived in some cases.

Notes

1 Dept. of Homeland Security, Homeland Threat Assessment, 17–18, (Oct. 2020), www.dhs.gov/sites/default/files/publications/2020_10_06_homeland-threat-assessment.pdf.

2 Seth G. Jones, Catrina Doxsee, Nicholas Harrington, Grace Hwang and James Suber, *The War Comes Home: The Evolution of Domestic Terrorism in the United States*, CSIS BRIEFS, (Oct. 22, 2020), www.csis.org/analysis/war-comes-home-evolution-domestic-terrorism-united-states.

3 Shelly Tan, Youjin Shin and Danielle Rindler, *How One of America's Ugliest Days Unraveled inside and outside the Capitol*, Washington Post, (Jan. 9, 2021), www.washingtonpost.com/nation/interactive/2021/capitol-insurrection-visual-timeline/.

4 Eric Tucker, *Biden Orders Review of Domestic Violent Extremism Threat*, (Associated Press, Jan. 22, 2021), https://apnews.com/article/joe-biden-donald-trump-jen-psaki-national-security-terrorism-8ac769920a5a945ed1ccaf44d09 06d99.

5 The White House, National Strategy for Countering Domestic Terrorism, (Jun. 2021), www.whitehouse.gov/wp-content/uploads/2021/06/National-Strategy-for-Countering-Domestic-Terrorism.pdf.

6 *See* Webber, Preventive Detention of Terror Suspects, 168–76.

7 U.S. v. Watson, 423 U.S. 411 (243), (1976); Payton v. New York, 445 U.S. 573, 583, (1980); Kentucky v. King, 31 S. Ct. 1849, 1854, (2011); Gerstein v. Pugh, 420 U.S. 103, 125, 126, (1975); County of Riverside v. McLaughlin, 500 U.S. 44, 56, (1991).

8 Harry Litman, *A Domestic Terrorism Statute Doesn't Exist. Congress Must Pass One – Now*, Washington Post, (Aug. 5, 2019), www.washingtonpost.com/opinions/2019/08/05/domestic-terrorism-statute-doesnt-exist-congress-must-pass-one-now/.

9 Robin Simcox and Emily Dyer, Al-Qaeda in the United States: A Complete Analysis of Terrorism Offenses, 675, Table 11C, (Henry Jackson Society, 2013).

10 18 U.S.C. §§2339A, 2339B. §2339A does not refer to foreign terrorist organizations but is predicated on 47 listed offenses such as killing people, bombing etc. To violate this section, a suspect must have provided support with the

intent or knowledge that the support would be used for, or in preparation for the predicate offense, or conspiracy to commit the predicate offense. Support encompasses tangible or intangible property and a wide range of services including those relating to currency, financial services, training, expert advice or assistance, documentation and weapons. §2339B deals with the provision of support to a foreign terrorist organization.

11 Robert M. Chesney, *Beyond Conspiracy? Anticipatory Prosecution and the Challenge of Unaffiliated Terrorism*, 80 S. CALIF. L. REV. 425, 493, (2007).

12 *See e.g.* Holder v. Humanitarian Law Project, 130 S. Ct. 2705, (2010).

13 United States v. Abu Khatallah, 151 F. Supp. 3d 116, (D.D.C. 2015).

14 *Id.*, ¶138.

15 *Id.*, ¶140.

16 *Id.*, ¶¶143–4.

17 18 U.S.C. §3144.

18 *See e.g.* David Cole, *Out of the Shadows: Preventive Detention, Suspected Terrorists and War*, 97 California Law Review 693, 704, (2009); Donald Q. Cochran, *Material Witness Detention in a Post 9/11 World: Mission Creep or Fresh Start?* 18 George Mason Law Review 1, 4–7, (2010); Adam Klein and Benjamin Wittes, *Preventive Detention in American Theory and Practice*, 2 Harvard National Security Journal 85, 138–40, (2011).

19 U.S. Dept. of Justice (DOJ), Office of the Inspector General, a Review of the Department's Use of the Material Witness Statute with a Focus on Select National Security Matters (Redacted), 92–3, (Sep. 2014), (OIG Report).

20 *Id.*

21 Al-Kidd v. Gonzales, 2006 U.S. LEXIS 70283, (D. Idaho, Sep. 27, 2006).

22 Ashcroft v. Kidd, 131 S. Ct. 2074, (2011).

23 *Id.*, 2079.

24 *Id.*, 2083–85.

25 OIG Report, 56, *citing* United States v. Paracha, No. 03-cr-1197, 2004 WL 1900336, (S.D.N.Y. 2004).

26 *Id.*, 58–60.

27 8 U.S.C. §1226.

28 *See e.g.* Dan E. Stigall, Counterterrorism and the Comparative Law of Investigative Detention, 55–6, (Cambria Press, 2009); Cole, *Out of the Shadows, Preventive Detention, Suspected Terrorists and War*, 719–22; *Jailed without Justice, Immigration Detention in the U.S.A.*, Amnesty International, (Mar. 2009), www.amnestyusa.org/pdfs/JailedWithoutJustice.pdf; *Jails and Jumpsuits, Transforming the U.S. Immigration Detention System: A Two Year Review*, Human Rights First, (2011), www.humanrightsfirst.org/wp-content/uploads/pdf/HRF-Jails-and-Jumpsuits-report.pdf.

29 Zadvydas v. Davis, 533 U.S. 678, 699, (2001).

30 *Jails and Jumpsuits*, Human Rights First, 13.

31 Turkmen v. Ashcroft, No. 02 Civ. 2307, 2006 WL 1662663, (E.D.N.Y. Jun. 14, 2006).

32 Turkmen v. Ashcroft, 589 F.3d 542, 550, (2d Cir. 2009).

33 This is an action where federal officials may be sued for damages in their individual capacities for depriving a plaintiff of certain constitutional rights. It derives from Bivens v. Six Unknown Named Agents, 403 U.S. 388 (1971). A Bivens action is not available if there is an adequate administrative or state remedy in tort, or if the defendant is not employed by the U.S. government.

34 Turkmen v. Ashcroft, 915 F. Sup. 2d 314, (E.D.N.Y., 2013).

35 Turkmen v. Hasty, 789 F.3d 18, (Jun. 17, 2015).

36 Ziglar v. Abbasi, 137 S. Ct 1843, (Jun. 19, 2017).

37 *Id.*, 1854, *citing* Davis v. Passman, 442 U.S. 228, (Jun. 5, 1979).
38 *Id.*, 1855, *citing* Carlson v. Green, 446 U.S. 14, (Apr. 22, 1980).
39 *Id.*, 1857, *citing* Ashcroft v. Iqbal, 556 U.S. 662, 675, (May 18, 2009).
40 *Id.*, 1860.
41 *Id.*
42 *Id.*, 1861.
43 *Id.*, 1862–3.
44 *Id.*, 1866, 1869.
45 *Id.*, 1884.
46 Turkmen v. Ashcroft, 2018 U.S. Dist. LEXIS 137492, (Aug. 13, 2018).
47 Hamdi v. Rumsfeld, 542 U.S. 507, 517, (2004).
48 Authorization for the Use of Military Force, Pub. L. No. 107–40, 115 Stat. 224, (2001).
49 Hamdan v. Rumsfeld, 548 U.S. 557, 629–30, (2006). Since then the United States did participate in the non-binding Copenhagen Process referred to above and there is some reference to them adhering to some of the provisions relating to treatment in detention set out in GC AP II in the Department of Defense (DOD) Law of War Manual, Chap. XVII, (Jun. 2015, updated Dec. 2016).
50 *See e.g.* Al-Bihani v. Obama, 590 F.3d 866, 874, (Jan. 5, 2010); Awad v. Obama, 608 F.3d 1, 11, (2010); Ali v. Obama, 736 F.3d 542, 552, (Dec. 3, 2013).
51 Al-Alwi v. Trump, 901 F.3d 294, 299, (2018).
52 *The Guantanamo Docket*, New York Times, www.nytimes.com/interactive/projects/guantanamo/detainees/current, (last accessed Nov. 10, 2020). For data relating to the detentions *also see Guantanamo By The Numbers*, Human Rights First, www.humanrightsfirst.org/resource/guantanamo-numbers, (last accessed May 25, 2021).
53 Carol Rosenberg and Charlie Savage, *Biden Administration Transfers Its First Detainee from Guantanamo Bay*, New York Times, (Jul. 19, 2021), www.nytimes.com/2021/07/19/us/politics/guantanamo-bay-detainee-released.html?action=click&module=Top%20Stories&pgtype=Homepage.
54 Spencer S. Hsu, Abigail Hauslohner and Missy Ryan, *Last 'Low-Value' Afghan Detainee Asks to Be Freed from Guantanamo Bay as U.S. Troops Leave Afghanistan*, Washington Post, (May 10, 2021), www.washingtonpost.com/local/legal-issues/last-low-value-afghan-detainee-asks-to-be-freed-from-guantanamo-bay-as-us-troops-leave-afghanistan/2021/05/10/4eb21328-b19d-11eb-ab43-bebddc5a0f65_story.html. All prisoners were released by the time the Taliban took over Afghanistan in August 2021, *see e.g.* Sophia Ankel, *Video Shows Thousands of Prisoners, Reportedly including Islamic State and Al Qaeda Fighters, Freed from Kabul Jail By the Taliban*, Business Insider, (Aug. 15, 2021), www.businessinsider.com/watch-afghan-prisoners-isis-al-qaeda-fighters-freed-by-taliban-2021-8.
55 Carol Rosenberg, *Biden Administration Clears 3 Guantanamo Detainees for Release*, New York Times, (May 17, 2021), www.nytimes.com/2021/05/17/us/politics/guantanamo-detainees-release.html.
56 Rosenberg and Savage, *Biden Administration Transfers Its First Detainee from Guantanamo Bay.*
57 Carol Rosenberg and Julian E. Barnes, *Guantanamo Detainee Agrees to Drop Call for C.I.A. Testimony*, New York Times, (May 14, 2021), www.nytimes.com/2021/05/14/us/politics/guantanamo-detainee-cia-testimony.html.
58 National Defense Authorization Act (NDAA) of 2012, Pub. L. 112–88, (NDAA, 2012).
59 *Id.*, §1023.
60 *Id.*, §1024.
61 NDAA of 2013, Pub. L. 112–239, §1033.

62 Respondents' Memorandum Regarding the Government's Detention Authority Relative to Detainees Held at Guantanamo Bay, *In re*: Guantanamo Bay Detainee Litigation, Misc. No. 08–442 (TFH) (D.D.C., Mar. 13, 2009).
63 Stephen W. Preston, General Counsel for US DOD, Address at Annual Meeting of the American Society of International Law, Washington, DC, "The Legal Framework for the United States' Use of Military Force Since 9/11," (Apr. 10, 2015).
64 Rasul v. Bush, 542 U.S. 466, (2004).
65 Detainee Treatment Act of 2005, Pub. L. 109–148, 119 Stat. 2739, (2005).
66 Hamdan v. Bush, 56.
67 Military Commissions Act of 2007, Pub. L. 109–366, 120 Stat. 2600, (2006).
68 Boumediene v. Bush, 553 U.S. 723, 732, 779, (2008). In order to facilitate the "meaningful opportunity" the judges of the D.C. District Court developed a standing case management order to manage discovery and protect classified information, In re Guantanamo Bay Detainee Litigation, Misc. No. 08–442, 2008 U.S. Dist. LEXIS, 2008 WL 4858241, (D.D.C., Nov. 6, 2008), as amended, 2008 U.S. Dist. LEXIS 109502, 2008 5245890, (D.D.C., Dec. 16, 2008).
69 Boumediene v. Bush, 766.
70 The White House, Executive Order 13567, Periodic Review of Individuals Detained at Guantanamo Bay Naval Station Pursuant to the Authorization for Use of Military Force, (Mar. 7, 2011), https://obamawhitehouse.archives.gov/the-press-office/2011/03/07/executive-order-13567-periodic-review-individuals-detained-guant-namo-ba.
71 Laura Dickinson, *Extraterritorial Counterterrorism: Policymaking v. Law*, Just Security, (Jul. 15, 2021), www.justsecurity.org/77357/extraterritorial-counterterrorism-policymaking-v-law/.
72 Ali v. Trump, 959 F. 3d 364, 366, (May 15, 2020).
73 Ali v. Obama, 741 F. Supp. 2d 19, 27, (D.D.C. 2011).
74 Ali v. Trump, 367, *citing* Ali v. Trump 317 F. Supp. 3d 480, (Feb. 22, 2019).
75 *Id.*, 368.
76 *Id.*
77 *Id.*, *citing* Qassim v. Trump, 927 F. 3d 522, 530, (D.C. Cir., 2019).
78 *Id.*
79 *Id.*, 369.
80 *Id.*
81 *Id.*, *citing* Foucha v. Louisiana, 504 U.S. 71, 80, (1992).
82 *Id.*, *citing* Estate of Phillips v. District of Columbia, 455 F. 3d. 397, 403, (D.C. Cir. 2006).
83 *Id.*, 370.
84 *Id.*, 370–1.
85 *Id.*, 372–3.
86 Ali v. Biden, No. 20–888, 2021.
87 Supreme Court Order List, 593 U.S., (May 17, 2021), www.supremecourt.gov/orders/courtorders/051721zor_6537.pdf.
88 Al-Hela v. Trump, 2019 U.S. Dist. LEXIS 42717, (D.D.C. Jan. 28, 2019), *citing* Kiyemba v. Obama, 555 F.3d 1022, 1026–7, (Feb. 18, 2009). This ruling relied on a line of decisions holding that the due process clause does not apply to aliens without property or presence in the sovereign territory of the United States.
89 Abdulsalam Ali Abdulrahman Al Hela v. Trump, 972 F.3d 120, (Aug. 28, 2020).
90 *Id.*, 30, *citing* Ali v. Obama, 736 F.3d 542, 544 (2013) *and* Al-Bihani v. Obama, 590 F.3d 866, 878, and n.4, (2010).

91 *Id.*, 137: "The Suspension Clause . . . does not guarantee an absolute right personally to access the government's access in a *habeas* proceeding."
92 *Id.*, 137–8.
93 *Id.*, 139, (*citing* USAID v. Alliance for Open Society International Inc, 140 S. Ct 2082, 2086 (2020)), *and* 147; See also the Concurring Judgment of Circuit Judge Randolph in Ali v. Trump, 373.
94 Charlie Savage and Carol Rosenberg, *Biden Legal Team Divided on Scope of Rights of Guantanamo Detainees*, New York Times, (Jul. 8, 2021), www.nytimes.com/2021/07/08/us/politics/biden-rights-guantanamo-detainees.html.
95 Ann. E. Marimow and Missy Ryan, *Appeals Court Appears Reluctant to Say Guantanamo Detainees Have Due Process Rights*, Washington Post, (Sep. 30, 2021), www.washingtonpost.com/politics/courts_law/guantanamo-due-process-case/2021/09/29/09ad4982-206a-11ec-8200-5e3fd4c49f5e_story.html.
96 Charlie Savage, *Biden Administration Punts on Due Process Rights for Guantanamo Detainees*, New York Times, (Jul. 9, 2021), www.nytimes.com/2021/07/09/us/politics/guantanamo-detainees-due-process.html.
97 Maqaleh v. Gates, 605 F.3d 84, 87, 98 (May 21, 2010): "the writ does not extend to Bagram confinement in an active theater of war in a territory under neither the *de facto* nor *de jure* sovereignty of the United States and within the territory of another *de jure* sovereign."
98 *Id.*, 95.
99 *Id.*
100 ACLU Foundation v. Mattis, 286 F. Supp. 3d 53, 60, (Dec. 23, 2017 D.D.C.).
101 Doe v. Mattis, 288 F. Supp. 3d 195, (Jan. 23, 2018 D.D.C.).
102 Doe v. Mattis, 889 F.3d 745, (May 7, 2018).
103 ACLU, Doe v. Mattis – Challenge to Detention of American by U.S. Military Abroad,(Oct.29,2018),www.aclu.org/cases/doe-v-mattis-challenge-detention-american-us-military-abroad.
104 Charlie Savage and Eric Schmitt, *Trump Officials Reconsider Prosecuting ISIS 'Beatles' without Death Penalty*, New York Times, (Jul. 31, 2020), www.nytimes.com/2020/07/31/world/middleeast/isis-beatles-hostages.html; U.S. Dept. of Justice, Office of Public Affairs, ISIS Militants Charged with Deaths of Americans in Syria, (Oct. 7, 2020), www.justice.gov/opa/pr/isis-militants-charged-deaths-americans-syria.
105 *See e.g.* Elgizouli v. Secretary of State for the Home Department (SSHD), [2020] UKSC 10, (Mar. 25, 2020).
106 Webber, Preventive Detention of Terror Suspects, 177, *citing* U.S. Dep. Of Justice, Office of Legal Counsel, Memorandum from John C. Yoo and Robert Delahunty for Alberto R. Gonzales, Counsel to the President, Re: Treaties and Laws Applicable to the Conflict in Afghanistan and to the Treatment of Persons Captured by U.S. Armed Forces in that Conflict, (Nov. 30, 2001).
107 David Cole, The Torture Memos, 8, (The New Press, 2009), *citing* Joint Investigation into 9/11: Fifth Public Hearing, Sep. 26, 2002, Joint House/Senate Intelligence Committee Hearing, statement of Cofer Black, former Chief of CIA's Counterterrorism Center.
108 *Id.*
109 *No More Excuses: A Roadmap to Justice for CIA Torture*, Human Rights Watch, (Dec. 1, 2015), www.hrw.org/report/2015/12/01/no-more-excuses/roadmap-justice-cia-torture.
110 *The Road to Abu Ghraib*, Human Rights Watch, (Jun. 8, 2004), www.hrw.org/report/2004/06/08/road-abu-ghraib#.
111 Cole, The Torture Memos, 8.

112 Convention Against Torture and Other Cruel, Inhuman or Degrading Treatment or Punishment, adopted and opened for signature, ratification and accession by General Assembly resolution 39/46 of 10 December 1984, entry into force June 26, 1987.
113 Cole, The Torture Memos, *OLC Opinions on the CIA Detention and Interrogation Program, Submitted by Senator John D. Rockefeller IV for Classification Review*, (Apr. 22, 2009), 287–8.
114 U.S. reservations, declarations and understandings, Convention against Torture and Other Cruel, Inhuman or Degrading Treatment or Punishment, Cong. Re. S17486–01, (daily ed, Oct. 27, 1990).
115 Cole, The Torture Memos, *U.S. Dep. of Justice, Office of Legal Counsel, Memorandum for John A. Rizzo, Senior Deputy General Counsel, Central Intelligence Agency*, (May 10, 2005), 155, 197.
116 Hamdan v. Rumsfeld, 548 U.S. 557 (2006).
117 The White House, E.O 13491 – Ensuring Lawful Interrogations, (Jan. 22, 2009).
118 NDAA for Fiscal Year 2016, §1045, Public Law 114–92, (Nov. 25, 2015).
119 Husayn v. Mitchell, 938 F.3d 1123, (Sep. 18, 2019).
120 United States v. Zubaydah, Docket No. 20–827, (2021).
121 Robert Barnes, *Supreme Court Considers Whether Information Widely Known Can Be State Secret*, Washington Post, (Oct. 6, 2021), www.washingtonpost.com/politics/courts_law/supreme-court-guantanamo-zubaydah/2021/10/05/9546913e-261d-11ec-8d53-67cfb452aa60_story.html.
122 David Luban, *Torture Evidence and the Guantanamo Military Commissions*, Just Security, (May 26, 2021), www.justsecurity.org/76640/torture-evidence-and-the-guantanamo-military-commissions/, *citing* USA v. Majid Khan, Military Commissions Trial, Judiciary Guantanamo Bay, AE 033K Ruling, (Jun. 4, 2020).
123 USA v. Majid Khan, ¶¶3(c) 1, 2, 4, 5, 6, 7, 13.
124 *Id.*, ¶4(c).
125 *Id.*
126 Luban, *Torture Evidence and the Guantanamo Military Commissions*, *citing* the case of Majid Khan, who, as a condition of his deal for early release, was required to seek the vacating of the ruling in USA v. Majid Khan, in which the judge had given him sentencing credit because of the torture he had suffered at the hands of the CIA. *See also* Scott Roehm, *How the Biden Administration Should Take Torture-Derived Off the Table*, Just Security, (Jun. 17, 2021), www.justsecurity.org/76985/how-the-biden-administration-should-take-torture-derived-evidence-off-the-table/, (referring to a pending habeas petition, Duran v. Trump, 1:20-cv-01186 D.D.C.).
127 Luban, *Torture Evidence and the Guantanamo Military Commissions*, *citing* USA v. Al Nashiri, Military Commissions Trial, Guantanamo Bay, AE 353AA Ruling, (May 18, 2021), in which the judge somewhat creatively decided that 10 U.S.C §948r(a) which precludes the admission into evidence of statements obtained by the use of torture in military commissions, did not prevent a military judge from considering such evidence in interlocutory proceedings. However, this decision was overruled in *In re Al-Nashiri*, U.S. Court of Military Commission Review, CMCR Case No. 21–001, (Sep. 20, 2021) on the grounds that the issue was “not ripe or ready for judicial review.” Luban also notes a similar approach of the willingness of the International Criminal Court to admit evidence obtained by torture in Prosecutor v. Al Hassan, Trial Chamber X, ICC-01/12–01/18, public redacted version of “Decision on requests related to the submission into evidence of Mr. Al Hassan’s statements,” (May 20, 2021).

128 *U.S. Contractor to Pay $5.28 Million to Abu Ghraib Prisoners*, CBS News, (Jan. 8, 2013), www.cbsnews.com/news/us-contractor-to-pay-528-million-to-abu-ghraib-prisoners/.
129 Ameziane v. Obama, 58 F. Supp. 99, 103 (Jul. 21, 2014 D.D.C.).
130 IACHR, Report No. 29/20, Case 12.865, Merits Report, Djamel Ameziane v. United States of America, OEA/Ser.L/V/II, Doc. 39 (Apr. 22, 2020).
131 *Id.*, ¶114.
132 *Id.*, ¶115.
133 *Id.*, ¶125.
134 *Id.*, ¶¶200, 206.
135 *Id.*, ¶¶222, 224.
136 *Id.*, ¶227.
137 *Id.*, ¶¶68–9.
138 H.M. Government, Home Office, Operation of Police Powers Under the Terrorism Act 2000 and Subsequent Legislation: Arrests, Outcomes, and Stop and Search. Great Britain, Year Ending September 2020, (Dec. 10, 2020), https://assets.publishing.service.gov.uk/government/uploads/system/uploads/attachment_data/file/942747/police-powers-terrorism-sep2020-hosb3820.pdf.
139 Terrorism Act 2000, c. 11, §§40, 41, (U.K.). *See* Webber, Preventive Detention of Terror Suspects, 97–116.
140 Terrorism Act 2000, Sched. 8, §§21–37.
141 *Id.*, §§26, 33.
142 *Id.*, §6.
143 *Id.*, §7.
144 Ireland v. United Kingdom, Appl. No. 5310/71, ECtHR, 34 (Dec. 13, 1977).
145 *Id.*, ¶68, *citing* Northern Ireland (Emergency Provisions) act 1973.
146 *Id.*, ¶79, *citing* United Kingdom Government's Notice of Derogation, 14 Yearbook of the Convention 32, (Aug. 20, 1971).
147 *Id.*, ¶96.
148 *Id.*, ¶147(iv).
149 *Id.*, ¶167.
150 *Id.*, ¶168.
151 Larissa Brown, *Hooded Men's Army Torture Claims go to Supreme Court*, The Times, (Jun. 14, 2021), www.thetimes.co.uk/article/hooded-mens-army-torture-claims-go-to-supreme-court-f5wngmmg7.
152 Christie v. Leachinsky, [1947] AC 573, 593.
153 This was established in 1997 by the Special Immigration Appeals Commission (SIAC) pursuant to section 6 of the Special Immigration Appeals Commission Act 1997, c.68. Special advocates are court appointed lawyers who have been security cleared, so that they can see material that cannot be made public for reasons of national security. Neither the detainee nor his counsel may see the materials, (called closed material) and the special advocate may not show this evidence to nor discuss it with the detainee or his lawyer. The special advocate will discuss the material and advocate for the detainee to the judge in a closed hearing, *i.e.* a hearing that the detainee and his regular lawyer may not attend.
154 Sher v. The Chief Constable of Manchester Police, [2010] EWHC 1859 (Admin.), ¶91.
155 Sher v. United Kingdom, Appl. No. 5201/11, ECtHR, (Oct. 20, 2015), ¶139.
156 *Id.*, ¶149.
157 *Id.*
158 For a discussion of control orders and the problems arising, *see* Webber, Preventive Detention of Terror Suspects, 102–6.
159 A. and Others v. United Kingdom, Appl. No. 3455/05 ECtHR, ¶¶218–220, (Feb. 19, 2009).

160 SSHD (Respondent) v. AF (Appellant), (FC) and another (Appellant), [2009] UKHL 28, ¶65.
161 R. (on the application of Hicks and others) (Appellants) v. Commissioner of Police for the Metropolis (Respondent), [2017] UKSC 9 (Feb. 17, 2017) ("Hicks").
162 *Id.*, ¶8.
163 Ostendorf v. Germany.
164 Hicks, ¶10.
165 *Id.*, ¶31.
166 *Id.*, ¶32.
167 *Id.*, ¶38.
168 S, V and A v. Denmark, ¶46.
169 R. (on the application of Al-Jedda) (FC) (Appellant) v. Secretary of State for Defence (Respondent) [2007] UKHL 58, (Dec. 12, 2007), "Al-Jedda v. SSD." The House of Lords ceased judicial business on July 30, 2009 and the Supreme Court opened on October 1, 2009.
170 U.N.S.C. Resolution 1546, ¶10, S/RES/1546, (2004), Jun. 8, 2004, (giving the Multinational Force "the authority to take all necessary measures to contribute to the maintenance of security and stability in Iraq in accordance with the letters annexed to this Resolution expressing *inter alia,* the Iraqi request for the continues presence of the Multinational Force and setting out its tasks, including by preventing and deterring terrorism").
171 Al-Jedda v. SSD, ¶¶23, 124, 135, 148.
172 *Id.*, ¶¶38, 118, 129, 136, 152.
173 *Id.*, ¶¶43, 119, 128, 131, 153.
174 Al-Jeddah v. The United Kingdom.
175 *Id.*, ¶86.
176 Jelena Pejic, *The European Court of Human Rights' Al-Jedda Judgment: The Oversight of International Humanitarian Law*, (2011) 90 IRRC 837, 847–8, 851.
177 Hassan v. United Kingdom. *See also* Diane Webber, *Hassan v. United Kingdom: A New Approach to Security Detention in Armed Conflict?*, (Apr. 2, 2015) 19(7) American Society of International Law Insights, www.asil.org/insights/volume/19/issue/7/hassan-v-united-kingdom-new-approach-security-detention-armed-conflict.
178 Hassan v. United Kingdom, ¶76. *See also* Al-Saadoon & Ors v. SSD and Rahmatullah & Anor v. SSD & Anor, [2016] EWCA Civ 811, ¶4, (Sep. 9, 2016) confirming the jurisdictional point in principle, but on the facts the appellants were not within the power and control of the British forces at the relevant time.
179 Hassan v. United Kingdom, ¶97.
180 *Id.*, ¶101. There have been derogations that were deemed necessary as a result of internal conflicts or terrorist threats, *see e.g.* Brannigan and McBride v. The United Kingdom; A v. The United Kingdom.
181 *Id.*, ¶102, *citing* Armed Activities on the Territory of the Congo, (Democratic Republic of the Congo v. Uganda), Judgment, ICJ Reports 168 (2005); Legal Consequences of the Construction of a Wall in the Occupied Palestinian Territory, Advisory Opinion, ICJ Reports 136, (2004).
182 *Id.*, ¶104.
183 *Id.*, ¶105.
184 *Id.*, ¶106.
185 *Id.*, ¶110.
186 Abd Ali Hameed Al-Waheed v. Ministry of Defence, Serdar Mohammed v. Ministry of Defence, [2017] UKSC 2 (Jan. 17, 2017), ¶2. ("Al-Waheed and Mohammed v. MOD"). After the British government received thousands of

reports of allegations of abuse and unlawful killings by British soldiers in Iraq, it launched an inquiry into the Iraq war, headed by Sir John Chilcot, The Chilcot Report was published in July 2006, (The report of the Iraq Inquiry, Executive Summary HC 264 (Jul. 6, 2016).) The Chilcot Report led to an inquiry by the International Criminal Court (ICC) into whether the activities in Iraq amounted to war crimes. In 2020 the ICC concluded that as the United Kingdom had not been unwilling to investigate and prosecute offenders, it would close its case. *See* International Criminal Court, Situation in Iraq/UK, Final Report, (Dec. 9, 2020), www.icc-cpi.int/itemsDocuments/201209-otp-fnal-report-iraq-uk-eng.pdf.

187 Ian Cobain, *MoD Pays Out Millions to Iraqi Torture Victims*, The Guardian, (Dec. 20, 2012), www.theguardian.com/law/2012/dec/20/mod-iraqi-torture-victims.

188 Al-Waheed and Mohammed v. MOD ¶1.

189 *Id.*, ¶2.

190 *Id.*, ¶3

191 *Id.*, ¶5.

192 *Id.*, ¶4.

193 *Id.*, ¶¶5, 6.

194 *Id.*, ¶13.

195 *Id.*, ¶¶14, 16, 235.

196 *Id.*, ¶30.

197 *Id.*, ¶¶33–8.

198 *Id.*, ¶¶38, 39.

199 *Id.*, ¶¶40–3.

200 *Id.*, ¶44.

201 *Id.*, ¶61.

202 *Id.*, ¶68.

203 *Id.*, ¶89.

204 *Id.*, ¶111.

205 *Id.*, ¶104. Lady Hale agreed with the entire judgment. Lord Wilson agreed with this, ¶133: "I can see no reason why, if an authorization for detention during a NIAC is valid under international law in that it emanates from the Security Council, art. 5(1) should hobble the authorization – so long, of course, that safeguards against arbitrary or unchallengeable detention remain in place," and that Art. 5(4) was violated in respect of Mohammed, ¶144. Lord Mance was not convinced that Art. 5(4) had been violated and thought that the issues relating to Mohammed should be remitted to trial for determination, ¶¶215, 223. Lord Hughes agreed with Lord Sumption and Lord Mance, ¶¶224, 226. Lord Toulson agreed with Lord Sumption and Lord Hughes, ¶231. Lord Hodge agreed with Lord Sumption, ¶232. Lord Reed dissented, (with whom Lord Neuberger agreed), and held that no right of detention arose under IHL, or UNSC Resolutions, and violated Art. 5(1)(c), ¶234.

206 *Id.*, ¶112. Lady Hale agreed with the entire judgment. Lord Wilson agreed with this, ¶140. Lord Mance agreed, ¶222. Lord Reed would have allowed this appeal, ¶360.

207 Rahmatullah (No. 2) (Respondent) v. MOD and another (Appellants), Mohammed and others (Respondent) v. MOD and another, [2017] UKSC 1 (Jan. 17, 2017) (Rahmatullah and Mohammed v MOD).

208 GC IV, Art 45 precludes the transfer of protected persons (civilians) to a Power not party to the GCs.

209 SSFCA v. Yunus Ramatullah, [2012] UKSC 48, (Oct. 31, 2012).

210 Rahmatullah and Mohammed.v, MOD, ¶1.

211 *Id.*, ¶4, *citing* Johnstone v. Pedlar, [1921] 2 AC 262, 271.

212 *Id.*, ¶80.
213 *Id.*, ¶¶6–7.
214 *Id.*, ¶75.
215 Belhaj and another (Respondents) v. Straw and others (Appellants) and Rahmatullah (No. 1) (Respondent) v. MOD and another (Appellants), [2017] UKSC 3 (Jan. 17, 2017).
216 *Id.*, ¶¶3, 4.
217 *Id.*, ¶197.
218 *Id.*, ¶266.
219 *Id.*, ¶268.
220 *Id.*, ¶¶269–72.
221 *Id.*, ¶278.
222 Alseran and Al-Waheed and others v. MOD, [2017] EWHC 3289 (QB), (Dec. 14, 2017), (Alseran and Al-Waheed v. MOD).
223 *Id.*, ¶3.
224 Al-Waheed and Mohammed v. MOD.
225 Rahmatullah and Mohammed v. MOD; Alseran and Al-Waheed v. MOD, ¶4.
226 Human Rights Act 1998, §6, c.42 (U.K.): "It is unlawful for a public authority to act in a way which is incompatible with a Convention right."
227 Alseran and Al-Waheed v. MOD, ¶¶17, 719–20, 972–82.
228 Overseas Operations (Service Personnel and Veterans) Act 2021, c.23 (U.K.). *See also* Lucy Fisher, *Tory MPs Revolt over Bill to Curb Military Prosecutions*, The Times, (Nov. 2, 2020), www.thetimes.co.uk/article/tory-mps-revolt-over-bill-to-curb-military-prosecutions-3fhncqhvk; David Davis and Dan Jarvis, *Blocking Torture Investigations Will Damage the Army's Standing*, The Times, (Nov. 2, 2020), www.thetimes.co.uk/edition/news/blocking-torture-investigations-will-damage-the-armys-standing-zghf8wcvv.
229 Amichai Cohen and Stuart Cohen, Israel's National Security Law: Political Dynamics and Historical Development, 11, (Routledge, 2011).
230 Emanuel Gross, The Struggle of Democracy against Terrorism, 124, (University of Virginia Press, 2006).
231 Israel Ministry of Foreign Affairs, Wave of Terror 2015–2020, https://mfa.gov.il/MFA/ForeignPolicy/Terrorism/Palestinian/Pages/Wave-of-terror-October-2015.aspx, (last accessed Dec. 9, 2020).
232 Shabak, Monthly Reports, www.shabak.gov.il/english/publications/Pages/monthlyreports.aspx, (last accessed Jul. 15, 2021).
233 Dvir Saar and Ben Wahlhaus, *Preventive Detention for National Security Purposes in Israel*, 9 Journal of National Security Law & Policy 413, (2018); Diane Webber, Preventive Detention of Terror Suspects, 142–54.
234 *Id.*, 142–3.
235 *Id.*, 144, *citing* Daphne Barak-Erez, *Israel's Anti-Terrorist Law: Past, Present and Future*, 604, *in* Global Anti-Terrorism Law and Policy (Victor V. Ramraj, Michael Hor, Kent Roach and George Williams, eds., Cambridge University Press, 2012); Gross, The Struggle of Democracy against Terrorism, 122; Stephanie Cooper Blum, The Necessary Evil of Preventive Detention in the War on Terror, 120, (Cambria Press, 2008).
236 Webber, Preventive Detention of Terror Suspects, 144, *citing* the Defence (Emergency) Regulations 1945, Palestine Gazette No. 1442, Supp. No. 2. The British enacted these emergency regulations to deal with resistance and they were incorporated into Israeli law after independence in 1948. It permitted detention without trial by order of military commanders for renewable periods of six months, with a limited power to appeal to a military committee.
237 Emergency Powers (Detention) Law, 5739–1979, §1, S.H. 76, 33 L.S.I. 89–92 (Isr. 1979), ("EPDL").

238 Saar and Wahlhaus, *Preventive Detention for National Security Purposes in Israel*, 417.
239 EPDL, §2.
240 Saar and Wahlhaus, *Preventive Detention for National Security Purposes in Israel*, 420: pointing to cases requiring that "convincing evidentiary material must indicate to 'a degree of near certainty' that unless the detention order is issued, national or public security would be seriously harmed, *citing* AdminA 7/88 Anonymous v. Minister of Defense 42(3) PD 133, 136, (1988); AdminA 4/96 Ginzberg v. Minister of Defense, 50(3) PD 221, 223, (1996); AdminA 8788/03 Federman v. Minister of Defense 58(1) 176, 190–1, (2003); AdminA 4/94 Ben-Horin v. State of Israel 48(5) PD 329, ¶7, (1994); AdminA Fahima v. State of Israel, 59(3) PD 258, ¶8, (2004).
241 *Id.*, 422–3, *citing* AdminA 2/82 Lerner v. Minister of Defense 42(3) PD 529, 531 (1982).
242 *Id.*, 420, *citing* HCJ 3280/94 Federman v. Ilan Biran, Commander of IDF Forces in Judea and Samaria, 5, (1994, unpublished). They note that between 2011 and 102 one order was issued, but 38 were ordered in 2015 and 26 in 2016 after the spike in terror attacks at that time.
243 EPDL, §1(b).
244 EPDL, §4.
245 *Id.*, §5.
246 *Id.*, §7.
247 Criminal Procedure Law (Powers of Enforcement – Arrest) 1996, §35(A).
248 *Id.*, §35(C).
249 *Id.*, §35(D).
250 EPDL, §9.
251 *Id.*, §5.
252 *Id.*, §2(d).
253 *Id.*, §6(c).
254 Webber, Preventive Detention of Terror Suspects, 152, *citing* Daphne Barak-Erez and Matthew C. Waxman, *Secret Evidence: The Due Process of Terrorist Detentions*, 48 Columbia Journal of Transnational Law 3, 21–23, (2009).
255 Shiri Krebs, *Lifting the Veil of Secrecy: Judicial Review of Administrative Detentions in the Israeli Supreme Court*, 45(3) Vanderbilt Journal of Transnational Law 639, 643 (2012).
256 Webber, Preventive Detention of Terror Suspects, 145, *citing* John Does v. Ministry of Defense, CrimFH 7048/97, ¶1, (Apr. 12, 2000).
257 *Id.*, ¶3.
258 *Id.*, ¶18.
259 *Id.*, ¶19.
260 *Id.*, ¶21.
261 *Id.*, ¶25.
262 Incarceration of Unlawful Combatants Law, 5762–2002, ("UCL"), §1, (Isr.).
263 *Id.*, §2.
264 Saar and Wahlhaus, *Preventive Detention for National Security Purposes in Israel*, 433, *citing* A v. State of Israel, CrimA 6659/06, 6, (Jun. 11, 2008). The Court interpreted the law to encompass foreign nationals, who are not specifically mentioned in the UCL.
265 UCL, §3.
266 *Id.*, §5.
267 *Id.*, §6.
268 *Id.*, §5 (e) and (f).

269 A v. State of Israel, 1. *See also* Webber, Preventive Detention of Terror Suspects, 146–9; Saar and Wahlhaus, *Preventive Detention for National Security Purposes in Israel*, 433, 436, 438–9, 442, 444–6.
270 Basic Law (5752–1992): Human Dignity and Liberty (Isr.).
271 A v. State of Israel, ¶¶6, 11.
272 *Id.*, ¶8.
273 *Id.*, ¶9, *citing* Public Committee against Torture ("PCAT") v. Government of Israel, HCJ 769/02, ¶¶18, 21, (unreported judgment of Dec. 14, 2006).
274 *Id.*, ¶12.
275 *Id.*
276 *Id.*, ¶13.
277 *Id.*, ¶14.
278 *Id.*, ¶¶15, 17.
279 *Id.*, ¶19.
280 *Id.*, ¶20.
281 Report of the Commission of Inquiry Regarding the GSS' Interrogation Practices with Respect to Hostile Terrorist Activities, Vol. 1 Landau Book 269, (1995) (Commission of Inquiry).
282 PCAT v. Government of Israel, H.C 5100/94, (May 26, 1999). The "Shabach" position involves a suspect with his head covered by a sack being seated on a small low chair tilted forward, with one hand tied behind the suspect in the gap between the chair's seat and back support, and the other hand tied behind the chair against the back support and exposing the suspect to very loud music.
283 *Id.*, ¶23.
284 *Id.*, ¶24.
285 *Id.*, ¶25.
286 *Id.*, ¶¶26–30.
287 *Id.*, ¶33, *citing* Penal Law 5737/1977, Art. 34(1): "A person will not bear criminal responsibility for committing any act immediately necessary for the purpose of saving the life, liberty, body or property, of either himself or his fellow person, from substantial danger of serious harm, imminent from the particular state of things [circumstances], at the requisite timing, and absent alternative means for avoiding the harm.:
288 *Id.*, ¶34.
289 *Id.*, ¶36.
290 *Id.*, *citing* Commission of Inquiry, 328.
291 *Id.*, ¶38.
292 *Id.*, ¶39, containing the much-quoted passage: "Although a democracy must often fight with one hand tied behind its back, it nevertheless has the upper hand. Preserving the Rule of Law and recognition of an individual's liberty constitutes an important component in its understanding of security. At the end of the day they strengthen its spirit and its strength and allow it to overcome its difficulties."
293 PCAT v. The Government of Israel, HCJ 5100/94, 4054/95, 518/96, (Jul. 6, 2009) ("PCAT v. Israel 2009").
294 *See e.g. The Occupation's Fig Leaf: Israel's Military Law Enforcement System as a Whitewash Mechanism*, B'tselem, (May 2016), www.btselem.org/sites/default/files/publications/201605_occupations_fig_leaf_eng.pdf; *Addameer Collects Hard Evidence on Torture and Ill-Treatment Committed against Palestinian Detainees at Israeli Interrogation Center*, Addameer, (Dec. 23, 2019), www.addameer.org/news/addameer-collects-hard-evidence-torture-and-ill-treatment-committed-against-palestinian.
295 A (F.C.) and Others (F.C.) v. SSHD, [2004] UKHL 56.
296 *See e.g.* SSHD v. JJ, [2007] UKHL 47; SSHD v. MB (FC) [2007].

Part III
Targeted killing

Although unmanned systems had been used for many years in combat situations predominantly for the purposes of reconnaissance and gathering information, 9/11 was the trigger for armed unmanned system or drones to be used in an ever-expanding scope and quantity by many countries, and for targeted killing by drone to become a predominant method of countering terrorism.[1] However, it is a counter-terrorism strategy that remains mostly cloaked in secrecy. In June 2020, the majority of drone strikes were still triggering little public reaction or scrutiny, despite the fact that the strikes frequently generated fundamental challenges to international legal standards.[2] One journalist has commented on the general indifference of the public, while conflating the lawful targeting of enemy fighters who are unlawful combatants, with assassinations which are essentially unlawful killings: "The public in Britain as well as in America seems surprisingly untroubled by state assassinations of our prospective foes, even when their families or friends are obliterated with them."[3]

Part III examines the judicial trends in targeted killing cases, both in the international context that underpins domestic law of many countries, and gives three domestic perspectives, of the United States, United Kingdom, and Israel. A number of the cases discussed below are examples of targeted killings using methods other than drones to combat terrorism prior to and post 9/11, because the jurisprudence in them is relevant and pertinent to the targeting measures delivered by drones.

Notes

1 Stuart Casey-Maslen, *Introduction*, 2–3 *in* Drones and Other Unmanned Weapons Systems under International Law, (Stuart Casey-Maslen, Maziar Homayounnejad, Hilary Stauffer and Nathalie Weizmann, eds., Brill Nijhoff, 2018).

2 U.N. Human Rights Council, *Report of the Special Rapporteur on Extrajudicial, Summary or Arbitrary Executions*, A/HRC/44/38, 1, (Jun. 29, 2020).

3 Max Hastings, *There Are No Good Choices in the Hunt for Terrorists*, The Times, (Apr. 27, 2021), www.thetimes.co.uk/article/there-are-no-good-choices-in-hunt-for-terrorists-v8nmkcmb6.

DOI: 10.4324/9780367817275-6

4 The international law framework for targeted killing

"The proliferation of weaponized remotely piloted aircraft technology, taken together with the increasingly asymmetrical nature of modern conflicts, poses challenges for the framework of international law."[1] Drones with their technological capabilities, are programed to distinguish between military and civilian objects but human commanders must still make the proportionality decisions.[2]

Although the focus of this book is on human rights, it is pertinent to discuss all three international legal frameworks that regulate targeted killings: use of force by one state on another's territory (*ius ad bellum*); International Humanitarian Law (IHL); and International Human Rights Law (IHRL). For a particular drone strike to be lawful under international law, it must satisfy the legal requirements under *all* applicable international legal regimes.[3] It is necessary to underscore the limits of the international framework before the domestic perspectives can be fully understood.

Use of force (*ius ad bellum*): an overview

This is the body of international law that determines whether the use of force of one state against another on another's state territory is legal.[4] Before 9/11, acts in self-defense were only permissible against another state. Since 9/11, there has been a shift in State practice, with "broad and extensive" use of force against non-State armed groups.[5] The "cornerstone"[6] of and starting point for the use of force framework is Article 2(4) of the U.N. Charter and customary international law which ban the threat or use of force against another State.[7] If there is consent, Article 2(4) does not apply. In the absence of consent by State A that State B may use force on the territory of State A, force may be used in two situations: if the Security Council authorizes enforcement action pursuant to Article VII of the Charter; or in self-defense pursuant to Article 51 of the Charter. A number of criteria must be satisfied in accordance with rules established by the International Court of Justice (ICJ) and customary international law.[8]

First, acting in self-defense may be justified where an armed attack occurs against the retaliating State,[9] or if one is imminent. However, the scale and

DOI: 10.4324/9780367817275-7

effects of the "attack" must reach a certain level of gravity.[10] Second, the ICJ has frequently said that for the use of force to be lawful, the measures taken must be both necessary and proportionate: rules well established in customary international law.[11] Necessity means that measures such as diplomacy and sanctions have proved unsuccessful or are believed to result in failure.[12] Thus the law of self-defense allows responses to emergency situations if States are facing immediate or imminent attack.[13] This was traditionally understood to mean that "a threatened State can take military action as long as the threatened attack is imminent, no other means would deflect it, and the action is proportionate."[14] The definition of imminence has been modified by some countries, as discussed below. These modifications have been said to create "troubling legal distortions."[15] Anticipatory self-defense can only be lawful in response to an existing threat, rather than acting to prevent something that might happen in the future.[16]

In the case of self-defense against a non-state actor, before 9/11 this would only have been permissible if an attack by a non-state actor could be attributed to a state, on the basis that that state exercised "effective control" over the non-state actor.[17] For example, in *D.R.C. v. Uganda*, the ICJ did not consider it necessary to address the contention of the parties on the issue of whether international law applied in the case of large-scale attacks by irregular forces: it proceeded on the presumption that the right of self-defense did apply.[18] Similarly, in the *Wall Advisory Opinion*, it was suggested that the attacks by a non-state actor should be scrutinized using the test applied to evaluating attacks made by state actors.[19] However, *ius ad bellum* only deals with obligations between States under the UN Charter. It does not deal with obligations owed to individuals. This means that even if a strike may be lawful under Article 51 of the UN Charter, it still could be unlawful under IHL or IHRL.[20]

International Humanitarian Law: an overview

One of the main purposes of IHL, also called the law of armed conflict (LOAC),[21] is to protect civilians from the effects of hostilities. It regulates both lawful and unlawful acts of violence in armed conflict.[22] An international armed conflict (IAC) describes the situation when two or more states engage in armed force against each other. The International Criminal Tribunal for the Former Yugoslavia (ICTY) has opined that an IAC exists "whenever there is a resort to armed force between States."[23] In IACs, the Hague Conventions and Geneva Conventions apply to the conduct of hostilities.[24] The four key principles that are applicable to all combat operations[25] are distinction (which means distinguishing between combatants and civilians),[26] military necessity (which means using all measures that are not prohibited by LOAC needed to defeat the enemy as quickly and efficiently as possible),[27] avoidance of unnecessary suffering (which is applicable to combatants rather than civilians),[28] and proportionality (which means that the loss of life and damage to property incidental to attacks must not be excessive in relation to the expected military advantage).[29]

Experts disagree whether the conflict can extend beyond the territory of the State parties.[30]

In the context of counter-terrorism strategies, the relevant area of IHL is that relating to non-international armed conflicts (NIACs). Common Article 3 of the Geneva Conventions and the 1997 Additional Protocol II apply. The IHL framework in a NIAC (by a State against an armed non-state group) only applies if there is protracted armed violence between governmental authorities and organized armed groups or between such groups within a State,[31] and the violence must reach a certain level of intensity that is higher than internal disturbances and tensions.[32]

Questions arise as to the applicability of IHL in situations where a State wishes to use drones against members of armed groups or their associates operating in different countries. Applicability would depend on a number of factors, including whether in each country, the armed group had the required level of organization.[33] In a NIAC, the rules of proportionality, military necessity, unnecessary suffering and distinction must be observed.[34] Distinction in the NIAC context means that persons may only be targeted if they are directly participating in hostilities, or if they are recognized as having a continuous combat function.[35] This is a particularly thorny and controversial issue as it is often difficult to identify civilians who directly participate in hostilities, and what direct participation actually entails.[36]

As regards IHL, Gary Solis defines targeted killing as "the intentional killing of a specific enemy combatant, or civilian directly participating in hostilities, who cannot reasonably be apprehended, the targeting done at the direction of the state, in the context of an international or non-international armed conflict."[37] He lists four guiding principles: either an "IAC or a NIAC must be in progress" at the time of the targeting;[38] the "targeted individual must be a specific individual," who, in the case of a NIAC, has been positively identified and selected because of his confirmed activities in connection with an armed conflict;[39] no reasonable possibility exists for arrest instead of killing;[40] and a senior military commander must authorize the targeted killing.[41]

Most drone strikes have been undertaken in the context of NIACs, against armed groups.[42] As mentioned above, a conflict can only be classed as a NIAC if the armed group has a certain level of organization,[43] and intensity, which is a balance between duration and magnitude.[44] Furthermore the rules relating to proportionality must be complied with in both IACs and NIACs, so in the case of targeting this means that precautions must be taken to avoid civilian (or those not directly participating in hostilities, or those not having continuous combat function) injury or death.[45] In IHL the aim of the proportionality rule is to limit collateral damage while recognizing that an operation may be carried out even if some collateral damage is likely, provided that it is not "excessive in relation to the concrete and direct military advantage anticipated."[46] Customary humanitarian law mandates that injured civilians must be cared for and dead civilians must be identified.[47]

Existing IHL governs the use of armed drones in NIACs.[48] This means that the IHL prohibition on attacking civilians or non-military objects applies,[49] and that every reasonable thing should be done to ensure that the objective of the strike is a lawful target, as opposed to a civilian.[50] In theory these prohibitions could limit the use of drones, but it is unclear to what extent IHL standards are being adhered to. Some say that no clear legal principles exist that might assist in assessing the legality of an attack directed at civilians and civilian objects.[51] However, the problem is more likely to derive from the secrecy surrounding targeted killing, which impedes meaningful oversight, as well as a lack of any mechanism to enforce legal standards.

One particular challenge relates to "signature strikes" in which people are targeted because of certain characteristics associated with so-called terrorist activity, such as their appearance or location, but not necessarily their actual identity or activity.[52] The inability to confirm the identity and combatant status of persons hit and killed by signature strikes means that the IHL requirement of distinction cannot be complied with.[53] The effects of these deficiencies are discussed further below in the sections dealing with specific countries.

International Human Rights Law

IHRL provides the third legal framework relevant to targeted killing, but as will be seen below, there is frequently a blurring of the boundaries between IHRL and IHL, and much controversy about which framework governs. Because IHRL mandates that the use of force must be a measure of last resort, it has been said that outside of an armed conflict, lethal drone strikes will rarely be lawful. In situations of armed conflict, where IHL operates alongside (and in a complementary fashion to) IHRL, there may be occasions in which a lethal drone strike would be a lawful operation according to the applicable targeting rules of IHL.[54] However, according to the current Special Rapporteur Agnes Callimard, in order for a targeted killing to comply with IHRL, there are additional slightly different criteria:

> assessing necessity, proportionality and precaution through a situational analysis that takes into account the location, circumstances, possibilities of armed resistance and the planning involved. It also means that the lethal use of force cannot be justified or allowed when it is not necessary, it is likely to cause disproportionate harm, or it reasonably could have been avoided by feasible precautionary measures.[55]

The right to life, as discussed in depth below, the right not to be subjected to cruel, inhuman treatment,[56] the right to private and family life,[57] and the duty to investigate and account for civilian casualties and fatalities,[58] together with relevant guidance and jurisprudence are all relevant to assessing the lawfulness of targeting killing.

International Covenant on Civil and Political Rights (ICCPR)

Table 4.1 Right to life provisions in IHRL

International Covenant on Civil and Political Rights
Art. 6(1):
Every human being has the inherent right to life. This right shall be protected by law. No one shall be arbitrarily deprived of his life.
This is non-derogable (Art. 4(2))

European Convention on Human Rights
Art. 2(1): Everyone's right to life shall be protected by law. No one shall be deprived of his life intentionally other than in the execution of a court-imposed sentence after conviction of a crime carrying the death penalty.
Art. 2(2):
Deprivation of life shall not be regarded as inflicted in contravention of this Article when it results from the use of force which is no more than absolutely necessary . . . in defense of any person from unlawful violence . . . [or] in action lawfully taken for the purpose of quelling a riot or insurrection.
This is non-derogable except in respect of deaths resulting from lawful acts of war (Art. 15(2))

American Convention on Human Rights
Art. 4(1):
Every person has the right to have his life respected. This right shall be protected by law and, in general, from the moment of conception. No one shall be arbitrarily deprived of his life.
This is non-derogable (Art. 27(2)).

African Charter on Human and Peoples Rights
Art. 4:
Human beings are inviolable. Every human being shall be entitled to respect for his life and the integrity of his person. No one may be arbitrarily deprived of this right.
No derogation is permitted in this Charter.

Arab Charter on Human Rights
Art. 5:
Human beings are inviolable. Every human being shall be entitled to respect for his life and the integrity of his person. No one may be arbitrarily deprived of this right.
This right is non-derogable (Art. 4 (2)).

As Article 6(1) is non-derogable,[59] it applies at all times, even in armed conflicts.[60] States are required to ensure that all activities that take place in their territory or in other places subject to their jurisdiction are consistent with Article 6,[61] including "persons located outside any territory effectively controlled by the State, whose right to life is nonetheless affected by its military or other activities in a direct and foreseeable manner."[62] Despite the fact that the United States and Israel maintain that the ICCPR does not apply extraterritorially,[63] generally both IHRL and customary law appear to govern the use of armed drones either within a state's territory or extraterritorially.[64] This is discussed further in the sections dealing with specific countries.

The meaning of "arbitrarily" has been the subject of scholarly discussion[65] and HRC guidance. The 2018 HRC General Comment No. 36 notes:

> Although it inheres in every human being, the right to life is not absolute. While the Covenant does not enumerate the permissible grounds for deprivation of life, by requiring that deprivations of life must not be arbitrary, article 6(1) implicitly recognizes that some deprivations of life may be non-arbitrary . . . . Even those exceptional measures leading to deprivations of life that are not arbitrary per se must be applied in a manner that is not arbitrary. Such exceptional measures should be established by law and accompanied by effective institutional safeguards designed to prevent arbitrary deprivations of life.[66]

The HRC commented that arbitrariness should be interpreted broadly to include elements of inconsistency with international or domestic law, inappropriateness, injustice, lack of predictability and due process of law, reasonableness, necessity and proportionality. Furthermore, lethal force for law enforcement purposes is an extreme measure that is only permissible if strictly necessary to protect life from an imminent threat.[67] Some scholars have suggested that precaution, meaning that a warning should be given if reasonably feasible, should be an additional test for arbitrariness.[68] States are required to enact a protective legal framework that outlaws *inter alia* terrorist activity.[69]

The obligation to protect also includes a requirement to investigate and prosecute perpetrators of unlawful deprivations of life.[70] Ian Park has identified the relevant criteria for investigating Article 6 violations.[71] Investigations must be "independent,[72] impartial,[73] prompt,[74] thorough,[75] effective,[76] credible,[77] and transparent."[78] If a violation is found the remedy must include "adequate measures of compensation, rehabilitation and satisfaction, including guarantees for non-repetition."[79]

To some extent the HRC has addressed the tension relating to when IHL and IHRL apply during armed conflicts, commenting that they are "complementary, not mutually exclusive."[80]

Commentators are divided as to whether GC 36 goes far enough to clarify this complicated issue.[81] The use of lethal force must be "strictly necessary in view of the threat posed by the attacker; it must represent a method of last resort after other alternatives have been exhausted or deemed inadequate; the amount of force applied cannot exceed the amount strictly needed for responding to the threat; the force applied must be carefully directed only against the attacker; and the threat responded to must involve imminent death or serious injury."[82] There is a dearth of HRC jurisprudence on this topic but relevant HRC Observations are analyzed below in the discussion about the use of armed drones in several countries.

European Convention on Human Rights (ECHR)

Intentional deprivation of life includes negligent as well as intentional acts by a state that result in death.[83] The seminal case is *McCann v. United Kingdom*,[84] even though it does not relate to targeted killing by drones. In 1988 British, Spanish and Gibraltar authorities suspected that three members of the Provisional IRA, who were known to British police, were planning an attack involving a car bomb on British forces stationed in Gibraltar with a radio-controlled device. Special Air Service (SAS) officers were deployed to Gibraltar to assist the local police. Their goal was to foil the attempt, arrest the offenders, and collect evidence for a trial. Two of the suspected terrorists were shot dead after one of the soldiers interpreted the suspects' actions as being about to detonate the bomb, and acted to stop what he believed to be an imminent threat of the bomb. A while later another officer saw the third suspect move his hand towards his hip, and as the soldier believed that the suspect was about to detonate the bomb, he shot the suspect dead to neutralize the threat. After the shootings no detonating material was found on the bodies of any of the suspects, nor did a suspicious car contain a bomb, although a bomb was later found in a car in a Spanish town close to the Gibraltar border.

The European Court of Human Rights (ECtHR) noted that Article 2(2) ECHR ranked as "one of the most fundamental provisions" in the ECHR and the provisions had to be "strictly construed."[85] It considered that the exceptions in Article 2(2) indicate that the provision

> extends to, but is not concerned exclusively, with intentional killing. . . . The text of Article 2(2), read as a whole does not primarily define instances where it is permitted intentionally to kill an individual, but describes the situations where it is permitted to "use force" which may result, as an unintended outcome, in the deprivation of life. The use of force, however, must be no more than "absolutely necessary" for the achievement of one of the purposes set out in sub-paragraphs (a), (b) or (c).[86]

The use of the expression "absolutely necessary" indicated that a "stricter and more compelling test of necessity" had to be applied than the test of necessity referred to in Articles 8–11 ECHR. The force used had to be "strictly proportionate to the achievement of the aims" set out in Article 2(2).[87] In assessing the facts, the Court had to consider the acts of the persons using the force as well as all the surrounding circumstances, including the planning and control of the operation.[88]

The Court examined the acts of the soldiers involved in the shooting, which were based on an honest belief that the shooting was absolutely necessary to save lives. Although the belief turned out to be mistaken, the Court decided that the actions did not amount to a violation of Article 2.[89] However, the Court did find a violation of Article 2(2) by the authorities because of a lack of appropriate care in the control and organization of the operation.[90]

European case law continues to mandate non-arbitrariness and reinforces the interpretations of necessity and proportionality. For example, *Finogenov v. Russia* was a case resulting from the hostage-taking by Chechen terrorists of more than 900 people in a Moscow theatre in 2002.[91] The claim was brought by relatives of hostages killed during the storming of the theater and rescue operation conducted by Russian security forces. The operation involved pumping a narcotic gas into the auditorium which was expected to send everyone to sleep, but in fact killed 125 hostages. Although lethal force by law enforcement officers may be justified in certain circumstances, including in combating terrorism, the ECtHR said that "Article 2 does not grant them carte blanche."[92]

In addition to the requirements of necessity, and proportionality, it is equally important that suffering should not be caused and that complaints be investigated. In *Benzer*, the activities that took place in March 1994 under the guise of combating terrorism in two Turkish villages are an example of multiple egregious substantive and procedural human rights violations.[93] At that time frequent armed clashes were taking place between the Kurdistan Workers Party (PKK), which was an illegal organization and Turkish security forces. The security forces employed villagers as village guards to assist them in the fight against the PKK. Places with village guards were often attacked by PKK members, so in some locations residents refused to act as village guards. Where the security forces suspected that villagers were providing logistical support to the PKK, they evacuated the villages. In the two villages in issue, (Kl and K2) the applicants had refused to be village guards.

On March 26, 1994, with many people working outside in the fields, military planes and a helicopter circled Kl and K2. The aircraft bombed and strafed the village, killing 13 people in Kl and 25 people in K2, most of which were children, women and the elderly, and injuring 13. Thirty-four of the dead were relatives of the applicants. No national authority offered any help to the villagers. Members of the military warned the villagers not to complain to judicial authorities. Journalists were prevented from speaking to villagers. Despite the facts that the PKK did not have any fighter jets and that it would have been impossible for another state's military to have bombed the villages, the Turkish Prime Minister announced that the military jets that had bombed Kl and K2 did not belong to Turkey. It was also suggested by state prosecutors that the PKK had attacked the villages. No official investigators visited the villages or spoke to survivors, nor were any effective investigations opened by national authorities.[94]

In 2004, after a state prosecutor again urged an investigation into the PKK attacks on K2 (with domestic Turkish law permitting the file to remain open for 20 years), the applicants instructed new lawyers to file official complaints and requested an investigation and prosecution of the perpetrators and repeatedly, over a period of eight years, fruitlessly sought disclosure of documents and evidence.[95]

Despite applying to the ECtHR 12 years after the incident, (instead of within six months of the exhaustion of domestic measures pursuant to Article 35(1) ECHR), the Court ruled that in the exceptional circumstances of this case, the complaints relating to indiscriminate bombing and the failure to investigate, under Article 2 and 13 (which is the right to an effective remedy) were admissible.[96]

The Court concluded that there had been a violation of Article 2 since the evidence supported the applicants' claim that the bombing had been perpetrated by the Turkish Air Force, and that

> an indiscriminate aerial bombardment of civilians and their villages cannot be acceptable in a democratic society) and cannot be reconcilable with any of the grounds regulating the use of force which are set out in Article 2(2)

> of the Convention or, indeed, with the customary rules of international humanitarian law or any of the international treaties regulating the use of force in armed conflicts.[97]

Furthermore, the Court concluded that the investigation had been totally inadequate,[98] and that the terror, fear and panic caused by the bombardment amounted to inhuman treatment.[99] The Court concluded that its Committee of Members should supervise a new criminal investigation,[100] and awarded damages in compensation amounting to over two million Euros for the violations of Articles 2 and 3.[101] The latest status report seems to indicate that the payments have been made.[102] Ten years after the event the claimants in this case were fortunate that the ECtHR had ruled in their favor, because the Court had rejected many Turkish cases where compensation had been sought by victims of PKK terrorism after the enactment of the Turkish Compensation Law – a law that the ECtHR deemed adequate[103] for three years when it reverted to its previous approach.[104] Perhaps *Benzer* was exceptional because "the very nature of the violation found was such as to leave no real choice between measures capable of remedying it."[105]

The claim to the ECtHR was the only effective path to recourse to compensation: there was no viable route using IHL, and ICCPR mechanisms offered little help. The essence of Article 2 has very similar meaning to the ICCPR Article 6 right to life, but the prescriptive text of Article 2 ECHR makes "it more difficult – although not impossible – to interpret . . . a state's right to life obligations with reference to IHL."[106] For example, procedural IHRL obligations relating to investigating loss of life are more expansive than those in IHL.[107]

Unlike the right to life under the ICCPR, the right to life in the ECHR is derogable in times of war or public emergency, subject to the provisions of Article 15.[108] This subject, in the context of armed conflict, is discussed further below in the section on the United Kingdom.

American Convention on Human Rights (ACHR)

The Inter-American Court of Human Rights (IACtHR) has frequently discussed the relevant criteria for the legitimate use of force by governmental security forces.[109] For example, in 2007 it examined the alleged extrajudicial execution of four persons in the course of a security operation by armed forces and national police in a state of emergency, together with a failure to conduct a proper investigation.[110] The Court noted that in addition to observing the duty not to deprive persons of their lives arbitrarily, States must "adopt any and all necessary measures to protect and preserve the right to life of the individuals within their jurisdiction."[111] This means that

> States must adopt all necessary measures to create a legal framework that deters any possible threat to the right to life; establish an effective legal system to investigate, punish and redress deprivation of life by State officials or private individuals; and guarantee the right to unimpeded access to

> conditions for a dignified life. Especially, States must see that their security forces, which are entitled to use legitimate force, respect the right to life of the individuals under their jurisdiction.[112]

The Court reiterated that for the use of force to be legitimate, it had to satisfy the criteria of exceptionality, necessity, proportionality and humanity:

> The use of force must be limited by the principles of proportionality, necessity and humanity. Excessive or disproportionate use of force by law enforcement officials that result in the loss of life may therefore amount to arbitrary deprivations of life. The principle of necessity justifies only those measures of military violence which are not forbidden by international law and which are relevant and proportionate to ensure the prompt subjugation of the enemy with the least possible cost of human and economic resources. The principle of humanity complements and inherently limits the principle of necessity by forbidding those measures of violence which are not necessary (i.e. relevant and proportionate) to the achievement of a definitive military advantage. In peacetime situations, state agents must distinguish between persons who, by their actions, constitute an imminent threat of death or serious injury and persons who do not present such a threat, and use force only against the former.[113]

In cases involving lethal use of force, the State has a fundamental obligation "to initiate, *ex officio* and without delay, a serious, independent, impartial and effective investigation."[114] Deficiencies in this due process will constitute "an arbitrary deprivation of life, and thus violate the right to life."[115] In this case, the use of force was illegitimate, and the absence of both a satisfactory and convincing explanation for the use of the force and an effective investigation, resulted in a finding of arbitrary deprivation of life in violation of Article 4.[116]

In 1998, in the course of a counterinsurgency operation, a Colombian Air Force helicopter dropped six fragmentation bombs on the village of Santo Domingo, killing 17 civilians including children, and injuring 27. The injured and survivors were machine-gunned from a helicopter as they tried to flee. Having noted that the ACHR applies "in times of peace or armed conflict,"[117] the IACtHR's examination of these actions in a NIAC involved interpreting applicable IHRL in a way that complemented IHL,[118] analyzing the facts in the light of the IHL principles of distinction, proportionality and precaution.[119] Having found that the State had neither complied with the principles of distinction[120] nor precaution,[121] the Court ruled that the State's actions violated Article 4.[122] More recently the IACtHR noted that it was appropriate to turn to IHL, especially in NIACs, in order to understand a State's obligations relating to the right to life in an armed conflict, particularly as the ACHR does not define "arbitrary."[123] However, IHL is not generally taken into account in interpreting the obligation to investigate allegation of right to life violations.[124]

African Charter on Human and Peoples' Rights

The African Commission on Human Rights (AfCHR) adopted guidance on Article 4 in 2015. On the issue of arbitrary deprivation of life, the guidance states

(12) A deprivation of life is arbitrary if it is impermissible under international law, or under more protective domestic law provisions. Arbitrariness should be interpreted with reference to considerations such as appropriateness, justice, predictability, reasonableness, necessity, and proportionality. Any deprivation of life resulting from a violation of the procedural or substantive safeguards in the African Charter, including on the basis of discriminatory grounds or practices, is arbitrary and as a result unlawful.

(13) The right to life continues to apply during armed conflict. During the conduct of hostilities, the right to life needs to be interpreted with reference to the rules of international humanitarian law. In all other situations the intentional deprivation of life is prohibited unless strictly unavoidable to protect another life or other lives.

(14) A State shall respect the right to life of individuals outside its territory. A State also has certain obligations to protect the right to life of such individuals. The nature of these obligations depends for instance on the extent that the State has jurisdiction or otherwise exercises effective authority, power, or control over either the perpetrator or the victim (or the victim's rights), or exercises effective control over the territory on which the victim's rights are affected, or whether the State engages in conduct which could reasonably be foreseen to result in an unlawful deprivation of life. In any event, customary international law prohibits, without territorial limitation, arbitrary deprivation of life.[125]

In armed conflict, IHL is to be used to determine whether a deprivation of life was arbitrary. Any violation of IHL resulting in a death will be classed as arbitrary deprivation of life. In any situation outside of armed conflict, IHRL will apply.[126] This is spelt out to include situations "where military necessity does not require parties to an armed conflict to use lethal force in achieving a legitimate military objective against otherwise lawful targets."[127] In 2015, targeted killing by drone must have been a rare event in Africa as the wording of the following paragraph suggests:

> The use during hostilities of new weapons technologies such as remote controlled aircraft should only be envisaged if they strengthen the protection of the right to life of those affected. Any machine autonomy in the selection of human targets or the use of force should be subject to meaningful human control. The use of such new technologies should follow the established rules of international law.[128]

The guidance emphasizes the requirement of accountability, mandating "prompt, impartial, thorough and transparent investigations," as well as prosecution and reparation.[129] States also are obliged to protect individuals from violations or threats by non-State actors, and States are responsible for killings by such individuals "that are not adequately prevented, investigated or prosecuted by authorities."[130]

Summary

Fundamentally, a drone strike must satisfy the legal requirements under *all* applicable international legal regimes.[131] However, each of the three international law frameworks discussed above are problematic to some extent. Relatively little international case law exists that relates specifically to targeted killing by drone, although there is a body of domestic litigation dealing with this in each of the three countries discussed. The main focus of this book is on the relationship of counter-terrorism strategies and human rights law, but the picture would be incomplete without some discussion of IHL because the question has frequently arisen in IHRL cases as to whether IHL or IHRL applies, and whether one framework has primacy over the other. In the cases discussed above, it can be seen there has been a shift towards concern for, and the application of human rights in IHL situations. Furthermore, the international jurisprudential bodies have not been particularly deferential to governmental policies and practices.

The *ius ad bellum* regime permits the use of force only if it is necessary and proportionate.[132] Self-defense is permitted if an attack is immediate or imminent, but the meaning of "imminence" has frequently been stretched or distorted.[133] The effect of such distortions has legal implications, some of which are discussed below in the domestic perspectives. In the context of counter-terrorism, if the attacker is a non-State actor, *ius ad bellum* will not be applicable, although IHL will be. The more limited NIAC rules will apply in drones strikes conducted in counter-terrorism situations and the rules of proportionality, military necessity, unnecessary suffering, and distinction must be observed.[134] Particular difficulties arise with distinguishing a lawful target from a civilian and identifying if the civilian activity amounts to directly participating in hostilities or continuous combat function (which would disqualify them from POW status if captured),[135] because IHL prohibits the killing of civilians.

Certain rules in IHRL and the customary law relating to distinction and proportionality apply to the use of armed drones either within a state's territory or extraterritorially.[136] Fundamentally, everyone has the right not to be arbitrarily deprived of their life. States are required to ensure that this right is protected and to investigate and hold perpetrators accountable for every arbitrary deprivation of life. In all the treaties mentioned above except the ECHR, in cases in involving deaths resulting from lawful acts of war, the right to life is non-derogable. Targeted killing "cannot be justified or allowed when it is not necessary, it is likely to cause disproportionate harm, or it reasonably could have been avoided by feasible precautionary measures."[137]

Notes

1 UNGA Human Rights (HR) Council, *Report of the Special Rapporteur on the Promotion and Protection of Human Rights and Fundamental Freedoms While Countering Terrorism*, A/68/389, ¶22, (Sep. 18, 2013).
2 Gary D. Solis, The Law of Armed Conflict, 551–2, (Cambridge University Press, 2nd ed., 2016).
3 Christof Heyns, Dapo Akande, Lawrence Hill-Cawthorne and Thompson Chengeta, *The International Law Framework Regulating the Use of Armed Drones (Drone Framework)*, 65(4) International and Comparative Law Quarterly, 791, 795, (2016).
4 Stuart Casey-Maslen, *Armed Unmanned Weapons Systems under Jus ad Bellum*, 62 *in* Drones and Other Unmanned Weapons Systems under International Law, (Stuart Casey-Maslen, Maziar Homayounnejad, Hilary Stauffer and Nathalie Weizmann, eds., Brill Nijhoff, 2018).
5 Heyns and Ors, *Drone Framework*, 802–3.
6 Armed Activities on the Territory of the Congo (Democratic Republic of the Congo v. Uganda), Judgment, (Dec. 19, 2005), ICJ Reports, (2006) 168, 223, ¶148.
7 Heyns and Ors, *Drone Framework* 797, *citing* U.N. Charter of the United Nations, Art. 2(4), Oct. 24, 1945, 1 U.N.TS. XVI.
8 *Id.*, 800–5.
9 *Id.*
10 *See e.g.* Case Concerning Oil Platforms, (Iran v. United States), [2003] I.C.J. Rep. 161, ¶¶51, 62.
11 *Id.*, ¶74; Also see Legality of the Threat or Use of Nuclear Weapons, Advisory Opinion, (Nuclear Weapons case) [1996] I.C.J. Rep. 226, ¶41; Case Concerning Armed Activities on the Territory of the Congo, (D.R.C. v. Uganda), Judgment, I.C.J. Rep. 2005, 168, ¶147.
12 Casey-Maslen, *Armed Unmanned Weapons Systems under Jus ad Bellum*, 77.
13 Heyns and Ors, *Drone Framework*, 801.
14 *Id.*, *citing* U.N. Doc. A/59/565, Report of the High-level Panel on Threats, Challenges and Change, A More Secure World: Our Shared Responsibility, ¶188 (2004). *See also* Case Concerning Gabcikovo-Nagymaros Project, International Court of Justice, (Hungary/Slovakia) Judgment of 25 Sep. 1997, ICJ Reports 1997 7, ¶54: "'Imminence' is synonymous with 'immediacy' or 'proximity' and goes far beyond the concept of 'possibility.' As the International Law Commission emphasized in its commentary, the 'extremely grave and imminent' peril must have been a threat to the interest at the actual time.' (Yearbook of the International Law Commission, 1980, Vol. II, Part 2, 49, ¶33). That does not exclude, in the view of the Court, that a 'peril' appearing in the long term might be held to be 'imminent' as soon as it is established, at the relevant point in time, that the realization of that peril, however far off it might be, is not thereby any less certain and inevitable."
15 HR Council, *Report of the Special Rapporteur on Extrajudicial, Summary or Arbitrary Executions*, 2020, ¶¶53–9, *describing* 'distortions' of time, geography and the principle of sovereignty.
16 Heyns and Ors, *Drone Framework*, 801.
17 Casey-Maslen, *Armed Unmanned Weapons Systems under Jus ad Bellum*, 78, *citing* Military and Paramilitary Activities in and against Nicaragua, Nicaragua v. United States of America, ICJ Reports 1986, 14, ¶¶109, 115, 195 *and* Legal Consequences of the Construction of a Wall in the Occupied Palestinian Territory, Advisory Opinion. ICJ Reports 1996 226, ¶193 (Wall Advisory Opinion).
18 *Id.*, 80, *citing* D.R.C. v. Uganda, 147.

19 *Id.*, citing Wall Advisory Opinion, Judge Simma, ¶11, Judge Kooijmans, ¶31.
20 U.N. HR Council, *Report of the Special Rapporteur on Extrajudicial, Summary or Arbitrary Executions*, 2020, ¶31.
21 This book does not claim to do justice to this very complex topic. The essential elements of IHL or LOAC are explained briefly in Part I.
22 Jelena Pejic, *Extraterritorial Targeting by Means of Armed Drones: Some Legal Implications*, 96(893) International Review of the Red Cross 67, 85, (2014).
23 Prosecutor v. Tadic, (Decision on the Defense Motion for Interlocutory Appeal on Jurisdiction) ICTY-94–1, ¶70, (Oct. 2, 1995).
24 Hague Convention II with respect to the Laws and Customs of War on Land, (Jul. 29, 1899, entered into force Sep. 1900, 187 CTS); Hague Convention IV with respect to the Laws and Customs of War on Land and its annexed regulations, (Oct. 18, 1907, entered into force Jan. 26, 1910); Geneva Convention for the Amelioration of the Condition of the Wounded and Sick in Armed Forces in the Field, (Aug. 12, 1949), 6 U.S.T. 3114, 75 U.N.T.S. 31 (GC I); Geneva Convention for the Amelioration of the Condition of the Wounded, Sick and Shipwrecked Members of Armed Forces at Sea, (Aug. 12, 1949). 6 U.S.T. 3217, 75 U.N.T.S. 85 (GC II); Geneva Convention Relative to the Treatment of Prisoners of War, (Aug. 12, 1949), 6 U.S.T. 3316, 75 U.N.T.S. 135 (GC III); Geneva Convention Relative to the Protection of Civilian Persons in Time of War, (Aug. 12, 1949), 6 U.S.T. 3516, 75 U.N.T.S. 287 (GC IV); Protocol Additional to the Geneva Conventions of August 12, 1949 and Relating to the Protection of Victims of International Armed Conflicts, (Jun. 8, 1977), 1125 U.N.T.S. 3 (API); Protocol Additional to the Geneva Conventions of Aug. 12, 1949 and Relating to the Protection of Victims of Non-International Armed Conflicts, (Jun. 8, 1977), U.N.T.S. 609 (APII).
25 Solis, The Law of Armed Conflict, 268.
26 API, Art. 48. *Also see* Nuclear Weapons case, Advisory Opinion, ¶78, emphasizing the importance of this principle.
27 Dept. of Defense, (DOD), Law of War Manual, ¶2.2, (Jun. 2015, updated 2016); It is also recognized as customary international law, *see also* Solis, The Law of Armed Conflict at 277, *citing* Commentary ON THE Additional Protocols, 392, (Yves Sandoz, Christophe Swinarski and Bruno Zimmermann, eds., Martinus Nijhoff, 1987).
28 Solis, The Law of Armed Conflict, 289; API, Art. 35(2).
29 API, Art. 51(5)(b), 57(2)(b).
30 Nathalie Weizmann, *Armed Drones and the Law of Armed Conflict*, 92 *in* Drones and Other Unmanned Weapons Systems under International Law, (Stuart Case-Maslen, Maziar Homayounnejad, Hilary Stauffer and Nathalie Weizmann, eds., Brill Nijhoff, 2018).
31 Prosecutor v. Tadic, ¶70.
32 Prosecutor v. Musema (Appeals Judgment) ICTR- 96–13-A, ¶248, (Nov. 16, 2001).
33 Heyns and Ors, *Drone Framework*, 809; ICRC, International Humanitarian Law and the Challenges of Contemporary Armed Conflicts, (2015).
34 APII, Art. 13(1) on distinction; proportionality is required under customary international law, *see e.g.* Prosecutor v. Kupreskic. IT-95–16-T, ¶524 (Jan. 14, 2000); military necessity is required under customary international law, *see* Commentary on the Additional Protocols, 392.
35 Nils Melzer, Interpretive Guidance on the Notion of Direct Participation in Hostilities under International Humanitarian Law, 33–4, (International Committee of the Red Cross, (ICRC) 2009); ICRC, IHL and the challenges of contemporary armed conflict, 43, 31IC/11/5.1.2; AP II Art. 13(2) & (3); Jean-Marie Henkaerts and Louise Doswwald-Beck, ICRC., Customary International

Humanitarian Law: Rules, Rule 6, (Cambridge University Press, 2009); Heyns and Ors, Drone Framework, 810–14.

36 *See e.g.* Pejic, *Extraterritorial Targeting by Means of Armed Drones*, 88–93; Melzer, Interpretive Guidance, which concluded that persons who merely participate in hostilities sporadically, spontaneously or on some unorganized basis are civilians who may not be targeted unless engaged in an act of participation of hostilities at the time of an a targeted attack. The Guidance also explains what conduct amounts to direct participation in hostilities.

37 Solis, The Law of Armed Conflict, 555, 558–60.

38 *Id.*

39 *Id.*

40 *Id.*

41 *Id.*

42 International Bar Association (IBA), The Legality of Armed Drones under International Law, 20. (May 25, 2017).

43 *Id.*, 21, *citing* relevant criteria set out in cases such as Prosecutor v. Boskovski & Tarculovski, IT-04–82-T, Trial Chamber Judgment, ¶197, (Jul. 10, 2008); Prosecutor v. Limaj, IT-03–66-T, Judgment, ¶¶90, n101–03, 145 (Nov. 30, 2005); Prosecutor v. Haradinaj & Ors, I -04–84-T, Judgment, ¶¶60, 65, 71–72, 129, (Apr. 3, 2008).

44 *Id.*, 22, *citing* Abella v. Argentina, IACHR Report No. 55/97, Case No. 11.137, ¶¶147, 155, (Oct. 30, 1977).

45 Pejic, *Extraterritorial Targeting by Means of Armed Drones*, 86.

46 *Id.*, 86–7.

47 Henkaerts and Doswwald-Beck, ICRC., Customary International Humanitarian Law, Rules 109, 116.

48 Weizmann, *Armed Drones and the Law of Armed Conflict*, 114.

49 *Id.*, 116.

50 Pejic, *Extraterritorial Targeting by Means of Armed Drones*, 87.

51 Casey-Maslen, *Unmanned Weapons Systems and the Right to Life*, 172–5 *in* Drones and Other Unmanned Weapons Systems under International Law, *citing* Prosecutor v. Gotovina, (Appeals Chamber) (Case No. IT-06–90-A), Dissenting Opinion of Judge Pocar, ¶13, (Nov. 16, 2012).

52 Weizmann, *Armed Drones and the Law of Armed Conflict* 118–19, *citing* UNGA *Report of the Special Rapporteur on the Promotion and Protection of Human Rights and Fundamental Freedoms While Countering Terrorism*, ¶74, UNGA, *Report of the Special Rapporteur on Extrajudicial, Summary or Arbitrary Executions*, U.N. Doc. A/68/382, ¶72, (Sep. 13, 2013).

53 Solis, The Law of Armed Conflict, 561.

54 Ben Emmerson, *New Counter Terrorism Measures: New Challenges for Human Rights*, 129, *in* Using Human Rights to Counter Terrorism, (M. Nowak and A. Chabord, eds., Edward Elgar, 2018).

55 HR Council, *Report of the Special Rapporteur on Extrajudicial, Summary or Arbitrary Executions*, 2020, ¶50.

56 ICCPR, Art. 10; ECHR, Art. 3; ACHR, Art. 5; AfC, Art. 5; ArC, Art. 8.

57 ICCPR, Art. 23; ECHR, Art. 8; ACHR, Art. 17; AfC, Art. 18.

58 IBA, The Legality OF Armed Drones under International Law, 40, *citing* Isayeva v. Russia, Appl. No. 57950/00, ¶209, ECtHR. (2005).

59 *Id.*, Art. 4(2); CCPR/C/GC/36, Human Rights Committee, General Comment No. 36 (2018) on Art. 6 of the International Covenant on Civil and Political Rights, on the right to life, ¶2, (Oct. 30, 2018) (HRC GC No. 36).

60 *Id.*, ¶67; Nuclear Weapons case, Advisory Opinion, ¶25: "In principle, the right not arbitrarily to be deprived of one's life applies also in hostilities. The test of what is an arbitrary deprivation of life, however, then falls to be determined by

the applicable *lex specialis*, namely, the law applicable in armed conflict which is designed to regulate the conduct of hostilities."

61 HRC GC No. 36, ¶23.
62 *Id.*, ¶63.
63 For a detailed discussion about the controversy concerning the interpretation of jurisdiction under the ICCPR, see Part II on Preventive Detention *infra*.
64 Stuart Casey-Maslen, *Unmanned Weapons Systems and the Right to Life*, 167.
65 *See e.g.* Ian Park, The Right to Life in Armed Conflict, 20–32, (Oxford University Press, 2018); Sarah Joseph, *Extending the Right to Life under the International Covenant on Civil and Political Rights: General Comment 36*, 19(2) Human Rights Law Review 347, (Jun. 2019).
66 HRC GC No. 36, ¶10.
67 *Id.*, ¶12.
68 *See e.g.* Nils Melzer, Targeted Killing in International Law, 223–39, (Oxford University Press, 2008); Jessica Lynn Corsi, *Drone Deaths Violate Human Rights: The Applicability of the ICCPR to Civilian Deaths Caused by Drones*, 6(2) International Human Rights Review 205, 231, (Dec. 2017), commenting that "most lethal drone strikes are likely arbitrary as they forgo required precaution in applying lethal force."
69 HRC GC No. 36, ¶20.
70 *Id.*, ¶27.
71 Park, The Right to Life in Armed Conflict, 60.
72 HRC Concluding Observations: Cameroon, (2019) 15.
73 HRC Concluding Observations: Bolivia, (2013) 15.
74 HRC Concluding Observations: Russia, (2009) 14; HRC Communication No. 1556/2007 Novakovic v. Serbia, ¶7.3, (Oct. 21, 2010).
75 HRC Concluding Observations: Mauritania, (2013) 13.
76 HRC Concluding Observations: U.K. (2015) 8.
77 HRC Concluding Observations: Israel, (2010) 9.
78 HRC Concluding Observations: U.K. (2015) 8.
79 Park, The Right to Life in Armed Conflict, 60, *citing* HRC Communication No. R11/45, Suarez de Guerrero v. Colombia, (Mar. 31, 1982).
80 HRC GC No. 36, ¶64.
81 See e.g. Ryan Goodman, Christof Heyns and Yuval Shany, *Human Rights, Deprivation of Life and National Security: Q&A with Christof Heyns and Yuval Shany on General Comment*, 36, Just Security, (Feb. 4, 2019), www.justsecurity.org/62467/human-life-national-security-qa-christof-heyns-yuval-shany-general-comment-36/; Shaheed Fatima, *Targeted Killing and the Right to Life: A Structural Framework*, Just Security, (Feb. 6, 2019), www.justsecurity.org/62485/targeted-killing-life-structural-framework/; Janina Dill, *General Comment 36: A Missed Opportunity?*, Just Security, (Feb. 11, 2019), www.justsecurity.org/62473/general-comment-36-missed-opportunity/.
82 HRC GC No. 36, ¶12.
83 Park, The Right to Life in Armed Conflict, 34.
84 McCann v. United Kingdom, Appl. No. 18984/91, ECtHR, (Sep. 27, 1995).
85 *Id.*, ¶147.
86 *Id.*, ¶148.
87 *Id.*, ¶149.
88 *Id.*, ¶150.
89 *Id.*, ¶200.
90 *Id.*, ¶213.
91 Finogenov and Ors. v. Russia., Appl. Nos. 18299/03, 27311/03, ECtHR, Final Judgment, (Jun. 4, 2012).
92 *Id.*, ¶207.

93 Benzer v. Turkey, Appl. No. 23502/06 ECtHR, (Mar. 24, 2014).
94 *Id.*, ¶¶9–14, 20, 31, 36–7.
95 *Id.*, ¶¶40–87.
96 *Id.*, ¶¶131–5.
97 *Id.*, ¶¶183–5.
98 *Id.*, ¶¶186–98.
99 *Id.*, ¶¶199–213.
100 *Id.*, ¶¶219.
101 *Id.*, ¶¶223–48.
102 Benzer v. Turkey, *see* http://hudoc.exec.coe.int/eng?i=004-34747 (last accessed Jan. 4, 2021).
103 Icyer v. Turkey, Appl. No. 18888/02 ECtHR, (Jan. 12, 2006). *See* Dilek Kurban, *Forsaking Individual Justice: The Implications of the European Court of Human Rights' Pilot Judgment Procedure for Victims of Gross and Systematic Violation*, 16(4) Human Rights Law Review, 731–69, (Dec. 2016).
104 *Id*, *citing* Gasyak v. Turkey, Appl. No. 27872/03, ECtHR, (Jan. 13, 2010), ¶¶68, 71, noting that the obligation to conduct an effective investigation would be rendered illusory if the sole remedy available to victims was an award of damages. The Compensation Law did not afford adequate redress.
105 Benzer v. Turkey, ¶217.
106 Park, The Right to Life in Armed Conflict, 62.
107 *Id.*, 116.
108 ECHR, Art. 15: "In time of war or other public emergency threatening the life of the nation any High Contracting Party may take measures derogating from its obligations under the Convention to the extent strictly required by the exigencies of the situation, provided that such measures are not inconsistent with its other obligations under international law."
109 *See e.g.* Case of Villagran-Morales v. Guatemala, Ser. C No. 63, ¶144 IACtHR, (1999); Case of Montero Aranguren (Detention Center of Calia) v. Venezuela, Ser. C No. 150, ¶63 IACtHR, (2006); Case of Baldeon-Garcia v. Peru, Judgment, Ser. C No. 147, ¶82, IACtHR, (2006).
110 Case of Zambrano Velez v. Ecuador, IACtHR Ser. C No. 166, (2007).
111 *Id.*, ¶80.
112 *Id.*, ¶81.
113 *Id.*, ¶87, *citing* IACHR, Report on Terrorism and Human Rights, OEA/ser.4 V/II.116, (Oct. 22, 2002).
114 *Id.*, ¶88.
115 *Id.*, ¶90, *citing* UNGA, *Extrajudicial, Summary or Arbitrary Executions*, Report of Philip Alston, Special Rapporteur, UN Doc. A/61/311 (Sep. 5, 2006), ¶36.
116 *Id.*, ¶110.
117 Case of the Santo Domingo Massacre v. Colombia, Judgment (Preliminary objections, merits and reparations) Ser. C No. 159 IACtHR, 22, (Nov. 30, 2012).
118 *Id.*, ¶187.
119 *Id.*, ¶211.
120 *Id.*, ¶213.
121 *Id.*, ¶229. The Court considered it did not have sufficient information and stated that it was inappropriate to comment on the issue of proportionality, (¶215).
122 *Id.*, ¶230.
123 Giovanna Maria Frisso, *The Duty to Investigate Violations of the Right to Life in Armed Conflicts in the Jurisprudence of the Inter-American Court of Human Rights*, 51(2) Israel Law Review, 169, 182, (Jul. 2018), *citing* Case of Cruz Sanchez v. Peru, Ser. C No. 292, IACtHR, ¶¶272–3, (Apr. 17, 2015) (in Spanish only).
124 *Id.*, 185, 188, *noting that* one exception to this is found in *Cruz Sanchez* at ¶350 where the Court said that "the fact that deaths occurred in the context of a NIAC

did not exempt the State from its obligation to initiate an investigation . . . on the use of force that had lethal consequences."

125 African Commission on Human and Peoples' Rights (AfCHR), General Comment No. 3 on the African Charter on Human and Peoples' Rights: The Right to Life (Art. 4), ¶¶B 12, 13, 14, (adopted during the 57th Ordinary Session of the African Commission on Human and Peoples' Rights held from November 4 to 18 in Banjul, The Gambia, 2015, (AfCHR GC 3).

126 *Id.*, ¶¶F32, 33.

127 *Id.*, ¶F34.

128 *Id.*, ¶F35.

129 *Id.*, ¶¶C15–21.

130 *Id.*, ¶¶H38–40

131 Heyns and Ors, *Drone Framework*, 791, 795.

132 *See e.g.* Nuclear Weapons case, Advisory Opinion, ¶41; D.R.C. v. Uganda, Judgment, ¶147.

133 HR Council, *Report of the Special Rapporteur on Extrajudicial, Summary or Arbitrary Executions*, 2020, ¶¶53–9, *describing* "distortions" of time, geography and the principle of sovereignty.

134 APII, Art. 13(1) on distinction; proportionality is required under customary international law, *see e.g.* Prosecutor v. Kupreskic. IT-95–16-T, ¶524 (Jan. 14, 2000); military necessity is required under customary international law, *see* Commentary on the Additional Protocols, 392.

135 Solis, The Law of Armed Conflict, 222; AP I Art. 45(3).

136 Casey-Maslen, *Unmanned Weapons Systems and the Right to Life*, 167.

137 *Suggested in* HR Council, *Report of the Special Rapporteur on Extrajudicial, Summary or Arbitrary Executions*, 2020, ¶50.

5 Domestic perspectives on targeted killing

This chapter examines the laws and practices of three countries that have used drones to kill terror suspects: the United States; the United Kingdom; and Israel. These countries have been selected for analysis because each has interpreted the relevant international law differently, yet in the twenty years since 9/11 increasing judicial attitudes of deference to each government can be perceived.

United States

> More than 17 years after the first U.S. drone strike, the drone program remains shrouded in secrecy, complicating effective oversight and making independent assessments of the legitimacy and efficacy of the U.S. drone program extraordinarily challenging.[1]

The United States is the world's most prolific user of armed drones. Some are launched by the U.S. Air Force, but increasingly since 2009, many are operated by the Central Intelligence Agency (CIA) outside the active battlefield.[2] Statistics from a number of NGOs or other non-official sources suggest that the United States, through its military forces and the CIA, has carried out thousands of strikes since 2002 in Afghanistan, Iraq, Libya, Niger, Pakistan, Somalia, Syria, and Yemen.[3] The CIA and their contractors are U.S. sponsored fighters, but they are classified for the purposes of IHL as civilians. This means that they are unprivileged belligerents, meaning that if they were captured in an IAC, they would not be entitled to prisoner of war status, and they could be prosecuted in respect of unlawful deaths, injuries or damage to property that occur in both IACs and NIACs.[4]

A report by the human rights NGO Civilians in Conflict ("CIVIC") examined CIA participation in drone activity in three contexts: their covert use of force pursuant to statutory authority; their support to other government or irregular forces; and their support to regular and irregular partner forces by U.S. special operations forces pursuant to statutory fiscal authority.[5] Covert action is defined as "an activity or activities of the United States to influence political, economic or military conditions abroad, where it is intended that the role of the United States will not be apparent or acknowledged publicly."[6]

DOI: 10.4324/9780367817275-8

Covert operations, either conducted alone or as a partner, are believed to have taken place in Afghanistan, Iraq, Libya, Niger, Pakistan, Somalia, Syria, and Yemen "with few legal impediments, scant congressional oversight and little public accountability."[7] Allowing the CIA to operate drones pursuant to covert action enables the United States to officially deny participation.[8] Although the military are required to investigate and report civilian deaths, which is discussed below, the CIA are not.[9] CIVIC comments:

> The operational character and immediate operational effects of covert lethal drone strikes conducted by the CIA and those conducted in secret by the Defense Department, are practically indistinguishable. In fact, for most drone strikes, the two agencies cooperate at every step of the process, making it difficult for the public to understand the specific role played by each . . . . Beyond the implausibility of accountability for covert action, the statutory authority by which a strike is conducted, and the agency that oversees it, also impair consistent congressional oversight. Covert CIA strikes conducted under Title 50 are subject to the rigid requirements of the covert action statute, but oversight is limited to only a handful of congressional leaders. Meanwhile, military strikes are subject to a more arcane system of congressional reporting (e.g. for sensitive and non-sensitive military operations), but more clearly subject to provisions requiring public estimates of civilian casualties (under §1057 of the 2018 NDAA, as amended) and more plainly subject to requirements under the War Powers Resolution.[10]

CIVIC highlights the fact that in many cases where the CIA have provided paramilitary support to other state forces or armed groups, those groups have perpetrated many serious human rights violations, but any information that might set out the extent to which the CIA are required to ensure that such violations do not take place, or to report violations, is not publicly available.[11] CIA involvement with Special Operations Forces under fiscal statutory authority[12] is thought to include classified operations in a number of countries in Africa and the Middle East, some of which are believed to have been combat missions against suspected terrorists or terrorist groups in places where there were hostilities with armed groups.[13] These operations are viewed as incidental to U.S. counterterrorism operations and exempt from many oversight and reporting requirements.[14]

Other than in cases where states have consented to the use of force in their territories by the United States,[15] three successive administrations have maintained that targeted killings have been carried out lawfully either in compliance with self-defense, or IHL relating to NIACs with al-Qaeda and ISIS.

Covert targeted killing during the Bush administration was minimal, directed at high value al-Qaeda targets, mainly in Pakistan and Yemen, as a subordinate part of the response to 9/11.[16] The program expanded exponentially under President Obama.[17] In 2013 President Obama decided to reduce the role of the CIA and transferred many drone operations to the Department of Defense.[18]

> The President himself oversaw the design of a new bureaucracy responsible for nominating suspected militants to government "kill lists". . . . The National Counter-Terrorism Center developed a "disposition matrix," a database that associated the names of suspected terrorists with the resources being used to "track them down" . . . . The President himself approved the criteria used by the committee [at the National Security Council] as well as the kill lists . . . . In bureaucratizing the program, the President normalized it.[19]

The targeting standards were loosened, to allow for "signature strikes" targeting groups or individuals thought to be involved in militant activity, rather than being directed at specific persons.[20]

Imminence

Different Administrations have had varying interpretations of "imminence." The Bush Administration concept of imminent threats in the 2002 National Security Strategy[21] had "blurred the distinction between pre-emption and prevention," effectively "sidelin[ing]" imminence.[22] The Obama Administration redefined the usual temporal meaning of the term "imminence"[23] in the context of self-defense which

> does not require the United States to have clear evidence that a specific attack on U.S. persons and interests will take place in the immediate future . . . . Decision makers must take into account that certain members of al-Qaeda . . . are continually plotting attacks against the United States . . . . A high level official could conclude, for example, that an individual poses an 'imminent threat' of violent attack against the United States where he is an operational leader of al-Qaeda or an associated force and is personally and continually involved in planning terrorist attacks against the United States.[24]

This "stretched meaning of imminence turns the traditional international law interpretation of the concept on its head."[25] The refined notion of imminence was used to justify the targeting of an American citizen, Anwar al-Aulaqi.[26] The Attorney General sought to explain the action on the grounds that al-Aulaqi's "direct personal involvement in the continued planning and execution of terrorist attacks against the U.S. homeland" justified the action taken by the United States.[27] In essence, this meant that al-Aulaqi was a lawful LOAC target because he was a "leader of enemy fighters with a continuous combat function."[28] President Obama endorsed this view, saying,

> America does not take strikes to punish individuals; we act against terrorists who pose a continuing and imminent threat to the American people, and when there are no other governments capable of effectively addressing the threat. And before any strike is taken, there must be near-certainty that no civilians will be killed or injured – the highest standard we can set.[29]

After President Obama's speech, Presidential Policy Guidance (PPG) was released. The PPG does not carry the force of law, and still does not reach IHRL standards,[30] but it reflects the policy of the time that moved in an IHRL direction.[31] It required that the "United States only use lethal force, including drone strikes, against terrorism suspects that pose a 'continuing, imminent threat,' when capture is infeasible, when there is 'near certainty' that no civilians will be injured or killed."[32] It also required that all operations would have to go through a multi-step interagency review, including by members of the Principals and Deputies Committees of the National Security Council before the President would give approval.[33] It has been estimated that 542 targeted strikes against terrorist targets were made during the Obama Administration, although that number does not reflect strikes in Afghanistan, Iraq, and Syria.[34]

Secrecy

At that time the reporting of civilian casualties was shrouded in mystery, with official numbers differing wildly from NGO estimates – a practice that had generated some complaints from human rights organizations.[35] President Obama issued an Executive Order in July 2016 which mandated additional measures to reduce civilian casualties, to investigate and take responsibility for such casualties, including the making of *ex gratia* payments to the injured or the families of civilians who were killed, and to report annually about the number of strikes and the numbers of civilians injured or killed as a result of government operations, including those conducted by the CIA.[36] Hina Shamsi has assessed the Obama Administration's approach in areas outside of active hostilities (i.e. in places other than recognized battlefields where LOAC would apply) as one in which "a set of made-up rules that cherry-picked from a variety of legal frameworks" applied (i.e. IHL, IHRL, and use of force in self-defense).[37]

In the Trump administration, the strikes intensified[38] and drone killing became even more secretive.[39]

> In the first half of the Trump administration, the United States demonstrated its continued reliance on lethal drones to respond to perceived terrorist threats, yet with no overarching strategy to guide such use. The Trump administration has placed a primacy on immediate military action, resulting in a U.S. drone policy that appears less restrained, less transparent, and less accountable.[40]

Media reports in 2017 suggested that the Trump drone policy planned to revise the Obama era rules in the form of Principles, Standards and Procedures (PSP) in a number of respects: eliminating the requirement that intended targets of drone strikes pose an "imminent threat"; modifying the requirement of "near certainty" that the target is present at the time of the strike to a "reasonable certainty"; downgrading the level of person with authority to make strike decision, from a senior policy maker to an operational commander;[41] and expanding the type of target from a high-level militant to persons who were rank-and-file.[42]

Reports of the content of the PSP could not be confirmed because of the secrecy surrounding the subject.[43] The extraordinary efforts to keep the PSP secret went on for more than three years. In October 2017 the ACLU filed a request under the Freedom of Information Act ("FOIA")[44] for the public disclosure of the PSP.[45] As the Government did not release the information, the ACLU filed a lawsuit to force disclosure in December 2017.[46] The Government's response did not acknowledge the existence of the PSP by neither confirming nor denying the existence of this guidance.[47] In 2019 the Department of Defense ("DOD") issued to journalists a redacted report relating to the 2017 ambush of U.S. soldiers and local partners in Niger,[48] which confirmed the existence of the PSP. The New York Times made a FOIA request for the PSP, which was denied and resulted in consolidating their lawsuit with the claim of the ACLU. It was not until September 2020 that a federal court ruled that the Government was not entitled to keep the new targeted killing rules secret. In a Memorandum Opinion in October 2020, the District Court explained the reasons for making the Order.[49] In essence, because the content of the DOD Niger ambush report referred to the PSP guidance, the continued official response that would neither confirm nor deny the existence of the PSP was "illogical and implausible."[50] Without the DOD report, it is clear that the Court would have upheld the Government's position and denied the FOIA requests. On April 30, 2021, a heavily redacted version of the PSP document was released by the Biden Administration.[51]

Hina Shamsi has analyzed that document and the changes made to the Obama rules. The Trump rules did not mention areas outside of active hostilities, so the rules applied to all parts of the world, including in those places where armed conflicts were taking place with their more permissive IHL killing rules. Shamsi notes that the Trump rules "departed from law by allowing force in response to a mere 'threat,'" rather than a "continuing and imminent threat."[52] The Obama policy constraints were abandoned, and civilian protections were watered down by removing the minimal operating principles that were in the Obama rules. The Obama requirement that there should be near certainty that a target would be in a strike location, was reduced to the requirement that there should be "reasonable certainty" that a male target would be present.[53] Shamsi suggests that the rules provided an "open-ended authorization for the United States to kill virtually anyone it designates as a terrorist threat, anywhere in the world, without reference to the laws prohibiting extrajudicial killing under human rights law."[54]

President Trump also permitted the CIA to resume covert drone operations.[55] It is not known exactly how many covert strikes were made during the Trump administration, because that information is also classified. As to civilian casualties, President Trump issued an Executive Order in March 2019 that revoked the reporting requirement relating to civilian casualties mandated in President Obama's 2016 Executive Order.[56] All the Trump era modifications to the practice of targeted killing had profound adverse IHL and IHRL implications.

President Biden suspended the Trump rules on January 20, 2021,[57] and is reportedly revising the policy governing use of force against terrorists outside the United States.[58] However, according to the Pentagon, on February 25, 2021 President Biden authorized airstrikes in eastern Syria "in response to the rocketing in Iraq and to continuing threats to American and coalition personnel."[59] The rocket attack had killed one Filipino contractor and injured four American contractors and one U.S. soldier. The resulting strike killed several people and destroyed several buildings. There was immediate confusion as to whether the attack was conducted in retaliation or self-defense. The White House Press Secretary said that the strike was conducted in self-defense and was "proportionate to the prior attacks."[60] President Biden's letter to Congress suggested that the strike was in response to the rocket attacks:

> in response [to the attacks], I directed this military action to protect and defend our personnel and our partners against these attacks and future such attacks. The United States always stands ready to take necessary and proportionate action in self-defense, including when, as is the case here, the government of the state where the threat is located is unwilling or unable to prevent the use of its territory by non-state militia groups responsible for such attacks.[61]

On the same day, the U.S. Ambassador to the United Nations sent a letter to the U.N. Security Council reporting the strike as having been conducted pursuant to "its inherent right of self-defense." She stated that this "necessary and proportionate action was taken to defend U.S. personnel and to deter further attacks."[62] One commentator, Ryan Goodman, examined sources in order to evaluate whether the right of self-defense extends to using force to stop more attacks days after an initial attack occurred, but did not reach a conclusion.[63]

However, Adil Ahmad Haque commented that the strikes violated international law because

> The airstrikes did not repel an ongoing armed attack, halt an imminent one, or immediately respond to an armed attack that was in fact over but may have appeared ongoing at the time. And the airstrikes were carried out in the territory of another State without its consent, against a non-State actor (or two, or more).[64]

Another commentator, John Bellinger, considered that the strike complied with both domestic and international law and commended the inaugural war powers report as a "model of war powers practice and transparency."[65] Yet as of March 2, 2021, some members of Congress were complaining that they were not satisfied with the official rationale for the strikes.[66]

On March 3, 2021, the White House released its Interim National Security Strategic Guidance.[67] It is somewhat vague and broad brush and the only oblique reference to targeted killing is found in the following passage:

> In advancing America's interests globally, we will make smart and disciplined choices regarding our national defense and the responsible use of our military, while elevating diplomacy as our tool of first resort. A powerful military matched to the security environment is a decisive American advantage. The United States will never hesitate to use force when required to defend our vital national interests. We will ensure our armed forces are equipped to deter our adversaries, defend our people, interests, and allies, and defeat threats that emerge. But the use of military force should be a last resort, not the first; diplomacy, development, and economic statecraft should be the leading instruments of American foreign policy. Military force should only be used when the objectives and mission are clear and achievable, when force is matched with appropriate resources and as part of an integrated strategy, when it is consistent with our values and laws, and with the informed consent of the American people. Decisions will be grounded in our strong tradition of civilian control of the military and healthy civil-military relations. And, when force is required, we will employ it alongside international and local partners wherever possible to bolster effectiveness and legitimacy, share burdens, and invest others in success.[68]

However, the New York Times reported that the Biden Administration had "quietly imposed temporary limits on counterterrorism drone strikes and commando raids outside conventional battlefield zones like Afghanistan and Syria." Drone strikes on terror suspects in places where there are not many United States ground troops may not take place without White House prior permission.[69] On June 28, 2021, in response to recent drone attacks on U.S. troops on both sides of the Iraq-Syria border, the United States forces launched airstrikes on facilities used by Iran-backed militia.[70] President Biden said the action had been taken to defend U.S. troops pursuant to Article II of the U.S. Constitution.[71]

With the United States withdrawal of all its troops from Afghanistan in August 2021, and the Taliban taking control of the country,[72] it remains to be seen what legal basis will be relied on to justify future drone strikes; either as reprisals for the ISIS-K attack on Kabul airport on August 26, 2021,[73] or to prevent future terror attacks by ISIS-K, al-Qaeda, or the Taliban itself on U.S. interests.[74] The Taliban were quick to state that both the U.S. reprisal strike on August 27, and a preventive strike on ISIS-K on August 29 before the last departure of remaining U.S. military personnel on August 31, were a "violation of sovereignty."[75] That final drone strike had been carried out in order to prevent what the United States believed to be an imminent attack by ISIS. Unfortunately, the strike killed ten civilians, including seven children.[76] However, this was one instance where the United States did admit that the strike had been a "tragic mistake."[77]

"High-value" strikes

Over the years the U.S. alone or with partners has made some "high value" drone strikes, such as the targeted killing of Mohammed Emwazi or "Jihadi John."[78]

One of the highest profile strikes was the targeted killing near Baghdad airport of Qasem Soleimani, the head of the Iranian Islamic Revolutionary Guard-Quds Force on January 2, 2020. Five other people were also killed, including Abu Mahdi al-Muhandis, deputy commander of Iraqi militia, who had been in a car with Soleimani. Was this an extrajudicial killing?[79] Did it comply with international law? Was it necessary? Was it proportionate, and were the principles of distinction and non-arbitrariness observed?

The DoD immediately issued a statement to justify "decisive defensive action to protect U.S. personnel abroad."[80] The statement claimed self-defense but also sought to justify the action because of Soleimani's past deeds:

> General Soleimani was actively developing plans to attack American diplomats and service members in Iraq and throughout the region. General Soleimani and his Quds Force were responsible for the deaths of hundreds of American and coalition service members and the wounding of thousands more. He had orchestrated attacks on coalition bases in Iraq over the last several months – including the attack on December 27th – culminating in the death and wounding of additional American and Iraqi personnel. General Soleimani also approved the attacks on the U.S. Embassy in Baghdad that took place this week.[81]

Over the next ten days the Administration provided a jumbled justification, according to the New York Times:

> They had to kill him because he was planning an "imminent" attack. But how imminent they could not say. Where they could not say. And really, it was more about what he had already done. Or actually it was to stop him from hitting an American embassy. Or four embassies. Or not.[82]

On February 14, 2020, the White House issued a notice pursuant to a mandatory statutory reporting requirement.[83] It justified the Soleimani attack in domestic law under Article II of the U.S. Constitution, which empowers the President to use force to protect the United States from an attack or threat of an imminent attack, and under the 2002 Authorization for Use of Military Force against Iraq, which authorizes the President to use the Armed Forces of the United States "as he determines to be necessary and appropriate" to defend the national security of the country. It also justified the attack under international law as self-defense "in response to a series of escalating armed attacks that Iran and Iran-supported militias had already conducted against the United States."[84] This report prompted the Chairman of the House Committee on Foreign Affairs to issue a statement saying:

> This official report directly contradicts the President's false assertion that he attacked Iran to prevent an imminent attack against United States personnel and embassies. The administration's explanation in this report makes no

> mention of any imminent threat and shows that the justification the President offered to the American people was false, plain and simple.
>
> To make matters worse, to avoid having to justify its actions to Congress, the administration falsely claims Congress had already authorized the strike under the 2002 Iraq war resolution. This legal theory is absurd. The 2002 authorization was passed to deal with Saddam Hussein. This law had nothing to do with Iran or Iranian government officials in Iraq. To suggest that 18 years later this authorization could justify killing an Iranian official stretches the law far beyond anything Congress ever intended.[85]

Immediately after the strike, Agnes Callimard, the U.N. Special Rapporteur on extra-judicial, summary or arbitrary executions, noted that for a drone strike to be lawful, it had to comply with the requirement in all applicable international legal frameworks.[86] For this targeted killing to be justified as one of self-defense, the *ius ad bellum* would require there to have been an imminent threat, i.e. an imminent future threat. Although the word "imminent" was used by several spokespersons, there was scant information about any actual imminent threat.[87] In addition to imminence, the use of the drone would have to be both necessary and proportionate. In the case of pre-emptive self-defense, pursuant to Article 51 of the U.N. Charter, the United States would have to inform the U.N. Security Council of their actions, which they did on January 8.[88] Agnes Callimard commented that the few details publicly available in the few days after the attack "did not establish a factual basis for the claim that any attacks were imminent, let alone that Soleimani was key to their implementation."[89]

Imminence is also relevant when examining whether the strike would be lawful under IHRL, (the right to life under Article 6 ICCPR in particular) because a strike would only be lawful if strictly necessary to protect against an imminent threat to life, with no option other than using lethal force.[90] The presence of the other five individuals who were killed along with Soleimani is problematic to satisfy the requirements of IHRL because collateral damage is not generally permitted.[91]

Agnes Callimard next considered whether IHL might have been applicable, but she concluded that it was highly unlikely that either an IAC or an NIAC were in existence between the United States and Iran (because Soleimani was Iranian) or Iraq (where the strike happened). If IHL was applicable, the United States would have to show that the attack was militarily necessary, and proportionate.[92] This killing therefore appears to have failed the tests in each of the frameworks.

On the same day as the Soleimani strike, the United States attempted and failed to kill by drone a second Iranian Commander, Abdul Reza Shahla'i, in Yemen.[93] Little has been reported on this, or the legal basis for this attempt, which is unclear.[94]

Redress

A number of the strikes led to litigation in U.S. courts seeking information, investigation, and/or compensation, none of which yielded anything of real consequence for the claimants. As mentioned above, in 2011 dual United States and Yemeni citizen Anwar al-Aulaqi was killed in Yemen. He was a Muslim cleric who was alleged to have strong ties with al-Qaeda, facilitating terror attacks and encouraging and inciting others to commit acts of terror. In July 2010 the U.S. Treasury titled him a Specially Designated Global Terrorist ("SDGT"). Before his death, his father brought an action in the Washington D.C. District Court in which he sought an injunction prohibiting the U.S. Government from intentionally killing his son.[95] Although he did not challenge his son's SDGT designation, the father claimed that his son had been placed on military and CIA "kill lists" without charge, trial, or conviction. The United States neither confirmed nor denied the existence of any order to kill Anwar al-Aulaqi.

The claim before the court was that the alleged policy of authorizing the targeted killing of U.S. citizens outside of armed conflict "in circumstances in which they do not present concrete, specific, and imminent threats to life or physical safety, and where there are means other than lethal force that could reasonably be applied to neutralize any such threat," violated Aulaqi's Fourth Amendment right to be free from unreasonable seizures, his Fifth Amendment right not to be deprived of life without due process of law, and his Fifth Amendment due process right for failing to disclose the criteria by which he was selected for targeted killing. The Plaintiff also claimed that the policy of targeted killing violated treaty and customary international law in breach of the Alien Tort Statute ("ATS").[96] Although Judge Bates mused "How is it that judicial approval is required when the United States decides to target a U.S. citizen overseas for electronic surveillance, but that . . . judicial scrutiny is prohibited when the United States decides to target a U.S. citizen overseas for death,"[97] he dismissed all claims as not being justiciable because the plaintiff lacked standing.[98] The ATS claim would also have been dismissed because it raised non-justiciable political issues.[99]

The Obama Administration had sought legal advice before authorizing the targeted killing of al-Aulaqi. A secret Office of Legal Counsel ("OLC") Memorandum apparently provided the basis for a DOJ White Paper, that a journalist at NBC News obtained in February 2013.[100] The DOJ concluded that

> where the following three conditions are met, a U.S. operation using lethal force in a foreign country against a U.S. citizen who is a senior operational leader of al-Qaeda or an associated force would be lawful: (1) an informed, high-level official of the U.S. government has determined that the targeted individual poses an imminent threat of violent attack against the United States; (2) capture is infeasible and the United States continues to monitor whether capture becomes feasible; and (3) the operation would be conducted in a manner consistent with applicable law of war principles.[101]

The DOJ therefore decided that this targeted killing could be justified as a lawful act of national self-defense. In its explanation of the meaning of "imminent threat" the DOJ opined that the United States was not required "to have clear evidence that a specific attack on U.S. persons and interests will take place in the immediate future," because a "broader concept of imminence was required."[102] Furthermore, feasibility of capture would be a "highly fact-specific and potentially time-sensitive inquiry."[103] In the discussion about conducting the operation in accordance with LOAC principles of necessity, distinction, proportionality and avoidance of unnecessary suffering, the DOJ noted that "it would not be consistent with those principles if anticipated civilian casualties would be excessive in relation to the anticipated military advantage."[104] Finally, the memo concluded that this type of lethal operation mounted against a U.S. citizen in these circumstances would not result in an unlawful killing.[105]

Two weeks after killing Anwar al-Aulaqi and American citizen Samir Khan, another U.S. drone apparently targeted an Egyptian national in Yemen, but it happened to kill at least seven people, including al-Aulaqi's teenage son. Their representatives sued a number of officials in their personal capacity on the ground that the authorization of the drone strikes violated the Fifth Amendment rights of the deceased.[106] Judge Collyer stated that "the powers granted to the Executive and Congress to wage war and provide for national security does not give them *carte blanche* to deprive a U.S. citizen of life without due process and without any judicial review."[107] The Court found the case was justiciable and that it had subject matter jurisdiction.[108] However the Court rejected the Fifth Amendment claims relating to negligence in the deaths of al-Aulaqi's son and Samir Khan, for failing to state a claim.[109] The Court went on to find no available remedy under U.S. law for the claim relating to Anwar al-Aulaqi's death. The Plaintiffs had sought a *Bivens* remedy, but Judge Collyer opined that this would

> impermissibly draw the Court into "the heart of executive and military planning and determination" as the suit would require the Court to examine national security policy and the military chain of command as well as operational combat decisions regarding the designation of targets and how best to counter threats to the United States.[110]

The Court therefore issued a judgment deferential to the government, stating

> In this delicate area of warmaking, national security, and foreign relations, the judiciary has an exceeding limited role. This Court is not equipped to question, and does not make a finding, concerning Defendants' actions in dealing with AQAP generally or Anwar al-Aulaqi in particular. Its role is much more modest: only to ensure that the circumstances of the exercise of war powers against a specifically targeted U.S. citizen overseas do not call for the recognition of a new area of *Bivens* relief.[111]

In 2017 the families of another two men killed by a drone in Yemen in 2012 claimed that their relatives were collateral damage of an attack intended for other people. They sought only a declaratory judgment that their family members had been killed during a U.S. drone attack in violation of IHL, the Torture Victim Protection Act and the Alien Tort Statute. The D.C. District Court rejected the clams primarily on deferential political question grounds.[112] The D.C. Circuit Court of Appeals, in a judgment for the court by Judge Brown, upheld the district court's decision, because

> in matters of political and military strategy, courts lack the competence necessary to determine whether the use of force was justified. . . . And it is the Executive, and not a panel of the D.C. Circuit, who commands our armed forces and determines our nation's foreign policy. . . . Courts are not constitutionally permitted to encroach upon Executive powers.[113]

However, most unusually, Judge Brown gave a separate concurring opinion in which she commented on the deferential approach using the political question ground to reject claims:

> In other liberal democracies, courts play (or seem to play) a significant supervisory role in policing exercises of executive power. . . . In this country, however, strict standing requirements, the political question doctrine, and the state secrets privilege confer such deference to the Executive in the foreign relations arena that the Judiciary has no role to play. These doctrines may be deeply flawed. In fact, I suspect that technology has rendered them largely obsolete, but the Judiciary is simply not equipped to respond nimbly to a reality that is changing daily if not hourly.[114]

She reviewed the state and extent of the U.S. drone program and wondered "if judges will not check this outsized power, then who will?" Judge Brown lamented the fact there was "pitifully little oversight within the Executive" and the fact that operations were "shrouded in secrecy," and ended by saying that the "Executive and Congress must establish a clear policy for drone strikes and precise avenues for accountability."[115] A lone judicial voice.

The subject of the "Kill List" is something that has also personally affected a number of journalists. In 2018 two journalists, Ahmad Zaidan, a Syrian and Pakistani citizen and Bilal Kareem, a U.S. citizen, who reported on terrorism and conflict in the Middle East, believed that in 2016 their names were on the U.S. "Kill List," the former because his name was on a list of suspected terrorists, and the latter because he had been the victim or near victim of at least five aerial bombings.[116] Their complaint related to alleged violations of the Administrative Procedure Act ("APA"),[117] the First, Fourth and Fifth Amendments, as well as domestic statutory infringements that would result in violations of IHRL and IHL, and they sought injunctions that would remove them from the list and to stop them from being targeted for killing.

The D.C. District Court ruled that Ahmad Zaidan had no standing to pursue his claim because he failed to establish an actual or imminent injury.[118] Because Bilal Kareem was able to show that one of the near misses came from a U.S. drone, he had shown the required standing to proceed.[119] The defendants sought to dismiss on the grounds that the APA did not apply to military authority exercised in the field in time of war or occupied territory. However, the Court accepted the argument that the case concerned the decision to put Bilal Kareem on the "Kill List" – a decision made in Washington D.C. made in accordance with the known Obama PPG procedures, within the jurisdiction of the APA. Furthermore, the court noted that the defendants had not developed their facts and arguments sufficiently to justify dismissal of the claim.[120] The statutory claims were all dismissed because of the Court's inability to hear cases regarded as a political question, but the Court ruled that the constitutional claims could proceed.[121]

The D.C. District Court dismissed Bilal Kareem's case after applying the state secrets privilege which precluded both discovery as well as the actual litigation on the grounds of national security.[122] Matters worsened for him still further when he appealed that decision. The Appeal Court revisited the issue of standing and took the traditional, more deferential stance. They remanded the case for dismissal on the grounds that Kareem had no standing to proceed because he had failed to allege "a sufficiently factual basis to create a plausible inference that the described missile attacks were attributable to the United States and specifically targeted Kareem."[123]

Although families seeking compensation from U.S. courts for the deaths of innocent victims are not generally successful, there is some evidence that the United States has made condolence payments funded by Congress or "solatia" payments as an expression of sympathy to innocent victims out of military funds.[124] In the drone era, payments have been made to families in Iraq from about 2003 onwards and in Afghanistan from 2005 onwards. The amount of a condolence payment for a death seems to range from $2,500 to $6,000. Little public data exists to show how many have received these payments. However, it is believed that in 2012 the U.S. made 219 condolence payments in Afghanistan totaling $891,000, and the families of more than 30 people killed in Pakistan each received approximately $3,000.[125] In 2016 the U.S. reportedly paid $1.2 million to the family of an Italian aid worker accidentally killed in a drone strike in Pakistan.[126] After the admission by the U.S. military that they committed a "horrible mistake" in the drone strike that killed ten civilians in Kabul as mentioned above,[127] it remains to be seen if the families of the deceased will be compensated for their loss. This subject is still cloaked in secrecy, as the DoD has not supplied details of any payments in their annual reports to Congress.[128]

United Kingdom

In 1988, British military officers shot and killed three IRA terror suspects suspected of planning an attack in Gibraltar. This episode led to the 1995 European Court of Human Rights (ECtHR) ruling that the U.K. had violated the right to life of the suspects,[129] as discussed above. Since 9/11 the United Kingdom has been using armed drones for targeted killing either alone, or as part of a coalition force, predominantly with the United States, in areas such as Iraq and Afghanistan, where at the time the United Kingdom was involved in armed conflict,[130] and in Syria, where it was not. The United Kingdom's involvement in targeted killing is also somewhat shrouded in secrecy.[131]

Investigations and redress

In 2003, while a Coalition of armed forces from the United States, United Kingdom and other countries were administering security in Iraq, there were a number of shooting incidents in which Iraqi citizens were killed by British soldiers in Basra. In *Al-Skeini*, relatives of six victims sought judicial review of the Secretary of State's decision not to conduct an independent inquiry into the deaths, not to accept liability for the deaths, and not to pay compensation.[132] Although these deaths were not caused by drone, the legal issues are applicable to cases of targeted killing by drone, both relating to the right to life substantively, as well as the right to investigate.

Use of force by British troops during operations is governed by military rules of engagement. In June 2003 the Commander of the brigade in Iraq issued a formal policy for the investigation of shooting incidents. If the Commander was satisfied on the basis of the available information that the soldier had acted lawfully within the rules of engagement, there was no requirement to instigate a Special Investigation Branch ("SIB") investigation.[133]

In the case of Al-Skeini and two other victims, the incidents did not result in a SIB investigation.[134] In respect of the fourth victim, the SIB recommended the prosecution of the officer concerned. This did not proceed because in the circumstances the lack of sufficient evidence made the prospect of conviction unrealistic.[135] The officers involved in the shooting of the fifth victim were investigated by the SIB and tried by court-martial, but they were acquitted due to the unreliability of a prosecution witness. The victim's family sued the Ministry of Defense for damages and the claim was settled without a trial for a compensatory payment of GBP 115,000.[136]

The sixth victim Baha Mousa, a hotel receptionist who had been detained with nine other hotel workers, was tortured and killed in custody at a British military base. Seven soldiers involved were charged with a number of criminal offenses. Charges were dropped against four, two were acquitted, and one pleaded guilty to the war crime of inhumane treatment and was sentenced by the court-martial to one year's imprisonment and dismissal from the army.[137] A public inquiry into the treatment and killing of Mousa followed, resulting in severe condemnation of the treatment of detainees together with a set of recommendations.[138] In 2010 the Ministry of Defense paid a total of GBP 2.83 million to the families of Mousa and the other hotel workers.[139]

The judicial review litigation worked its way through the strata of domestic courts,[140] with most of the arguments centered on whether the victims had been within the control and authority of the United Kingdom, and thus concerned the jurisdictional scope of the ECHR at the time of the killings. All of the domestic courts concluded that the only victim who had been within the relevant scope, was Mousa, in respect of whom the investigative duty had been complied with.

The ECtHR concluded that at the time of all the killings, the United Kingdom exercised authority and control over the persons killed in security operations, such as to establish a jurisdictional link between the victims and the United Kingdom pursuant to Article 1 ECHR.[141] The Grand Chamber reiterated that

> Article 2, which protects the right to life and sets out the circumstances when deprivation of life may be justified, ranks as one of the most fundamental provisions of the Convention. No derogation from it is permitted under Article 15, "except in respect of deaths resulting from lawful acts of war." Article 2 covers both intentional killing and also the situations in which it is permitted to use force which may result, as an unintended outcome, in the deprivation of life. Any use of force must be no more than "absolutely necessary" for the achievement of one or more of the purposes set out in sub-paragraphs (a) to (c).[142]

The Court remarked that the general prohibition on arbitrary killing would be ineffective without a procedure that reviewed the lawfulness of the use of lethal force. This means that there must be "some form of effective official investigation,"[143] even in difficult security conditions, including armed conflict. In those difficult situations, "all reasonable steps must be taken to ensure that an effective, independent investigation is undertaken into alleged breaches of the right to life."[144] Furthermore authorities must act "of their own motion" once they have been made aware of the matter.[145] The ECtHR found that the procedural duty of Article 2 had been violated in respect of all except the sixth victim.[146]

Hassan v. United Kingdom[147] has been discussed in the context of detention in Part II, but the case also contained a complaint that Hassan's death had violated the investigatory procedural aspect of Article 2 ECHR. However, the ECtHR found no violation of Article 2 on the basis that there was no evidence to suggest that British forces were responsible in any way for Hassan's death, because the death had occurred in a part of Iraq that was not controlled by British forces, four months after his release from British military custody.[148]

In 2015 a United Kingdom RAF drone strike killed two British citizens, Reyaad Khan and Ruhul Amin in Syria, where the United Kingdom was not fighting a war, without Parliamentary approval.[149] The then Prime Minister David Cameron commented that the strike marked "a new departure," and that it was "the first time . . . that a British asset has been used to conduct a strike in a country where we are not involved in a war."[150] He stated that Khan's death had occurred in an act of self-defense to protect the British people from a direct threat of terrorism action in the United Kingdom being plotted and directed by Khan.[151]

This justification of self-defense seemed to reflect a complete change of British counter-terrorism strategy. Up to this point, only the United States and Israel had a policy of using drone strikes against terror suspects outside areas of armed conflict. Because there was such a lack of clarity about the Government's policy, the Parliamentary Joint Committee on Human Rights (JCHR) conducted an inquiry into the Government's policy on the use of drones, and this paid great attention to identifying the appropriate legal framework.[152] Despite failing to receive adequate detailed answers from the Government, the JCHR established that it was the Government's policy to use lethal force abroad, even outside of armed conflict, against individuals suspected of planning an imminent terrorist attack against the United Kingdom, when there is no other way of preventing the attack.[153]

In order to justify that an attack by Khan was imminent, a Government Memorandum had described the evidence against him to have been clear, indicating the existence of a genuine threat: "the threat of attack was current; and an attack could have been a reality at any moment and without warning."[154] The Memorandum went on to state that when using military force the United Kingdom always adheres to the IHL principles of military necessity, distinction, humanity and proportionality.[155] That definition of imminence appears to have the implicit support of the U.N. Security Council.[156] However the JCHR expressed concerns about having too flexible an interpretation of imminence, because it risked leading to an overbroad policy that could be used to justify any member of ISIS anywhere being considered a legitimate target, in respect of a remote threat of an attack that is at the earliest stages of preparation.[157] The JCHR also established that unlike the United States, the United Kingdom does not consider that it is "in a global war against ISIS/Da'esh such that it can use lethal force against them anywhere in the world."[158]

In the course of the inquiry, the Secretary of State asserted that where the United Kingdom uses force abroad outside of armed conflict, it will comply with IHL (where imminence is not required), and that compliance will be sufficient to meet the United Kingdom's obligations under IHRL.[159] The JCHR noted that in principle it is correct that outside of armed conflict, IHRL will apply and in an armed conflict, compliance with IHL may indeed meet the relevant IHRL obligations.[160] However, the issue is whether using lethal force by drone abroad would bring the victims within the jurisdiction of the United Kingdom, and its obligations pursuant to the European Convention. If it does, the lethal force must comply with the higher IHRL standards mentioned above.

However, according to the most recent case on this issue in 2016, the question turned on whether the United Kingdom had the required level of authority and control in the place where the act occurred, and in the absence of that, the ECtHR, in their interpretation of jurisdiction on a set of facts that were not exactly analogous,

> required a greater degree of power and control than that represented by the use of lethal or potentially lethal force alone . . . the intention of the Strasbourg court was to require that there be an element of control of the individual prior to the use of lethal force.[161]

However, it seems that each case adjudicated by the ECtHR will turn on its own facts.

A second all party Parliamentary inquiry into the use of armed drones by the United Kingdom in 2018 noted that during the Iraq War and the Afghanistan campaigns, the United Kingdom's use of drones had been regarded as "a model of responsible and ethical use . . . strictly according to battlefield needs for the protection and facilitation of United Kingdom forces operating in designated areas."[162] However, the United Kingdom's reputation has been tarnished by the mode of operating during post-withdrawal campaigns in Iraq, Afghanistan, and Syria, raising "serious questions about the legality, efficacy, and strategic coherence of the U.K.'s use of drones."[163]

As in the United States, transparency and accountability in the United Kingdom's use of drones are lacking.[164] For example, in 2018, the United Kingdom incredibly asserted that only one confirmed civilian casualty occurred in 1,700 drone strikes in Iraq and Syria, and that only one drone strike in Afghanistan killed four and injured two.[165] The Government consistently denied that it operated a targeted killing program until about 2017, when some ministers seemed to suggest support for using lethal force to hunt down and kill suspected terrorists. These conflicting comments caused confusion as to what Government policy was on this subject.[166] Furthermore, the Government refused to supply any information or answer questions about its lethal operations on the grounds that "disclosure would, or would be likely to, prejudice the capability, effectiveness or security of the armed forces."[167]

The inquiry concluded that many of the questions posed in the conclusions to the JCHR Report still remained unanswered, and called for clarity and information from the Government on *inter alia* (i) its policy on the use of drones for legal strikes; (ii) the geographical scope of lethal drone strikes in armed conflicts with non-state armed groups; (iii) the interpretation of imminence; (iv) the principle of distinction in conflicts with non-state armed groups; (iv) how to apply IHRL in armed conflicts; and (v) accountability for civilian casualties.[168]

"High-value" strikes

At least three British citizen ISIS fighters were killed by United States drone strikes with the assistance of United Kingdom intelligence.[169] Junaid Hussain was killed in August 2015,[170] and his wife Sally Jones, the "White Widow" was killed in June 2017.[171] Mohammed Emwazi, or "Jihadi John" was killed in a United States drone strike in November 2015 with the assistance of British intelligence. David Cameron described "Jihadi John's" killing as an "act of self-defense" and "the right thing to do."[172]

Over a period of 18 months starting in mid-2012, the British government started interviewing Iraqi civilians who brought complaints relating to unlawful killing or serious abuse at the hands of British soldiers.[173] 280 Iraqis were alleged to have been unlawfully killed.[174] The British, through the Iraq Historic Allegations (IHAT) team, investigated 1,374 allegations,[175] and although reports in the media vary, it seems that by mid-2017, the U.K. government had paid almost

£22 million in compensation to Iraqi families, although it is not known how many of those payments related to unlawful killings.[176]

The provision of intelligence by the United Kingdom to assist United States drone strikes has generated litigation in the United Kingdom. For example, in 2011 a CIA operated drone strike killed 40, including Malik Khan, a peaceful Pakistani tribal elder in the Federal Administered Tribal Area of Pakistan. His son, Noor Khan, who also lives there, sued the British government, claiming judicial review of "a decision by [the Foreign Secretary] to provide intelligence to the United States authorities for use in drone strikes in Pakistan, among other places."[177] The High Court claim was dismissed in December 2012,[178] and the claim was reformulated to seek leave to appeal, by requesting (a) a declaration that a British national who kills a person in a drone strike is not entitled to rely on a defense of combatant immunity, with the result that an employee of the United Kingdom's Government Communications Headquarters (GCHQ) or any other Crown employee in the United Kingdom could commit an offense under sections 44–46 Serious Crimes Act 2007[179] by passing locational information to an agent of the United States Government for use in drone strikes in Pakistan; or (b) a declaration that if a defense of combatant immunity applies, the passing of information as set out in (a) may give rise to an international war crime, and therefore, before authorizing the passing of such information to the United States, the Foreign Secretary must formulate and publish a lawful policy setting out the circumstances for transmitting the information.[180]

The Court pointed out that it would not consider, let alone decide, whether United States drone strikes are lawful. This is because the British courts do not examine or sit in judgment on sovereign acts of a foreign state, pursuant to a principle that always applies except in exceptional circumstances, such as where foreign acts of state "are in breach of clearly established rules of international law or are contrary to English principles of public policy, as well as where there is a grave infringement of human rights."[181] The Court analyzed the claim as being one where, although it was being asked to decide a hypothetical question of whether a United Kingdom national who as a matter of secondary liability killed a person in a drone strike in Pakistan would be guilty of murder, in reality the Court was being asked to condemn the acts of the drone operators.[182] The Court dismissed the appeal:

> a finding by our court that the notional U.K. operator of a drone bomb which caused a death was guilty of murder would inevitably be understood (and rightly understood) by the U.S. as a condemnation of the U.S. In reality, it would be understood as a finding that (i) the U.S. official who operated the drone was guilty of murder and (ii) the U.S. policy of using drone bombs in Pakistan and other countries was unlawful. The fact that our courts have no jurisdiction to make findings on either of these issues is beside the point. What matters is that the findings would be understood by the U.S. authorities as critical of them. Although the findings would have no legal

> effect, they would be seen as a serious condemnation of the U.S. by a court of this country. . . . There is no escape from the conclusion that, however the claims are presented, they involve serious criticisms of the acts of a foreign state. It is only in certain established circumstances that our courts will exceptionally sit in judgment of such acts. There are no such exceptional circumstances here.[183]

Israel

Israel's policy of targeted killing has been carried out openly since 2000,[184] without the secrecy seen in other countries, and with a clearly set out legal framework[185] that is unique. Whereas a large body of literature supports the view that targeted killing produces more radicalization and retaliatory terror attacks,[186] some commentators contend that in Israel, where 200 targeted killing operations were conducted between 2000 and 2010, the result was a reduction in suicide bombing attacks.[187]

Legal framework

The United States and the United Kingdom have determined that the IHL rules relative to NIACs are applicable to the use of armed drones. In Israel, the law derives from 2006 Israel's Supreme Court (sitting as the High Court) in what is widely referred to as the "Targeted Killing" case.[188] It is the only national Supreme Court in the world to have addressed the issues of targeted killing openly and head-on, and despite much criticism of the judgment,[189] many commentators view the decision as setting an international standard.[190]

After the start of the second Intifada in September 2000, a policy of targeted killing became Israel's counter terrorist measure of choice.

> By means of this policy, the security forces operate in order to kill operatives in terrorist organizations who are involved in the planning, dispatching or commission of terror attacks against Israel. During the second Intifada, preventative attacks have been carried out throughout Judaea, Samaria and the Gaza Strip.[191]

The petitioners in the Targeted Killing case sought a declaration from the Court that the policy was illegal under international law, together with an order that the practice of targeting policy should cease. They claimed that between 2000 and 2005, approximately 300 operatives in terrorist organizations and 150 civilians close to the location of the targets were killed.[192] The petition was denied:

> It has therefore been decided that it cannot be determined *ab initio* that every targeted killing is prohibited under customary international law, just as it cannot be determined *ab initio* that every targeted killing is permitted under customary international law. The laws relating to targeted killings are

> determined in customary international law, and the legality of each individual attack needs to be decided in accordance with them.[193]

The Court held that the rules of international law governing *international* armed conflicts apply to the continuous fight between Israel and the armed terrorist groups in the Occupied Territories that has existed since the beginning of the Intifada in 2000, because the conflict crosses the border of a state.[194] President (Emeritus) Barak said that these laws include the laws of belligerent occupation and

> apply to every case of an armed conflict of an international character – i.e. one that crosses the borders of the state – whether the place where the armed conflict is occurring is subject to a belligerent occupation or not. These laws constitute a part of the laws of the conduct of war (*ius in bello*). From the humanitarian viewpoint, they are a part of international humanitarian law. This humanitarian law is a special law (*lex specialis*) that applies in an armed conflict. Where this law has a lacuna, it can be filled by means of international human rights law.[195]

President Barak stated that other applicable laws included basic principles of Israeli public law, as well as customary international law, which are part of Israeli law, as well as the relevant parts of the Geneva Conventions and API.[196] Israel has acknowledged that this classification is problematic, and that various courts, states and experts have classified conflicts between Israel and Palestinian terror organizations in the Gaza Strip as NIACs. Israel, in its report of the 2014 Gaza conflict, (Gaza Report) stated that it conducted those operations in accordance with IHL rules governing both IACs and NIACs, "including the rules relating to distinction, precaution and proportionality."[197] Although the specific IHL rules that pertain in the two forms of conflict vary to an extent, it appears to be generally accepted that the bulk of those governing attacks apply in both.[198]

Even more controversially, President Barak considered the status of the terrorists: were they combatants or civilians? He concluded that they did not fall into the traditional definition of combatants because they did not carry or wear anything to distinguish themselves as combatants, nor did they conduct themselves according to the laws of war.[199] Under the normal rules of IHL, everyone who is not a combatant is deemed a civilian. But President Barak took a different view: although acknowledging that a third category of "unlawful combatant" was not officially recognized in international law, he undertook a "dynamic interpretation" to adapt the existing rules to what he considered to be the new reality of "civilians who are unlawful combatants."[200]

These persons may be attacked for such time as they are directly participating in hostilities, which include using weapons or not, collecting intelligence and preparing to take part in hostilities, or acting voluntarily as a human shield, not only against the army or state, but also against the civilian population of the state.[201] In 2009 the ICRC's Interpretive Guidance contained echoes of the descriptions of persons who may described as member of armed groups on the basis of a continuous combat function in the Targeted Killing case.[202] Some say that the Israeli criteria relating to participation are more demanding than the ICRC guidance.

However, this was not the approach taken by Israel in the 2014 Gaza conflict, where the basis for targeted killing depended not solely on direct participation in hostilities, but appeared to shift from conduct, to mere membership of the organized armed groups.[203] Thus the members of organized armed groups in the military wing of Hamas were stated to be legitimate targets under customary international law, even when they were not in the act of preparing or conducting military activities.[204] So Israel, like the U.S. armed forces, takes a broader view of acts that qualify as direct participation than the test set forth in the Interpretive Guidance.[205]

President Barak also referred to the importance and duty of verifying the status of the person before targeting, and of considering under the duty of proportionality, whether a less harmful measure could be used.[206] In the Gaza Report, Israel stated that it went to great lengths whenever feasible to verify the targets, including the cancellation of attacks in appropriate situations, to analyze the proportionality of strikes, and minimize collateral damage by issuing warnings and attempting to time attacks to mitigate the risk of harm to civilians.[207] Despite this, there were many civilian casualties, but both sides dispute the actual numbers.[208] Israel took a number of steps to mitigate civilian suffering[209] and conduct an extensive investigation of alleged violations of IHL.[210]

However, Israel was widely condemned for their actions in the Gaza conflict, and this led to an inquiry pursuant to a United Nations Human Rights Council resolution. The HRC Report considered *inter alia* that Israel had released insufficient information relating to targeting decisions,[211] that Israeli military policy violated IHL,[212] that Palestinian armed groups violated IHL due to the inherently indiscriminate nature of projectiles aimed towards Israel and to targeting of civilians,[213] and that Palestinian authorities had failed to bring to justice perpetrators of violators of IHL and IHRL.[214] In the Recommendations, both parties were urged *inter alia* to respect IHL and IHRL and conduct investigations into violation of international law that complied with IHRL standards.[215] By contrast, the independent Schmitt and Merriam study of 2015 concluded that the Israel Defense Force (IDF) operations are clearly well-regulated and subject to the rule of law, with extremely robust systems of examination and investigation of operational incidents, with significant civilian oversight, both by the Attorney General and the Supreme Court.[216]

Israel was again engaged in intense fighting in 2021 with the terrorist group Hamas which controls Gaza. Approximately 4,340 rockets were fired into Israel from Gaza between May 10, 2021,[217] until the announcement of a cease fire on May 20, 2021.[218] A number of rockets were also fired from Lebanon into Israel by parties supporting Hamas.[219] The impact of many of about 90% of the rockets were neutralized by Israel's Iron Dome defense system, but at May 20, 2021, Israel had suffered 12 fatalities including 2 children[220] with hundreds injured,[221] and at least 230 Palestinians (of which 170 were combatants, according to the

Israel Defense Forces,)[222] had been killed, including 65 children and 1710 people wounded.[223] Unsurprisingly, many voiced justified concerns about the intensity of the fighting and level of fatalities. News stations and NGOs have protested about the high number of Palestinian casualties, and some allege Israeli war crimes, but brush off the fact that Israel was defending itself against a continuous barrage of thousands of armed rockets.[224] What if there had been no Iron Dome? If there had been equal numbers of dead and injured on each side, or if the number of rockets had resulted in 4,000 deaths, would there have been a similar outcry? It remains to be seen how the 2021 conflict will be analyzed.

In terms of the law, there were no findings about the 2014 Gaza conflict that would mark Israel as an outlier with respect to any particular norm. On the contrary, in most cases Israel's legal position on its customary law obligations is in accord with the targeting laws set forth in Additional Protocol I, as the Parties thereto typically interpret them. On a number of issues, Israel takes a different approach than the Parties to Additional Protocol I, but none of its stances is unique; in most cases other non-Parties to the Additional Protocol, such as the United States, share them.[225]

A number of commentators have criticized the *Targeted Killing* case for its "judicial activism."[226] The Israel Supreme Court was known for its activist judgments in which it did not baulk at faulting official policy, particularly in the period from the late 1990s to 2008.[227] However, Yahli Shereshevski has discerned a swing towards deference to the executive in cases involving the conduct of hostilities since 2009.[228]

Whereas up to 2009 the Court prided itself on its accessibility and the range of cases that were considered justiciable, it appears that since 2009, the hitherto extensive judicial review of military operations "decreased dramatically" both in the number of cases and regarding the "willingness of the Court to intervene . . . and actively interfere with Israeli conduct of hostilities policy.[229] For example, in 2003 human rights organizations filed a petition requesting an order that Military Police be required to investigate civilian deaths that occurred during Israel Defense Force activity. At that time Israeli policy merely required an operational debriefing in these circumstances. It was not until 2011 that the Court rejected this petition, after official policy had changed to require the opening of an investigation in any cases of civilian deaths in the West Bank that had not occurred as a result of acts clearly committed in the context of hostilities.[230] The rejection of the petition can be viewed as a deviation from the approach in the *Targeted Killings* case, which had mandated that any deaths arising out of a targeted strike should be independently investigated.[231] Shereshevsky suggests the shift towards deference stems from "the increased involvement of the international community since the 2009 Gaza conflict, and especially the threat of international criminal adjudication."[232]

Some say that the activist human rights approach of the Court was a response to the many petitions filed between 2000 and 2008 by human rights NGOs such as B'Tselem.[233] Two suggestions have been offered for the more deferential approach of the Court since 2009. First, the approach of the NGOs changed after 2009, by an extensive reduction in the number of petitions. Some thought the petitions were detrimental to the NGOs' causes as they resulted in judgments that reflected a functioning legal system,[234] that seemed to have human rights at its center. Second, as a result of international criticism, and "a significant threat of external intervention, it is possible that the domestic identity of the Court, as a part of Israeli society, has strengthened, making it more protective and thus more deferential to the government position in national security issues."[235]

Summary

Targeted killing by drones is still "wrapped up in a secrecy that extends to the investigation of civilian deaths."[236] The opacity includes counting the number of strikes and ascertaining how many have been injured or killed, as various NGOs' numbers differ enormously both from organization to organization and from official data.

Of the three countries, Israel alone has faced undisputed immediate threats, most recently in 2021, albeit from a non-state actor. Over the years since 9/11, the notions of imminence and self-defense have frequently been stretched and contorted by the United States and the United Kingdom almost beyond credulity. Despite this, their judiciaries have been almost always routinely and increasingly deferential to government policy. However even Israel's judiciary, which up to 2009 had taken a deliberate human rights compliant approach, has become more deferential in the last 12 years. The judicial approach and reactions of the public in general to targeted killing will be discussed in detail in Part V.

Notes

1 Shannon Dick and Rachel Stohl, *U.S. Drone Policy: Transparency and Oversight*, (Stimson, Feb. 11, 2020), www.stimson.org/2020/u-s-drone-policy/.
2 Christopher J. Fuller, See It/Shoot It: The Secret History of the CIA's Lethal Drone Program, 210–46, (Yale University Press, 2017), *noting that* during the Obama Administration the CIA mainly focused its drone operations in Pakistan and Afghanistan; *Exception(s) to the Rule(s): Civilian Harm, Oversight, and Accountability in the Shadow Wars,* Center for Civilians in Conflict ("CIVIC"), Stimson Center and Security Assistance Monitor, (Nov. 2020).
3 A number of organizations such as Airwars, The Bureau of Investigation, The Long War Journal, New America and Statistica have reported number of strikes but in respect of allegedly confirmed strikes the numbers from 2002 to date range from at least 8,346 to 33,843 or more.
4 Solis, The Law of Armed Conflict, 548.
5 *Exception(s) to the Rule(s)*, CIVIC, 1, *citing* 50 U.S.C. §3093 (the covert action statute) which states that Presidential approval of covert action may only be given if the action "is necessary to support identifiable foreign policy objectives of the United States and is important to the national security of the United States," *and* 10 U.S.C. §127e which gives U.S. Special Operations Command the fiscal authority to give financial aid to foreign partner forces in counterterrorism operations.
6 50 U.S.C. 3093(3e). This does not include routine support to traditional activities of the U.S. government.

7 *Exception(s) to the Rule(s),* CIVIC, 15.
8 *Id.*, 8.
9 *Id.*, 16.
10 *Id.*, 19–20. Sensitive military operations in Afghanistan, Iraq and Syria are exempt from the reporting requirements in 10 U.S.C. §130f.
11 *Id.*, 11–13. *Also see* Marten Zwanenburg, *The "External Element" of the Obligation to Ensure Respect for the Geneva Conventions: A Matter of Treaty Interpretation*, 97 International Law Studies 621, (2021), which discusses the extent to which Common Art. 1 of the Geneva Conventions requires all states to take all possible steps to ensure compliance with the GCs. That would mean that the United States would have a duty to ensure that the CIA respected the GCs.
12 *Id.*, 13, *citing* 10 U.S.C. §127e.
13 *Id.*, 13–14.
14 *Id.*, 17. *See also The Humanitarian Impact of Drones*, Women's International League for Peace and Freedom (WILPF), (WILPF, International Disarmament Institute, Pace University, Oct. 2017).
15 The United States has said that a number of States, such as Pakistan, Iraq, Yemen, Afghanistan, and Somalia have consented at times to the U.S. carrying out drone strikes on their territories. *See e.g.* Lynn E. Davis, Michael McNerney and Michael D. Greenberg, *Clarifying the Rules for Targeted Killing*, 11–12 (Rand Corporation, 2016); Max Brookman-Byrne, *Drone Use 'Outside Areas of Active Hostilities': An Examination of Legal Paradigms Governing US Covert Remote Strikes*, 64(3) Netherlands International Law Review 3, 19, 21, 31, (2017); Fred Aja Agwu, Armed Drones and Globalization in the Asymetric War on Terror, 176 (Routledge, 2018).
16 CIVIC, Exception(s) to the Rule(s), 8.
17 *Id.*, During the first three years of President Obama's first term, "the CIA conducted 300 lethal strikes in Pakistan, or at least one every three days," and also expanded to strikes in Yemen, *citing* Robert Chesney, *Military Intelligence Convergence and the Law of the Title 10/Title 50 Debate*, 5 Journal of National Security Law and Policy 539, 567, (2012).
18 *Exception(s) to the Rule(s)*, CIVIC, 9, *citing* Charlie Savage and Peter Baker, *Obama, in a Shift, to Limit Targets of Drone Strikes*, New York Times, (May 23, 2013), www.nytimes.com/2013/05/23/us/us-acknowledges-killing-4-americans-in-drone-strikes.html.
19 Jameel Jaffer (ed.), The Drone Memos: Targeted Killing, Secrecy and the Law, 10, (The New Press, 2016).
20 *Id.*, 10–11.
21 U.S. Government, The National Security Strategy, (Sep. 2002), available at: www.state.gov/ documents/organization/63562.pdf.
22 Luca Trenta, *The Obama Administration's Conceptual Change: Imminence and the Legitimation of Targeted Killings*, European Journal of International Security, 69, 80–1, (2017).
23 Under international law, the long-established understanding of the meaning of imminence is "instant, overwhelming, leaving no choice of means and no moment for deliberation." This meaning derives from a diplomatic incident in 1837 known as the "Caroline" case, *see* The Avalon Project, *The Caroline*, https://avalon.law.yale.edu/19th_century/br-1842d.asp.
24 Trenta, *The Obama Administration's Conceptual Change*, 87, *citing* U.S. Dept. of Justice White Paper, Lawfulness of a Lethal Operation Directed Against a U.S. Citizen Who Is a Senior Operational Leader of Al-Qaeda or an Associated Force, (draft Nov. 8, 2011).
25 Rosa Brooks, *Drones and the International Rule of Law*, 28(1) Ethics and International Affairs, 69, 94, (2014).

26 Another American citizen, Samir Khan, was killed at the same time. See below for further discussion relating to litigation resulting from the deaths.
27 Solis, The Law of Armed Conflict, 599, *citing* Letter from Eric H. Holder Jr., Attorney General of the United States to Patrick J. Leahy. Senator, (May 22, 2013).
28 *Id.*, 600.
29 The White House, Remarks by the President at the National Defense University, (May 23, 2013), https://obamawhitehouse.archives.gov/photos-and-video/video/2013/05/23/president-obama-speaks-us-counterterrorism-strategy#transcript.
30 Brett Max Kaufman and Ana Durkin, *United States Targeted Killing Litigation Report*, *in* Litigating Drone Strikes: Challenging the Global Network of Remote Killing, 121, www.ecchr.eu/fileadmin/Publikationen/Litigating_Drone_Strikes_PDF.pdf, (European Center for Constitutional and Human Rights, 2017).
31 Laura Dickinson, *Extraterritorial Counterterrorism: Policymaking v. Law*, Just Security, (Jul. 15, 2021), www.justsecurity.org/77357/extraterritorial-counterterrorism-policymaking-v-law/, noting that although the Obama Administration considered that as a matter of international law, drone strikes should be governed by IHL, the standards that applied as a matter of policy were more protective of human rights.
32 White House, Presidential Policy Guidance, Procedures for Approving Direct Action against Terrorist Targets Located Outside the United States and Areas of Active Hostilities, (May 22, 2013).
33 *Id.*, §1B.
34 Elena Chachko, *Administrative National Security*, 108 Georgetown Law Journal 1063, 1080, (2020), *citing* Micah Zenko, *Obama's Final Drone Strike Data*, Council on Foreign Relations Policy, Power and Preventative Action, (Jan. 20, 2017), www.cfr.org/blog/obamas-final-drone-strike-data.
35 *Exception(s) to the Rule(s)*, CIVIC, 9, *citing* "*Will I Be Next?' U.S. Drone Strikes in Pakistan*, Amnesty International, (Oct. 2013), www.amnesty.org/download/Documents/12000/asa330132013en.pdf. *See also e.g.* Larry Lewis and Diane Vavrichek, Rethinking the Drone War: National Security, Legitimacy, and Civilian Casualties in U.S. Counterterrorism Operations, (CNA Corporation, Marine Corps University Press, 2016). This practice continues. *See* Annie Shiel and Chris Woods, *A Legacy of Unrecognized Harm: DoD's 2020 Civilian Casualties Report*, Just Security, (Jun. 7, 2021), www.justsecurity.org/76788/a-legacy-of-unrecognized-harm-dods-2020-civilian-casualties-report/, which comments that the number of civilian casualties in 2020 had been extensively undercounted.
36 *Id.*, *citing* Executive Order No. 13732 of Jul. 1, 2016, 81 U.S. Fed. Reg. 130, ¶¶2, 3.
37 Hina Shamsi, *Trump's Secret Rules for Drone Strikes and Presidents' Unchecked License to Kill*, Just Security, (May 3, 2021), www.justsecurity.org/75980/trumps-secret-rules-for-drone-strikes-and-presidents-unchecked-license-to-kill/.
38 Chachko, *Administrative National Security*, 1081, *citing* Micah Zenko, *The (Not-So) Peaceful Transition of Power: Trump's Drone Strikes Outpace Obama*; Council on Foreign Relations, Policy, Power and Preventative Action, (Mar. 2, 2017), www.cfr.org/blog/not-so-peaceful-transition-power-trumps-drone-strikes-outpace-obama.
39 Rachel Stohl, *An Action Plan on U.S. Drone Policy: Recommendations for the Trump Administration*, 5, (Stimson, Jun. 2018), www/stimson.org/sites/default/files/fileattachments/Stimson%20Action%20Plan%20US%20Drone%20Policy.pdf.
40 Rachel Stohl, *Drones and the Development of International Standards*, (Stimson, Feb. 4, 2020), www.stimson.org/2020/drones-and-the-development-of-international-standards/.

41 *See e.g.* Charlie Savage and Eric Schmitt, *Trump Poised to Drop Some Limits on Drone Strikes and Commmando Raids*, New York Times, (Sep. 21, 2017), www.nytimes.com/2017/09/21/us/politics/trump-drone-strikes-commando-raids-rules.html; Charlie Savage, *Will Congress Ever Limit the Forever-Expanding 9/11 War?* New York Times, (Oct. 28, 2017), https://nytimes.com/2017/10/28/us/politics/aumf-congress-niger.html; Luke Hartig, *Trump's New Drone Strike Policy: What's Any Different? Why It Matters*, Just Security, (Sep. 22, 2017), www.justsecurity.org/45227/trumps-drone-strike-policy-different-matters/.

42 Chachko, *Administrative National Security*, 1085.

43 Stohl, *An Action Plan on U.S. Drone Policy* 15. *See also* Shannon Dick and Rachel Stohl, *U.S. Drone Policy: Transparency and Oversight*, (Stimson, Feb. 11, 2020).

44 Freedom of Information Act, 5 U.S.C. §552.

45 ACLU, ACLU v. DOD – FOIA Case Seeking Trump Administration's Secret Rules for Lethal Strikes Abroad, (Oct. 6, 2020), www.aclu.org/cases/aclu-v-dod-foia-case-seeking-trump-administrations-secret-rules-lethal-strikes-abroad.

46 American Civil Liberties Union (ACLU) and American Civil Liberties Foundation (ACLF) v. Department of Defense, (DOD) Department of Justice (DOJ), Department of State (DOS), Complaint for Injunctive relief. Case 1:17-cv-09972, S.D.N.Y. (Dec. 21, 2017).

47 ACLU and ACLF v. DOD, DOJ, DOS, Answer, Case 1:17-cv-09972-ER, S.D.N.Y, (Feb. 1, 2018).

48 *See e.g.* Eric Schmitt and Thomas Gibbons-Neff, *Fourth U.S. Soldier Is Found Dead after Ambush in Niger*, New York Times, (Oct. 6, 2017), www.nytimes.com/2017/10/06/world/africa/green-berets-niger-soldiers-killed.html; Rukmini Callimachi, Helene Cooper, Eric Schmitt, Alan Binder and Thomas Gibbon-Neff, *'An Endless War': Why 4 U.S. Soldiers Died in a Remote African Desert*, New York Times, (Feb. 20, 2018), www.nytimes.com/interactive/2018/02/17/world/africa/niger-ambush-american-soldiers.html; Eric Schmitt, *Pentagon Ends Review of Deadly Niger Ambush, Again Blaming Junior Officers*, New York Times, (Jun. 6, 2019), www.nytimes.com/2019/06/06/world/africa/niger-ambush-pentagon-review.html.

49 ACLU and ACLF v. DOD, DOJ, DOS; The New York Times Company v. DOD, Memorandum Opinion, Case 1:17-cv-09972-ER, (Oct. 5, 2020).

50 *Id.*, 10–11.

51 Charlie Savage, *Trump's Secret Rules for Drone Strikes Outside War Zones Are Disclosed*, New York Times, (May 1, 2021), www.nytimes.com/2021/05/01/us/politics/trump-drone-strike-rules.html; ACLU Comment on Release of Trump Administration Lethal Force Rules, ACLU, (May 1, 2021) (attaching PSP FOIA Document – Apr. 30, 2021), www.aclu.org/press-releases/aclu-comment-release-trump-administration-lethal-force-rules.

52 Shamsi, *Trump's Secret Rules for Drone Strikes and Presidents' Unchecked License to Kill.*

53 *Id.*

54 *Id.*

55 Gordon Lubbold and Shane Harris, *Trump Broadens CIA Powers, Allows Deadly Drone Strikes*, Wall Street Journal, (Mar. 13, 2017), www.wsj.com/articles/trump-gave-cia-power-to-launch-drone-strikes-1489444374.

56 Exception(s) to the Rule(s), CIVIC, 10, *citing* Executive Order No. 13862 of Mar. 6, 2019, Revocation of Reporting Requirement, §2, 84 FR 8789. The Biden Administration reintroduced this, *see* DoD, Annual Report on Civilian Casualties in Connection with United States Military Operations in 2020, 16, (Jun. 2, 2021), https://media.defense.gov/2021/Jun/02/2002732834/-1/-1/0/ANNUAL-REPORT-ON-CIVILIAN- CASUALITIES-IN-CONNECTION-WITH-UNITED-STATES-MILITARY-OPERATIONS-IN-2020.PDF.

57 Ellen Nakashima and Missy Ryan, *Biden Orders Temporary Limits on Drone Strikes Outside War Zones*, Washington Post, (Mar. 4, 2021), www.washingtonpost.com/national-security/biden-counterterrorism-drone-strike-policy/2021/03/04/f70fedcc-7d01-11eb-85cd-9b7fa90c8873_story.html.
58 Dickinson, *Extraterritorial Counterterrorism: Policymaking v. Law*.
59 Helene Cooper and Eric Schmitt, *U.S. Airstrikes in Syria Target Iran-Backed Militias That Rocketed American Troops in Iraq*, New York Times, (Feb. 25, 2021), www.nytimes.com/2021/02/25/us/politics/biden-syria-airstrike-iran.html, *citing* Pentagon Press Secretary John F. Kirby.
60 Ryan Goodman, *Legal Questions (and Some Answers) Concerning the U.S. Military Strike in Syria*, Just Security, (Mar. 1, 2021), www.justsecurity.org/75056/legal-questions-and-some-answers-concerning-the-u-s-military-strike-in-syria/, *citing* The White House Briefing Room, Statements and Releases, Press Gaggle by Pres Secretary Jen Psaki and Homeland Security Advisor and Deputy National Security Advisor, Dr. Elizabeth Sherwood-Randall, Aboard Air Force One, *en route* Houston, Texas, (Feb. 26, 2021), www.whitehouse.gov/briefing-room/statements-releases/2021/02/26/press-gaggle-by-press-secretary-jen-psaki-and-homeland-security-advisor-and-deputy-national-security-advisor-dr-elizabeth-sherwood-randall/.
61 *Id.*, *citing* The White House Briefing Room, Statements and Releases, A Letter to the Speaker and President pro tempore of the Senate Consistent with the War Powers Resolution, (Feb. 27, 2021), www.whitehouse.gov/briefing-room/statements-releases/2021/02/27/a-letter-to-the-speaker-of-the-house-and-president-pro-tempore-of-the-senate-consistent-with-the-war-powers-resolution/.
62 *Id.*, *citing* Letter from Ambassador Linda Thomas-Greenfield, Representative of the United States to the United Nations, to Dame Barbara Woodward DCMG, OBE, President of the Security Council, United Nations, New York, (Feb. 27, 2021), www.justsecurity.org/wp-content/uploads/2021/02/united-states-of-america-letter-to-united-nations-on-27-february-2021-syria-strike-under-article-51.pdf.
63 *Id.*
64 Adil Ahmad Haque, *Biden's First Strike and the International Law of Self-Defense*, Just Security, (Feb. 26, 2021), www.justsecurity.org/75010/bidens-first-strike-and-the-international-law-of-self-defense/.
65 John Bellinger, *President Biden's Inaugural War Powers Report*, Lawfare, (Mar. 1, 2021), www.lawfareblog.com/president-bidens-inaugural-war-powers-report.
66 Andrew Desiderio, *Biden Administration Still Hasn't Briefed Top Senators on Syria Strike*, Politico, (Mar. 2, 2021), www.politico.com/news/2021/03/02/syria-strike-senators-briefing-472745.
67 The White House Briefing Room, Statements and Releases, Interim National Security Strategic Guidance, (Mar. 3, 2021), www.whitehouse.gov/briefing-room/statements-releases/2021/03/03/interim-national-security-strategic-guidance/.
68 *Id.*, 14.
69 Charlie Savage and Eric Schmitt, *Biden Secretly Limits Counterterrorism Drone Strikes Away From War Zones*, New York Times, (Mar. 3, 2021), www.nytimes.com/2021/03/03/us/politics/biden-drones.html, noting that the new interim rules had been issued on January 20, 2021, although not publicly announced. The Administration is still reviewing legal and policy frameworks at time of writing. *See also* Ellen Nakashima and Missy Ryan, *Biden Orders Temporary Limits on Drone Strikes Outside War Zones*, Washington Post, (Mar. 4, 2021), www.washingtonpost.com/national-security/biden-counterterrorism-drone-strike-policy/2021/03/04/f70fedcc-7d01-11eb-85cd-9b7fa90c8873_story.html; Eric Schmitt and Christoph Koettle, *Remote C.I.A. Base in the Sahara Steadily*

Grows, New York Times, (Mar. 8, 2021), www.nytimes.com/2021/03/08/us/politics/cia-drones-sahara-niger-libya.html?searchResultPosition=2, which reports that the C.I.A. is continuing to conduct secret drone flights from an air base in the Sahara but there is no evidence to show these are anything other than surveillance missions.

70 Alex Horton, Louisa Loveluck and John Hudson, *U.S. Targets Iran-Backed Militia in Iraq, Syria Strikes*, Washington Post, (Jun. 28, 2021), www.washingtonpost.com/national-security/2021/06/27/us-airstrike-iraq-syria/.

71 Michael R. Gordon and Jared Malsin, *Iran-Backed Militias Fire Rockets in New Attack Aimed at U.S. Forces*, Wall Street Journal, (Jun. 28, 2021), www.wsj.com/articles/iran-backed-militias-threaten-revenge-after-u-s-airstrikes-in-iraq-syria-11624877977.

72 *Afghanistan: Joe Biden Defends US Pull-Out as Taliban Claim Victory*, BBC News, (Sep. 1, 2021), www.bbc.com/news/world-asia-58403735; Jim Huylebroek, Najim Rahim and Eric Nagourney, *The Taliban Celebrate Victory, With a Crisis Looming*, New York Times, (Sep. 1, 2021), www.nytimes.com/2021/08/31/world/asia/afghanistan-taliban-airport.html.

73 *Islamic State Claims Responsibility for Rocket Attack on Kabul Airport*, Reuters, (Aug. 30, 2021), www.reuters.com/world/asia-pacific/islamic-state-claims-responsibility-rocket-attack-kabul-airport-2021-08-30/.

74 Catherine Philp, *Joe Biden Needs Fresh Rules for Remote Strikes on Afghan Targets*, The Times, (Aug. 30, 2021), www.thetimes.co.uk/article/biden-needs-fresh-rules-for-remote-strikes-on-afghan-targets-cvkph2ddm.

75 Courtney Kube, Dartunorro Clark and Chantal Da Silva, *2 High Profile ISIS Targets Killed in U.S. Drone Strike In Afghanistan, Pentagon Says*, NBC News, (Aug. 28, 2021), www.nbcnews.com/news/world/u-s-retaliates-against-isis-drone-strike-afghanistan-n1277844; Susannah George, *10 Civilians Killed by U.S. Drone Strike in Kabul, Family Says*, Washington Post, (Aug. 21, 2021), www.washingtonpost.com/world/2021/08/30/drone-civilians-islamic-state/.

76 Eric Schmitt, *A Botched Drone Strike in Kabul Started with the Wrong Car*, New York Times, (Sep. 21, 2021), www.nytimes.com/2021/09/21/us/politics/drone-strike-kabul.html.

77 Eric Schmitt and Helene Cooper, *Pentagon Acknowledges Aug. 29 Drone Strike in Afghanistan Was a Tragic Mistake That Killed 10 Civilians*, New York Times, (Sep. 17, 2021, updated Sep. 28, 2021), www.nytimes.com/2021/09/17/us/politics/pentagon-drone-strike-afghanistan.html.

78 Phil Stewart and Mark Hosenball, *Strike on 'Jihadi John' Unfolded Quickly, But Hunt Took Months*, Reuters, (Nov. 13, 2015), www.reuters.com/article/us-mideast-crisis-jihadijohn-operation/strike-on-jihadi-john-unfolded-quickly-but-hunt-took-months-idUSKCN0T227920151114.

79 William J. Aceves, *When Death Becomes Murder: A Primer on Extrajudicial Killing*, 50 Columbia Human Rights Law Review 116, (2018), explaining what constitutes extrajudicial killing, although this does not specifically deal with targeted killing by drones.

80 DoD, Press Release, Statement, (Jan. 2, 2020).

81 *Id.*

82 Peter Baker and Thomas Gibbons-Neff, *Esper Says He Saw No Evidence Iran Targeted 4 Embassies, as Story Shifts Again*, New York Times, (Jan. 12, 2020), www.nytimes.com/2020/01/12/us/politics/esper-iran-trump-embassies.html.

83 White House, Notice on the Legal and Policy Frameworks Guiding the United States' Use of Military Force and Related National Security Operations: United States Military Action Against Qassem Soleimani, (Feb. 14, 2020), https://foreignaffairs.house.gov/_cache/files/4/3/4362ca46-3a7d-43e8-a3ec-be024

5705722/6E1A0F30F9204E380A7AD0C84EC572EC.doc148.pdf, *as mandated by* NDAA 2018 §1264.

84 *Id.*

85 U.S. House of Representatives Committee of Foreign Affairs, Press Release, Engel Statement on the White House's Latest Justification for Soleimani Killing, (Feb. 14, 2020), https://foreignaffairs.house.gov/2020/2/engel-statement-on-the-white-house-s-latest-justification-for-soleimani-killing. For comments on the domestic law justifications, *see* Scott R. Anderson, *Did the President Have the Domestic Legal Authority to Kill Qassem Soleimani?* Lawfare, (Jan. 3, 2020), www.lawfareblog.com/did-president-have-domestic-legal-authority-kill-qassem-soleimani; Oona Hathaway, *The Soleimani Strike Defied the Constitution*, The Atlantic, (Jan. 4, 2020), www.theatlantic.com/ideas/archive/2020/01/soleimani-strike-law/604417/.

86 Agnes Callimard, *The Targeted Killing of General Soleimani: Its Lawfulness and Why It Matters*, Just Security, (Jan. 8, 2020), www.justsecurity.org/67949/the-targeted-killing-of-general-soleimani-its-lawfulness-and-why-it-matters/.

87 Adam Taylor, *The Key Word in U.S. Justifications for the Killing of Iranian General: 'Imminent,'* Washington Post, (Jan. 5, 2020), www.washingtonpost.com/world/2020/01/05/key-word-us-justifications-killing-iranian-general-imminent/.

88 Letter from U.S. Ambassador Kelly Craft to Ambassador Dang Dinh Quy, President of United Nations, (Jan. 8, 2020), https://assets.documentcloud.org/documents/6609712/Art-51-Letter.pdf.

89 Callimard, *The Targeted Killing of General Soleimani: Its Lawfulness and Why It Matters.*

90 *Id.*

91 *Id.* However, the United States has claimed that the jurisdiction of the ICCPR does not apply extraterritorially.

92 *Id.*

93 John Hudson, Missy Ryan and Josh Dawsey, *On the Day U.S. Forces Killed Soleimani, They Targeted a Senior Iranian Official in Yemen*, Washington Post, (Jan. 10, 2020), www.washingtonpost.com/world/national-security/on-the-day-us-forces-killed-soleimani-they-launched-another-secret-operation-targeting-a-senior-iranian-official-in-yemen/2020/01/10/60f86dbc-3245-11ea-898f-eb846b7e9feb_story.html.

94 Robert Chesney, *Targeting Shahla'I in Addition to Soleimani: Unpacking the Legal Questions*, Lawfare, (Feb. 10, 2020), www.lawfareblog.com/targeting-shahlai-addition-soleimani-unpacking-legal-questions.

95 Al-Aulaqi v. Obama, 727 F. Supp. 2d 1 (Dec. 7, 2010).

96 *Id.*, 12.

97 *Id.*, 8.

98 *Id.*, 35.

99 *Id.*, 44–52. But Chachko, in *Administrative National Security* at 1086–7 questioned the relevancy of the examples of cases that the judge used in his opinion.

100 Ryan Goodman, *Backgrounder for Release of OLC's Targeted Killing Memo*, Just Security, (Jun. 23, 2014), www.justsecurity.org/12061/backgrounder-release-justice-departments-targeted-killing-memo/; *attaching* DoJ White Paper, Lawfulness of a Lethal Operation Directed against a U.S. Citizen Who Is a Senior Operational Leader of Al-Qaeda or an Associated Force, (Draft, Jun. 8, 2011), *and setting out* various criticisms of the White Paper.

101 DoJ White Paper, 1.

102 *Id.*, 7.

103 *Id.*, 8.

104 *Id.*

105 *Id.*, 10, 13, 15.
106 Al-Aulaqi v. Panetta, 35 F. Supp. 3d 56, 60, (Apr. 4, 2014).
107 *Id.*, 69.
108 *Id.*, 70.
109 *Id.*, 73.
110 *Id.*, 74–80. The Plaintiffs had tried to rely on Bivens v. Six Unnamed Agents of Federal Bureau of Narcotics, 403 U.S. 388 (1971) but the categories of permissible claims were limited and the Supreme Court has consistently refused to apply Bivens liability to new contexts or categories.
111 *Id.*, 78.
112 Ahmed Salem Bin Jaber v. United States, 155 F. Supp. 3d 70, (Feb. 22, 2016).
113 Ahmed Salem Bin Ali Jaber v. United States, 861 F.3d 241, 247, 249, (Jun. 30, 2017).
114 *Id.*, 250. Judge Brown was talking specifically about Israel in her reference to other democracies. See below.
115 *Id.*, 252–3.
116 Zaidan v. Trump, 317 F. Supp. 3d 8, (Jun. 13, 2018).
117 Administrative Procedure Act ("APA"), 5 U.S.C. §551.
118 Zaidan v. Trump, 18–19.
119 *Id.*, 20.
120 *Id.*, 22–3.
121 *Id.*, 23–9.
122 Kareem v. Haspel, 412 F. Supp. 3d 52, (Sep. 24, 2019).
123 Kareem v. Haspel, 2021 U.S. App. LEXIX 1128, 10, (Jan. 15, 2021).
124 Cora Currier, *Hearts, Minds and Dollars: Condolence Payments in the Drone Strike Age*, Propublica, (Apr. 5, 2013), www.propublica.org/article/hearts-minds-and-dollars-condolence-payments-in-the-drone-strike-age, *citing* www.documentcloud.org/documents/627368-gao-report-on-condolence-payments-2007.html#document/p15/a98457.
125 *Id.*
126 Joshua Keating, *Obama Administration Makes Rare Payment to Family of Aid Worker Killed in U.S. Drone Strike*, Slate, (Sep. 16, 2016), https://slate.com/news-and-politics/2016/09/obama-administration-makes-rare-payment-to-family-of-aid-worker-killed-in-drone-strike.html.
127 Alex Horton, Joyce Sohyun Lee, Elyse Samuels and Karoun Demirjian, *U.S. Military Admits 'Horrible Mistake' in Kabul Drone Strike That Killed 10 Afghans*, Washington Post, (Sep. 17, 2021), www.washingtonpost.com/national-security/2021/09/17/drone-strike-kabul-afghanistan/.
128 Joanna Naples-Mitchell, *New DoD Policy on Amends Needs to Address Transparency Gap*, Just Security, (Apr. 23, 2019), www.justsecurity.org/63723/new-dod-policy-on-amends-needs-to-address-transparency-gap/. No *ex gratia* (either condolence or *solatia*) payments were made during 2020, *see* U.S. Dept. of Defense (DoD) Annual Report on Civilian Casualties in Connection with United States Military Operations in 2020, 16, (Jun. 2, 2021), https://media.defense.gov/2021/Jun/02/2002732834/-1/-1/0/ANNUAL-REPORT-ON-CIVILIAN-CASUALITIES-IN-CONNECTION-WITH-UNITED-STATES-MILITARY-OPERATIONS-IN-2020.PDF.
129 McCann v. United Kingdom, Appl. 18984/91, ECtHR, Judgment, (Sep. 27, 1995).
130 House of Lords, House of Commons, Joint Committee on Human Rights, (JCHR), The Government's Policy on the Use of Drones for Targeted Killing, HL Art. 141, HC 574, 1.7d1, (2016).
131 Joanna Frew, *In the Frame*, Drone Wars 10, 40, (Jan. 2020), https://dronewars.net/wp-content/uploads/2020/01/InTheFrame-Web.pdf, "a form of

'quasi-secrecy' surrounds the UK's drone targeted killings." *Also see below* the discussion on the Reyaad Khan targeted killing and aftermath.

132 The history of these claims is set out in Al-Skeini v. United Kingdom, Appl. No. 55721/07 EctHR, (Jul. 7, 2011).

133 *Id.*, ¶¶25–32. *See also regarding SIB investigations* Park, The Right to Life in Armed Conflict, 142–58.

134 Al-Skeini v. United Kingdom, ¶¶34–46.

135 *Id.*, ¶¶47–54.

136 *Id.*, ¶¶55–62.

137 *Id.*, ¶¶63–71.

138 *Baha Mousa Inquiry: "Serious Discipline Breach' by Army*, BBC News, (Sep. 8, 2011), www.bbc.com/news/uk-14825889,*citing* The RT Hon Sir William Gage (Chairman), The Report of the Baha Mousa Inquiry, Presented to Parliament pursuant to Section 26 of the Inquiries Act 2005, Ordered by the House of Commons to be printed on Sep. 8, 2011.

139 *UK Pays £9m in Compensation to Iraqi Civilians*, BBC News, (Jun. 16, 2010), www.bbc.com/news/10332224. Nearly £9m was paid between 2003 and 2009 to compensate Iraqi civilians injured or killed by British military operations.

140 R. (on the application of Al-Skeini and Others) v. Secretary of State for Defense, [2004] EWHC 2911 (Admin) (Dec. 14, 2004); R. (on the application of Al-Skeini and Others) v. Secretary of State for Defense [2005] EWCA Civ 1609 (Dec. 21, 2005); Al-Skeini and Others v. Secretary of State for Defense, [2007] UKHL 26 (Jun. 13, 2007).

141 Al-Skeini v. United Kingdom, ¶¶149–150. For a discussion on ECHR jurisdiction see the discussion relating to jurisdiction in preventive detention in Part II.

142 *Id.*, ¶162.

143 *Id.*, ¶163, *citing* McCann v. United Kingdom, ¶¶150, 161–2.

144 *Id.*, ¶164.

145 *Id.*, ¶165.

146 *Id.*, ¶177.

147 Hassan v. United Kingdom, Appl. No. 29750/09, EctHR, (Sep. 16, 2014).

148 *Id.*, ¶¶62–4.

149 JCHR, The Government's Policy on the Use of Drones for Targeted Killing, ¶1.2. Parliament had approved the use of military force in Iraq, but not in Syria without a separate vote in the House of Commons. A Belgian national was also killed in the RAF strike. Armed strikes in Syria were approved by Parliament in December 2015.

150 House of Commons Debate, Hansard, vol. 599 c30, (Sep. 7, 2015).

151 JCHR, The Government's Policy on the Use of Drones for Targeted Killing, ¶1.3.

152 *Id.*, ¶1.28; *Also see* All-Party Parliamentary Group on Drones Inquiry Report, (APPG), The UK's Use of Armed Drones: Working with Partners, (2018).

153 *Id.*, JCHR, The Government's Policy on the Use of Drones for Targeted Killing, ¶2.2.

154 *Id.*, ¶3.16, *citing* Memorandum from the Government on Drones, (Dec. 2015).

155 *Id.*

156 *Id.*, ¶3.36, *citing* UNSCR 2249 (2015).

157 *Id.*, ¶¶3.40–1.

158 *Id.*, ¶3.52.

159 *Id.*, ¶3.54.

160 *Id.*, ¶3.55.

161 Al Sadoon v. Secretary of State for Defence, Rahmatullah v. Secretary of State for Defence, [2016] EWCA Civ 811, ¶69, (Sep. 9, 2016).

162 APPG, The UK's Use of Armed Drones, 3, 7.

163 *Id.*
164 *Id.*
165 *Id.*, 13, *citing Syria War: MoD Admits Civilian Died in RAF Strike on Islamic State*, BBC News, (May 2, 2018), www.bbc.com/news/uk-43977394; Nick Hopkins, *Afghan Civilians Killed by RAF Drone*, The Guardian, (Jul. 5, 2011), www.theguardian.com/uk/2011/jul/05/afghanistan-raf-drone-civilian-deaths.
166 *Id.*, 25.
167 *Id.*, 13.
168 *Id.*, 5.
169 *Id.*, 26.
170 *Id. See also: UK Jihadist Junaid Hussain killed in Syria Drone Strike, Says US*, BBC News, (Aug. 27, 2015), www.bbc.com/news/uk-34078900.
171 *Id. See also: British ISIS Recruiter Sally-Anne Jones 'Killed by Drone*, BBC News, (Oct. 12, 2017), www.bbc.com/news/uk-41593659.
172 Matt Dathan, *Jihadi John 'Dead': David Cameron Says Targeting ISIS Executioner Was 'Act of Self-Defense'*, Independent, (Nov. 13, 2015), www.independent.co.uk/news/uk/home-news/jihadi-john-dead-david-cameron-says-targeting-isis-executioner-was-act-self-defence-a6733056.html.
173 Andrew Williams, *British Soldiers Accused of Torture and Abuse during Iraq Occupation*, Newsweek Magazine, (Dec. 17, 2014), www.newsweek.com/2014/12/26/british-soldiers-caught-further-torture-allegations-during-iraqi-occupation-292323.html. This topic has also been discussed in Part II.
174 Richard Norton-Taylor, *How Many Iraqis Were Killed or Abused by British Soldiers? We May Never Know*, The Guardian, (Jan. 13, 2016), www.theguardian.com/news/defence-and-security-blog/2016/jan/13/how-many-iraqis-were-killed-or-abused-by-british-soldiers-we-may-never-know.
175 Iraq Historic Allegations Team, Allegations under Investigation, (Mar. 31, 2016), https://assets.publishing.service.gov.uk/government/uploads/system/uploads/attachment_data/file/523972/20150512-IHAT_Allocated_Cases_as_per_31_March_2016.pdf. There is no breakdown in the document showing how many cases related to killing.
176 *Ministry of Defence Paid Nearly £22 Million in Iraq War Compensation Claims*, ITV News, (Jun. 13, 2017), www.itv.com/news/2017-06-13/ministry-of-defence-paid-nearly-22-million-in-iraq-war-compansation-claims.
177 R. (on the Application of Noor Khan) v. Secretary of State for Foreign and Commonwealth Affairs, [2014] EWCA Civ 24, ¶¶1, 4 (Jan. 20, 2014) ("Khan v. SSFCA").
178 R. (on the Application of Khan) v. Secretary of State for Foreign and Commonwealth Affairs, [2012] 3728 (Admin), (Dec. 21, 2012).
179 Serious Crime Act 2007, c. 27 §§44–46 which related to encouraging or assisting offences when a person believes that one or more offenses will be committed and that his act will assist the commission of those offences.
180 Khan v. SSFCA, ¶6.
181 *Id.*, ¶¶25–8.
182 *Id.*, ¶¶35, 36.
183 *Id.*, ¶¶37, 53.
184 Ronen Bergman, Rise and Kill First, xii, (Random House, 2018), *noting* that between 1947 and 2000, Israel had conducted 500 targeted killing operations. Since 2000 and 2018, at least 1800 strikes were caried out.
185 Ophir Falk, Targeted Killings, Law and Counter-Terrorism Effectiveness: Does Fair Play Pay Off?, 3, (Routledge, 2021).
186 *Id.*, 5, *citing e.g.* Audrey Kurth Cronin, *Why Drones Fail: When Tactics Drive Strategy*, Foreign Affairs, (Jul./Aug. 2013), www.foreignaffairs.com/articles/somalia/2013-06-11/why-drones-fail; Shah Aqil, *Do U.S. Drone Strikes Cause*

Blowback? Evidence from Pakistan and Beyond, 42(4) International Affairs, 47 (2018). *See also* Emmerson, *New Counter-Terrorism Measures: Continuing Challenges for Human Rights*, 128; Ophir Falk and Amir Hefetz, *Minimizing Unintended Deaths Enhanced the Effectiveness of Targeted Killing in the Israel-Palestinian Conflict*, 42(6) Studies in Conflict and Terrorism 600 (2019); Anouk S. Rigterink, *The Wane of Command: Evidence on Drone Strikes and Control within Terrorist Organizations*, 115(1) American Political Science Review, 31, 32 (2021).

187 *Id.*, 7, *citing e.g.* Daniel Byman, *Do Targeted Killings Work?* 85(2) Foreign Affairs, 102, 103, (Mar./Apr. 2006); Daniel Jacobson and Edward H. Kaplan, *Suicide Bombings and Targeted Killings in (Counter-)Terror Games*, 51(5) Journal of Conflict Resolution 772 (Oct. 2007); Bryan C. Price, Targeting Top Terrorists: Understanding Leadership Removal in Counterterrorism Strategy, 150–79, (Columbia University Press, 2019), where he argues that leadership decapitation decreased the operational capability of Hamas. However, *see* Oldrich Bures and Andrew J. Hawkins, *Israeli targeted killing operations before and during the Second Intifada: A Contextualized Comparison*, 31(3) Small Wars & Insurgencies, 569 (2020), where the authors argue that during the Second Intifada between 2000 and 2005, when Israel had changed its legal basis, scale, methods and legal definition of a high value target, the new policy was less "successful" because it yielded more civilian casualties, more retaliatory responses and more adverse political consequences.

188 Public Committee Against Torture (PCAT) v. The Government of Israel, (2006) HCJ 769/02.

189 *See e.g.* Yael Stein, *Any Name Illegal and Immoral*, 17(1) Ethics and International Affairs 127 (Mar. 2003); Orna Ben-Naftali and Keren Michaeli, *Public Committee against Torture in Israel v. Government in Israel. Case No HCJ 769/02*, 101(2) American Journal of International Law, 459 (Apr. 2007); UNGA, HR Council, *Report of the Special Rapporteur on Extrajudicial, Summary or Arbitrary Executions*, Philip Alston, *Addendum, Study on Targeted Killings*, A/HRC/14/24/Add.6 (May 28, 2010), ¶¶13–17.

190 Falk, Targeted Killings, 32, *citing e.g.* Anthony Dworkin, *Israel's High Court on Targeted Killing: A Model for the War on Terror?*, Crimes of War Project, (Dec. 15, 2006); Tamar Meshel, *A Decade Later and Still on Target: Revisiting the 2006 Targeted Killing Decision*, 7 Journal of International Humanitarian Legal Studies 88 (2016); *see also* Tamar Meisels, *Targeted Killing with Drones? Old Arguments, New Technologies*, 29(1) Philosophy and Society, 1 (2017).

191 PCAT v. The Government of Israel, ¶2.

192 *Id.*

193 *Id.*, ¶64.

194 *Id.*, ¶¶16, 18.

195 *Id.*

196 *Id.*, ¶¶18, 19, 20.

197 State of Israel, The 2014 Gaza Conflict: Factual and Legal Aspects, (Gaza Report) ¶233, (May 2015), https://mfa.gov.il/ProtectiveEdge/Documents/2014GazaConflictFullReport.pdf.

198 Michael N. Schmitt and John J. Merriam, *Tyranny in Context: Israeli Targeting Practices in Legal Perspective*, 37 University of Pennsylvania Journal of International Law 53, 94, (2015).

199 PCAT v. The Government of Israel, ¶¶24, 25.

200 *Id.*, ¶¶27–41. *See also* Markus Gunneflo, Targeted Killing: A Legal and Political History, 18–24, (Cambridge University Press, 2016).

201 PCAT v. The Government of Israel, ¶33. Barak discusses a number of examples relating to the difference between direct and indirect participation. *See also* Schmitt and Merriam, *Tyranny in Context*, 109–14.

202 Yahli Shereshevsky, *Targeting the Targeted Killings Case: International Lawmaking in Domestic Contexts*, 39(2) Michigan Journal of International Law 242, 249 (2018), *citing* Melzer, Interpretive Guidance, 34: "continuous combat function requires lasting integration into an organized armed group acting as the armed forces of a non-state party to an armed conflict. Thus, individuals whose continuous function involves the preparation, execution, or command of acts or operations amounting to direct participation in hostilities are assuming a continuous combat function."
203 Shereshevsky, *Targeting the Targeted Killings Case*, 242, 245–9.
204 Gaza Report, ¶¶265, 268.
205 Schmitt and Merriam, *Tyranny in Context*, 113. *See also* Falk, Targeted Killings, 37–8.
205 Gaza Report, ¶406.
206 PCAT v. The Government of Israel, ¶40.
207 Gaza Report ¶¶282, 290, 291–304, 316, 330–33. This practice accords with evidence collected and analyzed by Schmitt & Merriam, *Tyranny in Context*.
208 *Id.*, ¶406.
209 *Id.*, ¶¶373–405.
210 *Id.*, ¶¶409–14, 444–57.
211 HR Council, *Report of the Independent Commission of Inquiry Established Pursuant to HR Council Resolution S-21/1*, U.N.G.A. A/HRC/29/52, ¶75 (Jun. 24, 2015).
212 *Id.*, ¶¶77–8.
213 *Id.*, ¶79.
214 *Id.*, ¶80.
215 *Id.*, ¶¶82–8.
216 Schmitt and Merriam, *Tyranny in Context*, 135.
217 Israel Defense Force (IDF), Guardian of the Walls, www.idf.il/en/minisites/operation-guardian-of-the-walls/second-week-summary/ (last accessed May 20, 2021).
218 Josef Federman and Fares Akram, *Israel, Hamas, Agree to Cease-Fire to End Bloody 11-Day War*, Associated Press, (May 20, 2021), https://apnews.com/article/israel-palestinian-cease-fire-hamas-caac81bc36fe9be67ac2f7c27000c74b.
219 Loveday Morris, Michael E. Miller and Shira Rubin, *Biden Tells Netanyahu He Expects 'Significant de-Escalation Today' as Israel, Hamas Continue Attacks*, Washington Post, (May 19, 2021), www.washingtonpost.com/world/2021/05/19/israel-gaza-conflict-latest-updates/.
220 Federman and Akram, *Israel, Hamas, Agree to Cease-Fire to End Bloody 11-Day War*.
221 *Ceasefire between Israel and Gaza Terror Groups Goes into Effect*, Times of Israel, (May 20, 2021), www.timesofisrael.com/liveblog-may-20-2021/.
222 Yaakov Katz, *Israel's Gaza Operation Is Like No Other Military Op. in History: Opinion*, Jerusalem Post, (May 20, 2021), www.jpost.com/opinion/israels-gaza-operation-is-like-no-other-military-op-in-history-opinion-668709.
223 Federman and Akram, *Israel, Hamas, Agree to Cease-Fire to End Bloody 11-Day War*.
224 *See e.g. Israel/OPT: Pattern of Israeli Attacks on Residential Homes in Gaza Must Be Investigated as War Crimes*, Amnesty International, (May 17, 2021), www.amnesty.org/en/latest/news/2021/05/israelopt-pattern-of-israeli-attacks-on-residential-homes-in-gaza-must-be-investigated-as-war-crimes/;*Israel Committing War Crimes in Gaza, Palestinian FM Tells UN*, Aljazeera, (May 16, 2021), www.aljazeera.com/news/2021/5/16/israel-committing-war-crimes-in-gaza-palestinian-fm-tells-un. Some news stations are more even-handed: Joseph Krauss, *Explainer: Are Israel, Hamas Committing War Crimes in Gaza?* ABC

News, (May 18, 2021), https://abcnews.go.com/International/wireStory/explainer-israel-hamas-committing-war-crimes-gaza-77748883; Declan Walsh, *When Fighting Erupts between Israel and Hamas, the Question of War Crimes Follows*, New York Times, (May 16, 2021), www.nytimes.com/2021/05/16/world/middleeast/israel-gaza-hamas-civilian-casualties.html.

225 Schmitt and Merriam, *Tyranny in Context*, 136–7.

226 *See e.g.* Jonathan Cohen, *Israel: Judicial Appointments, Standing and Political Questions*, The Jurist, (Jul. 30, 2010), http://jurist.org/dateline/2010/07israel-judicial-appointments-standing-and-political-questions.php; Yigal Mersel, *On Aharon Barak's Activist Image*, 47(2) Tulsa Law Review 339 (2011); Shereshevsky, *Targeting the Targeted Killings Case*, 255–6, *citing e.g.* Menachem Hofnung and Keren Weinshall Margel, *Judicial Setbacks, Material Gains: Terror Litigation at the Israeli High Court of Justice*, 7 Journal of Empirical Legal Studies, 664 (2020); Amichai Cohen and Stuart A. Cohen, *Israel and International Humanitarian Law: Between the Neo-Realism of State Security and the "Soft Power" of Legal Acceptability*, 16 Israel Studies 1, 11, (2011).

227 Shereshevsky, *Targeting the Targeted Killings Case*, 243. Examples of such cases are Anonymous Persons v. Minister of Defense, CrimA 7048/97, 54(1) PD 721 (2002); Physicians for Human Rights v. Israel Defense Force Commander in the Gaza Strip, HCJ 4764/04, 58(5) PD 385 (2004); Adalah Legal Center for Arab Minority Rights in Israel v. General Officer Commanding Central Command 60(3) PD 67 (2005); A v. State of Israel, (Unlawful Combatants) CrimA 6659/06 62(4) PD 329 (2008).

228 *Id.*

229 *Id.*, 257. *See also* Fidh (International Federation for Human Rights), Shielded from Accountability: Israel's Unwillingness to Investigate and Prosecute International Crimes, (Sep. 2011), www.fidh.org/IMG/pdf/report_justice_israel-final.pdf.

230 *Id.*, 258, *citing* B'Tselem v. Judge Advocate General, HCJ 9594/03, (Aug. 21, 2011).

231 *Id.*, 259, *citing* PCAT v. Government of Israel, ¶40.

232 *Id.*

233 *Id.*, 260, *citing* Cohen and Cohen, *Israel and International Humanitarian Law*, 14–15.

234 *Id.*, 261.

235 *Id.*, 262.

236 HR Council, *Report of the Special Rapporteur on Extrajudicial, Summary or Arbitrary Executions*, 2020, ¶22.

Part IV

Tackling the problems of foreign fighters

Since 2014 at least 40,000 people have travelled from more than 120 countries to join ISIS, of which at least 5,000 came from Europe.[1] By mid-2018, at least 7,366 people had returned home,[2] and a more recent report estimates that over 1,500 have returned to Europe.[3] In 2019 very few foreign fighters returned to Europe,[4] and it is unlikely that many, if any, returned during 2020–2021 because of restrictions on travel relating to the COVID-19 pandemic. Data at February 2021 show that a few thousand foreign fighters remain active in Iraq and Syria,[5] and that about 2,000 FTFs with 10,000 family members are held in deplorable conditions in displacement camps in Syria.[6] The al-Hol camp alone holds more than 60,000 people of dozens of nationalities, most of which are children,[7] but many countries do not want their citizens back.[8] The journalist Antony Loyd questions whether the ISIS brides in the Syrian camps are able to accept the level of their own responsibility for making the choice to go to live in the caliphate. He comments:

> Without that recognition of responsibility, and a commitment to some sort of atonement, western societies will never accept these women back, and efforts by lawyers or human rights groups to describe them merely as victims will only antagonize, just as accusations that all are perpetrators pointlessly, erroneously inflame.[9]

Because of fears that the camps could be "spawning a new generation of extremists" the Biden administration urged its western allies to repatriate its FTFs and their families.[10]

Part IV is structured slightly differently from the previous sections. It begins with an analysis of the international law framework, but because the topic is relatively new with limited data, and because countries are still struggling to discover how to deal with returning FTFs in a way that prevents future acts of terrorism, the domestic examples are dealt with in different way, providing a comparative overview of what is happening in twelve countries that have data in English.

DOI: 10.4324/9780367817275-9

Notes

1 Anthony Dworkin, *Beyond Good and Evil: Why Europe Should Bring ISIS Foreign Fighters Home*, European Council on Foreign Relations, 3, (Oct. 25, 2019), www.ecfr.eu/page/-/beyond_good_and_evil_why_europe_should_bring_isis_foreign_fighters_home.pdf. *See also* Richard Barrett, *ISIS Foreign Fighters after the Fall of the Caliphate*, 6(1) Armed Conflict Survey 23, 24, (2020), *noting that* since the fall of the caliphate, the mobilization of foreign fighters to Iraq and Syria has continued, and estimating that up to 3,000 foreign fighters remain, *citing* U.S. Dept. of Defense (DOD), Office of Inspector General, 'Operation Inherent Resolve:' Lead Inspector General Report to the United States Congress, April 1, 2019–June 30, 2019, 2 (Jul. 2019).

2 *How Many IS Foreign Fighters Are Left in Iraq and Syria*?, BBC News, (Feb. 20, 2019), www.bbc.com/news/world-middle-east-47286935.

3 Francesco Marone, *Tackling the Foreign Fighter Threat in Europe*, Italian Institute for International Political Studies (ISPI), (Jan. 9, 2020), https://ispionline.it/it/pubblicazione/tackling-foreign-fighter-threat-europe-24756.

4 Europol, European Union Terrorism Situation and Trend Report 2020, 44, www.europol.europa.eu/sites/default/files/documents/european_union_terrosm_situation_and_trend_report_te-sat_2020_0.pdf.

5 U.N. Office of Counter-Terrorism, Statement by Mr. Vladimir Voronkov, Under-Secretary-General of the United Nations Office of Counter-Terrorism, Twelfth Report of the Secretary-General on the threat posed by ISIL (Da'esh) to international peace and security and the range of United Nations efforts in support of Member States in countering the threat, ("Twelfth Report") (Feb. 10, 2021), www.un.org/counterterrorism/www.un.org/counterterrorism/sites/files/210210_usg-_voronkov_statement_sc_briefing_12th_ISIL.pdf.

6 Catherine Philp, *Joe Biden Urges Western Allies to Bring Back Isis Families Held in Syria*, The Times, (Mar. 31, 2021), www.thetimes.co.uk/article/joe-biden-urges-western-allies-to-bring-back-isis-families-held-in-syria-sng77cngg; Karen DeYoung, *Blinken Says the Number of ISIS Fighters and Family Members Being Held at Detention Camps in Syria is 'Untenable,'* Washington Post, (Jun. 28, 2021), www.washingtonpost.com/national-security/binken-isis-prisoners-syria/2021/06/28/a0faa66e-d7f8-11eb-8fb8-aea56b785b00_story.html.

7 U.S. Department of State, Office of the Spokesperson, Briefing with Acting Special Envoy for the Global Coalition to Defeat ISIS John Godfrey on U.S. Participation in the Upcoming D-ISIS Ministerial, Special Briefing, via Teleconference, ("FTF Briefing") (Mar. 29, 2021), www.state.gov/briefing-with-acting-special-envoy-for-the-global-coalition-to-defeat-isis-john-godfrey-on-u-s-participation-in-the-upcoming-d-isis-ministerial/.

8 Lila Hassan, *Repatriating ISIS Foreign Fighters Is Key to Stemming Radicalization, Experts Say, But Many Countries Don't Want Their Citizens Back*, PBS Frontline, (Apr. 6, 2021), www.pbs.org/wgbh/frontline/article/repatriating-isis-foreign-fighters-key-to-stemming-radicalization-experts-say-but-many-countries-dont-want-citizens-back/.

9 *Id.*

10 Philp, *Joe Biden Urges Western Allies to Bring Back Isis Families Held in Syria; See also* Matt Clinch, *Trump Urges European Allies to Take Back Hundreds of ISIS Fighters Captured in Syria*, CNBC, (Feb. 17, 2019), www.cnbc.com/2019/02/17/trump-urges-european-allies-to-take-back-hundreds-of-isis-fighters.html.

6 The international law framework for foreign fighters

This chapter analyzes the tools in international law that underpin the domestic counter-terrorism strategies that have been used in a selection of countries to deal with the threat of terrorism perceived to be posed by foreign terrorist fighters (FTF) and their families.

U.N. Resolutions

Concerned by the then growing threat of foreign fighters heading to Syria to fight with ISIS, the Security Council adopted Resolution 2178 in 2014. This Resolution defined FTFs as "individuals who travel to a State other than their States of nationality or residence for the purpose of the perpetration, planning or preparation for, or participation in terrorist acts, or the providing or receiving of terrorist training, including in connection with armed conflict."[1]

The Resolution *inter alia* stated that Member States shall

> consistent with international human rights law, international refugee law and international humanitarian law, prevent and suppress the recruiting, organizing, transporting or equipping of individuals who travel to a State other than their States of nationality or residence for the purpose of the perpetration, planning or preparation for, or participation in terrorist acts, or the providing or receiving of terrorist training, and the financing of their travel and their activities.[2]

Member States would be obliged to deny entry to individuals other than their own citizens or permanent residents if they had "credible information" that provided "reasonable grounds to believe" that the individual was seeking entry or transit in order to participate with the above mentioned terrorist activity, or if the activities indicated that an "individual, group, undertaking or entity was associated" with al Qaeda.[3] Member States were required to enact appropriate criminal legislation so that the perpetrators could be prosecuted.[4] Member States were also obliged to supply advance passenger information, as well as report to appropriate national authorities any actual or attempted departures from, or entries to, that Member State.[5]

A number of problematic issues have been identified, most of which are caused by imprecise or lack of definition in the Resolution, and this has affected how States have enacted legislation in response. For example, the term "foreign" in FTF is a blanket

DOI: 10.4324/9780367817275-10

description of persons involved and leaves no room for considering the situation of persons having dual nationality.[6] "Terrorism" and thus "terrorists" are not defined. Many have argued that this omission can result in States interpreting these terms in vague or overbroad ways, which in turn can lead to abuses in implementing the Resolution.[7] Furthermore, the Resolution appears to conflate terrorism and IHL. The International Committee of the Red Cross (ICRC) has made it clear that other than those offenses which are classified as terrorist under IHL, the term "acts of terrorism" should be reserved for acts of violence committed outside of armed conflict.[8]

In 2015 the U.N. Counter-Terrorism Committee met in Madrid to share best practices and developed 35 guiding principles that might assist countries in dealing with FTFs.[9] These were published as the Madrid Guiding Principles, focusing mainly on preventing FTFs from travelling, and on international cooperation with prosecuting and reintegrating returnees.[10]

In 2017 the Security Council adopted Resolution 2396,[11] which required Member States to enhance the advance passenger information and passenger name record systems, create watch lists, and collect biometric data. It also mandated the sharing of information about suspected FTFs and their families with relevant authorities,[12] whether or not the family members were alleged to have been involved in terrorist activity. This is very likely to have human rights implications in terms of the right to privacy. A further 17 guidelines were added to the Madrid Guidelines that updated and expanded the sections on prosecution, rehabilitation and reintegration in December 2018.[13]

International Human Rights Law (IHRL)

When implementing the U.N. Resolutions, States are obliged to act in compliance with IHRL. Many of the measures that States have enacted to deal with the FTF problem have involved restrictions on travel, both in respect of departing from and returning to the home country, as well as depriving persons of citizenship. A number of human rights conventions are relevant to the countries discussed in this chapter.

International Covenant on Civil and Political Rights (ICCPR)[14]

Table 6.1 Rights applicable to returning foreign fighters in the ICCPR

Liberty of movement	Art. 12(1) Everyone lawfully within the territory of a State shall, within that territory, have the right to liberty of movement and freedom to choose his residence. (2) Everyone shall be free to leave any country, including his own. (3) The above-mentioned rights shall not be subject to any restrictions except those which are provided by law, are necessary to protect national security, public order (ordre public), public health or morals, or the rights and freedoms of others, and are consistent with the other rights recognized in the present Covenant. (4) No one shall be arbitrarily deprived of the right to enter his own country.

Fair treatment	Art. 7 No one shall be subjected to torture or to cruel, inhuman or degrading treatment.
Family life	Art 17(1) No one shall be subjected to arbitrary or unlawful interference with his privacy, family, home, or correspondence.

Thus a number of rights are affected if states place restrictions on movement. For example, in *Ilyasov v. Kazakhstan*, a Russian with the right to permanently reside in Kazakhstan went to visit his parents in Russia and was refused re-entry into Kazakhstan in the interests of State security.[15] Although his complaints under ICCPR Articles 12, 19 (freedom of expression), and 23 (protection of family) were declared admissible, the majority of the HRC treated the case as one of violation of the family rights in Article 17 and 23[16] and did not "pronounce" on possible violations of Article 12 and 19.[17] Three judges separately opined that whilst Article 12 (4) "is designed to extend extraordinarily strong protection – more than the usual proportionality standard – to the right of a State's own nationals" to remain and return to their "own" country, Article 12(4) did not apply in this case because as a mere permanent resident, Ilyasov's own country was Russia, and not Kazakhstan.[18]

All the countries discussed in this chapter have ratified the ICCPR. Preventing individuals from leaving or returning to their own country for reasons of national security does not in principle violate IHRL. Freedom of movement includes the right to a passport,[19] but the restrictions set out in Art. 12(3) must be proportionate, necessary, appropriate, and the least intrusive measure for achieving the desired result.[20] In *El Dernawi v. Libya*,[21] the applicant, who was a member of the Muslim Brotherhood and who claimed he was being persecuted in Libya because of his political beliefs, was granted asylum with approval for family reunification in Switzerland in March 2000. In September 2000, the applicant's wife and three children were stopped at the Libya/Tunisia border, and her passport which also covered the children, was confiscated. She was told that she could not travel because her husband's name was on an internal security wanted list in connection with a political case. She tried to obtain the return of her passport, without success. The HRC noted that "a passport provides a national with the means practicably to exercise the right to freedom of movement, including the right to leave one's own State."[22] In this case, Libya had not shown any justification for either the confiscation or the failure to return the passport, in violation of Article 12(2).

The decision to prevent entry cannot be made arbitrarily according to Article 12(4). General Comment 27 states that even if prevention of entry is permitted by law, it should be

> in accordance with the provisions, aims and objectives of the Covenant and should be, in any event reasonable in the particular circumstances. The Committee considers that there are few, if any, circumstances in which deprivation of the right to enter one's own country could be reasonable. A State Party must not, by stripping a person of nationality or by expelling an individual to a third country, arbitrarily prevent this person from returning to his or her own country.[23]

General Comment 27 was adopted in 1999, but the meaning of "arbitrary" has been refined by General Comment No. 35[24] to encompass most of the elements of Article 12(3). In a 2018 case concerning Article 12(4), the HRC repeated its remarks in GC 27 in which "few if any circumstances" were envisaged where depriving a person of the right to enter their own country would be reasonable.[25] Since then, as of September 2021, no cases by returning foreign fighters claiming a violation of Article 12(4) or Article 17 appear to have been decided by the HRC. The limitations of that judicial body have been discussed in Part II.

Convention on the Rights of the Child ("CRC")[26]

Table 6.2 Rights applicable to children of foreign fighters in the CRC

Discrimination	Art. 2(1) States Parties shall respect and ensure the rights set forth in the present Covenant to each child within its jurisdiction without discrimination of any kind, irrespective of the child's or his or her parent's or legal guardian's race, color, sex, language, political or other opinion, national, ethnic or social origin, property, disability, birth, or other status. (2) States Parties shall take all appropriate measures to ensure that the child is protected against all forms of discrimination on the basis of the status, activities, expressed opinions, or beliefs of the child's parents, legal guardians, or family members.
Best interests of the child	Art. 3(1) In all actions concerning children, whether undertaken by public or private social welfare institutions, courts of law, administrative authorities or legislative bodies, the best interests of the child shall be a primary consideration.
Right to life	Art. 6(1) States Parties recognize that every child has the inherent right to life. (2) States Parties shall ensure to the maximum extent possible the survival and development of the child.
Identity	Art. 8(1) States Parties undertake to respect the right of the child to preserve his or her identity, including nationality, name, and family relations as recognized by law without unlawful interference.
Non-separation	Art. 9(1) States Parties shall ensure that a child shall not be separated from his or her parents against their will, except when competent authorities subject to judicial review determine, in accordance with applicable law and procedures, that such separation is necessary for the best interests of the child. (2) In any proceedings pursuant to paragraph (1) of the present article, all interested parties shall be given an opportunity to participate in the proceedings and make their views known.

Many of the measures taken to tackle the problem of FTFs have had significant adverse effects on children. In 2018 the U.N. Office of Counter-Terrorism (UNOCT) produced guidance in accordance with international law for dealing with children caught up in the foreign fighter issues, particularly those held in camps in Syria.[27] The guidance recommended that all such children should be treated as "victims entitled to special protection," with the goal of rehabilitating and reintegrating them in "normal" society.[28] Measures for children should be guided by the CRC principles of non-discriminatory treatment,[29] having the best interests of the child as a primary consideration,[30] the child's inherent right to life, survival and development,[31] and respect for the views of the child.[32] Significantly, if parents are FTFs, or even suspected of being such, the detaining of the children because of the "sins" of the parents would be discriminatory and violate Article 2 CRC.[33] However, this has to be balanced with the obligation to preserve family unity.[34]

Despite this guidance, the UNOCT reported in February 2021 that

> nearly two years after the territorial defeat of ISIL, some 27,500 foreign children are still in harm's way in the camps in northeast Syria, including about 8,000 children from some 60 countries other than Iraq. 90 per cent of them are under 12 years of age.[35]

The report noted that Kazakhstan, the Russian Federation and Uzbekistan had repatriated hundreds of children from Syria, but other States, particularly those in Europe, had taken very few.[36]

In two connected Communications to the U.N. Committee on the Rights of the Child, three French grandparents of eleven children with French nationality, (some of whom had been born in Syria), sought repatriation to France of their grandchildren detained in dire conditions in camps that were controlled by Kurdish forces in Syria.[37] The Committee noted that France was well aware of the children's situation, and that the deplorable detention conditions could cause irreparable harm to the children's lives and development. The Committee noted that France had the capability and power to protect the children be repatriating them, having already repatriated 17 French children in March 2019.

The Committee declared that these Communications were admissible because France had jurisdiction over these 11 children, with the obligation to protect their human rights, and by extension, the human rights of all French children in Syrian detention camps.[38] However, this decision raises the question of how, under international law, France could have jurisdiction over children in a camp that it did not control in any way.[39] One expert has commented that involving nationality in the tests to determine extraterritorial jurisdiction carries the risk of arbitrariness.[40]

European Convention on Human Rights (ECHR)[41]

Table 6.3 Rights applicable to returning foreign fighters in the ECHR

Family life	Art. 8(1) Everyone has the right to respect for his private and family life, his home and his correspondence. (2) There shall be no interference by a public authority with the exercise of this right except such as in accordance with the law and is necessary in a democratic society in the interests of national security, public safety, or the economic well-being of the country, for the prevention of disorder or crime, for the protection of health or morals, or for the protection of the rights and freedoms of others.
Fair treatment	Art. 3 No one shall be subjected to torture or to inhuman or degrading treatment or punishment·
Freedom of movement	Protocol 4, Art. 2(1) 1. Everyone lawfully within the territory of a State shall, within that territory, have the right to liberty of movement and freedom to choose his residence. (2) Everyone shall be free to leave any country, including his own. (3) No restrictions shall be placed on the exercise of these rights other than such as are in accordance with law and are necessary in a democratic society in the interests of national security or public safety, for the maintenance of ordre public, for the prevention of crime, for the protection of health or morals, or for the protection of the rights and freedom of others. (4) The rights set forth in paragraph 1 may also be subject, in particular areas, to restrictions imposed in accordance with law and justified by the public interest in a democratic society.[42] Protocol 4, Art. 3(1) No one shall be expelled by means of either an individual or of a collective measure, from the territory of the State of which he is a national. (2) No one shall be deprived of the right to enter the territory of the State of which he is a national.

Although Article 8 protects the rights to family life and the home, this right may be restricted in the interests of national security. The guarantees of Article 8 are frequently affected by all of the counter-terrorism strategies concerning restrictions of movement and citizenship.

In *Iletmis v. Turkey*, the applicant was a Turkish national.[43] He, his wife and two children had residence permits to live in Germany. He was suspected of being a sympathizer of and involved in the activities of the Kurds, and was the subject of a Turkish investigation into activities committed abroad detrimental to the national interest. While on a visit to Turkey to see family, he was arrested. Although he was initially released without charge, his passport was confiscated in 1992, and his family joined him in Turkey. He was charged later that year, and eventually acquitted of security offences in 1999 for lack of evidence, after which a new passport was issued. The ECtHR opined that the withdrawal of the passport in 1992 was legitimate in order to preserve national security at the time.[44] However, since the proceedings were so protracted without progress or evidence, the confiscation and failure to return the passport for so many years amounted to a violation of Article 8, because continuing to prevent him from leaving the country "no longer answered a pressing social need and was therefore disproportionate in relation to the aims pursued, legitimate though they were under Article 8."[45]

Deprivation of citizenship was a legal measure in several countries long before 9/11, although it was rarely used. One commentator has highlighted the fact that all citizens are not treated equally – the human rights of individuals with only one citizenship that has been acquired by birth, are in general more protected than those of naturalized persons who may have multiple nationalities.[46]

Statelessness is dealt with in a number of international instruments:

Universal Declaration of Human Rights

Article 15 states "Everyone has the right to a nationality. No one shall be arbitrarily deprived of his nationality nor denied the right to change his nationality."[47]

Convention Relating to the Status of Stateless Persons

In this Convention stateless means "a person who is not considered as a national by any State under the operation of its law."[48]

Convention on the Reduction of Statelessness

Article 8 provides that a Contracting State may not deprive a person of his or her nationality if such deprivation would render the individual stateless. However, this does not apply in situations where the Contracting State specified at the time of ratifying the Convention, that at that time, its law permitted it to deprive a person of nationality who "inconsistently with [their] duty of loyalty to the Contracting State, had conducted him [or herself] in a manner seriously prejudicial to the vital interests of the State." The United Kingdom, Belgium, Brazil, Italy, and Jamaica made such reservations or declarations at the time they ratified the Convention. A procedural protection applies in that no deprivation of nationality may be made without giving the individual concerned the right to a fair hearing by a court or other independent body.[49]

European Convention on Nationality

This guarantees that everyone shall have the right to a nationality, statelessness shall be avoided and that no one shall be arbitrarily deprived of his or her nationality, but only 21 European countries have ratified this Convention.[50]

The ECHR does not guarantee the right to citizenship but the ECtHR has stated that "it cannot be ruled out that an arbitrary denial of citizenship might in certain circumstances raise an issue under Article 8 of the Convention because of the impact of such a denial on the private life of the individual,"[51] and that "measures restricting the right to reside in a country may, in certain cases, entail a violation of Article 8 of the Convention if they create disproportionate repercussions on the private or family life, or both, of the individuals concerned."[52]

In 2020, in *Ghoumid v. France*, five individuals living in France who had dual nationality were convicted in Paris of participating in a criminal conspiracy to commit terrorism in 2007.[53] In 2015 the French citizenship of all the men was revoked. They complained to the ECtHR that the revocation had breached their right to respect for their private life and their family life, in violation of Article 8. The Court commented that in this case the deprivation of citizenship had no adverse consequences in the context of where these individuals could live and the impact on family life, because they had applied for residence permits and could contest any rejection if that occurred.

The Court examined the case to see if the deprivation of citizenship was arbitrary, which could have an impact on private life. They decided that the measures were lawful and that the individuals had been afforded substantial procedural safeguards and therefore the decision to revoke citizenship was not arbitrary. As the revocation did not render them stateless nor trigger deportation, it did not have disproportionate consequences for their family life. Despite the fact that the terrorist acts resulting in the convictions had occurred years before the stripping of citizenship, the Court was deferential to the Government's stance. Their justification for the revocation decision was that terrorist violence constituted a sufficiently serious threat to merit the stripping of citizenship, particularly as the decision to revoke was made in the wake of the increased terror attacks in France in 2015. The ECtHR did not find a violation of Article 8.[54]

In tandem with the substantive rights, the procedural guarantees that allow individuals to challenge how measures are imposed are equally important. In addition to guaranteeing rights to a fair trial in a criminal context, Article 6(1) ECHR extends this to the determination of a person's civil rights in a "fair and public hearing within a reasonable time by an independent and impartial tribunal established by law."

Sometimes civil, as opposed to human, political or public rights, may be affected by administrative measures taken by countries to deal with FTFs. However, this is quite a limited category. For example, Article 6 is not engaged in decisions involving "immigration or the entry, residence or removal of aliens,"[55] nor in cases concerning restrictions on movement,[56] but may apply in situations that may have "direct and significant repercussions on a private right belonging to an individual," as where restrictions might affect contact with family members.[57] If civil rights are affected, then any restriction affecting those rights must be open to challenge in judicial proceedings.[58] This means that if, for example, an individual claimed that his rights under Article 8 were violated, he would be entitled to a fair hearing to protect those civil rights.

Summary

The U.N. Resolutions were the trigger for states to enact legislation and issue regulations and policies to deal with the issues relating to FTFs both traveling to Iraq and Syria, as well as returning to their home countries. However, several of the terms used in the resolutions are unclear, particularly "foreign" and "terrorism." This could result in states crafting overbroad measures which have the potential for violating IHRL.

Turning to IHRL jurisprudence, the HR Committee, which has not opined on any cases relating to returning FTFs, does not appear to have been particularly deferential to State parties.[59] Furthermore, the U.N. Committee on the Rights of the Child decision on the admissibility of the case brought by the French grandparents, referred to above is very human rights-friendly, even though it is unclear how France would have jurisdiction over children in a Syrian camp.[60]

The ECtHR was even-handed in the 2006 Turkish case, in opining that the initial confiscation of the passport did not amount to a violation of Article 8 ECHR, but the delay of seven years to resolve the problem was deemed to violate Article 8.[61] However in the 2018 French citizenship deprivation case, the ECtHR was deferential to the decision to revoke the citizenship because of the seriousness of the threat of terrorism at a time when France was enduring an increase of terrorist acts and threats.[62]

Notes

1 U.N. S/RES/2178, (2014).
2 *Id.*, ¶5.
3 *Id.*, ¶8.
4 *Id.*, ¶6.
5 *Id.*, ¶9.
6 Organization for Security and Co-operation in Europe (OSCE), Guidelines for Addressing the Threats and Challenges of "Foreign Terrorist Fighters" within a Human Rights Framework (Ftf Guidelines) 22.
7 *Id., and see e.g.* Martin Scheinin, *Back to 9/11 Panic? Security Council Resolution on Foreign Terrorist Fighters*, Just Security, (Sep. 23, 2014), www.justsecurity.org/15407/post-911-panic-security-council-resolution-foreign-terrorist-fighters-scheinin/; Ben Emmerson, *New Counter Terrorism Measures: New Challenges for Human Rights*, 39, *in* Using Human Rights to Counter Terrorism, (Manfred Nowak and Anne Chabord, eds., Edward Elgar, 2018).
8 OSCE, FTF Guidelines, 24–5; Lisa Ginsborg, *One Step Forward, Two Steps Back: The Security Council, 'Foreign Fighters' and Human Rights*, 208, *in* Using Human Rights to Counter Terrorism; Elena Pokalova, Returning Islamist Foreign Fighters, 107, (Palgrave Macmillan, 2020).
9 Pokalova, Returning Islamist Foreign Fighters, 108.
10 *Id., citing* U.N.S.C. Counter-Terrorism Committee, Madrid Guiding Principles, S/2015/939, (Dec. 23, 2015).
11 U.N. S/RES/2396 (2017).
12 *Id.*, ¶¶5, 6, 11, 12, 13.
13 Pokalova, Returning Islamist Foreign Fighters, 110, *citing* U.N.S.C. Counter-Terrorism Committee, Annex to the letter dated December 28, 2018, from the Chair of the Security Council Committee established pursuant to resolution 1373 (2001) concerning counter-terrorism addressed to the President of the Security Council, 2018 Addendum to the 2015 Madrid Guiding Principles. S/2018/1177.

14 International Covenant on Civil and Political Rights, G.A. Res. 2200A (XXI), 21 U.N. GAOR Supp. (No. 16) at 52 U.N. Doc. A/6316 (1966), 999 U.N.T.S. 171 (entered into force Mar. 23, 1976), ("ICCPR"). As of March 2021, 173 countries are parties to this treaty, https://treaties.u.org/Pages/ViewDetails.aspx?src=TREATY&mtdmtdsgno=IV-4&chapter=4&clang=_en, (last accessed Mar. 16, 2021).

15 *See* Ilyasov v. Kazakhstan, HRC Communication No. 2009/2010, CCPR/C/111/D/2009/2010 (Sep. 4, 2014).

16 *Id.*, ¶¶6.11, 7.2, 7.3.

17 *Id.*, ¶7.8.

18 *Id.*, Joint opinion of Committee members Gerlad L. Neuman, Yuji Iwasawa and Walter Kälin, (concurring), ¶¶1–3.

19 Office of the High Commissioner for Human Rights, CCPR General Comment (GC) No. 27: Art. 12 (Freedom of Movement), Adopted at the Sixty-seventh session of the HRC on 2 November 1999, CCPR/C/21/Rev.1/Add.9, ¶9

20 *Id.*, ¶14.

21 Farag El Dernawi v. Libya, HRC Communication No. 1143/2002, CCPR/C/90/D/1143/2002 (Aug. 31, 2007).

22 *Id.*, ¶6.2.

23 HRC GC No. 27, ¶21.

24 HRC GC 35, CCPR/C/GC/35 (Dec. 16, 2014), ¶12, *noting that* the notion of arbitrariness includes elements of inappropriateness, injustice, lack of predictability and due process of law, reasonableness, necessity and proportionality.

25 *See e.g.* Deepan Budlakoti v. Canada, HRC Communication No. 2264/2013, CCPR/C/122/D/2264/2013, ¶9.4 (Aug. 29, 2018).

26 Convention on the Rights of the Child, ("CRC") adopted and opened for signature, ratification and accession by General Assembly resolution 44/25 of November 20, 1989, entry into force September 2, 1990, in accordance with art. 49. 197 states have signed it and all have ratified this except the United States.

27 U.N. Office of Counter-Terrorism, *Handbook, Children Affected by the Foreign-Fighter Phenomenon: Ensuring a Child Rights-Based Approach*, (Sep. 2018), www.un.org/counterterrorism/sites/www.un.org.counterterrorism/files/0918_ftf_handbook_web_reduced.pdf.

28 *Id.*, 27.

29 *Id.*, *citing* CRC, Art. 2.

30 *Id.*, *citing* CRC, Art. 3.

31 *Id.*, *citing* CRC, Art. 6.

32 *Id.*, *citing* CRC, Art. 12.

33 *Id.*, 31.

34 *Id.*, *citing* CRC, Art. 9.

35 U.N. Office of Counter-Terrorism, Statement by Mr. Vladimir Voronkov, Under-Secretary General of the U.N. Office of Counter-Terrorism, Twelfth Report of the Secretary General on the threat posed by ISIL (Da'esh) to international peace and security and the range of United Nations efforts in support of Member States in countering the threat, 3 (Feb. 10, 2021), www.un.org/counterterrorism/sites/www.un.org.counterterrorism/files/210210_usg_voronkov_statement_sc_briefing_12th_isil.pdf.

36 *Id.*

37 U.N. Committee on the Rights of the Child, Decision adopted by the Committee under the Optional Protocol to the Convention on the Rights of the Child on a communications procedure concerning communications No. 79/2019 and

No. 109/2019, CRC/C/85/D/79/2019 – CRC/C/85/D/109/2019 (Nov. 2, 2020) "CRC Decision 2020".

38 *Id.*, ¶¶9.7, 10.

39 *See e.g.* sections on extraterritorial jurisdiction in Part II. *See also* Agnes Callimard and Fionnuala Ni Aolain, Special Rapporteurs, *United Nations Human Rights Special Procedures, Extra-Territorial Jurisdiction of States over Children and Their Guardians in Camps, Prisons or Elsewhere in the Northern Syrian Arab Republic*, (2020), www.ohchr.org/Documents/Issues/Executions/UNSRsPublicJurisdictionAnalysis2020.pdf.

40 Marko Milanovic, *Repatriating the Children of Foreign Terrorist Fighters and the Extraterritorial Application of Human Rights*, EJIL: Talk! (Nov. 10, 2020), www.ejiltalk.org/repatriating-the-children-of-foreign-terrorist-fighters-and-the-extraterritorial-application-of-human-rights/.

41 European Convention for the Protection of Human Rights and Fundamental Freedoms, 213 U.N.T.S. 222 (entered into force Sep. 3, 1953), ("ECHR"). As of March 2021 47 states have ratified this Convention, https://coe.int/en/web/conventions/full-list/-/treaty/005/signatures, (last accessed Mar. 17, 2021).

42 Protocol No. 4 to the ECHR, ETS 46, (Sep. 16, 1963). As of March 2021 43 states have ratified Protocol 4. The United Kingdom and Turkey signed it, but have not ratified it, https://coe.int/en/web/conventions/full-list/-/treaty/046/signatures, (last accessed Mar. 17, 2021.

43 Iletmis v. Turkey, Appl. No. 29871/96, ECtHR, (Mar. 6, 2006).

44 *Id.*, ¶¶45–6.

45 *Id.*, ¶¶42, 50.

46 Laura van Waas and Sangita Jaghai, *All Citizens Are Created Equal, But Some Are More Equal Than Others*, 65 Netherlands International Law Review 413–30, (2018), https://doi.org/10.1007/s40802-018-0123-8.

47 Universal Declaration of Human Rights, Art. 15, U.N. Doc. A/RES/217 (III) (1948).

48 Convention Relating to the Status of Stateless Persons, Art. 1, U.N.T.S. Vol. 360, p. 117, (adopted Sep. 28, 1954, entry into force Jun. 6, 1960).

49 Convention on the Reduction of Statelessness, U.N.T.S., Vol. 989, p. 175 (adopted Aug. 30, 1961, entry into force Dec. 13, 1975). 73 countries have signed this Convention, including most European countries. The United States has not ratified this Convention.

50 European Convention on Nationality, ETS 166 (adopted Nov. 6, 1997, entry into force Nov. 6, 2000). Ratified by Albania, Austria, Bosnia, Bulgaria, Czech Republic, Denmark, Finland, Germany, Hungary, Iceland, Luxembourg, Montenegro, Netherlands, Norway, N. Macedonia, Norway, Portugal, Rep. of Moldova, Romania, Slovak Republic, Sweden, and Ukraine. Signed but not ratified by Croatia, France, Greece, Italy, Latvia, Malta, Poland, Russian Federation.

51 Ramadan v. Malta, Appl. No. 76136/12, ECtHR, ¶84, (Jun. 21, 2016).

52 Hoti v. Croatia, Appl. No. 63311/14, ECtHR, Final Judgment, ¶122, (Jul. 26, 2018).

53 Ghoumid and Others v. France, Appl. No. 52273/16 ECtHR, (Jun. 25, 2020) (in French only), ECtHR Press Release, Applicants stripped of nationality for terrorism-related offences: no violation of Covenant, ECtHR 191 (2020) (Jun. 25, 2020).

54 *Id.*

55 M.N. v. Belgium, Appl. No. 3599/18 ECtHR, ¶138, (May 5, 2020).

56 De Tommaso v. Italy, Appl. No. 43395/09. ECtHR, ¶146, ((Feb. 23, 2017).

57 *Id.*, ¶¶148, 151.
58 *Id.*, ¶149.
59 *See e.g.* Ilyasov v. Kazakhstan; Farag El Dernawi v. Libya.
60 CRC Decision 2020.
61 Iletmis v. Turkey.
62 Ghoumid v. France.

7 Domestic perspectives on foreign fighters

This chapter surveys the tools that are available for governments in a number of countries to use in order to keep their residents safe from the potential threat of terrorist activity from returning adult FTFs. The section will demonstrate the extent to which similar categories of measures – revoking citizenship and administrative measures that restrict liberty, freedom of movement, and association – are being used, and how countries are struggling to find effective deradicalizing, disengagement and reintegration programs. A sample of countries in Europe and elsewhere has been selected, based on availability of information in English. The largest amount of available data derives from the United Kingdom, and this is analyzed in depth.

Nearly all of the countries discussed would rather not repatriate their FTFs,[1] but if they did, prosecution of returnees would be their preferred way of dealing with the issue. Several countries, particularly France, wanted their nationals to be prosecuted by Iraqi courts in Syria and Iraq.[2] Table 7.1 shows that relatively few FTFs have been prosecuted.

Table 7.1 Prosecution of returning foreign fighters

Country	*Foreign fighters*	*Returnees*	*Prosecuted in home country*	*Most recent date of source of information*
Australia	230[3]	45[4]	2[5] = under 5%	March 2021
Belgium	478[6] (413)[7]	102 (125)[8]	30[9] = 29% maximum	March 2021
Canada	190[10]	60	13[11] = 21.6%	September 2020
Denmark	159[12]	67[13]	4[14] = 5.9%	March 2020
France	1,910	271 (302)[15]	200+[16] = 73.8%	January 2020
Germany	1050[17]	330+[18]	190+ in 2016[19] = 62.7%	January 2020
Israel	60	10	1[20] =10%	2019[21]
Italy	146[22]	12	3[23] = 25%	2019[24]

(*Continued*)

DOI: 10.4324/9780367817275-11

Table 7.1 (Continued)

Country	*Foreign fighters*	*Returnees*	*Prosecuted in home country*	*Most recent date of source of information*
Kazakhstan	500	125 voluntary returns, followed by repatriation of 516, comprising 22 men, 137 women, and 357 children[25]	57[26] adults = 15%	October 2019
United Kingdom	900+	400–425	Approximately 40[27] = 10%	April 2021
United States	129	28 comprising 12 adults and 16 children	10 = 83.3%	March 2021[28]

The main reason for the low rate of prosecution at home in many countries appears to be the difficulty of adducing sufficient admissible evidence to meet the criminal burden of proof in the different countries.[29] Therefore, the governments that are repatriating their FTFs are having to deal with the majority of their returnees in other ways.

A number of countries have introduced administrative measures such as travel bans and revocation of passports to prevent persons leaving and/or returning to their country of nationality or residence. Immigration law as a tool to control serious crime and terrorism seems attractive to governments because "in setting weaker procedural protections and lower standards of proof, it is regarded as more reliable than the slow, expensive, and uncertain passage of the criminal law process.[30] In addition to restricting movement, some countries have stripped citizenship from FTFs.

United Kingdom

Prosecution

As of May 2021, the United Kingdom had prosecuted about 10% of approximately 400 returning FTFs.[31] However, the only publicly available statistics comprise limited data displayed on the Crown Prosecution web site. An analysis conducted for the United Kingdom Independent Reviewer of the Terrorism Legislation of that data merely indicated that the number of successful prosecutions of returning FTFs were two in 2016, two in 2017, and two in 2018. Successful prosecutions of individuals who traveled or attempted to travel numbered eight in 2016, nine in 2017, and three in 2018, and of those who did not travel but were involved in support activity, prosecutions numbered nine in 2016 and two in 2017.[32]

The difficulties of prosecution have prompted a ministerial consultation to consider two proposals. The first concerns whether the outdated and largely defunct crime of treason should be redefined to cover membership or support of non-state actors such as terrorists who seek to harm the United Kingdom. The second proposal involves reversing the burden of proof required to prosecute a returning FTF.[33] The first proposal is not particularly controversial, but the second is. It remains to be seen if draft legislation will be published dealing with these proposals.

An unknown number of the other 90% of the returnees will have been assessed and dealt with in other ways. The table below[34] indicates that little is publicly known about how the United Kingdom has dealt with returning FTFs.

Table 7.2 Measures taken by United Kingdom to deal with returning foreign fighters

Year	*Denial of access to passport facilities*	*Seizing passports before travel*	*Temporary exclusion orders*	*Terrorism Prevention and Investigation Measures, maximum number during year*	*Deprivation of citizenship –on basis of being conducive to public good*
2013	6			9[35]	
2014	24			0 after February[36]	
2015	23	24		3[37]	
2016	17	15		7[38]	14
2017	14	14	9 (4 returned)	6	104
2018	5	5	16 (5 returned)	8	21
2019				6[39]	
2020				6, but 3 later in year[40]	

Restrictions on freedom to travel

The Counter-Terrorism and Security Act 2015 authorizes the seizure and temporary retention of travel documents of persons suspected of intending to leave the country in connection with terrorist-related activity for up to 14 days unless extended pursuant to a court order.[41] Passports do not confer citizenship; they are merely evidence of citizenship.[42] The British Home Secretary has the power to authorize the withdrawal of passport facilities for reasons that are necessary and proportionate, as for example in the case of persons who seek to harm the United Kingdom by travelling overseas to engage in terrorist activity, or who have travelled and who might wish to use those capabilities in an attack in the United Kingdom.[43]

Temporary Exclusion Orders (TEOs)

Temporary exclusion orders may be made in respect of overseas British residents or citizens with permission of a court, if the Secretary of State reasonably suspects that a person is or has been involved in terrorism-related activity outside the

United Kingdom and that such an order is necessary to protect the public from a risk of terrorism, provided that the person has a right of abode in the United Kingdom, and is outside the United Kingdom. In urgent cases an order may be made without court permission, provided all the other conditions are met.[44] TEOs can be in force for up to two years.[45] Their effect is also to invalidate the individual's passport during the exclusion period.[46] A notice must be served on the individual together with information on how to make an application for a permit to return.[47]

The Secretary of State may by notice impose some conditions on the permit to return. These consist of an obligation to report to a police station, to attend specified appointments, to notify police of the individual's place of residence and any change in the place of residence.[48] Returning without a permit or failure to comply with the conditions without a reasonable excuse are criminal offences punishable with up to five years imprisonment.[49]

An example of how this measure works is the case of QX, a British national, who was arrested in Istanbul in 2018 with his wife. The Secretary of State granted a TEO notice that banned QX on grounds of national security from returning to the United Kingdom for two years and invalidated his passport.[50] The notice was served on his solicitors. In 2019 he was deported from Turkey and he returned to the United Kingdom under a permit to return with a Notice of Obligations, including requirements to report to police daily, to notify police of any change of address and to attend appointments with a Home Office Desistance and Disengagement Program (DDP) mentor. QX was under criminal investigation at the same time.

QX complained about his mentor and the burden of daily reporting. The Notice of Obligations was varied by reducing the reporting obligations and changing the mentor to a theologian in October 2019. Two weeks later QX complained about the new mentor, questioning his qualifications and expressing concerns about protecting the privacy of any information given by QX to the mentor. The Home Office responded that the TEO would continue as it was, on the grounds of that it was still necessary and proportionate for protecting the public from a risk of terrorism.

QX applied to the High Court for a review of the TEO and the Obligations. In this type of application, the Court is permitted to use a "closed material" procedure.[51] In essence, sensitive material can be withheld from the individual and his legal representative, and such material is evaluated in a closed court session before a judge, attended by the prosecutor and a special advocate who represents the interests of the individual. The special advocate may only speak to the individual and his representative before the special advocate has seen the closed material.[52] If the prosecution wishes to rely on sensitive material in a closed session of the court, or withhold closed material from the individual and his representative on the grounds that disclosing it would be contrary to the public interest, the Secretary of State must obtain permission from the court.

QX's lawyer argued that Article 6 ECHR (right to a fair and public hearing in determining his civil rights) was engaged and that the obligations of the TEO violated Article 8 ECHR (interference with private life).[53] The British courts had previously ruled that "a breach of Article 8 is a breach of a civil right in the form of a statutory tort."[54] The Secretary of State argued *inter alia* that the admission of British citizens and the conditions for taking up the right to abode fall within a category of "hard core of public-authority prerogatives" which are outside the scope of the civil rights referred to in Article 6 ECHR.[55]

Here, the Court ruled that the right of abode of a citizen changes, or becomes "qualified," if the citizen returns to the United Kingdom pursuant to a TEO permit to return. The effect of this is that the qualified right of abode, an immigration measure, falls within the "hard core of public-authority prerogatives," outside the scope of Article 6.[56] However, the Court did not accept that the TEO Obligations were also immigration measures, commenting that the purpose of the Obligations is to protect national security.[57] The Court considered that the combination of Obligations in this case caused "direct and material" interference with QX's right to respect for private life under Article 8, and that Article 6(1) was engaged.[58]

The Court went on to consider QX's complaint relating to the closed material procedure, about the extent of disclosure of material that had been made to him and his legal representative. The guidelines for this derive from a European landmark decision in the context of preventive detention[59] and a British seminal case that evaluated closed material procedures in the now-repealed counter-terrorism measure of control orders:[60]

> the controlee must be given sufficient information about the allegations against him to enable him to give effective instructions in relation to those allegations. Provided that this requirement is satisfied there can be a fair trial notwithstanding that the controlee is not provided with the detail or the sources of the evidence forming the basis of the allegations. Where, however, the open material consists of purely general assertions and the case against the controlee is based solely, or to a decisive degree on closed materials, the requirements of a fair trial will not be satisfied, however cogent the case based on the closed materials may be.

In this case QX could give information to his legal advisors and his special advocate as to whether he traveled to Syria, and the reason for his travel. However, the Court considered that the closed material that it had seen contained more specific information that might have an impact on whether the Obligations were necessary and proportionate. The Court requested the Secretary of State to provide clarification and adjourned its decision on this issue.[61] A further open hearing took place some months later limited to a determination of whether a substantive hearing to evaluate the Obligations would be compatible with Article 6, and the Court ruled that as it considered that there was no breach of Article 6, the matter could proceed.[62] As of September 2021, the substantive hearing had not yet taken place.

Terrorism Prevention and Investigation Measures (TPIMs)

These administrative restrictions,[63] which were introduced in 2012[64] to replace the previous, more stringent, control orders[65] are designed to disrupt terrorist activity and facilitate investigations.[66] TPIMS are imposed by a notice by the Home Secretary who must be satisfied on the balance of probabilities that an individual is or has been involved in terrorism-related activity, that some or all of the relevant activity is new terrorism-related activity, and that the Secretary of State reasonably considers that it is necessary to impose the measures, both for the purpose of protecting the public and for purposes connected with preventing or restricting the individual's involvement in terrorist-related activity.[67] Generally the Secretary of State must apply to a court for permission to impose TPIMs, but in urgent cases the Secretary may impose an order without prior permission.[68] In such situations the Secretary of State must apply to a Court for confirmation that decisions resulting in the imposition of the order were not flawed.[69] In all situations (other than the Court confirmation of an urgent order) the recipient of the TPIM order has the right to challenge the orders in court and to make applications to vary the terms during the currency of the order.[70]

TPIMS can last for up to two years,[71] and a number of restrictive measures can be imposed, relating to overnight residence, travel, exclusions from various locations, access to financial services, transferring property, the use of electronic communication devises, a ban on having firearms, associating with particular persons, not to do certain work or studies, reporting, and monitoring.[72] Failure to comply with the terms of TPIM without reasonable excuse is a criminal offense in itself, carrying a maximum sentence of five years imprisonment.[73] Four such prosecutions took place in 2019.[74]

As shown in Table 7.2, since the imposition of TPIMs, relatively few have been in force, considering the large numbers of open MI5 and police open investigations. In 2019, second TPIMs were made for the first time against two individuals, in respect of new terrorism-related activity.[75] There have been questions about whether TPIMs are sufficiently stringent for their purpose of managing the risk of FTFs. For example, in a 2019 case involving deprivation of citizenship, a SIAC panel commented that TPIMs were not the most effective way of managing the risk of someone perceived to be very dangerous.[76]

Not all investigations or imposition of TPIMs relate to returning FTFs, but details about TPIMs do not appear to be widely reported, or even reported at all. The Home Secretary was asked during a Parliamentary debate in February 2019 how many returning foreign fighters were subject to TPIMs. His response was that "it was something that was not appropriate to discuss."[77]

Surveillance

The cost both financially and in terms of human resources in providing daily round the clock surveillance of more than 400 returnees, in addition to the many persons in the United Kingdom currently suspected to be involved in Islamist and right-wing extremism,[78] is enormous if not prohibitive. It has been suggested that surveillance would only be possible for the highest-risk returnees, and perhaps this would have to be managed in the community by police and local council officials.[79] The problems surrounding surveillance were highlighted in the two instances where convicted terrorists who were released from prison and were under surveillance, carried out terror attacks: Usman Khan in London on November 29, 2019;[80] and Sudesh Amman in London on February 2, 2020.[81] The later attack prompted a review of whether control orders should be reintroduced.[82] Although these two attacks were not carried out by returning FTFs, the issues highlighted here are applicable to returnees.

Revoking citizenship

Between 2016 and the end of 2019 approximately 139 suspected jihadists had been stripped of their British nationality and prevented from returning to the U.K.,[83] including at least 20 currently held in camps run by Syrian Democratic Forces.[84] Since then no numbers have been publicized. One of the most well-known cases is that of Shamima Begum, which is discussed in depth below. However, other "household" names of suspected terrorists are also in the list, including Abu Hamza,[85] "Beatles" Shafee El Sheikh "George," and Alexanda Kotey "Ringo,"[86] and "Jihadi Jack" Letts.[87]

Under the British Nationality Act 1981 (as amended) a person may be deprived of British citizenship as a counter-terrorism measure in two situations: if the Home Secretary is satisfied that the deprivation is conducive to the public good, provided that such an order would not make the individual stateless;[88] or if, in respect of a naturalized British citizen, the Home Secretary is satisfied that the deprivation is conducive to the public good because the person has conducted him/herself in a manner that is seriously prejudicial to the vital interests on the United Kingdom, and that the Home Secretary has reasonable grounds for believing that the individual is able to become a national of another country.[89]

This last limb is subject to an obligation that this power must be independently reviewed after the first year and then every three years.[90] An Independent Review of the U.K. Terrorism Legislation in 2016 highlights the fact that this second power still has the capacity to render a person stateless.[91] It also notes that this power has been criticized for being extremely broad, and that it may be used without the need to obtain prior judicial approval.[92] The 2019 Review has not yet been published.

One of the first cases involving a naturalized British FTF reached the ECtHR in 2017. K2 was born in Sudan and was naturalized in 2000. He was arrested and released on bail for a public order offense arising from participating in protests against Israeli military action in Gaza in 2009. While on bail he was alleged to have travelled to Somalia where he was involved in terrorist activities linked to Al-Shabaab, before continuing on to Sudan.

In June 2010 he was notified of the Secretary of State's decisions to deprive him of his British citizenship on the grounds that it would be conducive to the public good, and to exclude him from the United Kingdom because of his involvement in terrorism-related activities and links to a number of Islamist extremists.[93] The court proceedings in the United Kingdom continued until the end of 2015, during which time K2's wife and child returned to Sudan. The multiple court proceedings ruled that the Secretary of State had been justified to deprive K2 of his citizenship, that K2 was aware of the allegations against him, that there was no requirement in EU law mandating that he be present for his appeal, and that his right to family life was not infringed.[94] His application to the ECtHR mainly concerned the issue of whether the fact that he was not present in the United Kingdom prevented him from participating in his appeal.

The ECtHR reiterated that it had accepted that

> an arbitrary denial of citizenship might, in certain circumstances, raise an issue under Article 8 of the Convention because of its impact on the private life of the individual. . . . In determining whether a revocation of citizenship is in breach of Article 8, the Court has addressed two separate issues: whether the revocation was arbitrary; and what the consequences of revocation were for the applicant.[95]

Arbitrariness in this context means a revocation that is not in accordance with the law, or a revocation that was not accompanied by necessary procedural safeguards, such as an opportunity to challenge the decision, and if the authorities had not acted diligently or swiftly.[96] It is also a "stricter standard than that of proportionality."[97]

In this case, the question whether the deprivation was in accordance with the law was not at issue, and there was no evidence that the authorities had not acted swiftly or diligently.[98] The ECtHR did not accept that the lack of his presence would necessarily render a decision to revoke citizenship arbitrary. It did not exclude the possibility that

> an Article 8 issue might arise when there exists clear and objective evidence that the person was unable to instruct lawyers or give evidence while outside the jurisdiction; however Article 8 cannot be interpreted so as to impose a positive obligation on Contracting States to facilitate the return of every person deprived of citizenship while outside the jurisdiction in order to pursue an appeal against that decision.[99]

Here, K2 had been able to judicially review the decision to exclude him from the United Kingdom, and the ECtHR could not ignore the fact that the procedural difficulties being complained of were "not a natural consequence" of the Secretary of State's decisions: the Court of Appeal had noted that K2 had to conduct his appeal from outside the United Kingdom because of "his decision to flee the country before he was required to surrender to his bail."[100] The Court found no breach of either Articles 8 or 14.[101]

The case of Shamima Begum created widespread interest in the U.K. from the moment she left Bethnal Green in East London in 2015 as a 15-year-old schoolgirl, together with two friends, to join ISIS.[102] Her parents were born and married in Bangladesh. Her mother was naturalized as a British subject, but her father was not naturalized, although he had been granted indefinite leave to remain.

Ms. Begum was born and grew up in the United Kingdom and acquired British citizenship by birth. When she arrived in Raqqa she applied to marry an ISIS fighter. She had three children, all of whom died. Since the fall of the Caliphate she has been detained by the Syrian Democratic Forces in a displaced person camp in dire conditions. To some people, she is a heartless, dangerous suspected terrorist who said "when I saw my first severed head in a bin it didn't faze me at all."[103] To others, she is a child soldier and victim deserving of some level of sympathy.[104]

On February 19, 2019, The Home Secretary signed an order that deprived Ms. Begum of her British citizenship on the grounds that the decision was in the public good. She was described as a British/Bangladeshi dual national (having acquired Bangladeshi citizenship by descent, according to Bangladeshi law)[105] who presented a risk to the United Kingdom because she had traveled to Syria and "aligned with ISIS," and because she had dual nationality, the order would not make her stateless.[106] However, the Bangladesh Ministry of Foreign Affairs is reported to have stated that she is not a Bangladeshi citizen and she will not be permitted to enter the country.[107] Ms. Begum sought leave to enter the United Kingdom, which was also refused. She had sought a waiver of a Home Office biometrics policy requiring the provision of her fingerprints and a photograph of her face. The request for a waiver was denied.

Leaving aside the very complicated technicalities of the way the case went through the courts via the Special Immigration Appeals Commission (SIAC), the High Court (Administrative Court), the Court of Appeal and the Supreme Court, she appealed both decisions, and three issues were directed to be determined in various hearings: (1) whether the deprivation decision rendered Ms. Begum stateless; (2) whether either of the deprivation or leave to enter decisions violated what was described as the "extra-territorial human rights policy," because she was exposed to a risk of death or degrading treatment if she returned to Bangladesh or Iraq; and (3) whether it was possible for her to have a fair and effective appeal against the deprivation decision without being in the United Kingdom. Both SIAC[108] and the Administrative Court rejected the appeals.[109]

Ms. Begum appealed again, in a complicated court procedure involving the Administrative Court sitting concurrently with the Court of Appeal with the same judges. The Court struggled to find a satisfactory way to resolve the competing issues of satisfying the national security concerns about Ms. Begum, alongside the Court's acknowledgment that she could not effectively mount a fair and effective appeal against the deprivation decision from a prison camp in Syria, where she was living in appalling conditions.

The solution the Court reached was to allow Ms. Begum's appeal against the decision that denied her the right to enter the U.K., because "given that the only way she can have a fair and effective appeal is to be permitted to come into the United Kingdom to pursue her appeal, fairness and justice must, on the facts of this case, outweigh the national security concerns."[110] The effect of that would be that the Secretary of State would be required to grant her leave to enter and provide her with necessary travel documents. The Court also ordered that there be judicial review by SIAC of its decision relating to whether the extraterritorial human rights policy was violated by the deprivation decision.[111] The Court also ordered that Ms. Begum should be given leave to enter and provided with travel documents.[112]

At this stage, a small shift towards human rights can be perceived. However, the Secretary of State appealed the decisions to the Supreme Court, which took a 180-degree turn. The Court reviewed the factual background, including material from the Security Service outlining the perceived risks of people returning from ISIS-controlled territory. That material suggested that persons who had spent a lengthy period of time in ISIS-controlled territory were deemed likely to have developed the capability to carry out an attack, and the resulting possible risks included involvement in the planning of ISIS-directed or enabled attacks, radicalizing and recruiting U.K.-based associates, providing support to ISIS operatives, and posing a latent threat to the U.K.[113] In March 2018 the Security Service had advised the Prime Minister that "the national security threat from UK-linked-ISIL-aligned individuals would increase significantly if they returned to the UK."[114]

The Government had been provided with Mistreatment Risk Statements that assessed whether Ms. Begum might be at risk of harm in violation of Articles 2 or 3 ECHR (right to life and right to fair treatment) as a direct consequence of a deprivation decision. In general, the statements concluded that a person who is deprived of their British citizenship is unlikely to be treated very differently from a person with British citizenship. As to the likelihood of Ms. Begum being transferred to Bangladesh, the Security Service did not consider that repatriation to Bangladesh was a foreseeable result of depriving her of British citizenship, so there was no real risk of her returning there and being mistreated.[115] In principle, leaving her to live nowhere but in the deplorable conditions of the Syrian camp might violate Articles 2 or 3 ECHR, but the Government's view was that as she was no longer a British citizen, the ECHR could not apply extraterritorially to her situation.[116]

The first hint that there would be a significant shift towards deference came in the Supreme Court's analysis of the powers of SIAC and the limitations of the complicated appeal process of SIAC decisions. The Court, through Lord Reed, favored the approach of Lord Hoffman in a landmark 2001 deportation decision, in which he had said that SIAC's appellate limitations "arise from the need, in matters of judgement, and evaluation of evidence, to show proper deference to the primary decision maker," which is not SIAC, but the Secretary of State,[117] and continued to reinforce that in many appeal issues before SIAC.

> An appellate body traditionally allows a considerable margin to the primary decision maker. Even if the appellate body prefers a different view, it should not ordinarily interfere with a case in which it considers that the view of the Home Secretary is one that could reasonably be entertained. . . . Such

> decisions [relating to national security], with serious potential results for the community, require a legitimacy which can be conferred only by entrusting them to persons responsible to the community through the democratic process.[118] However, SIAC can, on the basis of its own assessment determine if the Secretary of State has acted incompatibly with the ECHR.[119]

In considering the question of whether the deprivation decision would violate natural justice if Ms. Begum could not have a fair and effective appeal, Lord Reed commented that as justice is not one-sided, an appeal should not be allowed "merely because the appellant finds herself unable to present her appeal effectively: that would be unjust to the respondent."[120] In cases of a temporary problem, a court might stay the proceedings until the issue is resolved, but if it cannot be resolved the case will proceed. If the forensic disadvantage is sufficiently serious, an appellant is likely to lose the case.[121] If one party is at a forensic disadvantage and it is impossible for the case to be fairly tried, the proceedings may have to be stayed and struck out in the interests of justice, because it cannot be tried at all.[122]

In this case Lord Reed followed judicial precedent, commenting that

> It would be irresponsible for the court to allow the [deprivation] appeal without any regard to the interests of national security which prompted the decision in question, and it is difficult to conceive that the law would require it to do so.[123]

In relation to the appeal by the Secretary of State against the Court of Appeal's decision granting Ms. Begum leave to enter, Lord Reed concluded that the Court of Appeal had erred, first because the only basis for allowing Ms. Begum's appeal would have been if the original denial of entry was unlawful pursuant to British human rights legislation, and this had not been argued.[124] Second, the Court of Appeal "appears to have overlooked the limitations to its competence, both institutional and constitutional, to decide questions of national security."[125] Its approach had not given the Home Secretary's assessment of the facts and risks "the respect which it should have received."[126] The Court unanimously allowed the Secretary of State's appeals and dismissed Ms. Begum's cross-appeal, stating that the appropriate way to deal with her problems would be by staying her appeal until she was able to play an effective part in it without compromising public safety.[127] Shamima Begum therefore remains in the camp in Syria, but her case may not be over. She could try to re-open her case in the United Kingdom if circumstances merit it or petition the ECtHR for relief.

In another case in July 2021 Mr. Justice Chamberlain of the High Court adjudicated on the procedural requirement of notifying a person that their citizenship had been revoked.[128] The issue concerned the method of notifying a person whose whereabouts are unknown, where there is no address for correspondence and no known representative. Regulation 10(4), which sets out the methods of notification, states that "the notice shall be deemed to have been given" when the Secretary of State notes the circumstances and places a copy of the notice on the person's file.[129] The Judge concluded that "Parliament did not give the

Home Secretary power to make regulations that treat notice as having been given to the person affected when it has not been given to that person, but instead has simply been placed on a Home Office file." He declared Regulation 10(4) *ultra vires.*[130] He ruled that as a consequence, the Home Secretary had no power to make the order of removing British citizenship from a woman held in a Syrian camp, and that the actual order made was invalid and a nullity.[131] Unsurprisingly, the Home Office are considering whether or not to appeal this decision.[132]

Desistance and disengagement programs

In addition to the United Kingdom's Prevent program, which is designed to stop people becoming radicalized in the first place,[133] Desistance and Disengagement Programs (DDP) were launched in 2016, initially to support persons on probation license after conviction of a terrorist offence, and expanded to include persons on TPIMs, and returned FTFs subject to TEOs. The program provides a range of intensive, tailored interventions and practical support, including mentoring, psychological support as well as theological and ideological advice, and is mandatory in certain cases. In such cases, non-compliance can lead to charges for breach of conditions.[134] Deradicalization is not the goal of DDP; the aim is to "change behaviors."[135] Problems have arisen regarding the choice, qualification and utility of theological mentors, as well as the behavior and level of engagement of individuals attending DDPs.[136]

Thirty people went on the program in 2016–17, and 86 participated in 2017–18,[137] and at least 110 in 2018–19.[138] It is not yet known how many of those were returnees, nor how successful the program is in deterring terror attacks,[139] but its effectiveness has been questioned[140] following the terror attack perpetrated by Usman Khan in London on November 29, 2019,[141] and by Sudesh Amman in London on February 2, 2020.[142]

Australia

Prosecution

Australian authorities have stated that prosecution is the preferred option to deal with its returnees. As of March 2020, Australia had prosecuted two individuals, a mere 5% of its estimated 45 returnees, and no returnees have been charged with substantive offenses such as murder.[143] The reason given for the low number of prosecutions is the difficulty of collecting admissible evidence.[144]

Restrictions on freedom to travel

Specific FTF legislation had been enacted in 2014, which *inter alia* proscribes entering a foreign country with the intention of engaging in hostile activity, engaging in hostile activity in a foreign country, engaging in preparatory acts, and entering or remaining in declared areas where terrorist organizations are engaging in hostile activity.[145] The "declared area" provisions, which currently only apply to Mosul and were due to expire on September 7, 2021, were the subject of a parliamentary inquiry in September 2020.[146] Complaints had been made that these provisions do not just deter travel as intended, but criminalize mere travel without any showing of intent, thereby infringing freedom of movement and the right to family life.[147] The Committee decided that it was not prudent to repeal the provisions at this time, that the provisions would be extended for another three years and that it "*may* review the operation, effectiveness and proportionality of the provisions by 7 January 2024."[148]

Australian authorities can refuse the issue of, or cancel a passport on national security grounds.[149] Since 2014, if the Director General of Security suspects that a person may leave Australia to engage in conduct that might prejudice Australia or a foreign country, he may request the Minister to suspend travel documents for 14 days, and once suspended, an officer may request the surrender of the passport.[150] A suspension order can only be renewed if new information is discovered by Australian Intelligence.[151]

These powers pay little heed to human rights protections, even though an explanatory memorandum attached to the 2014 Foreign Fighters Bill maintained that the powers were consistent with the ICCPR and were "reasonable and necessary" to protect national security.[152] However, rights to administrative review of the powers are restricted, and the right to judicial review is non-existent.[153] Consequently, no case law exists to be reviewed in this section. In any event, Australian immigration jurisprudence is shrouded in secrecy. Between February 2014 and March 2017, 36 passports were suspended, and 137 passports cancelled.[154]

Temporary Exclusion Orders (TEOs)

Australia enacted legislation in 2019 permitting a temporary exclusion order (TEO) for up to two years to be made in relation to any Australian citizen over the age of 14 who is located outside the country.[155] A TEO may not be made unless either the Minister reasonably suspects that it would substantially assist in preventing a terrorist act, or preventing the giving of training to a listed terrorist group, or providing support for an act of terrorism or a terrorist group, or the Australian Security Intelligence Organization (AIO) has assessed that the person is a direct or indirect risk to security for reasons related to politically motivated violence.[156] If the Minister wishes to make an order in respect of a person aged between 14 and 17, regard must be had to the "protection of the community as a paramount consideration," and "the best interests of the person as a primary consideration," with specified criteria to be taken into account.[157]

Once the Minister has made the TEO, it must be reviewed as soon as is practicable by a judicial authority which must see a written statement of reasons supported by all the material justifying the order.[158] An application may be made to the Minister or relevant Department to revoke the TEO with a statement as to why.[159] The statute is silent as to the timing and process for an application to revoke.

The statute sets out the criteria for issuing permits to return if the Minister considers it appropriate.[160] Conditions may be imposed on return permits, provided that the Minister considers the impact of imposing conditions and is satisfied that the conditions are reasonably necessary, and reasonably appropriate for the purpose of preventing terrorist activity.[161] The conditions cover a range of restrictions and requirements,[162] some of which are similar to those in control orders which are mentioned below. Return permits can be varied or revoked in certain specified situations.[163] Failure to comply with a condition is a criminal offence, punishable by a sentence of imprisonment for two years.[164]

It is possible to make applications to obtain return permits, as well as to revoke or vary them,[165] but the statute is silent both as to the necessary criteria to achieve success in making such applications, and procedural requirements. Perhaps the most startling clause in the statute is section 26: "The Minister is not required to observe any requirements of procedural fairness in exercising a power or performing a function under this Act." Lack of procedural fairness in the administration of TEOs is likely to trigger complaints of violations of the ICCPR. In the year 2019–20, five TEOs were made. One was revoked and one return permit was issued.[166]

Preventative detention and control orders

Legislation creating preventative detention of terror suspects was enacted in 2005, but only one person has been subject to an interim preventative detention order, in 2015.[167] As far as can be discerned from available governmental annual reports, this has not been used as a method for dealing with returning FTFs.

A member of the Australian Federal Police (AFP) may apply for a preventative detention order to prevent an imminent terrorist act occurring within the next 14 days.[168] The officer must reasonably suspect that a person will engage in a terrorist act or possesses something connected with the preparation for or engagement in a terrorist act, or has done an act in preparation for, or in planning a terrorist act that is capable of being carried out and could occur within the next 14 days.[169] Federal detention may not exceed 48 hours in total,[170] but the states have enacted complementary legislation that permits detention to be extended to up to 14 days.[171] Rights to challenge a detention order are very limited. A person merely has the right to make representations to a senior AFP officer with a view to having the order revoked, but there appears to be no mechanism in the statute to have the order revoked.[172]

Control orders share many features of the United Kingdom's system of TPIMs, with a set of similar obligations, restrictions and prohibitions.[173] Since 2014, the regime has been adapted to make it useful for dealing with returning FTFs. A control order may not last more than 12 months, but there is no restriction on the number of successive control orders that may be imposed on the same person.[174]

An AFP officer must obtain the consent of the Attorney General before applying to a court for an interim control order[175] for anyone except those under the age of 14.[176] The foreign fighter phenomenon sparked a number of changes to the control order regime.[177] The evidentiary threshold for obtaining a control order is lower than that required for obtaining the British TPIM. The AFP must have a reasonable suspicion that the order would substantially assist in preventing a terrorist act, or the support for, or facilitation of a terrorist act, or that the person has provided or received training from, or participated in training with a listed terrorist organization, or has engaged in a hostile activity in a foreign country, or has been convicted in Australia or elsewhere of a terrorist offence, or has provided support for or otherwise facilitated the engagement in a hostile activity in a foreign country.[178] Once the Attorney General has given consent, the AFP officer can apply to a court for an interim order, and an order will only be issued if the court is satisfied on the balance of probabilities as to the above grounds, and that the each of the obligations to be applied are reasonably necessary and appropriate and are adapted for the purpose of protecting the public from a terrorist act or for preventing the provision of support for or the facilitation of a terrorist act in Australia or abroad.[179]

The interim control order, which contains a date upon which it will take effect,[180] must be served on the person concerned as soon as is reasonably practicable, but in any event at least 48 hours before the specified start date.[181] The person has the right to obtain legal advice and representation, and may adduce evidence in a hearing to prevent the confirmation of the control order.[182] In 2016 closed material proceedings with a special advocate scheme were introduced,[183] similar to the special advocate program in the United Kingdom. Only 16 control orders have been made up to August 2020, of which five were not confirmed.[184]

Revoking citizenship

Under the Australian Citizenship Amendment (Allegiance to Australia) Act 2015, persons over the age of 14 holding dual nationality can lose their Australian citizenship in three ways:[185] such individuals are deemed to have renounced Australian citizenship automatically, either by engaging in, recruiting for or financing terrorist activity;[186] or through service outside Australia in armed forces of an enemy country or of a declared terrorist organization;[187] and a Minister may determine that a person ceases to be an Australian citizen if that person has been convicted of a terrorism offense and received a sentence of at least six years imprisonment.[188]

Notice of the revocation, and the reasons for it, must be given to the affected person,[189] who is entitled to seek review of "the basis on which the notice was given" in the High Court of Australia or the Federal Court of Australia. However, a notice can be withheld if the relevant Minister is satisfied that the giving of a notice could prejudice the security, defense or international relations of Australia or Australian law enforcement operations, or contrary to the public interest.[190] It is therefore quite difficult to challenge the revocation of citizenship.[191]

Between December 2015 and February 2019, twelve Australian dual citizens had their citizenship revoked because of their involvement with terror groups.[192] There are a number of concerns whether adequate procedural safeguards exist to ensure that any affected individual does in fact have dual nationality. For example, the Parliamentary Joint Committee on Intelligence and Security acknowledged that some of the provisions in the legislation had an "automatic" nature, with the Minister having a role limited to exempting individuals from the provisions or restoring lost citizenship. The Committee accepted that while depriving citizenship could be a useful counter-terrorism tool in some circumstances, it may have unintended consequences and should be subject to limitations and safeguards as well as be regularly reviewed. The Committee opined that the current "operation of law" model of automatic renouncement of citizenship as a result of a person's actions should be replaced by a ministerial decision-making model.[193]

Deradicalization and disengagement

Australia started to move its focus from purely policing to deradicalization and disengagement as early as 2010.[194] In 2014 the government awarded grants to over 40 organizations to work on deradicalization efforts that focused on youth engagement, social cohesion and education with the aim of constructing a counter narrative that advocates a peaceful or moderate Islam.[195] Meaningful data that assess the effectiveness of these initiatives are unavailable. The existing programs may offer some opportunities to deal with returning foreign fighters, particularly programs that target at-risk youths, or those that challenge extremist narratives. It seems that some of these programs do complement the law enforcement approach to some extent,[196] but they still rely heavily on the security services and are not really adequate to address radicalization in the long term.[197]

Belgium

Prosecution

Belgium reportedly has the highest ratio of foreign FTFs and returnees in Europe.[198] As of 2019, it had prosecuted 29% of its returnees. As in the other countries discussed, it is likely that the reason for the low rate of prosecution stems from lack of evidence and the government would prefer that their FTFs are detained and prosecuted in the country where they committed crimes.[199]

Pre-trial preventive detention

A returning FTF is systematically arrested and appears before an investigating magistrate who will assess whether pre-trial preventive detention is necessary.[200] Pre-charge detention is limited to two days.[201] In August 2016 the law on preventive detention[202] was amended. This is authorized in cases of absolute necessity for public security in the case of terrorist offences for which the maximum penalty exceeds five years.[203] In March 2018 the Belgian Constitutional Court ruled that this provision was not unconstitutional in that the "legislation does not disproportionately infringe the rights of the people concerned due to the special circumstances of terrorist offences, which might require stronger preventive measures that may not apply in other criminal offences."[204]

There is no maximum duration for detention,[205] but it is reviewed first within five days of the order, then after one month, and then every two months. A number of procedural safeguards exist. The person must be told the reason for arrest and is entitled to legal representation in interviews and court hearings when the order is reviewed and at any appeals.[206] Since 2014 a person can be detained at their home under electronic monitoring. There is no limitation of time on this and in cases of non-compliance, this can be converted into detention in prison.[207]

Pre-trial detention is justified for individuals who pose a security threat or a risk of disappearing before a trial, so this is likely to mean that it will be deemed justified for every returnee. They will either remain in custody until trial or will be released on strict conditions and supervision.[208]

Enhanced individualized monitoring and surveillance can be ordered of returnees, as well as electronic tagging.[209]

Revoking citizenship

Since 1934 the Belgian government has been able to strip individuals of citizenship if those persons were found to have seriously breached their duties as Belgian citizens,[210] but this measure was first used for counter-terrorist purposes in 1996.[211] Since 2015, the law has been modified to permit the stripping of Belgian citizens who hold dual nationality, if they have been convicted of terrorism offenses and sentenced to at least five years imprisonment.[212] Seventeen individuals were reported to have lost their citizenship between November 2017 and January 2020,[213] and another 14 dual citizens FTFs were stripped of Belgian citizenship in December 2020. As the whereabouts of most of the 14 were unknown, the Belgian authorities published an announcement of the revocation of their Belgian citizenship in newspapers as the only way to convey the information.[214]

Disengagement and deradicalization

Although the overall approach to foreign fighters involves the criminal justice model, other programs are evolving slowly.[215] Generally, the response is "structured around three core principles: a multi-agency approach, subsidiarity, and information-sharing." Subsidiarity means that the most relevant level of agency should be in the lead.[216] Belgian authorities have stated that they wish to introduce disengagement and deradicalization programs with a socio-preventive dimension which involve monitoring and mentoring,[217] but these are tailored first and foremost to the prison population. These programs have not yet been rolled out over the whole country, and some of those that do exist are in the earliest stages.[218] One study concludes that the programs are more geared towards disengagement than deradicalization.[219]

Canada

Very little is known of the approach taken by the Canadian government. Canada is struggling to monitor its returnees,[220] and many are expressing frustration that Canada appears to be doing nothing.[221] However, reports suggest that not many are returning because Canada is very reluctant to bring its citizens – even its child citizens – home.[222] A report in June 2020 estimated that at least 47 Canadians, most of which are women and children, were being detained in camps in Syria by the Syrian Democratic Forces.[223] In October 2020, the Canadian government bowed to criticism and pressure, and repatriated a five-year old orphan to live with an aunt and uncle, with the caveat that the child was the only person in the family who would be permitted to return.[224]

Prosecution and other measures

As of August 2019, Canada had prosecuted 6.6% of its returnees. How much of this is caused by evidentiary problems as opposed to a lack of political will is not known.[225] Public Safety Minister Ralph Goodale has publicly stated that a "full suite of measures" are being used – including surveillance, interrogations, further investigations, intelligence-gathering and lawful sharing, continuing threat assessments, no-fly listings, Criminal Code listings, terrorism peace bonds[226] and legally authorized threat-reduction measures.[227] However, the detail is largely lacking.

Canceling passports

Canada began canceling passports of Canadians who traveled to join extremist groups in Syria and Iraq in 2014.[228] Under the Canadian Passport Order, the Minister of Public Safety may cancel a passport if he has reasonable grounds to suspect that this would be necessary to prevent the commission of a terrorist offense, or for the national security of Canada or of a foreign country or state.[229] Within 30 days of becoming aware of the cancellation, the passport holder may apply in writing for a reconsideration of the decision, and after considering the representations the minister shall decide if reasonable grounds still exist to justify the cancellation. The passport holder can appeal an unfavorable decision to the Federal Court within thirty days of receiving notice of the decision.[230] Public Safety Canada may conduct an investigation to consider if the passport should be revoked. The applicant will be given an unclassified statement of reasons together with an opportunity to respond. If a passport has been revoked, the decision is final, but the applicant can apply for judicial review of the decision by the Federal Court.[231] No data can be found about the number of passports of FTFs that have been canceled or revoked.

Revoking citizenship

In May 2014 Canada enacted legislation to revoke the citizenship of dual citizens convicted of terrorism.[232] This law was repealed in 2017, and citizenship can now only be revoked if the person committed fraud, misrepresented themselves or knowingly hid information in an immigration application.[233] The previous system of automatic revocation was replaced by a hearing in Federal Court prior to any order of revocation.[234]

Preventing radicalization and disengagement

In December 2018 Canada announced its National Strategy on Countering Radicalization to Violence.[235] Its main stated focus is on preventing radicalization in the first place. One small section is devoted to the issue of "Returning Extremist Travelers." The primary strategy is to prosecute them, but very few have been. In addition, the methods referred to above by Mr. Goodale are listed. The strategy ends with a brief reference to disengagement measures, which are not defined.[236] Some further but still nebulous details are found online that were last modified in December 2019, that refer to local-level programming that is designed to complement the work of law enforcement agencies.[237] None of the programs appear to be designed to assist specifically with returning foreign fighters.[238] However anti-radicalization centers in major cities are likely to be the first line of support for returnees and their families.[239] If a returnee is assessed as low risk by the security agencies, the families are encourage to contact relevant social services.[240]

Denmark

Prosecution

As of July 2019, Denmark had prosecuted 5.9% of its returnees. Little information is publicly available, or is in English, but at the end of 2020, the extradition of a FTF from Turkey to Denmark for prosecution was reported in English.[241]

Canceling passports

Since 2015 Denmark had legislation and temporary regulations that permitted the revocation of passports if there was reason to believe that a person intended to participate in activities that might pose a threat to Denmark's national security. In 2020 these regulations were made permanent, and the period of revocation was extended to a maximum of three years. The Danish Institute for Human Rights tried unsuccessfully to have the period limited to one year.[242] FTFs also may be refused consular assistance.[243]

Pre-trial detention

Individual monitoring of returnees has been implemented.[244] Although the detention law does not specifically mention returnees, there is no reason why it would not be useful as a counter-terrorism measure in relevant situations. Persons may be held in pre-charge detention for up to three days before appearing before a judge or release. Once charged, if the potential crime could result in a prison sentence in excess of 18 months, then pre-trial detention may be authorized by a judge for a period of up to four weeks. This can be extended for further periods of four weeks.[245] This does not appear to be capped.

Revoking citizenship

In October 2019, Denmark enacted legislation within three days permitting the revocation of citizenship of persons with dual nationality, who have acted in a manner seriously prejudicial to Denmark's vital interests, without a trial.[246] The attempts of the Danish Institute for Human Rights to ensure that all such administrative decisions should automatically be tested before a court were not successful.[247] Affected persons have four weeks to appeal against the decision.[248] At least one person has had his citizenship revoked under this new law, and as of November 2019, up to four cases were said to be under review.[249] One of these persons commenced legal action against the Danish immigration minister on the ground that the decision to revoke citizenship without a trial violates Article 3 of the Danish Constitution,[250] which vests judicial power in the courts, but the outcome of the proceedings are not known.[251]

The U.N. Special Rapporteur on extrajudicial, summary or arbitrary arbitrations sent written questions about the deprivation of nationality in 2019. The Danish Minister of Foreign Affairs responded in detail, emphasizing that a "specific and individual assessment" would be made as to whether the activity was seriously prejudicial to the vital interests of Denmark, as well as a "specific proportionality assessment of the significance of the deprivation of nationality for the person concerned seen in relation to the severity of the conduct."[252] As to the right to dispute the decision, the Minister stated that this could be challenged before the courts during the period of four weeks after the person has received notice of the decision. The Minister concluded that the law complied with all Denmark's international substantive and procedural obligations.[253]

Deradicalization and reintegration

One of the best-known programs to prevent persons becoming radicalized and to reintegrate them into society is the Aarhus model, which was launched in 2007. It has three main characteristics: "(1) close and flexible cooperation among several already existing institutions and authorities working with exposed and vulnerable young people; (2) inclusion; and (3) scientific foundation (psychology)."[254] It is an interdisciplinary collaboration between schools, social services and police and has been rolled out over all of Denmark.[255] Mentoring and life psychology are essential elements.

In 2013 a special exit program was introduced to deradicalize returning foreign fighters and reintegrate them into society.[256] This is based on preconditions that the returnee has not committed any criminal act, and that the person has been screened and determined not to pose a security risk. If criminal activity is suspected, then the person will be prosecuted. If the preconditions have been satisfied, and an exit program is approved, the case goes to a task force for assessment as to which specific services should be offered to the returnee. Before the appropriate services (including mentoring, education, housing, psychological counselling, and medical care) are offered, the returnee will have to sign a written exit-process cooperation agreement. This exit program is only offered to those who are genuinely motivated to deradicalize, and "strong measures" are said to be taken to prevent the program from being used as "a hiding place for people intending to commit terrorist acts."[257] The effectiveness of the schemes have been hard to measure.[258]

France

Prosecution

As of 2017 France had prosecuted approximately 73% of returnees. A January 2020 report highlighted that a number of prosecutions in France are of persons tried in absentia, some of whom are presumed dead.[259] In October 2019, the French Foreign Minister travelled to Baghdad to try to persuade the local government to take custody of and prosecute 60 French nationals who were detained in Syrian camps.[260] France has the highest number of prosecutions in Europe, perhaps because its terrorism crimes are so broadly drafted, and perhaps because the judiciary "leaves room for interpretation" and "in order to be prosecuted, it is enough to be linked to jihadist activities."[261]

Restrictions on travel

In 2014 France introduced legislation that restricted would-be FTFs from traveling. Individuals can be banned without judicial approval from traveling for up to six months if authorities have serious grounds to believe that a trip was planned for a terrorist purpose.[262] Since 2016 the six-month ban can be renewed without limitation.[263] Within 24 hours of the decision, the individual's passport and identity card will be invalidated and must be surrendered to the authorities, in return for a receipt. The individual is entitled to appeal for judicial review to an administrative court. In one such appeal in 2015, the law was declared constitutional.[264]

Detention

Preventive detention could be used in the case of returnees whilst assessing whether there is sufficient evidence to prosecute. A person suspected of having committed, or who is attempting to commit a terrorist offence, or who is involved with a terrorist group may be held preventively pre-charge in *Garde à Vue* for up to six days.[265] Once an investigating magistrate opens an investigation, a person can be held in *détention provisoire* – pre-trial detention, if a judge is satisfied that lesser measures would not suffice. This can last for up to four years, and it is subject to judicial review at six monthly intervals.[266]

House arrest has been used in France pursuant to a judicial process as a means of pre-trial detention for decades, but its scope expanded during the state of emergency that existed from 2015–17.[267] In 2016 the government was empowered to place under administrative control returnees who could not be charged with a criminal offense but were believed to pose a serious threat to public security. The law was amended in 2017 with the result that returnees (and others) can be placed under house arrest for up to one year for the sole purpose of preventing the commission of terrorist acts.[268] The criteria for imposing house arrest, are if the behavior constitutes a threat of "particular gravity" for security and public order, and if the person has been in habitual contact with persons or organizations inciting, facilitating, or participating in terrorist acts, or if the person has disseminated or adhered to ideologies inciting the commission of acts of terrorism or apology for such acts.[269] If insufficient evidence exists to warrant house arrest, persons may be put under surveillance.[270]

Other conditions may be imposed that limit movement, enforce a 12-hour curfew, limit contact with specific persons, and require attendance at a police station three times a day on seven days a week.[271] The Minister of the Interior can commute these conditions to wearing an electronic monitoring bracelet.[272] These powers have been used extensively, and do not only apply to returnees.[273]

House arrest is imposed by administrative judges without a proper judicial review process. There have been challenges to the way the measure has been imposed, on the grounds of violation of individual freedoms as set out in the French Constitution. For example, in 2015 the Constitutional Court held that house arrest was a limitation of freedom of movement, as opposed to a restriction on liberty. As house arrest was limited to 12 hours a day, the Court held that this did not deprive the complainant of his liberty.[274] In another case, indefinite house arrest was imposed on a person convicted of plotting to bomb the U.S. Embassy in Paris, after his release from prison. He has been under house arrest for more than ten years.[275] Although these cases are not related to returnees, they illustrate the potential scope of this administrative measure.

Revoking citizenship

France, too, enacted similar citizenship stripping legislation in 1996 in response to terrorist attacks in 1995, but this only applied to persons who had been convicted of a crime not more than ten years after acquiring French citizenship. In 1998 the law was modified so that it only applied to persons with dual nationality.[276] In 2016 the National Assembly and the Senate failed to agree on modifying the law to permit the deprivation of citizenship and expulsion of dual citizens who were deemed to pose a terrorist threat.[277]

However, French law permits the revocation of citizenship of a person with dual nationality, if that person has been convicted of a terrorist offence either before becoming a French citizen or within 15 years of attaining citizenship, or for acts against the fundamental interests of France.[278] Between 1996 and 2016 there were 13 reported cases of revoking citizenship, and between 2016 and January 2020, only another three.[279]

Deradicalization and reintegration

France started to include deradicalization programs in its response to terrorism in 2013–14, mainly by attempting to deal with people in prison.[280] In 2016 the government decided to open an experimental Center for Prevention, Integration, and Citizenship which was staffed with 25 social workers, psychologists, educators, and a Muslim chaplain. Radicalized persons were invited to enter this program voluntarily, to develop critical minds and appropriate citizenship and republican values. Unfortunately, but possibly not surprisingly, the program closed after five months.[281] It was a failure for a number of reasons, which included the voluntary nature of the program, and because residents living near the Center protested against having extremists residing in their vicinity.[282] Furthermore, the fact that the program was "top-down," run by the Ministry of the Interior, which is in charge of the police, may have also had an adverse effect on the prospects of success.[283]

In February 2018 the government unveiled a new plan designed to isolate extremists within prisons, and open centers dedicated to reintegrating former extremists into society.[284] The 60-point plan focused on education, youth engagement, detection, and professionalizing and standardizing reintegration programs. The plan for returnees was to have long-term, locally driven counselling and support programs, operated with multi-disciplinary teams, out of local prefectures in coordination with the Ministries of Health and Education.[285] Some commentators have complained that the programs do not deal with right wing extremism and are totally focused on Islamist extremism without actually mentioning Islam, that the plan is overly ambitious and lacking any way to measure success, and misses the point of the problem.[286]

Germany

Prosecution

As of March 2017, 62.7% of returnees had been prosecuted. Since December 2017 all returnees are subject to criminal investigation.[287] In addition to the range of terror charges frequently used in FTF cases, in 2020 a dual-nationality German and Tunisian woman also faced charges relating to crimes against humanity in connection with enslaving a 13-year-old Yazidi girl in Syria.[288]

Restrictions on travel

In 2015 Germany enacted legislation to prevent FTFs from traveling. National identity cards and passports of persons who constituted a threat to the internal or external security or other significant interests of Germany may be revoked. Substitute identity cards would be issued, with the words "not valid for travel outside Germany."[289]

Detention

The prosecuting authority opens a criminal investigation in respect of every returnee, and many are placed in pre-charge detention for up to two days,[290] and pre-trial detention.[291] In theory, this is not meant to exceed six months, but a court can extend this in cases of particular difficulty, or for some other important reason that justify an extension.[292]

Revoking citizenship

In 2019 Germany introduced legislation that effectively strips citizenship from adult foreign fighters with dual nationality.[293] Although Article 16 of the German Federal Basic Law prohibits deprivation of citizenship, the new law permits the "statutory forfeiture" of citizenship of future dual citizen foreign fighters who take part in combat operations abroad for a terrorist militia.[294] The decision to revoke citizenship is made by a state agency. The law is not retrospective, so it does not apply to people who traveled overseas to join ISIS before August 9, 2019.[295] This law will therefore not apply to many of Germany's FTFs, particularly as it has been estimated that very few of them hold dual citizenship.[296]

Deradicalization

The approach is decentralized, as the government supports a number of local and regional non-governmental organizations that conduct rehabilitation initiatives around the country.[297] In 2000 one such NGO launched EXIT-Deutschland to facilitate the deradicalization of right-wing extremists.[298] This operates relatively free of government control and focuses on helping extremists involve themselves in critical reflection and reassessment of and successfully challenge the beliefs in right wing ideology. It is directed to people who approach EXIT because they want to leave right-wing movements and start a new life. It is not known how, or if, this program could adapt to dealing with Islamist ideology.[299]

Hayat is a family counselling program that is also designed for highly radicalized persons, including foreign fighters. Its goal is to prevent them from turning violent on their return. The role of friends and family of the returnee is seen as fundamental to the deradicalization process.[300] Violence Prevention Network is another program dealing with both deradicalization and disengagement that targets returnees through advice centers in different areas. It involves group and individual sessions for mentoring, discussing ideology and future planning for life after prison.[301]

Israel

Prosecution

Ten FTFs have returned from Iraq and or Syria.[302] One woman is known to have been indicted in 2019 after her return from Syria where she had joined the Jabat al-Nusra terror organization.[303]

Revoking citizenship

In 2017 Israel enacted legislation that authorized the Minister of the Interior to revoke Israeli nationality of any person if they have committed a breach of loyalty towards the State.[304] Citizenship cannot be revoked if this would make the person stateless, but if such a person was stateless, they would be given a permit for permanent residence.[305] Breach of loyalty is defined as engaging in, assisting, or soliciting the perpetration of a terrorist act, or actively taking part in a terrorist organization, engaging in treason, or acquiring citizenship or permanent residence in a number of listed countries.[306]

The person concerned may attend a court hearing to consider whether revocation should be ordered, but if he cannot be located or is overseas, the hearing can be conducted without him. The person may have a legal representative attend, irrespective of whether the person concerned is present.[307] A person whose nationality was revoked in his absence, or his legal representative, may request the court to cancel that revocation decision within 45 days.[308] Out of 60 Israeli citizens who traveled to Syria or Iraq to fight with ISIS, at least 19 have had their citizenship revoked.[309] There are no documented specific deradicalization programs.

Italy

Prosecution

Out of 12 returnees, at least three people are known to have been prosecuted.[310]

Revoking citizenship

In 2018 Italy enacted legislation facilitating the revocation of citizenship of persons convicted of terrorism offenses. However, this law violates IHRL for two reasons: it is discriminatory in that it only applies to naturalized citizens, or to those who acquired Italian nationality because they married an Italian citizen or were born and resided in Italy until the age of 18; and the application of this law can result in statelessness.[311]

Deradicalization

Italy has one of the lowest levels of radicalization in Europe, as well as relatively low numbers of FTFs and returnees.[312] Italy is also one of the few places where a comprehensive deradicalization strategy has neither been adopted or even tried.[313] Some initiatives dealing with deradicalization and disengagement have been taken by isolated and local groups, but there is still no national strategy.[314]

Kazakhstan

Prosecution

As of 2019, Kazakhstan had prosecuted 15% of returnees.

Revoking citizenship

In 2017 legislation was enacted that permits the revocation of citizenship of persons convicted of "grave terrorism and extremism-related crimes."[315] As Kazakhstan law does not permit dual citizenship,[316] if this law is exercised, it will make people stateless,[317] thus violating international law. The law has been criticized for its vagueness and overbreadth.[318] It is not known how many people, if any, have had their citizenship revoked under this law.

Disengagement

The majority of more than 600 persons repatriated in Kazakhstan are women and children.[319] Under the aegis of the Ministry of Education which has collaborated with two NGOs, 17 regional rehabilitation and reintegration centers have been opened across the country. In each center, psychologists, social workers, psychiatrists, theologians, lawyers, nurses, and teachers are available to help the women and children as well as their extended families and host communities.[320] These programs are operating on a trial-and-error basis, with the theory that it is perhaps more feasible to achieve disengagement than deradicalization.[321]

Kazakhstan's model aims at striking the "right balance between governmental and non-governmental actors, between security and human rights, and between a focus on social and psychological drivers and one that primarily targets ideology."[322] However others say that the lenient approach in prosecution and paucity of measures to prevent the reoccurrence of radicalization might lead to challenges in the long term.[323]

The Netherlands

Prosecution

As of 2018, the Netherlands had prosecuted 30% of returnees. It is a country that is vehemently opposed to repatriating its nationals, and that stance was bolstered by a Court of Appeal decision in November 2019 that ruled that the Netherlands was not legally required to repatriate the children of women who had joined ISIS.[324]

One case of interest is that of Fatima H., a dual Dutch and Moroccan citizen, who traveled to Syria in 2013, aged 13. When the Caliphate fell in 2019, she wanted to return to the Netherlands. The Dutch government tried to stop her returning, but she was deported with two young children to the Netherlands, together with one other woman,[325] in November 2019, despite the fact that her Dutch citizenship had been revoked weeks earlier.[326] On her return she was prosecuted and convicted of participation in a terrorist organization and was sentenced to four years imprisonment.[327]

Restrictions on travel

If a person is reasonably suspected to be involved in terrorist activities abroad, this is sufficient to prevent his or her return for limited, but infinitely renewable periods.[328] Travel documents will be revoked, and the names of the persons are added to the Netherlands terrorist sanction list.[329]

Detention

Every returnee is arrested on return and may be detained in a high security detention center (a Terrorist Ward) for up to three days and 15 hours before a hearing in front of an investigative judge. If there is evidence that the person might have been involved in terrorist activity, the person will be placed in pre-trial detention whilst the investigation continues,[330] provided that there is a serious suspicion that the person committed an offence that carries a minimum penalty of four years imprisonment.[331] There are regular reviews and although the maximum period for pre-trial detention is stated to be 104 days, that deadline only marks what is supposed to be the start of the trial phase.[332] Parole supervision, electronic monitoring, and restrictions on movement are common.[333]

Revoking citizenship

Dutch citizenship of dual nationals involved with terrorist activity can be revoked in two situations: where a person has been convicted of a terrorism-related crime;[334] and since March 2017, where a person over the age of 16 is considered a danger to Dutch national security because they are allegedly involved in terrorist activities abroad. No prior conviction is required for this.[335] Between the introduction of the 2017 law and early 2020, 23 revocations took place.[336]

Deradicalization and reintegration

Persons are assessed by a variety of actors, including security services, education, health, and religious personnel. A reintegration program, Exit Facility was established in October 2015. This is a voluntary program for persons who wish to reject jihadist ideology based on a "buddy" system that involves intensive conversations to help them find work and a "healthy" social network. The family of the returnee are also offered help by the Family Support network radicalization.[337]

Another program was established in 2012, run by the Dutch Probation Service Terrorists, Extremists and Radicals team. It is aimed at persons convicted or suspected of involvement in terrorist offences, and returnees. Judicial, prison, police, and municipal authorities design tailor- made interventions which may include counselling and mentoring by externally contracted psychologists and religious personnel.[338] This approach has been described as a combination of preparation and denial – preparation for the potential return of foreign fighters and denial of responsibility.[339]

United States

Prosecution

The U.S. has the smallest number of foreign fighters in this study and the lowest number of returnees but prosecutes the highest percentage of returnees (76.4% as of November 2019). As of March 2021, 28 citizens from the U.S. have been repatriated, comprising 16 children and 12 adults, of which ten have been or are being prosecuted.[340] The Biden Administration has urged the Western allies of the U.S. to repatriate FTFs and their families.[341]

International terrorism crimes are broadly drafted, and perhaps the presence of U.S. military in Iraq and Syria has facilitated the collection of admissible evidence to use in the prosecutions of returnees. Some suggest that the Justice Department may not want to repatriate foreign fighters until it has sufficient evidence to charge them immediately upon arrival.[342] If insufficient evidence exists to prosecute on material support or conspiracy charges, which can result in lengthy sentences, the government may only be able to charge returnees with lesser charges, such as making false statements, which result in commensurately lower sentences.[343] The approach to returnees has been described as ad hoc, case by case, rather than strategically organized.[344]

Despite President Trump's campaign plans in 2016 to house captured ISIS fighters in Guantanamo,[345] his Administration opted to deal with returning foreign fighters in accordance with domestic criminal law, rather than the laws of war.

Administrative measures

No administrative measures are acknowledged apart from monitoring by the F.B.I. Detention pursuant to the laws of war has been analyzed in Part II. However, it is relevant to mention one FTF in this section. One dual unnamed U.S.-Saudi citizen was detained at a U.S. base in Iraq for 13 months, ostensibly pursuant to the laws of war. He attempted to challenge his detention in 2018 in habeas corpus proceedings in the United States District Court for the District of Columbia.[346] In October 2018, whilst the habeas proceedings were pending, he was freed and handed to the authorities in Bahrain, with his U.S. passport revoked, although it is claimed that he retained his U.S. citizenship.[347]

Revoking citizenship

A person who was born or was naturalized in the United States cannot be stripped of U.S. citizenship unless he voluntarily, with the intention of relinquishing U.S. nationality, commits an act of treason against the United States, or formally renounces U.S. citizenship, or swears allegiance to a foreign state, becomes naturalized in a foreign state if over the age of 18, or enters or serves in the armed forces of a foreign state if those forces are engaged in hostilities against the United States, or accepts a position working for the government of a foreign state after becoming a national of or swearing allegiance to that state.[348] Additionally naturalized citizens can have their naturalization revoked if it was procured illegally, or if there was concealment of a material fact or willful misrepresentation during the naturalization process.[349] Revocation, or denaturalization can only be made after a court hearing and a ruling by a federal judge.[350] It is unconstitutional to prevent U.S. citizens from entering the U.S., or to strip citizenship because of mere conduct, unless such conduct occurred before naturalization.[351]

The case of ISIS bride Hoda Muthana is the only U.S. litigation relating to deprivation of citizenship in the context of FTFs,[352] but it turns on unique facts. Her father, Yemeni citizen Ahmed Ali Muthana, worked as a diplomat in the United Nations. Some months before Hoda Muthana was born in the United States in 1994, her father was asked by the Yemini Ambassador to return his diplomatic identity card, but the United States Mission did not receive notice of the termination of his diplomatic status until February 1995. He applied for a U.S. passport for her, confirmed that his diplomatic status had terminated before his daughter's birth, and the application for the passport was granted in 2005 and renewed in 2014.[353] Her parents and older siblings were naturalized, but Hoda Muthana was not, because her parents thought she had acquired citizenship by birth.[354]

In 2014, twenty-year-old Hoda Muthana left her home in Alabama and traveled to ISIS controlled territory in Syria and Iraq where she consecutively married two different ISIS fighters and had a son with the second husband. She "became a prominent spokeswoman for ISIS on social media, advocating the killing of Americans and encouraging American women to join ISIS."[355]

In January 2016 the U.S. sent Hoda Muthana a letter at her parents' U.S. address, revoking her passport on the grounds that she "was not within the jurisdiction of the U.S." at the time of her birth and was therefore not a U.S. citizen. In December 2018, Hoda Muthana left ISIS controlled territory and surrendered to Kurdish forces, which detained her at one of its camps in Syria. In January 2019 her lawyer wrote to the Attorney General in Alabama, indicating her desire to return to the United States and her willingness to surrender to U.S. authorities for any contemplated charges. President Trump tweeted that he had instructed the Secretary of State not to let her back in.[356] Ahmed Muthana filed the case on his daughter's behalf seeking recognition of the U.S. citizenship of his daughter and grandson, as well as equitable relief in terms of an order that the United States should accept them back and take steps to bring them back.

Under the Fourteenth Amendment of the U.S. Constitution, "all persons born or naturalized in the United States, and subject to the jurisdiction thereof, are citizens of the United States." However, a number of cases have confirmed that the "jurisdiction clause was intended to exclude from its operation children of ministers . . . of foreign States born within the United States."[357] Thus if a child is born to a person who is a foreign official with diplomatic immunity, the child is not deemed to be within the jurisdiction of the United States, and the birth would not confer U.S. citizenship.[358]

The D.C. District Court opined that it must substantially defer to the State Department's interpretation of the international law relating to diplomats. In this case the relevant date of the end of diplomatic privileges was the date of notification of such termination.[359] Therefore because the State Department was not notified of the termination of Mr. Muthana's diplomatic status until February 2005 which was several months after his daughter's birth, the Court concluded that Hoda Muthana was not a United States citizen by virtue of having been born in the United States, and her infant son did not acquire United States citizenship from her, and consequently she was not entitled to equitable relief.[360] The United States was entitled to cancel a passport that was obtained erroneously, illegally, or fraudulently.[361]

Mr. Muthana appealed this decision to the U.S. Court of Appeals for the District of Columbia Circuit. The Court decided that whereas Mr. Muthana had no standing to act as "next friend" to his daughter (conferring the right to act on her behalf), he could act as next friend to his infant grandson, but in any event the issue of citizenship of the grandson had to be analyzed together with that of his mother.[362]

During this hearing Mr. Muthana had tried to persuade the Court that the date of notification of the termination of his diplomatic credentials should be taken as September 1, 1994 (i.e. before his daughter's birth) pursuant to a letter that informed the United States of the period of his tenure, but the Court accepted the Secretary of State's stance of relying on the later date, saying that it "declined to second-guess the Executive's recognition of diplomatic status" otherwise "the courts rather than the Executive would have the final say with respect to recognizing a diplomat's immunity."[363] The Court upheld the District Court's decision on the basis that Hoda Muthana and her son were not now, and had never been United States citizens.[364] The claims for equitable relief failed for lack of subject matter jurisdiction.[365]

Deradicalization and disengagement

As of 2018, no radicalization or disengagement programs were in existence in U.S. prisons. Outside of prisons, some small-scale programs are underway, such as one where a returnee is involved in conducting an experimental program aimed at deradicalizing other potential travelers.[366]

The first disengagement program in the United States was started in Minnesota in 2016 after a spate of terrorism trials, in consultation with the director of the German Institute on Radicalization and Deradicalization Studies. The probation service leads the program, which first assesses the vulnerabilities of persons leading to their radicalization, and then an individually tailored approach is created for each person, involving psychological testing, counselling, mentoring, all working towards reintegration.[367] No information appears to point to other similar programs in the United States.

Summary

The initial practice for dealing with adult returnees is fairly standard across the countries surveyed in this chapter. There will invariably be criminal investigations and risk assessments for each returnee that involve judicial, intelligence, and law enforcement personnel.[368] Where criminal proceedings are not feasible, countries adopt a case-by-case approach involving administrative measures and/or deradicalization/disengagement/reintegration initiatives, as deemed appropriate.[369]

The administrative measures in all the countries surveyed have become more stringent over the last few years. Revoking citizenship of dual citizens is a tool used by almost all countries. However, it is questionable whether this measure will prevent terrorism and radicalization, and may be counter-productive,[370] and it does not promote accountability for terrorist crimes.[371]

The unwillingness of many countries to repatriate their citizens could result in many problems, not least because leaving FTFs and their families in temporary camps in Syria could help FTFs to "deepen their networks in preparation for the next conflict."[372]

Pre-trial detention is used extensively as a terror prevention method, but in some countries the duration can be extremely lengthy and indeterminate (Belgium, France, Germany, and the Netherlands), and these practices are frequently subject to legal challenge for alleged violations of human rights. House arrest is used in the U.K., Belgium, and France. Electronic monitoring and restrictions on movement and association are used in many of the countries. Little is known or reported about the effectiveness of these measures, but resources, both in human and financial terms are likely play a part in determining the extent to which these measures can work in countries with the largest number of returnees if prosecution is not feasible.

Little is reported or known about the effectiveness of the programs dealing with deradicalization/disengagement/reintegration. Many of them are in their infancy, and the programs will not achieve instant results, but the greatest challenge must be to prove that they contribute to a reduced terror threat or that the paucity or reduction of terror attacks are due to the success of any of these programs.

A U.S. study in 2020[373] analyzed 30 programs in 26 countries[374] to see if any lessons could be learned from successful deradicalization programs which had been operative from the 1940s to 2020. The report noted a lack of consensus as to what constituted a successful program, and that more research was needed, and concluded that whilst there was no single model that would work for every country, several common characteristics seen in a number of programs indicated some levels of success. These included "creating a sense of hope and purpose, building a sense of community, providing individual attention and regimented daily schedules, and enduring sustainable long-term commitment following completion of the program."[375] Further research is needed urgently about this.

Notes

1 Rik Coolsaet and Thomas Renard, *The Homecoming of Foreign Fighters in the Netherlands, Germany and Belgium: Policies and Challenges*, (Egmont Institute, Apr. 12, 2018), www.egmontinstitute.be/the-homecoming-of-foreign-fighters-in-the-netherlands-germany-and-belgium-policies-and-challenges/; Marie-Danielle Smith, *'We're Doing Nothing': Canada Could Be a Leader in Handling Its Foreign Fighters, But Isn't, Say Experts*, National Post, (Aug. 19, 2019), https://nationalpost.com/news/were-doing-nothing-canada-could-be-a-leader-in-handling-its-foreign-fighter-but-isnt-say-experts/.

2 *See e.g.* Matteo Pugliese, *France and Foreign Fighters: The Controversial Outsourcing of Prosecution*, ISPI, (Jan. 9, 2020), www.ispionline.it/it/pubblicazione/framce-and-foreign-fighters-controversial-outsourcing-prosecution-24666; Michael R. Gordon and Benoit Faucon, *U.S., Europeans Clash Over How to Handle Islamic State Detainees*, Wall Street Journal, (Dec. 1, 2019), www.wsj.com/articles/u-s-europeans-clash-over-how-to-handle-islamic-state-detainees-11575201600.

3 Independent National Security Monitor, Annual Report 2019–2020, ¶27 (Feb. 11, 2021), www.inslm.gov.au/node/190.

4 *Id.*, ¶28.

5 Greg Barton, *Preventing Foreign Fighters from Returning Home Could Be Dangerous to National Security*, The Conversation, (Jul. 22, 2019), www.theconversation.com/preventing-foreign-fighters-from-returning-home-could-be-dangerous-to-national-security-120752; Kerstin Braun, *Prospects and Challenges of Prosecuting: Foreign Fighters in Australia*, *in* Counterterrorism Yearbook 2020, 40 (Isaac Kfir and John Coyne, eds., Australian Strategic Policy Handbook, Mar. 1, 2020).

6 Belgium: Extremism and Counter-Extremism, Counter Extremism Project, www.counterextremism.com/countries/belgium, (last accessed Mar. 11, 2021).

7 Francesco Ragazzi and Josh Walmsley, *Member States' Approach to Tackling the Return of Foreign Fighters*, 32, in The Return of Foreign Fighters to EU Soil, (European Parliamentary Research Service, May 2018), https://wb-iisg.com/wp-content/uploads/bp-attachments/5634/EPRS_STU2018621811_EN-1.pdf.

8 *Id.*

9 Belgium: Extremism and Counter-Extremism.

10 Government of Canada, Public Safety Canada, Canadian Extremist Travelers, (Sep. 10, 2020), www.publicsafety.gc.ca/cnt/trnsprnc/brfng-ntrls/primntry-bndrs/20200621/009/index-en.aspx.

11 *Id*; see also Smith, *'We're Doing Nothing.'*

12 Denmark: Extremism & Counter-Extremism, Counter Extremism Project, www.counterextremism.com/denmark, (last accessed Mar. 11, 2021).

13 *Id.*

14 Kenneth R. Rosen, *Harsh Homecoming*, Foreign Policy, (Jul. 2, 2019), https://foreignpolicy.com/2019/07/02/harsh-homecoming-islamic-state-denmark-european-union-syria/.

15 Pugliese, *France and Foreign Fighters*, *citing* Eman Ragab, *Les enjeux de securité associés au retour des terroristes étrangers*, Annuaire Iemed De La Mediterranee 93, 95, (2018), www.iemed.org/observatori/arees-danalisi/arxius-adjunts/anuari/med.2018/fr/securite_terroristes_etrangers_Ragab_medyearbook2018_fr.pdf.

16 Sharon Weill, *French Foreign Fighters: The Engagement of Administrative and French Criminal Justice in France*, 100 International Review of the Red Cross 211–36, (2018), http://international-review.icrc.org/articles/french-foreign-fighters-engagement-administrative-and-criminal-justice-france.

17 Jan Raudszus, *The Strategy of Germany for Handling Foreign Fighters*, ISPI, (Jan. 9, 2020), www.ispionline.it/en/pubblicazione/strategy-germany-handling-foreign-fighters-24761.

18 Daveed Gartenstein-Ross, Emelie Chace-Donahue and Colin P. Clark, *The Threat of Jihadist Terrorism in Germany*, International Centre for Counter-Terrorism: The Hague (ICCT), (May 22, 2020), https://icct.nl/publication/the-threat-of-jihadist-terrorism-in-germany/.

19 Kerstin Braun, *'Home Sweet Home': Managing Foreign Terrorist Fighters in Germany, the United Kingdom and Australia*, 20 International Community Law Review, 311–46, 324 (2018).

20 Israel Ministry of Foreign Affairs, *ISA Arrests Israeli Arab Suspected of Joining the Jabat al-Nusra Terrorist Group in Syria*, (Jun. 2, 2019), https://mfa.gov.il/MFA/ForeignPolicy/Terrorism/Pages/ISA-arrests-Israeli-Arab-suspected-of-joining-Jabat-al-Nusra-in-Syria-2-June-2019.aspx. Others may have been prosecuted but no details have been found.

21 The Soufan Center numbers were confirmed in 2019 by Jack Moore, *From Israel to ISIS*, The National Abu Dhabi, (2019), https://israeltoisis.thenational.ae.

22 *Number of Monitored Foreign Terrorist Fighters (FTFs) in Italy from August 2016 to July 2020*, Statista, www.statista.com/statistics/743716/monitored-foreign-fighters-italy/ (last accessed Apr. 28, 2021).

23 U.S. Dept. of State (DoS), Country Reports on Terrorism 2019: Italy, www.state.gov/reports/country-reports-on-terrorism-2019/italy/; Joe Snell, *Terror Charges Follow Islamic State Woman Repatriated to Italy*, Al-Monitor, (Sep. 30, 2020), www.al-monitor.com/originals/2020/09/syria-al-hol-islamic-state-isis-italy-repatriate-terrorism.html; Reuters Staff, *Italy Jails Suspected al Qaeda Foreign Fighter Caught in Turkey*, Reuters, (Jan. 20, 2021), www.reuters.com/article/italy-security-arrest-idINKBN29P1H6.

24 Francesco Marone and Lorenzo Vidino, *Destination Jihad: Italy's Foreign Fighters*, ICCT, (Mar. 2019), https://icct.nl/app/uploads/2019/03/Marone-Vidino-Italys-Foreign-Fighters-March2019.pdf, *noting* that less than 20% of these foreign fighters are Italian citizens.

25 Elena Zhirukhina, *Foreign Fighters from Central Asia: Between Renunciation and Repatriation*, ISPI, (Oct. 3, 2019), www.ispionline.it/en/pubblicazione/foreign-fighters-central-asia-between-renunciation-and-repatriation-24072.

26 *Concern in Kazakhstan over Returning Foreign Fighters from Syria*, Foreign Military Studies Office, https://community.apan.org/wg/tradoc-g2/fmso/w/o-e-watch-mobile-edition-v1/22555/concern-in-kazakhstan-over-returning-foreign-fighters-from-syria/ (last accessed Dec. 17, 2019).

27 Jonathan Hall Q.C., The Terrorism Acts in 2018, Report of Independent Reviewer of the Terrorism Legislation on the Operation of the Terrorism Acts 2000 and 2006, ¶7.9 (Mar. 2020); Lizzie Dearden, *Only One in 10 Jihadis Returning from Syria Prosecuted, Figures Reveal*, The Independent, (Feb. 21, 2019), www.independent.co.uk/news/uk/home-news/shamima-begum-isis-return-uk-syria-jihadis-terror-threat-prosecute-nationality-a8790991.html; Matthew Offord M.P., H.C. Deb. c.1193, *citing* Official Report, 11 June 2018, Vol. 642, c. 666, (Feb. 18, 2019).

28 U.S. DoS, Office of the Spokesperson, Briefing with Acting Special Envoy for the Global Coalition to Defeat ISIS John Godfrey on U.S. Participation in the Upcoming D-ISIS Ministerial, Special Briefing, via Teleconference, ("FTF Briefing") (Mar. 29, 2021), www.state.gov/briefing-with-

acting-special-envoy-for-the-global-coalition-to-defeat-isis-john-godfrey-on-u-s-participation-in-the-upcoming-d-isis-ministerial/.

See also Seamus Hughes and Devorah Margolin, *The Fractured Terrorist Threat to America*, Lawfare, (Nov. 10, 2019), www.lawfareblog.com/fractured-terrorism-threat-america. *See also* Robin Wright, *Despite Trump's Guantanamo Threats, Americans Who Joined ISIS Are Quietly Returning Home*, The New Yorker, (Jun. 11, 2019), www.newyorker.com/news/news-desk/americas-isis-members-are-coming-home, *noting* that ten adults and six minors had come home and that at least another 20 Americans including six fighters had been identified in Syria.

29 *See e.g.* Jessie Blackbourn, Deniz Kayis and Nicola McGarrity, Anti-Terrorism Law and Foreign Terrorist Fighters, 19, 22 (referring to the U.K. and Australia), (Routledge, 2018).

30 Lucia Zedner, *Citizenship Deprivation, Security and Human Rights*, 18 European Journal of Migration and Law 222, 227 (2016).

31 Matt Dathan and Fiona Hamilton, *Boris Johnson Seeks tougher Treason Laws to Punish Returning Islamic State Jihadists*, The Times, (May 1, 2021), www.thetimes.co.uk/article/boris-johnson-seeks-tougher-treason-laws-to-punish-returning-islamic-state-jihadists-29dhcfbm5; *See also*, Hall, The Terrorism Acts in 2018 ¶7.9.

32 *Id.*, ¶7.19.

33 Matt Dathan and Fiona Hamilton, *Boris Johnson Seeks tougher Treason Laws to Punish Returning Islamic State Jihadists*; Leading Article, *The Times View on Using the Treason Act to Tackle Terrorism: Ultimate Betrayal*, The Times, (May 1, 2021), www.thetimes.co.uk/article/the-times-view-on-using-the-treason-act-to-tackle-terrorism-ultimate-betrayal-qnxppltls.

34 The data for the table derives unless stated otherwise from H.M. Government Transparency Report 2018: Disruptive and Investigatory Powers, (Jul. 2018) and H.M. Government Transparency Report 2018: Disruptive Powers, 2018/19, (Mar. 2020).

35 David Anderson Q.C., Second Report of Independent Reviewer, Terrorism Prevention and Investigative Measures in 2013, ¶3.3, (Mar. 2014).

36 David Anderson Q.C., Third Report of Independent Reviewer, Terrorism Prevention and Investigative Measures in 2014, (Mar. 2015).

37 Helen Fenwick, Explainer: *What's the Difference between Control Orders and TPIMs?*, The Conversation, (Jun. 8, 2017), https://theconversation.com/explainer-whats-the-difference-between-tpims-and-control-orders-79068.

38 H.M. Parliament, Rt. Hon. Amber Rudd M.P., Written Statement HCWS 362 (15 Dec. 2016), www.parliament.uk/business/publications/written-questions-answers-statements/written-statement/Commons/2016-12-15/HCWS362.

39 Jonathan Hall Q.C., The Terrorism Acts in 2019, Report of Independent Reviewer of the Terrorism Legislation on the Operation of the Terrorism Acts 2000 and 2006, ¶8.79.

40 UK Parliament, *House of Commons, Written Questions, Answers and Statements*, (Jan. 12, 2021), https://questions-statements.parliament.uk/written-statements/detail/202101-12/hcws698, showing that between Sep. 1 and Nov. 30, 2020, 3 TPIMs were in place, but between March and May 2020, six had been in place, https://questions-statements.parliament.uk/written-statements/detail/2020-07-16/HCWS374.

41 Counter-Terrorism and Security Act 2015, c.6, §1, Sch. 1. (U.K.).

42 Terry McGuiness and Melanie Gower, Deprivation of British Citizenship and Withdrawal of Passport Facilities, 12, (House of Commons Library Briefing Article No. 06820, Jun. 9, 2017).

43 Counter-Terrorism and Security Act 2015, §§2–4.
44 *Id.*, Sch. 2.
45 *Id.*, §4 (3).
46 *Id.*, §4 (9) & (10).
47 *Id.*, §4(1).
48 Counter-Terrorism and Security Act 2015, §9 (1) and (2).
49 *Id.*, §10.
50 QX v. Secretary of State for the Home Department (SSHD), [2020] EWHC 1221 (Admin), (May 15, 2020).
51 *Id.*, ¶27, *citing* Counter-Terrorism and Security Act 2015, Sch. 3. The power to use a closed material procedure derives from the Justice and Security Act 2013, c.18 and is also referred to in Part II.
52 The rules relating to special advocates for TEOs are found in Civil Procedure Rules (CPR), Part 88 – Proceedings Under the Counter-Terrorism and Security Act 2015.
53 QX v. SSHD, ¶¶49–51.
54 *Id.*, ¶44, *citing* SSHD v. BC and BB, [2009] EWHC 2926 (Admin), ¶¶20, 25 (dealing with obligations imposed by the now repealed measure of control orders – even if the obligations were considered to be "light," they still interfered with civil rights if they disproportionately interfered with Art. 8 rights.)
55 QX v. SSHD, ¶52.
56 *Id.*, ¶56.
57 *Id.*, ¶¶59–68.
58 *Id.*, ¶¶73, 78.
59 A & Others v. United Kingdom, Appl. No.3455/05 ECtHR, (Feb. 19, 2009).
60 SSHD v. AF (FC) [2009] UKHL 28, ¶59.
61 QX v. SSHD, ¶86.
62 QX v. SSHD, [2020] EWHC 2508 (Admin), (Sep. 21, 2020).
63 Preventive detention to prevent terror attacks as analyzed in Part II has not specifically been used to deal with returning FTFs.
64 Terrorism Prevention Measures and Investigation Act 2011, c.23, as amended by Counter-Terrorism and Security Act 2015, c.6.
65 Prevention of Terrorism Act 2005, c.2.
66 H.M. Government, Review of Counter-Terrorism and Security Powers, *Review Findings and Recommendations*, CM 8004, ¶26, (Jan. 2011).
67 Terrorism Prevention Measures and Investigation Act 2011, §§2 §§ and 3.
68 *Id.*, §§3 (5)(b), 6, 7.
69 *Id.*, Sch. 2.
70 *Id.*, §§8, 9, 12.
71 *Id.*, §5.
72 *Id.*, Sch.1.
73 *Id.*, §23.
74 Hall, The Terrorism Acts in 2019, ¶8.73.
75 *Id.*, ¶¶8.27, 8.34, *citing inter alia* SSHD v. JM and LF, [2021] EWHC 266 (admin), (Feb. 10, 2021). *See also* ¶¶8.23–8.76 for a thorough evaluation of the current issues, strengths and concerns relating to TPIMs.
76 U2 v. SSHD, SIAC Appeal No. SC/130/2016, ¶144, (Dec. 19, 2019).
77 Rt. Hon. Sajid Javid, H.C. Deb. c.1202 (Feb. 18, 2019, 3.58 p.m.).
78 H.M. Government, Contest: The United Kingdom's Strategy for Countering Terrorism, CM 9608, 6 (MI5 and Counter-Terrorism Policing were handling over 500 live investigations, involving some 3,000 people as of June 2018), (Jun. 2018). In 2021, MI5 were still reported as monitoring over 3,000

people who were feared to be plotting a terrorist attack, *see e.g.* Josh Glancy, Dipesh Gadher, Caroline Wheeler, John Simpson, and Katie Tarrant, *Father's Shock after Son Held over Sir David Amess Murder*, The Sunday Times, (Oct. 17, 2021), www.thetimes.co.uk/article/father-s-shock-after-son-held-over-sir-david-amess-murder-gr8rj7whq.

79 Helen Warrell, *UK Faces Uphill Challenge in Resettling ISIS Jihadis*, Financial Times, (Nov. 17, 2019), www.ft.com/content/11fd7c00-0790-11ea-a984-fbbacad9e7dd.

80 *See e.g.*, Helen Warrell, *London Bridge Attack Exposes Flaws in UK Terror Oversight*, Financial Times, (Dec. 1, 2019), www.ft.com/content/b1e1a534-137a-11ea-9ee4-11f260415385.

81 David Brown, Harry Shukman and Ben Ellery, *Streatham, Suspected Terrorist Shot Dead by Police after Stabbing Rampage in South London*, The Times, (Feb. 2, 2020), www.thetimes.co.uk/article/streatham-suspected-terrorist-shot-dead-by-police-after-stabbing-rampage-in-south-london=96s3pthss.

82 Sean O'Neill, Matthew Bradley, Richard Ford and Fariha Karim, *Jihadist Told Inmates He Wanted to Murder an MP*, The Times, (Feb. 4, 2020), www.thetimes.co.uk/article/streatham-terror-attack-jihadist-told-inmates-he-wanted-to-murder-an-mp-5tg6xkc6s.

83 H.M. Government Transparency Report 2018: Disruptive and Investigatory Powers, (Jul. 2018) and H.M. Government Transparency Report: Disruptive Powers, 2018/19. *See also* David Batty and Poppy Noor, *Who Has Been Stripped of UK Citizenship before Shamima Begum?* The Guardian, (Feb. 20, 2019), www.theguardian.com/uk-news/2019/feb/20/who-has-been-stripped-of-uk-citizenship-before-shamima-begum.

84 Fiona Hamilton and Jonathan Ames, *Shamima Begum Barred from Britain*, The Times, (Feb. 27, 2021), www.thetimes.co.uk/article/shamima-begum-cannot-return-to-britain-from-syria-to-fight-for-citizenship-6bblxlv5j. Sixteen of them may be women, *see* David Rose, *Nicole Jack, an ISIS Bride being Held in a Syrian Detention Camp, Pleads for Return to Britain*, The Times, (Oct. 7, 2021), www.thetimes.co.uk/article/nicole-jack-an-isis-bride-being-held-in-a-syrian-detention-camp-pleads-for-return-to-britain-pgk702v0k.

85 From Reuters, *Radical Loses Citizenship*, Los Angeles Times, (Apr. 6, 2003), www.latimes.com/archives/la-xpm-2003-apr-06-fg-masri6-story.html. Abu Hamza had originally held Egyptian citizenship. He was stripped of British citizenship in 2003. In the next seven years he was involved in extradition to the United States and criminal proceedings there, so it was not until 2010 that he was able to pursue his appeal against the loss of British citizenship. He won his appeal because he was able to show that he had been stripped of Egyptian citizenship in 2004, and the effect of the British deprivation order would render him stateless. *See* Abu Hamza v. Secretary of State for the Home Department, Special Immigration Appeals Commission, Appeal No. SC/23/2003, (Nov. 5, 2010).

86 *Islamic State 'Beatles' Duo Complain about Losing UK Citizenship'*, BBC News, (Mar. 31, 2018), www.bbc.com/news/uk-43601925.

87 Dan Sabbagh, *Jack Letts Stripped of British Citizenship*, The Guardian, (Aug. 18, 2019), www.theguardian.com/world/2019/aug/18/jack-letts-stripped-british-citizenship-isis-canada. He had dual British/Canadian citizenship, and was stripped of British citizenship while being held in a Syrian prison. The Canadian government indicated that they will not assist Letts in returning to Canada, *see* Reuters Staff, *Canada Says It Will Not Help 'Jihadi Jack' Come to the Country*, Reuters, (Aug. 20, 2019), www.reuters.com/article/us-canada-britain-islamist/canada-says-it-will-not-help-jihadi-jack-come-to-the-country-idUSKCN1VA2BW. Jihadi Jack's parents were sentenced to 15 months

imprisonment, suspended for 12 months, for sending money to their son in Syria, *see* Crown Prosecution Service, *Sally Lane and John Letts Sentenced for Sending Money to Daesh Supporting Son*, (Jun. 21, 2019), www.cps.gov.uk/cps/news/sally-lane-and-john-letts-sentenced-sending-money-daesh-supporting-son.

88 British Nationality Act 1981, c.61, §40 (2) and (4), as amended by S. 40(2) substituted (16.6.2006) by Immigration, Asylum and Nationality Act 2006 (c. 13) §§56(1), 62; S.I. 2006/1497, art. 3, Sch.

89 *Id.*, §40 (4A), as amended by S. 40(4A) inserted (28.7.2014) by Immigration Act 2014 (c. 22), §§66(1), 75(3); S.I.2014/1820, art.3(t) as amended by S.I. 2014/2771 art 14.

90 *Id.*, §40(B).

91 David Anderson Q.C., Citizenship Removal Resulting in Statelessness, First Review of the Independent Reviewer of the Operation of the Power to Remove Citizenship Obtained by Naturalisation from Persons Who Have No Other Citizenship, 14, ¶3.12, (Apr. 2016).

92 *Id.*, ¶¶15, 3.16, 3.18. *See also* Maarten P. Bolhuis and Joris van Wijk, *Citizen Deprivation as a Counterterrorism Measure in Europe; Possible Follow-Up Scenarios, Human Rights Infringements and the Effect on Counterterrorism*, 22 European Journal of Migration and Law 338, 347–8, (2020).

93 K2 v. United Kingdom, Appl. No. 42387/13, ECtHR, Decision, ¶¶1–8, (Mar. 9, 2017).

94 *Id.*, ¶¶9–35.

95 *Id.*, ¶49.

96 *Id.*, ¶50.

97 *Id.*, ¶61.

98 *Id.*, ¶¶52–3.

99 *Id.*, ¶57.

100 *Id.*, ¶60.

101 *Id.*, ¶¶67, 72.

102 Anthony Loyd, *Shamima Begum: Bring Me Home, Says Bethnal Green Girl Who Left to Join ISIS*, The Times, (Feb. 13, 2019), www.thetimes.co.uk/article/shamima-begum-bring-me-home-says-bethnal-green-girl-who-fled-to-join-isis-hgvqw765d.

103 *Id.*

104 John Reynolds, *Shamima Begum Begs British Public for Forgiveness: Former ISIS Bride Wants to Clear Her Name in UK Court*, The Times, (Sep. 15, 2021), www.thetimes.co.uk/article/shamima-begum-begs-british-public-for-forgiveness-xbzjvvlkr; Anthony Loyd, *Shamima Is Not a Threat: She Is Totally Broken*, The Times, (Jun. 3, 2021), referring to a British television documentary on ISIS brides, www.thetimes.co.uk/article/shamima-begum-is-not-a-threat-shes-totally-broken-she-needs-help-w7hd8fj9l; Mercedes Masters and Salvador Santino F. Regilme Jr, *Human Rights and British Citizenship: The Case of Shamima Begum as Citizen to Homo Sacer*, 12 Journal of Human Rights Practice 341, 352, (Sep. 2020); Sarah St. Vincent, *In Shamima Begum Case, UK Supreme Court Dismisses Rights and Overlooks Potential Victimhood*, Just Security, (Feb. 26, 2021), www.justsecurity.org/75016/in-shamima-begum-case-uk-supreme-court-dismisses-rights-and-overlooks-potential-victimhood/.

105 Shamima Begum v. SSHD, SIAC (Appeal No. SC/163/2019), ¶¶1, 10–12, 121–8. The case contains evidence of two experts with different views relating to Bangladeshi immigration law and after analyzing the evidence and Bangladeshi law, SIAC concluded that Shamima Begum still held Bangladeshi citizenship.

106 R. (on the application of Begum) v. Special Immigration Appeals Commission (SIAC), R (on the application of Begum) v. SSHD, [2021] UKSC 7 (Feb. 26, 2021), *summarized in* ¶¶1, 16 ("Begum Supreme Court case").

107 Esther Addley and Redwan Ahmed, *Shamima Begum Will Not Be Allowed Here, Says Bangladesh*, The Guardian, (Feb. 20, 2019), www.theguardian.com/uk-news/2019/feb/20/rights-of-shamima-begums-son-not-affected-says-javid.
108 Begum v. SSHD, SIAC, (Appeal No. SC/163/2019).
109 R. (Begum) v. SSHD, [2020] EWHC 74 (Admin), (Feb. 7, 2020).
110 R. (Begum) v. Special Immigration Appeals Commission (UN Special Rapporteur on the Promotion and Protection of Human Rights and Fundamental Freedoms While Countering Terrorism intervening) [2020] EWCA Civ 918, ¶121, (Jul. 16, 2020).
111 *Id.*, ¶129.
112 Begum Supreme Court case, ¶11.
113 *Id.*, ¶¶18–19.
114 *Id.*, ¶20.
115 *Id.*, ¶24.
116 *Id.*, ¶27.
117 *Id.*, ¶60, *citing* SSHD v. Rehman, (Rehman) [2001] UKHL 47, ¶49.
118 *Id.*, ¶¶61–2, *citing* Rehman ¶¶57, 62.
119 *Id.*, ¶69.
120 *Id.*, ¶90.
121 *Id.*
122 *Id.*, ¶¶91–3, *citing* Carnduff v. Rock, [2001] EWCA Civ 680, where a plaintiff's claim was struck out because a fair trial would have been impossible without the police disclosing information which had to be kept confidential in the public interest, and this factor overrode the public interest in having the plaintiff's claim litigated. This decision resulted in Carnduff v. United Kingdom, Appl. No. 18905/02 ECtHR, (unreported, Feb. 10, 2004) where a complaint of an unfair trial in violation of Art. 6 ECHR was dismissed, and Tariq v. Home Office, [2011] UKSC 35 which upheld and followed the principle in Carnduff v. Rock.
123 *Id.*, ¶94.
124 *Id.*, ¶107, *citing* Human Rights Act 1998, c.42, §6 (U.K.).
125 *Id.*, ¶¶108–11.
126 *Id.*, ¶134.
127 *Id.*, ¶¶135, 137.
128 R. (on the application of D4) v. SSHD, [2021] EWHC 2179 (Admin), (Jul. 30, 2021), referring to the duty to notify before service a notice of deprivation of citizenship, pursuant to British Nationality Act 1981, §40 (5).
129 *Id.*, ¶2, *citing* British Nationality (General) Regulations, SI 2018/851, 10(4).
130 *Id.*, ¶51.
131 *Id.*, ¶¶61, 62, 68.
132 Tim Shipman and Dipesh Gadher, *Jihadists Given Hope of Return to UK*, The Sunday Times, (Aug. 1, 2021), www.thetimes.co.uk/article/jihadists-given-hope-return-syria-isis-vqzlr9zkw; Lizzie Dearden, *Britain Cannot Remove ISIS Members' Citizenship without Telling Them, High Court Rules*, The Independent, (Jul. 30, 2021), www.independent.co.uk/news/uk/home-news/isis-syria-british-citizenship-begum-d4-b1894038.html.
133 H.M. Government, Contest, ¶16.
134 *Id.*, ¶¶166–72; U.K. Home Office, *Factsheet: Desistence and Disengagement Program*, (Nov. 5, 2019), https://homeofficemedia.blog.gov.uk/2019/11/05/fact-sheet-desistence-and-disengagaement-program/.
135 Hall, The Terrorism Acts in 2019, ¶8.5.
136 *Id.*, ¶¶8.7–8.16, *citing* QX v. SSHD.
137 Richard Ford, *Number of Terrorists Sent for 'Detoxification' Triples*, The Times, (Apr. 6, 2019), www.thetimes.co.uk/article/number-of-terrorists-sent-for-detoxificatio-triples-5n7002c2k.

138 Ian Drury and David Barrett, *More Than 100 Fanatics Are on Anti-Terror Scheme: Calls Grow for Review of De-Radicalisation Program That Usman Khan Was Placed on Amid Fears Public Could Be Put at Risk*, Daily Mail, (Dec. 3, 2019), www.dailymail.co.uk/news/article-7752665/More-100-fanatics-anti-terror-scheme.html.
139 Hall, The Terrorism Acts in 2019, ¶¶8.17–8.20.
140 Nazir Afzal, *With Sufficient Resources We Can Deradicalize Extremists*, The Times, (Feb. 4, 2020), www.thetimes.co.uk/article/streatham-terror-attack-extremists-can-be-deradicalised-but-it-takes-resources-t7gkwdm07.
141 *See e.g.* Warrell, *London Bridge Attack Exposes Flaws in UK Terror Oversight.*
142 David Brown, Harry Shukman and Ben Ellery, *Streatham: Suspected Terrorist Shot Dead by Police after Stabbing Rampage in South London*, The Times, (Feb. 2, 2020), www.thetimes.co.uk/article/streatham-suspected-terrorist-shot-dead-by-police-after-stabbing-rampage-in-south-london-96s3pthss.
143 Kerstin Braun, *Prospects and Challenges of Prosecuting: Foreign Fighters in Australia*, *in* Counterterrorism Yearbook 2020, 40, (Isaac Kfir and John Coyne, eds., Australian Strategic Policy Handbook, Mar. 1, 2020).
144 *Id.*, 40–1.
145 Blackbourn & Ors, Anti-Terrorism Law, *citing* Criminal Code (Cwlth) §§119.1 (1), 119.1 (2), 119.4, 119.2, 119.3.
146 Parliament of Australia, Media Release, Public Hearing on Counter-Terrorism 'Declared Areas,' (Sep. 22, 2020), www.aph.gov.au/About_Parliament/House_of_Representatives/About_the_House_News/Media_Releases/Public_hearing_on_counter-terrorism_declared_areas.
147 Parliament of Australia, Parliamentary Committee on Intelligence and Security, Review of 'Declared Areas' Provisions, Sections 119.2 And 119.3 of the Criminal Code, ¶¶2.26–2.30, (Feb. 2021).
148 *Id.*, ¶¶2.40–2.42.
149 Blackbourn & Ors, Anti-Terrorism Law, 66, *citing* Australian Passports Act 2005, No. 5, 2005, §14.
150 *Id.*, *citing* Australian Passports Act 2005, §§22A, 24A.
151 *Id.*, 67, *citing* Australian Passports Act 2005, §§22A (3).
152 *Id.*, 68.
153 *Id.*
154 *Id.*
155 Counter-Terrorism (Temporary Exclusion Orders) Act 2019, No. 53, 2019, §10, (Austrl.).
156 *Id.*, §10(2).
157 *Id.*, §10(3), (4) and (5).
158 *Id.*, §14.
159 *Id.*, §13.
160 *Id.*, §15.
161 *Id.*, §16.
162 *Id.*
163 *Id.*, §17.
164 *Id.*, §20.
165 *Id.*, §18.
166 Australian Government, Department of Home Affairs, Control Orders, Preventative Detention, Continuing Detention Orders, Temporary Exclusion Orders, and Powers in Relation to Terrorist Acts and Terrorist Offences, Annual Report, 2019–2020, 8, (Australian Government, Annual Report 2019–2020).
167 Blackbourn & Ors, Anti-Terrorism Law, 46, *citing* IMO an Application for a Preventative Detention Order in Respect of Causevic, (2015) 251 A Crim. R. 481.

168 Criminal Code Act (Cth) §105.1.
169 *Id.*, §105.4.
170 *Id.*, §105.12.
171 Diane Webber, Preventive Detention of Terror Suspects, a New Legal Framework, 117–19, (Routledge, 2016).
172 *Id.*, 118, *citing* Criminal Code Act (Cth) §105.17(7).
173 Criminal Code Act (Cth) §104.5(3).
174 *Id.*, §104.16.
175 *Id.*, §§104.2–104.6.
176 *Id.*, §104.28.
177 Blackbourn & Ors, Anti-Terrorism Law, 46.
178 Criminal Code Act (Cth) §104.2.
179 *Id.*, §104.4.
180 *Id.*, §104.5.
181 *Id.*, §104.12.
182 *Id.*
183 National Security Information (Criminal and Civil Proceedings) Act 2004 (Cth), §§38J (2)-(4), 38PC-PF.
184 Australian Human Rights Commission, Review of Federal Powers, Submission to the Parliamentary Joint Committee on Intelligence and Security, 94–5, (Sep. 10, 2020), https://humanrights.gov.au/sites/default/files/ahrc_afp_powers_submission_to_pjcis_2020.pdf.
185 Timna Baker, *Deprivation on National Security Grounds in Australia: Part of a Wider Trend*, European Network on Statelessness, (Apr. 11, 2019), www.statelessness.eu/blog/deprivation-nationality-national-security-grounds-australia-part-wider-trend; David J. Trimbach and Nicole Reisz, *Unmaking Citizens: The Expansion of Citizenship Revocation in Response to Terrorism*, Center for Migration Studies, (Jan. 30, 2018), https://cmsny.org/publications/unmaking-citizens/#_ftn7.
186 Australian Citizenship Amendment (Allegiance to Australia) Act 2015, No. 166, 2015, §33AA, (Austrl.).
187 *Id.*, §35.
188 *Id.*, §35A.
189 Australian Citizenship Act 2007, §35B.
190 *Id.*, §§35(7), 35B (3).
191 Blackbourn & Ors, Anti-Terrorism Law, 79.
192 John Coyne and Isaac Kfir, *Australia's Citizenship-Stripping Legislation May Be Doing More Harm Than Good*, The Strategist, (Australian Strategic Policy Institute, Aug. 8, 2019), https://.www.aspistrategist.org.au/australias-citizenship-stripping-may-be-doing-more-harm-than-good/. However, in contrast, BLACKBOURN & ORS, 80, state that at the time of writing their book, the citizenship stripping laws had only been used once, in early 2017.
193 Parliament of the Commonwealth of Australia, Parliamentary Joint Committee on Intelligence and Security, Annual Report of Committee Activities 2019–2020, ¶1.78, (Oct. 2020).
194 Ido Levy, *Deradicalization Programs in Australia and the Foreign Fighter Phenomenon*, 8, International Institute for Counter-Terrorism, IDC Herzliya, Israel, (Apr. 2018), www.ict.org/il/images/Australia%20foreign%20fighters.pdf.
195 *Id.*, 9, 14.
196 *Id.*, 33–4.
197 *Id.*, 5.
198 Thomas Renard and Rik Coolsaet, *From the Kingdom to the Caliphate and Back: Returnees in Belgium*, 19, *in* Who Are They, Why Are They (Not) Coming Back and How Should We Deal with Them? Assessing Policies on Returning Foreign

Terrorist Fighters in Belgium, Germany and the Netherlands, (Thomas Renard and Rik Coolsaet, eds., Egmont, Feb. 2018).

199 Daveed Gartenstein-Ross, Colin P. Clarke and Emily Chace-Donahue, *The Enduring Legacy of French and Belgian Islamic State Foreign Fighters*, Foreign Policy Research Institute (FPRI), (Feb. 5, 2020), www.fpri.org/article/2020/02/enduring-legacy-french-belgian-isis-foreign-fighters/.

200 Renard and Coolsaet, *From the Kingdom to the Caliphate and Back: Returnees in Belgium* 29.

201 Constitution of Belgium, Art. 12, amended Oct. 24, 2017: "Except in the case of a flagrant offence, no one can be arrested except on the strength of a reasoned judge's order, which must be served at the latest within forty-eight hours from the deprivation of liberty and which may only result in provisional detention." *See* www.dekamer.br/kvvct/pdf_sections/publications/constitution/GrondwetUK.pdf.

202 Pre-trial Detention Act of 1990. (Be.)

203 Loi portant des dispositions des dispositions diverses en matière de lutte contre le terrorisme, 2016–08–03/15, Art. 6, (Be).

204 Maria Roson, *Belgium Constitutional Court Decision on the Concept of Incitement to Terrorism*, EDRi, (May 30, 2018, *citing* Constitutional Court of Belgium, 31/2018, (preventive detention was also challenged in this case), https://edri.org/belgium-constitutional-court-decision-on-the-concept-of-incitement-to-terrorism/.

205 Eric Maes, Alexia Jonckheere, Magali Deblock and Morgane Hovine, *DETOUR: Towards Pre-Trial Detention as Ultima Ratio*, National Institute for Criminality and Criminology, 4, 8, (Oct. 2016), www.irks.at/detour/Uploads/BE_1st_National_Report.pdf.

206 *Id.*, 8–9.

207 *Id.*, 10–11.

208 Renard and Coolsaet, *From the Kingdom to the Caliphate and Back: Returnees in Belgium*, 29.

209 Ragazzi and Walmsley, *Member States' Approach to Tackling the Return of Foreign Fighters*, 86.

210 Patrick Wautelet, *Deprivation of Citizenship for 'Jihadists:' Analysis of Belgian and French Practice and Policy in the Light of the Principle of Equal Treatment*, *in* Jihad, Islam and the Law: Jihadism and Reactions from the Netherlands and Belgium, 49, (Pauline Kruiniger, ed. B.J.U., 2017).

211 *Id.*, 50, *citing* Code de la Nationalité Belge §23/1.

212 *Id.*, *citing* Code de la Nationalité Belge §23/1 and 23/2.

213 Bolhuis and van Wijk, *Citizenship Deprivation as a Counterterrorism Measure in Europe*.

214 NWS, *Another 14 IS Members Stripped of Their Belgian Citizenship*, Flandersnews.be, (Dec. 18, 2020), www.vrt.be/vrtnws/en/2020/12/18/another-14-is-members-stripped-of-their-belgian-citizenship/.

215 Ragazzi and Walmsley, *Member States' Approach to Tackling the Return of Foreign Fighters*, 25–7.

216 *Id.*, 26.

217 Matthew Campbell, *How 'Speed Dating' Is Preventing ISIS Radicalization in Belgium*, The Sunday Times, (Oct. 3, 2021), www.thetimes.co.uk/article/how-speed-dating-is-preventing-isis-radicalisation-in-belgium-hn8l5qzzj, *noting that* one town's mayor has pioneered a "speed dating" program that requires immigrants and returnees to be matched with a "buddy" to assist with reintegration and support.

218 Ragazzi and Walmsley, *Member States' Approach to Tackling the Return of Foreign Fighters*, 33–7.

219 Rik Coolsaet and Thomas Renard, *Foreign Fighters and the Terrorist Threat in Belgium*, ISPI, (Jan. 9, 2020), www.ispionline.it/en/pubblicazione/foreign-fighters-and-terrorist-threat-belgium-24663.
220 Douglas Quan, *Canada's Ability to Monitor Returning Foreign Fighters Is 'on the Margins' Ex-CSIS Chief Says*, National Post, (Apr. 2, 2019), https://nationalpost.com/news/canada/canadas-ability-to-monitor-returning-foreign-fighters-is-on-the-margins-ex-csis-chief-says/.
221 Marie-Danielle Smith, *'We're Doing Nothing': Canada Could Be a Leader in Handling Its Foreign Fighters, But Isn't, Say Experts.*
222 *See e.g.* Genevieve Zingg, *Canada Increasingly an Outlier by Keeping Its Child Citizens Detained in Syria*, Opencanada.Org, (Dec. 4, 2019), www.opencanada.org/features/canada-increasingly-outlier-heeping-its-child-citizens-detained-syria/.
223 Human Rights Watch, Bring Me Back to Canada, (Jun. 29, 2020), www.hrw.org/report/2020/06/29/bring-me-back-canada/plight-canadians-held-northeast-syria-alleged-isis-links#_ftn3.
224 Amanda Coletta, *Canada to Bring 5-Year-Old Orphan Home from Syrian Camp While Others Remain Stranded*, Washington Post, (Oct. 5, 2020), www.washingtonpost.com/world/the_americas/canada-amira-syria-orphan-repatriated/2020/10/05/bafe08ea-0723-11eb-859b-f9c27abe638d_story.html.
225 Kyle Matthews, *Justice for the Victims: How Canada Should Manage Returning "Foreign Fighters,"* Canadian Global Affairs Institute Policy Paper, (Sep. 2018), www.cgai.ca/justice_for_the_victims_how_canada_should_manage_returning_foreign_fighters.
226 Peace bonds are a Canadian cousin of the British control order, a court-imposed recognizance with conditions. *See* Webber, Preventive Detention of Terror Suspects, 126–9.
227 Janice Dickson, *Terrorism Experts Applaud Minister's Clarifications on Returned Foreign Fighters*, The Globe and Mail, (Jan. 16, 2019), www.theglobeandmail.com/politics/article-terrorism-experts-applaud-public-safety-ministers-clarifications-on/.
228 Stewart Bell, *Canadian Government Begins Invalidating Passports of Citizens Who Have Left to Join Extremist Groups*, National Post, (Sep. 20, 2014), https://nationalpost.com/news/canada/canadian-government-revoking-passports-of-citizens-trying-to-join-extremist-groups.
229 Government of Canada, Cancellation and Revocation of Passports and Refusal of Passport Services on Grounds of National Security, *citing* Canadian Passport Order, SI81–6, §11(2), www.canada.ca/en/immigration-refugees-citizenship/services/canadian-passports/security/refusal-revocation/national-security.html, (last accessed Apr. 21, 2021).
230 *Id.*
231 *Id.*
232 Phil Gurski, *The Foreign Terrorist Fighter Repatriation Challenge: The View from Canada*, International Centre for Counter-Terrorism: The Hague, (Feb. 21, 2019), https://icct.nl/publication/the-foreign-terrorist-fighter-repatriation-challenge-the-view-from-canada/.
233 Trimbach and Reiz, *Unmaking Citizens*, *citing* Strengthening Canadian Citizenship Act 2014 c.24, amending Citizenship Act 1977, §10.2.
234 *Id.*, *citing* Bill C-6, June 2017, amending Citizenship Act, §10.3.
235 Government of Canada, Public Safety Canada, National Strategy on Countering Radicalization to Violence, www.publicsafety.gc.ca/cnt/rsrcs/pblctns/ntnl-strtg-cntrng-rdclztn-vlnc/index-en-aspx, (last accessed Jan. 20, 2020).
236 *Id.*
237 Government of Canada, Public Safety Canada, Mitigating the Threat Posed by Canadian Extremist Travellers, www.publicsafety.gc.ca/cnt/ntnl-scrt/cntr-trrrsm/cndn-xtrmst-trvllrs/index-en.aspx. (last accessed Jan. 20, 2020).

238 Government of Canada, Public Safety Canada, Intervention Programs in Canada, www.publicsafety.gc.ca/cnt/bt/cc/ntrvntn-en.aspx. (last accessed Jan. 20, 2020).
239 Rabiyah Mirza, *Canadian Women in ISIS: Deradicalization and Reintegration for Returnees*, 34, University of Ottawa, 2018; Azra Rashid, *Canadian Women Who Joined ISIS Should Be Repatriated, Investigated and Rehabilitated*, The Conversation, (Mar. 31, 2021), https://theconversation.com/canadian-women-who-joined-isis-should-be-repatriated-investigated-and-rehabilitated-158026.
240 *Id.*, 30.
241 *Suspected Foreign Fighter Extradited to Denmark from Turkey*, Associated Press, (Dec. 18, 2020), https://apnews.com/article/turkey-copenhagen-denmark-islamic-state-group-arrests-f9e719415f4c34fe7241dcbea79330e6.
242 *Human Rights in Denmark 2020*, 19, The Danish Institute for Human Rights, (2020), www.humanrights.dk/sites/humanrights.dk/files/media/dokumenter/udgivelser/annual_report/imr_beretning_uk_web.pdf.
243 *Id.*
244 Hector de Rivoire *et al.*, *Returning Foreign Terrorist Fighters in Europe: A Comparative Analysis*, 19, Council of Europe and University of Strasbourg, (2017).
245 U.S. DoS, Denmark 2018 Human Rights Report, 3–4, www.state.gov/wp-content/uploads/2019/03/DENMARK-2018-HUMAN-RIGHTS-REPORT.pdf.
246 U.S. DoS, Bureau of Counterterrorism, Country Reports on Terrorism 2019: Denmark, www.state.gov/reports/country-reports-on-terrorism-2019/denmark/.
247 *Human Rights in Denmark 2020*, 19, The Danish Institute for Human Rights.
248 *Denmark Approves Stripping IS Fighters of Citizenship*, Deutsche Welle, (Oct. 24, 2019), https://p.dw.com/p/3RrhZ.
249 *Denmark Strips Citizenship from Man under New Anti-Jihadist Law*, The Local, (Nov. 26, 2019), www.thelocal.dk/20191126/denmark-strips-citizenship-from-man-under-new-anti-jihadist-law;*Denmark Strips 2 ISIS Adherents of Citizenship under New Law*, The Defense Post, (Nov. 26, 2019). https://thedefensepost.com/2019/11/26/denmark-isis-citizenship/.
250 W. Christian, *Foreign Fighter Stripped of Citizenship Sues Immigration Minister*, CPH Post Online, (Dec. 20, 2019), cphpost.dk/tag/foreign-fighters.
251 The Constitution of Denmark 1953, Art. 3: "the legislative power shall be vested in the King and the Folketing conjointly. The executive power shall be vested in the King. The judicial power shall be vested in the courts of justice."
252 Ministry of Foreign Affairs of Denmark, *Appendix A: Response by the Government of Denmark to Questions Two and Three from the United Nations Special Rapporteur on Extrajudicial, Summary or Arbitrary Executions on Foreign Fighters*, (2019), https://spcommreports.ohchr.org/TMResultsBase/DownLoadFile?gId=35114.
253 *Id.*
254 Preben Bertelsen, *Danish Preventive Measures and De-Radicalization Strategies: The Aarhus Model*, Panorama Insights into Asian and European Affairs, 241, 242 (Jan. 2015), https://psy.au.dk/fileadmin/Psykologi/Forskning/Preben_Bertelsen/Avisartkler_radikalisering/Panorama.pdf.
255 *Id.*
256 *Id.*, 244.
257 *Id.*
258 Ahmad Saiful Rijal Bin Hassan, *Denmark's Deradicalisation Programme for Returning Foreign Terrorist Fighters*, 11(3) Counter Terrorist Trends and Analyses 13 (International Centre for Political Violence and Terrorism Research, Mar. 2019).
259 Constant Meheut, *France Judges Dead Jihadists But Refuses to Repatriate the Living*, New York Times, (Jan. 26, 2020), www.nytimes.com/2020/01/26/world/europe/framce-ghost-trials-isis.html?

260 Pugliese, *France and Foreign Fighters: The Controversial Outsourcing of Prosecution.*
261 Meheut, *France Judges Dead Jihadists But Refuses to Repatriate the Living.*
262 Sharon Weill, *Terror in Courts, French Counter-Terrorism: Administrative and Penal Avenues, Report for the Official Visit of the U.N. Special Rapporteur on Counter-Terrorism and Human Rights*, 9, (May 2018), *citing* Loi No. 2014–1353, Art. L224–1 (Nov. 13, 2014) (Fr.), www.sciencespo.fr/psia/sites/sciencespo.fr.psia/files/Terror%20in%20Courts_2.pdf; *see also* Elena Pokalova, Returning Islamist Foreign Fighters, 112, (Palgrave Macmillan, 2020).
263 Loi No. 2016–987 (Jul. 21, 2016).
264 Weill, *Terror in Courts, French Counter-Terrorism*, 11, *citing* Conseil Constitutionel, Decision No. 2015–490 QPC of Oct. 14, 2015, M. Omar K.
265 Code de Procédure Pénale, (CPP) Arts. 706–88 (Fr.), *and see* Webber, Preventive Detention of Terror Suspects, 161–8.
266 *Id.*, *citing* CPP Art. 144.
267 Sharon Weill, *French Foreign Fighters: The Engagement of Administrative and Criminal Justice in France*, 100 International Review of the Red Cross 211, 216. (2018).
268 *Id.*, *citing* Art. L228(1–7) Law of Internal Security, introduced by Art. 3 of Law No. 2017–1510 (Oct. 30, 2017).
269 *Id.*, 217, *citing* Law on Internal Security, Art. L 228–1 (2017).
270 Fabien Merz, *Dealing with Jihadist Returnees: A Tough Challenge*, 210 Center for Security Studies Analyses in Security Policy, (ETH Zurich, 2017).
271 Weill, *French Foreign Fighters*, 217.
272 *Id.*
273 *Id.* For example, 754 persons were under house arrest in November 2017, and as of April 2019, the measures were being used on 127 persons.
274 *Id.*, 218, *citing* Constitutional Council, *M. Cedric D.*, Decision No. 2015–52, Appeal for Judicial Review, (QPC), 22 (Dec. 2015).
275 Eda Seyhan, *Liberté, Egalité, Absurdity*, Amnesty International, (Nov. 22, 2018), www.amnesty.org/en/latest/news/2018/11/liberty-egality-absurdity/.
276 Wautelet, *Deprivation of Citizenship for 'Jihadists'*, 52, *citing* Art No. 96–647 of Jul. 22, 1996 (Fr.).
277 Jade Maillet-Contoz, *Terrorism and Counter-Terrorism: French Policy after the 2015 Attacks*, E-International Relations, (Dec. 7, 2018), www.e-ir.info/2018/12/07/terrorism-and-counterterrorism-french-policy-after-the-2015-attacks/#_ftn16, *citing* Yohan Blavignat, *Déchéance de nationalité: un abandon en six actes*, Le Figaro, (Mar. 30, 2016), www.lefigaro.fr/politique/le-scan/2016/03/30/25001-20160330ARTFIG00296-decheance-de-nationalite-un-abandon-en-six-actes.php.
278 Code Civil, Art. 25 (Fr.).
279 Bolhuis and Wijk, *Citizenship Deprivation as a Counterterrorism Measure in Europe.*
280 Merz, *Dealing with Jihadist Returnees.*
281 H.J. Mai, *Why European Countries Are Reluctant to Repatriate Citizens Who Are ISIS Fighters*, NPR, (Dec. 10, 2019), www.npr.org/2019/12/10/783369673/europe-remains-reluctant-to-repatriate-its-isi-citizens-here-s-why/.
282 Maddy Crowell, *What Went Wrong with France's Deradicalization Program?* The Atlantic, (Sep. 28, 2017), www.theatlantic.com/international/archive/2017/09/france-jihad-deradicalization-macron/540699/; Elena Souris and Spandana Singh, *Want to Deradicalize Terrorist? Treat Them Like Everyone Else*, Foreign Policy, (Nov. 23, 2018), https://foreignpolicy.com/2018/11/23/want-to-deradicalize-terrorists-treat-them-like-everyone-else-counterterrorism-deradicalization-france-sri-lanka-pontourny-cve.

283 Alastair Reed and Johanna Pohl, *Tacking the Surge of Returning Foreign Fighters*, NATO Review, (Jul. 14, 2017), www.nato.int/docu/review/articles/2017/07/14/tackling-the-surge-of-returning-foreign-fighters/index.html.
284 *French Prime Minister Unveils New Deradicalization Program*, France 24, (Feb. 23, 2018), www.france24.com/en/20180223-france-deradicalisation-program-jihad-extremists-prisons-centres-philippe.
285 U.S. DoS Publication, Bureau of Counterterrorism, Country Reports on Terrorism 2018, 85 (Oct. 2019), www.justice.gov/eoir/page/file/215411/download#page85.
286 *See e.g.* Brandee Leon, *The Challenge of Deradicalization: What Happens After?* Real Clear Defense, (Jul. 2, 2019), https:www.realcleardefense.com/articles/2019/07/02/the_challenge_of_deradicalization_what_happens_after_114553.html; Lisa Louis, *Is France's Deradicalization Strategy Missing the Point?* Deutsche Welle, (Dec. 12, 2018), www.dw.com/en/is-frances-deradicalization-strategymissing-the-point/a-43772816.
287 Mais Masadeh, *A Lost Phone Brings a Female ISIS Returnee to Trial for Crimes against Humanity*, Just Security, (May 22, 2020), www.justsecurity.org/70280/a-lost-phone-brings-a-female-isis-returnee-to-trial-for-crimes-against-humanity/.
288 *Id.*
289 Library of Congress, *Legal Monitor, Germany: New Anti-Terrorism Legislation Entered into Force*, (Jul. 10, 2015), www.loc.gov/law/foreign-news/article/germany-new-anti-terrorism-legislation-entered-into-force/.
290 Ragazzi and Walmsley, *Member States' Approach to Tackling the Return of Foreign Fighters.*
291 Daniel H. Heinke and Jan Raudszus, *Germany's Returning Foreign Fighters and What to Do about Them*, *in* Returnees: Who Are They, Why Are They (Not) Coming Back and How Should We Deal with Them? 50, (Thomas Renard and Rik Coolsaet, eds., Egmont Institute, Feb. 2018).
292 Christina Morgenstern, Hans Kromrey, *Detour: Towards Pre-Trial Detention as Ultima Ratio*, 13, University of Greifswald, (2016), *citing* §§ 121, 122 Code Criminal Procedure (Ger.).
293 *Germany Toughens Citizenship Laws for Terrorists and Polygamists*, Deutsche Welle, (Jun. 26, 2019), www.dw.com/en/germany-toughens-citizenship-laws-for-terrorists-and-polygamists/a-49386785; Nationality Act of July 22, 1913, §17, as amended June 2019. [citation needed].
294 Kilian Roithmaier, *Germany and Its Returning Foreign Fighters: New Loss of Citizenship Law and the Broader German Repatriation Landscape*, International Centre for Counter-Terrorism: The Hague, (Apr. 19, 2019), https://icct.nl/publication/germany-and-its-returning-foreign-terrorist-fighters-new-loss-of-citizenship-law-and-the-broader-german-repatriation-landscape/.
295 Bolhuis and Wijk, *Citizenship Deprivation as a Counterterrorism Measure in Europe.*
296 *Id.*
297 Reed and Pohl, *Tackling the Surge of Returning Foreign Fighters.*
298 *Germany: Extremism & Counter-Extremism*, Counter Extremism Project, www.counterextremism.com/countries/germany.
299 Ragazzi and Walmsley, *Member States' Approach to Tackling the Return of Foreign Fighters*, 94.
300 Daniel Koehler, *Family Counselling as Prevention and Intervention Tool against Foreign Fighters: The German 'Hayat' Program*, Journal Exit-Deutschland, (Mar. 2013).
301 *Id.*, 95–6.

302 Ido Levy, *Why Are There So Few Islamic State Recruits from Israel?* Georgetown Public Policy Review, (Apr. 1, 2019), http://gppreview.com/2019/04/01/islamic-state-recruits-israel/.
303 Israel Ministry of Foreign Affairs, *ISA Arrests Israeli Arab Suspected of Joining the Jabat al-Nusra Terrorist Group in Syria*, (Jun. 2, 2019), https://mfa.gov.il/MFA/ForeignPolicy/Terrorism/Pages/ISA-arrests-Israeli-Arab-suspected-of-joining-Jabat-al-Nusra-in-Syria-2-June-2019.aspx. A number of other persons who were ISIS supporters other than returnees have been prosecuted since 2017, see https://mfa.gov.il/MFA/ForeignPolicy/Terrorism/Pages/default.aspx?WPID=WPQ4&PN=6, (last accessed Apr. 28, 2021).
304 Library of Congress, *Global Legal Monitor, Israel: Amendment Authorizing Revocation of Israeli Nationality Passed*, (Mar. 23, 2017), www.loc.gov/law/foreign-news/article/israel-amendment-authorizing-revocation-of-israeli-nationality-passed/, *citing* Nationality (Amendment No. 13) Law 5777–2017, §11(a).
305 *Id.*, *citing* §11(b).
306 *Id.*, *citing* §11(b)(2).
307 *Id.*, *citing* §11(2)(d) (1)-(4).
308 *Id.*, *citing* §11(2)(d)(3).
309 Anna Ahronheim, *19 Israelis to Have Citizenship Revoked for Fighting with ISIS*, The Jerusalem Post, (Aug. 22, 2017), www.jpost.com/arab-israeli-conflict/19-israelis-to-have-citizenship-revoked-for-fighting-with-isis-503145; Times of Israel Staff, *Israeli Islamic State Fighter Stripped of Citizenship in Absentia*, The Times of Israel, (Apr. 5, 2019), www.timesofisrael.com/israeli-islamic-state-fighter-stripped-of-citizenship-in-absentia/.
310 U.S. DoS, Country Reports on Terrorism 2019: Italy, www.state.gov/reports/country-reports-on-terrorism-2019/italy/; Joe Snell, *Terror Charges Follow Islamic State Woman Repatriated to Italy*, Al-Monitor, (Sep. 30, 2020), www.al-monitor.com/originals/2020/09/syria-al-hol-islamic-state-isis-italy-repatriate-terrorism.html; Reuters Staff, *Italy Jails Suspected al Qaeda Foreign Fighter Caught in Turkey*, Reuters, (Jan. 20, 2021), www.reuters.com/article/italy-security-arrest-idINKBN29P1H6.
311 Arianna Vedaschi and Chiara Graziani, *Citizenship Revocation in Italy as a Counter Terrorism Measure*, Verfassungsblog on Matters Constitutional, Verfassungsblog, (Jan. 29, 2019), https://verfassungsblog.de/citizenship-revocation-in-italy-as-a-counter-terrorism-measure/.
312 Valentina Cominetti, *The Italian Approach to De-Radicalization*, 12, International Institute for Counter-Terrorism, IDC Herzliya, (Dec. 2018), www.ict.org.il/images/Valentina%20Cominetti%20-%20final%20version.pdf.
313 *Id.*
314 *Id.*, 56.
315 U.S. DoS Publication, Bureau of Counterterrorism, Country Reports on Terrorism 2018, 169 (Oct. 2019).
316 Law of the Republic of Kazakhstan on Citizenship of the Republic of Kazakhstan 1991 as amended, Art. 17(7).
317 Almaz Kumenov, *Kazakhstan: Terror Suspects Found among Syrian Evacuees*, Eurasianet, (Jan. 10, 2019), https://eurasianet.org/kazakhstan-terror-suspects-found-among-syrian-evacuees. See also.
318 OSCE, ODIHR, *Guidelines for Addressing the Threats and Challenges of "Foreign Terrorist Fighters: Within a Human Rights Framework*, fn 169, (2018), www.osce.org/files/f/documents/4/7/393503_2.pdf, *citing Nations in Transit 2018, Kazakhstan, Country Profile*, Freedom House, www.rferl.org/a/kazakhstan-citizenship-law-nazarbaev/28610008.html; C. Putz, *Kazakhstan Considers Revoking Terrorists'*

Citizenship, The Diplomat, (May, 24, 2017), https://thediplomat,com/2017/05/kazakhstan-considers-revoking-terrorists-citizenship/.

319 Ashley Burke, *American Who Freed Canadian Girl Calls on World to Repatriate Children Stranded in Syrian Camps*, CBC News, (Mar. 17, 2021), www.cbc.ca/news/politics/former-us-diplomat-wants-children-freed-syria-detention-camps-1.5951716; Georgi Gotev, *Kazakhstan Prepatriates 'Foreign Fighters' from Syria*, Euractiv, (Apr. 2, 2021), www.euractiv.com/section/central-asia/news/kazakhstan-repatriates-foreign-fighters-from-syria/.

320 Anna Gussarova, *Repatriating Foreign Fighters: The Case of Kazakhstan*, European Eye on Radicalization, (Apr. 17, 2020), https://eeradicalization.com/repatriating-foreign-fighters-the-case-of-kazakhstan/; Stevan Weine, *Rehabilitating the Islamic State's Women and Children Returnees in Kazakhstan*, Just Security, (Dec. 12, 2019), www.justsecurity.org/67694/rehabilitating-the-islamic-states-women-and-children-returnees-in-kazakhstan/.

321 *Id.*

322 *Id.*

323 Asim Kashgarian, *Could Kazakhstan Efforts to Repatriate Foreign Fighters Be a Model?*, Voice of America, (Jan. 15, 2021), www.voanews.com/extremism-watch/could-kazakhstan-efforts-repatriate-foreign-fighters-be-model.

324 Goos Hofstee, *The Debate around Returning Foreign Fighters in the Netherlands*, ISPI, (Jan. 9, 2020), www.ispionlinee.it/en/pubblicazione/debate-around-returning-foreign-fighters-netherlands-24665.

325 Society, *Minister Says IS Women Deportation Is 'Very Disappointing'*, Dutch News.Nl, (Nov. 20, 2019), www.dutchnews.nl/news/2019/11/minister-says-is-women-deportation-is-very-disappointing/.

326 Bolhuis and Wijk, *Citizenship Deprivation as a Counterterrorism Measure in Europe*, 362–3.

327 Crime, *Rotterdam Woman Who Joined ISIS Given 4 Years in Prison*, NL Times, (Apr. 7, 2021), https://nltimes.nl/2021/04/17/rotterdam-woman-joined-isis-given-4-years-prison.

328 Ragazzi and Walmsley, *Member States' Approach to Tackling the Return of Foreign Fighters*, 55, *citing* Interim Act on Counterterrorism Administrative Measures 2017 (N.L.).

329 Bibi Van Ginkel and Simon Minks, *Addressing the Challenge of Returnees: Threat Perceptions, Policies and Practices in the Netherlands*, 64, Egmont Institute, 2018.

330 *Id.*, 65.

331 Jan Crijns, Bas Leeuw and Hilde Wermink, *Pre-Trial Detention in the Netherlands: Legal Principles versus Practical Reality*, 22–5, University of Leiden, (Mar. 2016), https://fairtrials.org/wp-content/uploads/j.h.crijns2c-b.j.g.-leeuw-h.t.wermink-pre-trial-detention-in-the-netherlands-legal-principles-versus-practical-reality.pdf.

332 *Id.*, 24–5, *citing* Code of Criminal Procedure, Art. 67.

333 *Id.*, 22–5, *citing* Code of Criminal Procedure, Art. 80; Ragazzi and Walmsley, *Member States' Approach to Tackling the Return of Foreign Fighters*, 46.

334 *The Legality of Revocation of Dutch Nationality of Dual Nationals Involved in Terrorist Organizations*, 5, Migration Law Clinic, University of Amsterdam, (Jul. 2018), https://migrationlawclinic.files.wordpress.com/2018/09/mlc-nationality-case-final-version.pdf, *citing* Dutch Nationality Act, Art. 14(2).

335 *Id.*, 7, *citing* Dutch Nationality Act, Art. 14(4).

336 Bolhuis and Wijk, *Citizenship Deprivation as a Counterterrorism Measure in Europe*, 346.

337 Ragazzi and Josh Walmsley, *Member States' Approach to Tackling the Return of Foreign Fighters*, 66–7.
338 *Id.*, 97.
339 Hofstee, *The Debate around Returning Foreign Fighters in the Netherlands.*
340 U.S. DoS, FTF Briefing, (Mar. 29, 2021).
341 *Id.*; Catherine Philp, *Joe Biden Urges Western Allies to Bring Back ISIS Families Held in Syria*, The Times, (Mar. 31, 2021), www.thetimes.co.uk/article/joe-biden-urges-western-allies-to-bring-back-isis-families-held-in-syria-sng77cngg.
342 Robin Wright, *Despite Trump's Guantanamo Threats, Americans Who Joined ISIS Are Quietly Returning Home*, The New Yorker, (Jun. 11, 2019), https://newyorker.com/news/news-desk/americas-isi-members-are-coming-home.
343 Alexander Meleagrou-Hitchens, Seamus Hughes and Bennett Clifford, *The Travelers: American Jihadists in Syria and Iraq*, 75–6, George Washington University Program on Extremism, (Feb. 2018), https://extremism.gwu.edu/sites/g/files/zaxdzs2191/f/TravelersAmericanJihadistsinSyriaandIraq.pdf.
344 *Id.*, 71, 79.
345 Robin Wright, *Despite Trump's Guantanamo Threats, Americans Who Joined ISIS Are Quietly Returning Home.*
346 John Doe v. Gen. James N. Mattis, Case 1:17-cv-2069 (TSC), filed in DDC Feb. 14, 2018.
347 Wright, *Despite Trump's Guantanamo Threats, Americans Who Joined ISIS Are Quietly Returning Home.*
348 8 U.S.C. §1481.
349 8 U.S.C. §1451.
350 U.S. Const. amend. XIV, ¶1; Tim O'Shea, *Immigrants: Can the Government Revoke Your Citizenship?*, Bipartisan Policy Center, (Jul. 5, 2018), https://bipartisanpolicy.org/blog/immigrants-can-the-government-revoke-your-citizenship/.
351 *See e.g.* United States v. Ahmed, 2019 U.S. Dist. LEXIS 175388, Case No. 18-cv-4598 (Sep. 20, 2019). The defendant had been convicted in 2009 for providing material support to terrorists during the statutory five-year period of having a good moral character required before naturalization.
352 *See e.g.* Saul Elbein, *The Un-American*, The New Republic, (Mar. 23, 2020), https://newrepublic.com/article/156793/isis-american-hoda-muthana-trump-birthright-citizenship; Rukmini Callimachi and Catherine Porter, *2 American Wives of ISIS Militants Want to Return Home*, New York Times, (Feb. 19, 2019), www.nytimes.com/2019/02/19/us/islamic-state-american-women.html; Nadia Al Faour, Kin Hjelmgaard, Revor Hughes and Deirdre Shesgreen, *The Making of an American Terrorist: Hoda Muthana Joined ISIS: Now She Can't Come Back*, USA Today, (Apr. 6, 2019), www.usatoday.com/story/news/world/2019/04/06/hoda-muthana-married-isis-fighters-so-trump-wont-let-her-back-usa/3350233002/.
353 Muthana v. Pompeo, 2019 U.S. Distr. LEXIS 218098, Civil Action No. 19–445 (RBW), 4, D.D.C. (Dec. 17, 2019) (Muthana v. Pompeo 2019).
354 Muthana v. Pompeo, 985 F.3d 893, 899 (Jan. 19, 2021), (Muthana v. Pompeo 2021).
355 *Id.*
356 Mutana v. Pompeo 2019, 5.
357 *Id.*, 23–4, *citing* Nikoi v. Att. Gen of United States, 939 F.2d 1065, 1066 (1991), *quoting* Slaughter-House Cases, 83 U.S. 36, 73 (1873), *citing* United States v. Wong Kim Ark, 169 U.S. 649, 693 (1898).
358 *Id.*, *citing* Raya v. Clinton, 703 F. Supp. 2d 569, 576 (W.D. Va 2010), "if the plaintiff's father was entitled to diplomatic privileges and immunities in this country on the date the plaintiff was born, the plaintiff is not a United States citizen."
359 *Id.*, 25–7, *citing* The Vienna Convention on Diplomatic Relations, Art. 39(2).

360 *Id.*, 32–3.
361 *Id.*, 35–7, *citing* 8 U.S.C. §1504; Atem v. Ashcroft, 312 F. Supp. 2d 792, 799 (E.D. Va. 2004), on passport cancellation and Hizam v. Kerry 747 F.3d 102, 110, (2d Cir. 2014) which confirmed that a court cannot confer citizenship nor order the issue of a passport in these circumstances.
362 *Id.*, 901–2.
363 *Id.*, 908.
364 *Id.*, 898–9, 903, 910.
365 *Id.*
366 Meleagrou-Hitchens and Ors, *The Travelers: American Jihadists in Syria and Iraq*, 81.
367 Ivy Kaplan, *An Inside Look at the First US Domestic Deradicalization Program*, The Defense Post, (Feb. 12, 2019), https://thedefensepost.com/2019/02/12/us-minnesota-deradicalizatio-porogram-inside-look/.
368 Ragazzi and Walmsley, *Member States' Approach to Tackling the Return of Foreign Fighters*, 40.
369 *Id.*
370 Meghan Benton and Natalia Banulescu-Bogdan, *Foreign Fighters: Will Revoking Citizenship Mitigate the Threat?* Migration Policy Institute, (Apr. 2019), www.migrationpolicy.org/article/foreign-fighters-will-revoking-citizenship-mitigate-threat.
371 Anthony Dworkin, *Beyond Good and Evil*, 10.
372 Nate Rosenblatt, *'A Caliphate That Gathered:' Addressing the Challenge of Jihadist Foreign Fighter Hubs*, 5, The Washington Institute for Near East Policy, Policy Notes No. 104, (Apr. 2021), www.washingtoninstitute.org/media/4462.
373 George Popp, Sarah Canna and Jeff Day, *Common Characteristics of "Successful" Deradicalization Programs of the Past*, NSI Reachback Report, (Feb. 2020), https://nsiteam.com/social/wp-content/uploads/2020/02/NSI-Reachback_B2_Common-Characteristics-of-Successful-Deradicalization-Programs-of-the-Past_Feb2020_Final.pdf.
374 *Id.* The first six listed countries are discussed in this chapter: Denmark, France, Germany, the Netherlands, Kazakhstan, Uzbekistan, Norway, Sweden, Northern Ireland, Saudi Arabia, Egypt, Iraq, Yemen, Algeria, Morocco, Nigeria, Congo, Pakistan, Sri Lanka, Bangladesh, Indonesia, Singapore, Tajikistan, China, Colombia.
375 *Id.*, 3.

Part V
Conclusions

Part V analyzes the judicial trends in cases dealing with counter-terrorism policies as discussed in Parts I, II, III, and IV and examines the public attitudes to the strategies. It concludes that the judicial approach has shifted from back and forth between security and liberty and settled at being predominantly deferential to government policy, and that a fairly large percentage of the public is not particularly concerned about any human rights implications arising out of these counter-terrorism measures. The section goes on to discuss the implications of the judicial and public trends and argues that the failure to respect human and humanitarian rights adequately may provide some explanation as to why the threat of terrorist activity has not decreased in response to current counter-terrorism strategies, that some of these strategies may actually encourage individuals to resort to use terrorist violence, and finally offers suggestions to address the problem.

DOI: 10.4324/9780367817275-12

8 Conclusions

1. Judicial trends

The role of the judiciary in democratic societies is traditionally understood to be one of interpreting the law and deciding disputes. In the United States, in 1787, Alexander Hamilton's vision was that the judiciary should be a "watchdog for liberty."[1] This could be construed as merely suggesting that judges should be mindful of human rights in their interpretation of the law. But how far can and should the judiciary go? Although a particular interpretation of a statute may result in a perception that the law has altered, in most, if not all countries, judges cannot change the law: that is the job of the legislature. Of the three countries discussed in this book, in the United States, the judges can strike down a law that is incompatible with the terms set out in the United States Constitution and its Amendments. In the United Kingdom, the judges can declare that a law is incompatible with the European Convention of Human Rights. In Israel, the judges can declare that a law is inconsistent with the Basic Law. In the 20 years since 9/11, the liberty/security balance has not remained static.

Preventive detention

Even in international human rights judicial bodies, shifting trends of judicial attitudes can be discerned; most noticeably in the jurisprudence of the European Court of Human Rights (ECtHR). Some might assume that international human rights judicial bodies would always rule in a human rights friendly manner, according to how they interpreted provisions in the relevant human rights Conventions. However, in cases involving national security in particular, the ECtHR has always recognized what is termed a "margin of appreciation" where it has been reluctant to interfere with government discretion in certain counter-terrorism policies.[2]

In the 2009 judgment of *A. v. United Kingdom* the ECtHR departed from its more usual stance of governmental deference in the area of national security.[3] After 9/11 the United Kingdom had enacted a number of counter-terrorism laws, one of which permitted the indefinite detention of international suspected terrorists.[4] The applicants had appealed their detention all the way through the domestic United Kingdom courts to the then-named House of Lords, where a

DOI: 10.4324/9780367817275-13

majority of judges had ruled that the detention was incompatible with Article 5 European Convention (ECHR).[5] That determination was not binding on the United Kingdom government, and because the applicants remained in detention, their only recourse was to petition the ECtHR. The ECtHR noted that "a wide margin of appreciation should be left to the national authorities. Nonetheless Contracting Parties do not enjoy an unlimited discretion."[6] The Court agreed that there was a public emergency that threatened the life of the nation,[7] but the derogating measures were disproportionate because they discriminated between U.K. nationals and non-nationals.[8] Following this finding of a violation of Article 5, the United Kingdom changed its law.

However, a significant shift in ECtHR opinion in the other direction was seen in the 2018 case of *S., V. and A. v. Denmark*. The Court queried the long line of a more restrictive, but what was actually a more human rights-friendly interpretation of preventive detention pursuant to Article 5(1)(c) that mandated that detention had to be connected with criminal proceedings. The Court commented that there was a need to revisit and clarify its confusing case law on this topic, not only to ensure greater consistency and coherence, but also to "address more appropriately modern societal issues."[9] Although that case concerned a short period of detention to prevent football hooliganism, there is no reason why any changes in interpretation would not apply to all cases of preventive detention pursuant to Article 5(1)(c). A more expansive interpretation that does not tie detention to criminal proceedings is more deferential to governments that wish to detain persons to prevent a terrorist act (or any other crime). However, if the protections against arbitrary detention were retained, human rights protections would be unaffected.

In the United States domestic criminal jurisprudence relating to material witness detention[10] and immigration detention,[11] the cases have been mainly deferential to government policy, apart from one short period involving cases deriving from the Guantanamo detentions. Between 2004 and 2008 the Supreme Court pushed back from the governmental stance adopted after 9/11, that detainees at Guantanamo had no rights whatsoever, particularly as regards duration of detention, treatment of detainees and challenging detention. A series of human rights-friendly rulings were delivered starting in late June 2004, a month after CBS had released shocking photographs relating to the treatment of detainees at Abu Ghraib prison.[12]

The first of these cases was *Hamdi v. Rumsfeld*, in which a plurality of the Supreme Court held that United States citizens who fought against the United States in Afghanistan as part of the Taliban could not be held in indefinite detention but could only be detained "for the duration of the conflict."[13] The Court was treating the case as one grounded in international humanitarian law (IHL) but referred to principles relating to detention as set out in Art. 118 of Geneva Convention III, which would be applicable only to an international armed conflict (which this was not). The Court went on to hold that a citizen-detainee must receive notice of the factual basis for his designation as a detainee, must be given a fair opportunity to challenge the detention, and have access to a lawyer.[14] Two days later, in *Rasul v. Bush*, statutory *habeas corpus* protection was given to all detainees in Guantanamo.[15]

In 2006 in *Hamdan v. Rumsfeld*, the Supreme Court acknowledged that the conflict with al-Qaeda was in fact a non-international armed conflict where only Common Article 3 applied. This provision prohibits torture and cruel treatment, and requires that detainees should be tried by a "regularly constituted court."[16] Legislation was enacted in 2006 establishing a procedure to challenge detention in a military commission,[17] but the 2008 ruling in *Boumediene v. Bush* determined that the legislation was not an adequate or effective substitute for *habeas corpus*, and that detainees in Guantanamo should have the right to challenge detention by claiming the constitutional privilege of *habeas corpus* in a U.S. federal court.[18]

The Supreme Court did not accept any other Guantanamo cases after Boumediene until 2021, and most of the *habeas* litigation has been conducted in the District of Columbia federal courts. *Boumediene* ended the run of human rights-friendly decisions. Since 2008 there has been a shift back to governmental deference as seen in the cases analyzed in Part II. The first Guantanamo case to come before the Supreme Court since 2008 was that of Abu Zubayda. The Court heard argument in October 2021 about whether the government could refuse to give him information relating to his detention and torture, on the grounds that this information was a state secret.[19] It remains to be seen whether the Supreme Court will take a deferential approach to this case.

The United Kingdom's Supreme Court is the highest court in England, Scotland, Wales, and Northern Ireland, but since 1998 it has not been the end of the road for persons claiming that their human rights have been violated. If the domestic courts have produced results involving deference to government policy, some aggrieved litigants have achieved greater satisfaction at the hands of the ECtHR.[20] In the United Kingdom the judicial trend has also moved for a time from deference, to more human rights-friendly decisions, often as a result of taking ECtHR rulings into account.[21] For example, in *Secretary of State v. JJ* concerning the imposition of an eighteen hour curfew in the now-abolished control orders[22] as an attempt to prevent terrorist activity, the court took notice of ECtHR rulings concerning Article 5 ECHR, and ruled that the curfew violated Article 5.[23] In 2007 the House of Lords ruled that control orders could be quashed if they violated the Article 6 ECHR right to a fair trial,[24] and in 2009, in *A. v. United Kingdom*, the ECtHR ruled that Article 6 ECHR required that a controlee must be given sufficient information about his case for him to give effective instructions to his lawyer in judicial review hearings.[25] This ruling prompted the House of Lords to acknowledge that this procedural change was necessary and applicable to control orders, and subsequently to other administrative measures cases.[26]

The 2017 case of *Hicks* which is discussed in Part II is an example of a move back to deference, as are the cases relating to detention overseas by British forces.[27] Further examples of the shift can be seen in cases relating to Terrorism Prevention and Investigation Measures (TPIMs), which were introduced in 2012 to replace control orders.[28] They do not deprive persons of liberty but can restrict movement and various activities. Frequently, persons subject to TPIMs complain about the severity of conditions, but in the majority of those cases, the courts have made rulings deferential to the government, purportedly in the interests of national security.[29]

In Israel, although a number of procedural safeguards exist that give detainees some rights relating to judicial review, there is a unique "judicial management model" where the judge alone sees and reviews the evidence against a detainee. However, out of 322 cases adjudicated between 2000 and 2010, no case resulted in the release of a detainee.[30] The importance of human rights is seen in the "Bargaining Chips" case, which outlawed indefinite detention[31] and the "Torture" case, which prohibited certain interrogation techniques.[32] However, in 2009 the court took a more deferential approach, by refusing to hear a petition that claimed that the "Torture" case ruling had been violated in many cases.[33]

Targeted killing

The international IHRL decisions have not been particularly deferential to policies of State parties and focus on the requirements of not acting in an arbitrary fashion, and of using force only when it is absolutely necessary and in a proportionate manner,[34] and ensuring that investigations take place into alleged violations.[35] There is a dearth of cases relating to the IHL aspects of targeted killing by drones. However, a trend has been discerned in IHRL cases since about 2014 whereby the relationship between IHL and IHRL has been discussed with an acknowledgement that certain elements of IHRL may apply in LOAC cases.[36]

In the United States, all the cases relating to targeted killing that have taken place outside of places where U.S. forces are not actually participating in an armed conflict have been treated as being governed either by IHL or *ius in bello*. However, the federal court judiciary has in principle acknowledged the human rights-friendly stance that the government does not have "*carte blanche* to deprive a U.S. citizen of life without due process and without any judicial review."[37] Yet even though relatives of those killed as collateral damage can in theory make a claim, in practice, the courts have been totally deferential to government policy, with cases failing. This is because claimants could not pierce the mist of secrecy surrounding drone strikes and because they encountered many technical legal obstacles, including standing, state secrets privilege and political question doctrine relating to foreign policy.[38]

The United Kingdom's participation in drone strikes is also lacking in transparency and accountability. Many of the United Kingdom's targeted killing cases relate to shooting incidents, but the IHL and IHRL principles are the same as they would be in cases about killing by drones. Again, prompted by an ECtHR ruling, the United Kingdom was forced to accept that in places where there was a jurisdictional link between the victims and the United Kingdom, the ECHR would apply, and the activities of British troops would be assessed through a human rights lens. Even if there was no substantive violation of Article 2 ECHR, a failure to comply with ECHR procedural requirements would result in the ECtHR finding a violation of Article 2 ECHR.[39]

The United Kingdom courts have, like the United States, deferred to government policy in cases involving questions relating to any form of United Kingdom involvement in U.S. drone strikes, including cases where the only British involvement was the provision of information.[40] There have not been a large number of targeted killing cases litigated in the British courts, not least because as mentioned in Parts II and III, the United Kingdom government has settled hundreds of claims relating to abusive treatment and unlawful treatment by British soldiers, including killings, although the breakdown between abusive treatment and killing claims is not known.

Unlike the secrecy surrounding targeted killing in the United States and the United Kingdom, Israel's practice of targeted killing for counter-terrorism purposes has been conducted openly since 2000. The legality of the policy and practice was confirmed in a landmark "Targeted Killing" case to be in accordance with customary international law, with a unique interpretation of IHL,[41] as discussed in Part III. One human rights element that can be discerned in the case is the requirement that any deaths arising out of a targeted strike should be independently investigated.[42] This reflects a more human rights approach than found in IHL provisions, which merely requires an official enquiry.[43]

Although one could not describe the judiciary as having taken a human rights approach in the "Targeted Killing" case, it can be said that they were "activist" and many activist judgments did emanate from the court with elements of human rights, such as in the "Bargaining Chips" and "Torture" cases as described above in the context of preventive detention. However, as discussed in Part III, after the 2009 Gaza conflict a shift towards deference to governmental policy has been perceived.[44]

Foreign fighters

A human rights approach has not featured heavily in the way most of the countries discussed in Part IV have handled the issue of repatriating their foreign terrorist fighters (FTFs), as many countries do not want their citizens back.[45] In some European countries where adults or children have been denied entry, petitions have been issued in international courts, such as in the case where French grandparents petitioned the U.N. Committee on the Rights of the Child, to get their grandchildren removed from a Syrian detention camp and repatriated to France.[46] However, even the ECtHR has shown deference to the national security policy of a Member State in cases involving terrorism, as exemplified in the 2020 case of *Ghoumid v. France*.[47]

In Part IV it was mentioned that the method of choice of many countries for dealing with returning FTFs would be prosecution, but Table 7.1 showed that out of the 12 countries surveyed, the percentage of FTFs who had been or are being prosecuted was relatively low, with the United States having the highest percentage – 83%, with France not too far behind at 73.9%, and Germany at 62.7%, but the rest lagged a long way behind. The most commonly-stated reason for the low numbers of prosecution related to the difficulty of obtaining credible and admissible evidence. The countries therefore have resorted to using various administrative measures to give them some control over whether FTFs can return, and if they do return, over the FTFs' behavior and activities, as well as their mindsets, by way of disengagement and deradicalization programs.

All the litigation discussed in Part IV concerned the administrative measures employed by those 12 countries. The largest number of cases relating to returning foreign fighters with judgments in English are found in the United Kingdom (which has prosecuted about 10% of returning FTFs) and these cases all tend to be deferential to United Kingdom counter-terrorism policy. The example cases of *K2*[48] and *Shamima Begum*,[49] (cases in which much of previous litigation on the points under discussion had been cited and discussed) which were examined in detail in Part IV, show that each level of court thoroughly analyzed the facts and the law, and were mindful of the human rights considerations. However, in cases where the government adduced evidence to show that the FTFs posed a threat to the United Kingdom, the court almost always deferred to the government. In particular, the Supreme Court's decision in *Begum* displayed a remarkable deferential swing away from the earlier more human rights friendly Court of Appeal decision. One exception to the trend was seen in *D4*, where the High Court declared that a citizenship deprivation order of a woman held in a Syrian camp was a nullity. Because the regulation governing the procedural aspects of the law was declared *ultra vires*, D4 was not given the notice required by statute.[50] It may be that courts are more willing to deal with procedural human rights requirements than substantive issues which frequently bring the courts in collision with governmental interests.

In Belgium, in a case concerning preventive detention, the Constitutional Court assessed the constitutionality of legislation providing for stronger preventive measures in terrorism cases than those applicable in general criminal cases. The Court ruled that the stronger measures were constitutional, even though they might affect civil liberties.[51]

Other than prosecutions, virtually no cases relating to returning FTFs in the United States have been found. One case that generated some media attention concerned the deprivation of citizenship of ISIS bride *Hoda Muthana*, as discussed in Part IV. However, it was a case that turned on its own technical facts relating to how and when a child of a diplomat could acquire citizenship, and as such, adds nothing to the question of judicial trends in this section.

2. Political narrative and counter-terrorism policy after 9/11: public opinion and the press

This section now turns to an examination of trends in political narrative, public opinion, and press reporting in the United States and United Kingdom relating to the three counter-terrorism measures discussed in the book.

The response to 9/11 was "an unprecedented global phenomenon."[52] 9/11 was the trigger for many countries, even those that had been fighting terrorism for many years, to re-think their counter-terrorism laws and strategies, and create new stringent laws and policies. But in the United States, the political narrative changed too. Helen Duffy notes that a "certain form of argumentation was used to persuade the public, the legislature branches and the judiciary that certain changes had occurred that justified novel government action."[53] The United States Government even adopted a new and sometimes peculiar terminology in connection with these terror attacks, such as "War on Terror" and "enemy combatants."[54] The United States government's view was that the threat posed by the 9/11 attacks was "so new that it was entitled to treat the criminal justice system as inadequate."[55]

The use of secrecy expanded enormously after 9/11.[56] For example, monitoring of United States citizens pursuant to the Foreign Intelligence Surveillance Act (FISA)[57] expanded exponentially. In addition to the secrecy of the actual surveillance, the surveillance must be authorized by the FISA Court, a secret process that does not involve an actual court hearing, either public or *in camera*, but involves "scrutiny through informal telephone calls and meetings with the government."[58] Renditions to secret "black sites" where detentions and interrogations of terror suspects took place by the CIA,"[59] as well as targeted killing by the United States military and CIA, have been shrouded in secrecy. After 9/11 targeted killing became openly tolerated by the governments in the countries discussed in this book.[60]

In terms of counter-terrorism secrecy in the United Kingdom, the British Government also had a role in some of the secret renditions and interrogations conducted by the CIA.[61] As to targeted killing, the United Kingdom admitted that since 2012 it had been involved in drone strikes in Afghanistan,[62] and had carried out its first drones strike in Iraq in 2014,[63] but it did not admit that it participated in drone strikes in Syria, a place where the United Kingdom was not involved in a war, until September 2015.[64] Remarkably, parliamentarians and human rights organizations still have not succeeded in finding out exactly what the British government's policy on drone strikes actually is.[65]

Turning to public opinion in the United States, United Kingdom, and Israel, a number of surveys have been conducted. A few of these have been selected to show trends. In 2016 the International Committee of the Red Cross (ICRC) conducted a survey of 17,000 people in six countries about *inter alia* torture and collateral damage from targeted killing.[66] In answer to the question whether torture was wrong or part of war, 66% thought it was wrong and 27% thought it was part of war.[67] The answers to a number of questions posed in 2016 were compared with answers to the same questions in a previous ICRC survey in 1999. For example, in 1999 28% of responders thought a "captured enemy combatant could be tortured to obtain important military information," but in 2016 that number actually increased to 36%.

Out of the three countries discussed in Parts II and III, 50% of those polled in Israel thought enemy combatants could be tortured with 25% saying they could not, 46% of those polled in the United States thought enemy combatants could be tortured and 30% thought they could not, and in the United Kingdom 26% thought enemy combatants could be tortured and 40% thought they could not.[68] Finally on the subject of torture, participants were asked whether their views would change if they had been told that their country had ratified the Convention Against Torture, but 44% still thought torture was sometimes acceptable and 15% that torture was always acceptable as it was "part of war."[69]

The ICRC also asked if it was wrong, or just part of war to attack "enemy combatants in populated villages or towns to weaken the enemy, knowing that many civilians would be killed." In 1999 68% of responders said it was wrong, with 30% believing it was just part of war. In 2016, 59% thought it was wrong, with 34% believing it was just part of war.[70]

Specifically on targeted killing, in 2014 Statista polled approximately 1,000 persons over the age of 18 in each of 44 countries asking if they approved of United States drone strikes to target extremists in Pakistan, Yemen and Somalia. At that time, the vast majority of responders disapproved; the only countries where more than 50% approved the strikes were the United States (52%), Kenya (53%) and Israel (65%).[71]

In the United States, Pew Research Center reported in 2015 that 58% of Americans approved and 35% disapproved of drone strikes. This had not changed much from their previous survey on this topic in 2013. 48% were "very concerned" about collateral damage, and 32% were somewhat concerned about this.[72] In a 2017 survey conducted by Statista, although it is not shown how many people were polled, 58% of the public approved of drone strikes in Syria, out of which 77% were Republicans and 45% were Democrats.[73] In 2018, Helen Duffy noted that "while the targeted killing of a U.S. citizen evoked an especially strong response, some of this response appears to have muted in the United States as time has passed."[74]

However, public opinion of these counter-terrorism methods is totally dependent on what the public knows about the subject. So how have these issues been reported? The data from a number of selected surveys have produced some interesting results.

In 2016, Sarah Kreps and Geoffrey Wallace questioned whether the international legal arguments of the administration have any impact on public support for drone strikes, or are individuals more persuaded by arguments about the effectiveness of strikes.[75] They argued that appeals made by NGOs about the international legality of the strikes resonate more with the public than arguments about effectiveness.[76] In this particular survey the participants were asked to agree or disagree with the following two statements: (1) regarding effectiveness – "the strikes have been instrumental in killing suspected militants and making Americans safer;" and (2) regarding international legality – "these strikes violate international law because they do not take necessary measures to prevent the death of civilians."[77] When the questions were framed in that way, a number of the individuals polled were swayed more by the legality question. Yet even so, more than 40% of the public approved of the strikes.[78] The effectiveness question did not have much effect on public opinion.[79] When the authors undertook a smaller follow-up survey seeking agreement or non-agreement with the statement that "drone strikes had led to civilian death," an even larger group indicated their disapproval of drone strikes.[80] The authors therefore concluded that the framing of the question asked by surveyors is crucial to the answer.[81]

This hypothesis was taken further by Alexandria Nylen and Charli Carpenter, who analyzed 188 survey questions relating to human rights issues in the national security context relating to "enhanced interrogation" and "targeted killing."[82] They noted that international law or IHRL is rarely mentioned in the questions or background information, nor is accurate information offered about IHRL norms, making it very difficult for the responders to answer the questions properly without being adequately informed about the topic.

Building on that theme, Stephen Ceccoli and John Bing conducted a Transatlantic Trends Survey in 2013 where 75% of people in the United States approved of drone strikes, but only 56% in the United Kingdom, 52% in France, 50% in Netherlands, 45% in Poland, 36% in Germany, 34% in Italy, and 33% in Spain approved.[83] This survey predated most of the involvement of European countries in drone strikes, apart from the United Kingdom participation. The authors sought to explain why the public attitude in Europe differed so much from that in the United States. They offered several reasons: first, relating to the lack of public information about drone strikes; and second, relating to ideological core beliefs, and preferences about foreign policy.[84] They concluded that their analysis indicated that persons who prefer strong transatlantic ties were more likely to approve of drone strikes than those who did not.[85] However, they also concluded that drone strikes were not generally well understood by the mainstream public in the United States and Europe.[86]

A 2018 survey conducted by Charles Rowling and others explored the U.S. political and news discourse relating to drone warfare during the Obama Administration to see how the Administration framed the policy and whether the press were independent in its coverage of the issue.[87] They analyzed 248 White House and military texts (comprising speeches, press releases, and conferences generated by the White House, the CIA, Department of Defense, Department of Justice, and the Department of State) which provided "the universe of available texts" between January 1, 2009 and December 31, 2013.[88] They concluded that "The Obama Administration – with President Obama leading the way – regularly emphasized the strategic value, domestic and international legality and technical capability of drone strikes, while downplaying the collateral damage caused by such strikes."[89]

They analyzed press coverage in the same time period comprising 1,293 stories from the New York Times, 324 from ABC News, 419 from CBS News, 260 from NBC News and 611 from Time magazine.[90] They also reached out to foreign sources. The opposition from abroad tended to come from presumably persons canvassed in Pakistan, Yemen, Iran, Afghanistan, the United Nations, and foreign NGOs, but the specifics of those sources were not detailed.[91] The authors were unsure of how the American public accepted and interpreted views of foreign sources.[92] They concluded that the average tone of the news coverage was

> relatively positive towards drones . . . despite a strong presence of oppositional voices from abroad, Americans still received a pro-drone picture from the news; such an imbalance may help explain why there has been continued

> support among a majority of Americans for the drone policy, despite intense opposition abroad.[93]

In 2019 the Washington Post polled 3,000 U.S. adults, of which 1,000 were Trump supporters and the rest represented the general U.S. population. 64% of the general population, and 26% of the Trump voters agreed that the airstrikes should not be used if they resulted in the killing of innocent civilians. The Washington Post concluded that if more Americans were better informed about what was going on, more would oppose the then current policy.[94]

In 2020, Joanna Frew examined how the United Kingdom media covered the topic of drone killings, by collating data from four mainstream news outlets in the United Kingdom: the BBC, a public broadcasting service that has committed to impartial reporting; the Daily Mail, the most widely read tabloid conservative news source; The Times, the biggest-selling pro-Government, broadly conservative broadsheet; and the Guardian, the biggest-selling left-leaning broadsheet.[95] Frew searched for news coverage relating to eight British members of ISIS who had been targeted by the United Kingdom or the United States (almost always with U.K. support) for drone strikes in Syria or Iraq between August 2015 and July 2018.[96]

The survey showed that the press coverage of targeted killing receded over time after the killing of "Beatle" Mohammed Emwazi, possibly because the only person that the United Kingdom has actually admitted killing by drone is Reyaad Khan,[97] as discussed in Part III. Other than the killings of Khan, Emwazi, and Sally Jones, the others received very little coverage.[98] Frew concluded that "a form of 'quasi-secrecy' surrounds the United Kingdom's drone targeted killings,"[99] noting that

> While there has been a substantial amount of press coverage, it often focuses in a sensational way on the individuals targeted, and has often lacked in-depth analysis and a proper examination of the wider legal and ethical arguments. In fact, coverage of these wider questions, as well as actual UK policy on drone targeting killing is very limited. This . . . is due to the government refusing to engage in such discussion [and] has stymied legitimate debate.

On the subject of foreign fighters, the way that Shamima Begum has been portrayed by the British press, is seen by some as a "driving force behind the government's refusal to allow her to return."[100] In recent years, the majority of the coverage concerns the women and children held in camps in Syria in appalling conditions.[101]

In summary, these samples of surveys show that the number of people who thought torture was acceptable was not insignificant. 59% of the responders to the ICRC question in 2016 about whether it was acceptable to attack villages if there was a risk of collateral damage, thought it was not, but in the Pew and Statista surveys about collateral damage, about half or more approved of the strikes. However, as the other surveys showed, often the answer depended on how the question was framed, and it emerged that generally speaking, because of the secrecy surrounding the topic of targeted killing, the public were not sufficiently informed generally about the nuances of the topic, or they had read, or been given, inaccurate information.

3. Analysis

After 9/11 many countries enacted legislation that expanded and strengthened existing counter-terrorism legislation or created new laws to fill an existing void. Over the last 20 years, these laws and strategies have been modified to reflect changes in the terrorist threat and the needs of particular countries. The judicial bodies in the countries examined in this book have largely been deferential to the counter-terrorism policies of their governments, and this is totally unsurprising and to be expected.

From about 2004 through 2008–2010 there did appear to be a shift in the security/liberty balance towards human rights in the domestic detention and torture cases. Desperate times had led to desperate measures, and once reports had begun to trickle into the public domain, and human rights organizations had published reports drawing the violations to the attention of lawmakers, and to some degree the public, a judicial shift was perceived to try to reset the balance to some extent. But after about 2010, there has been a move back to deference. Although a number of the targeted killing cases have acknowledged that IHRL might be applicable in principle, and have cited instances of when and how human rights should be taken into account, most of the cases deferred to government policy. The same approach has been discerned in the FTF cases.

In conclusion, the examples of cases relating to all three counter-terrorism measures suggest that in all three countries the judicial bodies have taken human rights considerations into account as far as they can until they reach the block of a governmental assessment relating to the needs of national security or foreign policy, which will trump human rights. The only situation where human rights have trumped national security in each of the three countries is seen in cases relating to the treatment of detainees, particularly interrogation methods involving torture. Notably, an ECtHR judgment was needed to prompt the United Kingdom to change its interrogation methods in Northern Ireland.[102] Human-rights rulings have also been made in cases involving challenges to detention, but in the United States and Israel, the permitted procedural rights have been more limited than those afforded to detainees in the United Kingdom.

Public opinion was predominantly formed from media reports that comprised reports of counter-terrorism strategies in action, some press comment on the subject, as well as official comment. Media coverage relating to detentions and torture died down quite rapidly after bursts of activity following the publication of the Abu Ghraib photos, and after reports in the United States and United Kingdom emerged relating to the countries' participation in extraordinary renditions and enhanced interrogation methods. It certainly cannot be said that the public has been bombarded with press or other news reports about targeted killing. Reports appeared if a high-profile or well-known person had been killed, but coverage also receded swiftly. As to FTFs, most coverage has related to the facts that countries do not want their citizens back, which is possibly something that much of the public agrees with. There has also been a fair amount of coverage about the women and children held in Kurdish-run camps in Syria.

Public opinion has not largely been up in arms against the drastic measures. Several reasons may suggest why. First, people are not particularly sympathetic about how terrorists are being treated, although a limited amount of sympathy might be expressed for the innocent children of ISIS fighters and their brides. Second, although people are made aware from time to time that there is a threat of terrorism, there are too many other things at home for people to worry about, such as personal financial issues, the state of the economy, or COVID-19. Third, most of these cases concern matters that have occurred thousands of miles away and are not in the forefront of people's minds. Fourth, many of the counter-terrorism measures in question have been, and continue to be shrouded in secrecy, which means that the media cannot report them in sufficient detail to provide the public with what is needed for them to have an informed opinion.

Does any of this matter? The book has shown many examples where human rights have been disregarded or violated in the use of various counter-terrorism measures. A number of the human rights violations are substantive, relating to the fundamental rights to life, fair treatment and liberty. Other violations derive from procedural deficiencies: failing to permit any or adequate access to judicial tribunals to challenge detention and other administrative measures, including deprivation of citizenship and rights to return to one's country; lack of oversight of measures, and failure of counties to investigate alleged violations; and lack of enforcement mechanisms or effective sanctions.

Furthermore, much has been written to suggest that failure to honor human rights foments more terrorist activity, because denial of rights can contribute to feelings of alienation and other factors said to cause radicalization and the impetus to commit a terrorist act.[103] U.N. Special Rapporteurs and others have been claiming for more than four years that detention and harsh treatment in Guantanamo and drone strikes have been recruitment tools for acts of terrorism,[104] although others have argued that the evidence does not clearly support that proposition.[105]

In the foreign fighter context, Hoda Muthana's sister was reported to have been arrested in April 2021 for trying to leave the U.S. and travel to Yemen and join ISIS.[106] Was her attempt to join ISIS prompted by the treatment of her sister? For at least two years there have been concerns that not bringing home the FTFs and their families and abandoning them in the Kurdish-run camps in Syria might result in further radicalization and provide a large cohort of new fighters, if the Kurds closed the camps and released the inmates.[107]

It seems certain that the denial or restriction of human rights does make a significant contribution to the toxic mix of circumstances that coalesce to inspire terrorist activity. Now that the Taliban have taken over Afghanistan, where it is estimated that more than half of their cabinet are persons on the UNSC terrorism blacklist,[108] they bring a new risk of transnational terrorist activity from themselves,[109] al-Qaeda and ISIS,[110] particularly as thousands of terrorist prisoners have been released from the former U.S. base at Bagram.[111] It remains to be seen if, or to what extent, respect for human rights will factor into the Taliban's method of government and how they will deal with the terrorist groups,[112] and whether any denial of human rights which may have occurred as a result of the counter-terrorism strategies of any country previously occupying Afghanistan, would have any effect on decisions made by these groups to commit terrorist activity.

Despite all the many counter-terrorism, counter-radicalization, deradicalization, and disengagement measures that exist, the threat of terror attacks is still high. For repatriated FTFs, the existing programs to deradicalize, or disengage, or re-integrate are a beginning but are far from perfect. Leaving FTFs detained in camps overseas will only increase that threat. They must be brought home and each country must deal with their citizens.

For years scholars and commentators have been discussing the liberty/security balance, and how failure to incorporate human rights considerations into counter-terrorism measures will increase, and have increased, the terrorist threat. The judicial bodies generally do what they can to be "watchdogs of liberty," subject to the constraints of certain aspects of policy. Some say that respect for human rights may in itself be an effective preventive measure.[113] But is that enough?

The problems can only begin to be solved if certain steps are taken by governments: steps that should not have any adverse effect of keeping countries safe from terrorist activity. These steps include:

1) in respect of administrative measures such as detention, and other restrictions relating to day-to-day life, the right to return to one's country and deprivation of citizenship, each substantive measure must be accompanied by adequate procedures that include allowing affected persons to be told the reasons for the imposition of the measure, and affording them the right to challenge the measure promptly before an impartial independent judicial body, with the assistance of legal counsel. Even if at the end of the challenge, the measure is confirmed, a proper human-rights aware procedure will have taken place.
2) in respect of the treatment of persons subjected to administrative measure or affected by collateral damage in targeted killing, and any other perceived violations of all counter-terrorism measures, governments must conduct prompt, thorough, and independent examinations of all complaints. If the complaint is justified, governments should be held accountable, perpetrators should be brought to justice, and victims should be provided with a meaningful remedy.
3) although many matters must be kept classified for reasons of protecting national security, counter-terrorism measures must be more transparent, with governments explaining why particular counter-terrorism measures are justifiable, appropriate, proportionate, and reasonable in the circumstances. If the voting public and the press were able to understand more of what is happening and were able to see that human rights were being respected, this is likely to produce greater confidence and trust in the counter-terrorism policies.

Notes

1 Clint Bolick, *The Role of the Judiciary*, 16(2) Cato's Letter, (Spring, 2018), www.cato.org/sites/cato.org/files/pubs/pdf/catosletter-v16n2.pdf, *citing* Alexander Hamilton, Federalist No. 78: "where the will of the legislature, declared in its statutes, stands in opposition to that of the people, declared in the Constitution, the judges ought to be governed by the latter rather than the former."
2 *See e.g.* Andrew Legg, The Margin of Appreciation in International Human Rights Law, (Oxford University Press, 2012); Yutaka Arai-Takahashi, The Margin of Appreciation Doctrine and the Principle of Proportionality in the Jurisprudence of the ECHR, (Intersentia, 2002).
3 A. v. United Kingdom, Appl. No. 3455/05 ECtHR, (Feb. 19, 2009).
4 Anti-Terrorism, Crime and Security Act 2001, c.24, §23 (U.K.).
5 A(FC) and others (FC) v. Secretary of State for the Home Department (SSHD), [2004] UKHL 56.
6 A. v. United Kingdom, ¶173.
7 *Id.*, ¶181.
8 *Id.*, ¶¶184, 190.
9 S, V and A v. Denmark, Appl. Nos. 35553/12, 36678/12, 36711/12, ECtHR, (Oct. 22, 2018), ¶103.
10 *See e.g.* Ashcroft v. Kidd, 131 S. Ct. 2074, (2011).
11 *See e.g.* Turkmen v. Hasty, 789 F.3d 18, (Jun. 17, 2015).
12 *See* Part II. CBS showed photographs of detainee abuse at Abu Ghraib on April 22, 2004, *see e.g.* Rebecca Leung, *Abuse at Abu Ghraib*, 60 Minutes, CBS News, (May 5, 2004), www.cbsnews.com/news/abuse-at-abu-ghraib/.
13 Hamdi v. Rumsfeld, 542 U.S. 507, 518, 521, 539, (Jun. 28, 2004).
14 *Id.*, 533.
15 Rasul v. Bush, 542 U.S. 466, (Jun. 30, 2004).
16 Hamdan v. Rumsfeld, 548 U.S. 557, 629–32, (Jun. 29, 2006).
17 Military Commissions Act of 2006, Pub.L. 109–366.
18 Boumediene v. Bush, 553 U.S. 723, 732, (Jun. 12, 2008), *and see* Part II.
19 Jessica Gresko, *Justices Skeptical of Detainee's Request for Secret Records*, Washington Post, (Oct. 6, 2021), www.washingtonpost.com/politics/high-court-to-hear-guantanamo-prisoners-state-secrets-case/2021/10/06/55b37570-265c-11ec-8739–5cb6aba30a30_story.html.
20 *See e.g.* Sher v. United Kingdom, Appl. No. 5201/11 ECtHR, (Oct. 20, 2015).
21 The U.K.'s Human Rights Act 1998, §§2, 3, c.42, requires that British legislation must be read and given effect in a way that is compatible with the rights in the European Convention on Human Rights, and British courts must take into account decisions of the European Court of Human Rights.
22 The control order regime was created in the Prevention of Terrorism Act 2005, c.2 as a counter-terrorism strategy to prevent terrorist activity. Control orders were abolished in December 2011.
23 SSHD v. JJ, [2007] UKHL 45, ¶¶21, 23, 24.
24 SSHD v. MB (FC), [2007] UKHL 46, ¶66.
25 A. and Others v. United Kingdom, Appl. No. 3455/05, ECtHR, (Feb. 19, 2009).
26 SSHD (Respondent) v, AF (Appellant), FC and another (Appellant), [2009] UKHL 28, ¶65.
27 *See e.g.* Abd Ali Hameed Al-Waheed v. MOD, Serdar Mohammed v. MOD, [2017] UKSC 2, (Jan. 17, 2017), Rahmatullah (No. 2) (Respondent) v. MOD and another (Appellants), Mohammed and others (Respondent) v. MOD and another, [2017] UKSC 1, (Jan. 17, 2017); Belhaj and another (Respondents) v. Straw and others (Appellants) and Rahmatullah (No. 1) (Respondent) v.

MOD and another (Appellants), [2017] UKSC 3, (Jan. 17, 2017); Kamil Najim Abdullah Alseran and Abd Ali Hameed Al-Waheed and others v. MOD, [2017] EWHC 3289 (QB), (Dec. 14, 2017), (Alseran and Al-Waheed v. MOD).

28 Terrorism Prevention Measures and Investigation Act 2011, c.23, as amended by Counter-Terrorism and Security Act 2015, c.6. These are discussed in Part IV.

29 *See e.g.* IM, JM and LG v. SSHD, [2017] EWHC 1529 (Admin), (Jun. 30, 2017); LF v. SSHD, [2017] EWHC 2685 (Admin), (Oct. 30, 2017); QT v. SSHD, [2019] EWHC 2588 (Admin), (Jul. 10, 2019).

30 *See* Part II; Shiri Krebs, *Lifting the Veil of Secrecy: Judicial Review of Administrative Detentions in the Israeli Supreme Court*, 45(3) Vanderbilt Journal of Transnational Law 639, 643, (2012).

31 John Does v. Ministry of Defense, CrimFH 7048/97, ¶25, (Apr. 12, 2000).

32 Public Committee Against Torture (PCAT) v. Government of Israel, H.C 5100/94, (May 26, 1999).

33 PCAT v. The Government of Israel, HCJ 5100/94, 4054/95, 518/96, (Jul. 6, 2009).

34 *See e.g.* Finogenov & Ors. v. Russia., Appl. Nos. 18299/03, 27311/03, Final Judgment, (Jun. 4, 2012); Case of Zambrano Velez v. Ecuador, Ser. C No. 166, IACtHR, (2007).

35 *See e.g.* Benzer v. Turkey, Appl. No. 23502/06 ECtHR, (Mar. 24, 2014); Zambrano Velez v. Ecuador.

36 Hassan v. United Kingdom, Appl. No. 29750/09, EctHR, (Sep. 16, 2014); Giovanna Maria Frisso, *The Duty to Investigate Violations of the Right to Life in Armed Conflicts in the Jurisprudence of the Inter-American Court of Human Rights*, 51(2) Israel Law Review, 169, 182, (Jul. 2018), *citing* Case of Cruz Sanchez v. Peru, Ser. C No. 292, IACtHR, ¶¶272–3, (Apr. 17, 2015) (in Spanish only).

37 Al-Aulaqi v. Panetta, 35 F. Supp.3d 56, 69, (Apr. 4, 2014).

38 *See e.g.* Ahmed Salem Bin Ali Jaber v. United States, 861 F.3d 241, 247, 249, (Jun. 30, 2017); Zaidan v. Trump, 317 F. Supp. 3d 8, (Jun. 13, 2018); Kareem v. Haspel, 2021 U.S. App. LEXIX 1128, 10, (Jan. 15, 2021).

39 *See e.g.* Al-Skeini v. United Kingdom, Appl. No. 55721/07 ECtHR, ¶177, (Jul. 7, 2011); Al-Saadoon & Ors. v. SSD, [2016] EWCA Civ. 811.

40 *See e.g.* R (on the Application of Noor Khan) v. SSFCA, [2014] EWCA Civ 24, ¶¶1, 4, (Jan. 20, 2014), which cites many other cases.

41 PCAT v. Israel, (2006) HCJ 769/02.

42 *Id.*, ¶40.

43 Geneva Convention III, Art. 121, Geneva Convention IV, Art. 131, but in 2013 The International Committee of the Red Cross (ICRC) published guidelines for investigating deaths in custody focused on IHRL principles, ICRC, Guidelines For Investigating Deaths In Custody, (Oct. 2013).

44 B'Tselem v. Judge Advocate General, HCJ 9594/03, (Aug. 21, 2011). Only a very limited number of cases in Israel are now published in English.

45 *See e.g.* Lila Hassan, *Repatriating ISIS Foreign Fighters Is Key to Stemming Radicalization, Experts Say, But Many Countries Don't Want Their Citizens Back*, PBS Frontline, (Apr. 6, 2021), www.pbs.org/wgbh/frontline/article/repatriating-isis-foreign-fighters-key-to-stemming-radicalization-experts-say-but-many-countries-dont-want-citizens-back/.

46 U.N. Committee on the Rights of the Child, Decision adopted by the Committee under the Optional Protocol to the Convention on the Rights of the Child on a communications procedure concerning communications No. 79/2019 and No. 109/2019, CRC/C/85/D/79/2019 – CRC/C/85/D/109/2019 (Nov. 2, 2020).

47 Ghoumid and Others v. France, Appl. No. 52273/16 ECtHR, (Jun. 25, 2020) (in French only), ECtHR Press Release, Applicants stripped of nationality for terrorism-related offences: no violation of Covenant, ECtHR 191 (2020), (Jun. 25, 2020).
48 K2 v. United Kingdom, Appl. No. 42387/13, ECtHR, Decision, (Mar. 9, 2017). The ECtHR analyzed the domestic K2 cases in their judgment in their discussion on the history of the claim.
49 R. (on the application of Begum) v. SSHD, [2021] UKSC 7, (Feb. 26, 2021).
50 R. (on the application of D4) v. SSHD, [2021] EWHC 2179 (Admin), (Jul. 30, 2021), *and see* Part IV.
51 Maria Roson, *Belgium Constitutional Court Decision on the Concept of Incitement to Terrorism*, EDRi, (May 30, 2018), *citing* Constitutional Court of Belgium, 31/2018, (preventive detention was also challenged in this case), https://edri.org/belgium-constitutional-court-decision-on-the-concept-of-incitement-to-terrorism/.
52 Kent Roach, THE 9/11 Effect: Comparative Counter-Terrorism, 1, (Cambridge University Press, 2011).
53 Helen Duffy, Detention of Terror Suspects, 83, (Hart Publishing, 2018).
54 *Id.*, 85–7.
55 *Id.*, 109.
56 *Id.*, 138–40.
57 Foreign Intelligence Surveillance Act of 1978, 50 U.S.C. §§1801–11, 1821–29, 1841–46, 1861–62, 1871.
58 David Kris, *How the FISA Court Really Works*, Lawfare, (Sep. 2, 2018), www.lawfareblog.com/how-fisa-court-really-works.
59 Julie Vitkovskaya, *What Are 'Black Sites'? 6 Key Things to Know about the CIA's Secret Prisons Overseas*, Washington Post, (Jan. 25, 2017), www.washingtonpost.com/news/checkpoint/wp/2017/01/25/what-are-black-sites-6-key-things-to-know-about-the-cias-secret-prisons-overseas/; Editorial Opinion, *About Those Black Sites*, New York Times, (Feb. 17, 2013), www.nytimes.com/2013/02/18/opinion/about-those-black-sites.html, *citing Globalizing Torture: CIA Secret Detention and Extraordinary Rendition*, Open Society Justice Initiative, (Feb. 2013), www.justiceinitiative.org/uploads/655bbd41-082b-4df3-940c-18a3bd9ed956/globalizing-torture-20120205.pdf.
60 As regards the United States, *see* Gary D. Solis, The Law of Armed Conflict, 557, (Cambridge University Press, 2nd ed., 2016), "Once an anathema to America, after 9/11 targeted killing became tolerated and then embraced," *citing Self-Licensed to Kill*, Economist, 12, (Aug. 4, 2001); Abraham D. Sofaer, then US State Dept legal Adviser, *Terrorism, the Law and the National Defense*, 126 Military Law Review 89, 121, (1989); Craig R. Whitney, *War on Terror Alters U.S. Qualms about Assassination*, International Herald Tribune, 4, (Mar. 29, 2004).
61 *See e.g.* Declan Walsh, *Britain Apologizes for Role in Libyan Dissident's CIA Nightmare*, New York Times, (May 10, 2018), www.nytimes.com/2018/05/10/world/europe/britain-libya-apology-cia-rendition-torture.html; Ruth Blakeley and Sam Raphael, *British Torture in the 'War on Terror'*, 23(2) European Journal of International Relations, 243, (2017); Ruth Blakely and Sam Raphael, *Accountability, Denial and Future-Proofing of British Torture*, 96(3) International Affairs 691, (2020).
62 *Revealed: US and Britain Launched 1,200 Drone Strikes in Recent Wars*, Bureau of Investigative Journalism, (Dec. 12, 2012), www.thebureauinvestigates.com/stories/2012-12-04/revealed-us-and-britain-lainched-1-200-drone-strikes-in-recent-wars.
63 *UK Drone Carries Out First Strike in Iraq*, BBC News, (Nov. 10, 2014), www.bbc.com/world-middle-east-29992686.

64 Nicholas Winning, *U.K. Premier Says Drone Strike Killed Two British Members of ISIS in Syria*, Wall Street Journal, (Sep. 7, 2015), www.wsj.com/articles/u-k-premier-says-drone-strike-killed-two-british-members-of-isis-in-syria-1441640520.
65 Joanna Frew, *In the Frame*, Drone Wars 6, (Jan. 2020), https://dronewars.net/wp-content/uploads/2020/01/InTheFrame-Web.pdf.
66 International Committee of the Red Cross (ICRC), People on War, (2016), www.icrc.org/en/document/people-on-war. The sixteen countries were Afghanistan, China, Colombia, France, Iraq, Israel, Nigeria, Palestine, Russia, South Sudan, Switzerland, Syria, Ukraine, United Kingdom, United States and Yemen.
67 *Id.*, 10.
68 *Id.*
69 *Id.*, 11.
70 *Id.*, 7.
71 *Do You Approve or Disapprove of the United States Conducting Missile Strikes from Pilotless Aircraft Called Drones to Target Extremists in Countries Such as Pakistan, Yemen and Somalia?*, Statista, (Sep. 2014), www.statista.com/statistics/233004/global-opinion-on-us-drone-strikes/.
72 Pew Research Center, *Public Continues to Back U.S. Drone Attacks*, (May 28, 2015), www.pewresearch.org/politics/2015/05/28/public-continues-to-back-u-s-drone-attacks/.
73 *American Public Opinion on U.S. Airstrikes in Syria as of April 2017, by Political Party Affiliation*, Statista, (Apr. 11–17, 2017), www.statista.com/statistics/700086/us-public-opinion-on-airstrikes-in-syria/.
74 Helen Duffy, Detention of Terror Suspects, 153.
75 Sarah E. Kreps and Geoffrey R. Wallace, *International Law, Military Effectiveness and Public Support for Drone Strikes*, 53(6) Journal of Peace Research 830, 831, (2016).
76 *Id.*
77 *Id.*, 834–5.
78 *Id.*, 836.
79 *Id.*, 837.
80 *Id.*, 839.
81 *Id.*, 840.
82 Alexandria Nylen and Charli Carpenter, *Questions of Life and Death: (De)constructing Human Rights Norms through US Public Opinion*, 4(2) European Journal of International Security, (Jun. 2019).
83 Stephen Ceccoli and John Bing, *Taking the Lead? Transatlantic Attitudes towards Lethal Drone Strikes*, 16(3) Journal of Transatlantic Studies 247, 248 (2018).
84 *Id.*, 252–3.
85 *Id.*, 263.
86 *Id.*, 265.
87 Charles M. Rowling, Penelope Sheets, William Pettit and Jason Gilmore, *Consensus at Home, Opposition Abroad: Officials, Foreign Sources, and US New Coverage of Drone Warfare*, 95(4) Journalism and Mass Communication Quarterly, 886, 887, (2018).
88 *Id.*, 894.
89 *Id.*, 902.
90 *Id.*, 896.
91 *Id.*, 902, Fig. 4.
92 *Id.*, 903.
93 *Id.*

94 James Ron, Howard Lavine and Shannon Golden, *No, Americans Don't Support Airstrikes That Kill Civilians, Even When They Target Terrorists*, Washington Post, (May 6, 2019), www.washingtonpost.com/politics/2019/05/06/no-americans-dont-support-airstrikes-that-kill-civilians-even-when-they-target-terrorists/.

95 Frew, *In the Frame*, 15.

96 *Id.*

97 *Id.*, 23.

98 *Id.*, 34.

99 *Id.*, 40.

100 Anthony Loyd, *Shamima Is Not a Threat: She Is Totally Broken*, The Times, (Jun. 3, 2021), referring to a British television documentary on ISIS brides, www.thetimes.co.uk/article/shamima-begum-is-not-a-threat-shes-totally-broken-she-needs-help-w7hd8fj9l.

101 *See e.g. Thousands of Foreigners Unlawfully Held in NE Syria*, Human Rights Watch, (Mar. 23, 2021), www.hrw.org/news/2021/03/23/thousands-foreigners-unlawfully-held-ne-syria#; Elian Peltier and Constant Meheut, *Europe's Dilemma: Take In ISIS Families, or Leave Them in Syria?* New York Times, (May 28, 2021), www.nytimes.com/2021/05/28/world/europe/isis-women-children-repatriation.html; Stephanie Nebehay, *Red Cross Reveals That Children Held in Northeast Syria Prisons*, Reuters, (Jun. 30, 2021), www.reuters.com/world/middle-east/red-cross-reveals-that-children-held-northeast-syria-prisons-2021-06–30/.

102 Hamdan v. Rumsfeld; Ireland v. United Kingdom, Appl. No. 5310/71, ECtHR, (Dec. 13, 1977); PCAT v. Government of Israel, H.C 5100/94, (May 26, 1999).

103 *See e.g. Report of the Special Rapporteur on the promotion and protection of human rights and fundamental freedoms while countering terrorism,* Fionnuala Ni Aoilain, U.N.G.A. A/76/261, ¶31: "unmet rule of law needs and human rights violations provide the fuel for continued cycles of conflict, violent extremism and terrorism," and ¶38: "evidence demonstrate[es] that, although conflict is one of the strongest predictors of the impact of terrorism, so too are deficiencies in human rights protections, socioeconomic factors related to disenfranchisement, deficient rule of law and equality and more," (Aug. 3, 2021).

104 Martin Scheinin, *Impact of Post-9/11 Counter-Terrorism Measures on All Human Rights*, 96; U.N. Doc. A/HRC/34/61; *Report of Special Rapporteur* [Ben Emmerson Q.C.] on the promotion and protection of human rights and fundamental freedoms while countering terrorism, ¶63, (Feb. 21, 2017), U.N. Doc. A/73/361; *Report of Special Rapporteur* [Fionnuala Ni Aolain] on the promotion and protection of human rights and fundamental freedoms while countering terrorism, ¶10, (Sep. 3, 2018); *see also* Adam Goldman and Missy Ryan, *At Least 12 Released Guantanamo Detainees Implicated in Attacks on Americans*, Washington Post, (Jun. 8, 2016), www.washingtonpost.com/world/national-security/about-12-released-guantanamo-detainees-implicated-in-deadly-attacks-on-americans/2016/06/08/004d038e-2776-11e6-b989-4e5479715b54_story.html; David P. Stewart, *Terrorism and Human Rights: The Perspective of International Law*, Middle East Institute, (Jun. 2018), www.mei.edu/sites/default/files/publications/PP4_Stewart_humanrightsCT.pdf; *Between a Drone and Al-Qaeda: The Civilian Cost of U.S. Targeted Killings in Yemen*, Human Rights Watch, (Oct. 22, 2013), www.hrw.org/report/2013/10/22/between-drone-and-al-qaeda/civilian-cost-us-targeted-killings-yemen; U.S. Director of National Intelligence, *Summary of the Reengagement of Detainees Formerly Held at Guantanamo Bay, Cuba*, (2016), www.dni.gov/files/documents/Newsroom/reports%20and%20Pubs/Summary_of _the_Reengagement_of_Detainees_Formerly_Held_at_GTMO_Ma%204_2016.pdf.

105 *See e.g. Q&A: Guantanamo Bay, US Detentions and the Trump Administration*, Human Rights Watch, (Jun. 27, 2018), www.hrw.org/news/2018/06/27/qa-guantanamo-bay-us-detentions-and-trump-administration#q5; Aqil Shah, *Do U.S. Drone Strikes Cause Blowback? Evidence from Pakistan and Beyond*, 42(4) International Security 47, 49, 82–84, (Spring, 2018).

106 Carol Robinson and Jeremy Gray, *Sister of Alabama ISIS Bride Hoda Muthana Arrested with Husband While Allegedly Trying to Join Terrorists*, Alabama.com, (Apr. 1, 2021), www.al.com/news/2021/04/sister-of-alabama-isis-bride-hoda-muthana-arrested-with-husband-while-allegedly-trying-to-join-terrorists.html.

107 *See e.g.* Hassan Mneimneh, *Response to 'Al-Hawl Camp': A Potential Incubator of the Next Generation of Extremism*, Fikra Forum, Washington Institute for Near East Policy, (Oct. 10, 2019), www.washingtoninstitute.org/policy-analysis/response-al-hawl-camp-potential-incubator-next-generation-extremism.

108 *Taliban Government Dominated by Officials on U.N. Security Council Sanctions List*, Counter Extremism Project, (Sep. 15, 2021), www.counterextremism.com/press/taliban-government-dominated-officials-un-security-council-sanctions-list.

109 Sajjan M. Gohel, *The Taliban Are Far Closer to the Islamic State Than They Claim*, Foreign Policy, (Aug. 26, 2021), https://foreignpolicy.com/2021/08/26/afghanistan-kabul-airport-attack-taliban-islamic-state/.

110 Ben Hubbard, Eric Schmitt and Matthew Rosenberg, *After Decades of War, ISIS and Al Qaeda Can Still Wreak Havoc*, New York Times, (Aug. 26, 2021), www.nytimes.com/2021/08/26/world/asia/Afghanistan-isis-qaeda.html; Fazaz A. Gerges, *The Taliban Can't Control Afghanistan: That Should Worry the West*, Foreign Policy, (Aug. 31, 2021), https://foreignpolicy.com/2021/08/31/taliban-afghanistan-islamic-state-khorasan-isis-west-security-terrorism-attacks/.

111 Catherine Philp, *Terrorist Elite Set Free from Afghan Guantanamo Bay*, The Times, (Aug. 15, 2021), www.thetimes.co.uk/article/thousands-of-terrorism-suspects-freed-as-taliban-seize-bagram-prison-q98fbk7v0.

112 Aquil Shah, *How Will the Taliban Deal with Other Islamic Extremist Groups?*, Carnegie Endowment for International Peace, (Aug. 31, 2021).

113 A view advanced by Manfred Nowak and Anne Chabord, *Introduction*, 3–4, *in* Using Human Rights to Counter Terrorism, (Manfred Nowak and Anne Chabord, eds., Edward Elgar, 2018).

Select bibliography

Aceves, W.J., "When Death Becomes Murder: A Primer on Extrajudicial Killing," 50 *Columbia Human Rights Law Review* 116, 2018.

Addameer, *Addameer Collects Hard Evidence on Torture and Ill-Treatment Committed against Palestinian Detainees at Israeli Interrogation Center*, December 23, 2019.

Agwu, F.A., *Armed Drones and Globalization in the Asymmetric War on Terror*, Routledge, 2018.

All-Party Parliamentary Group on Drones Inquiry Report, *The UK's Use of Armed Drones: Working with Partners*, 2018.

Amnesty International, *Jailed Without Justice, Immigration Detention in the U.S.A.*, 2009.

Anderson, D., *Citizenship Removal Resulting in Statelessness, First Review of the Independent Reviewer of the Operation of the Power to Remove Citizenship Obtained by Naturalisation from Persons Who Have No Other Citizenship*, April 2016.

Anderson, D., *Second Report of Independent Reviewer, Terrorism Prevention and Investigative Measures in 2013*, March 2014.

Anderson, D., *Third Report of Independent Reviewer, Terrorism Prevention and Investigative Measures in 2014*, March 2015.

Arai-Takahashi, Y., *The Margin of Appreciation and the Principle of Proportionality in the Jurisprudence of the ECHR*, Intersentia, 2002.

Australian Government, Department of Home Affairs, *Control Orders, Preventative Detention, Continuing Detention Orders, Temporary Exclusion Orders, and Powers in Relation to Terrorist Acts and Terrorist Offences, Annual Report, 2019–2020*, Australian Government, Annual Report 2019–2020.

Australian Human Rights Commission, *Review of Federal Powers, Submission to the Parliamentary Joint Committee on Intelligence and Security*, September 10, 2020.

Barak-Erez, D., "Israel's Anti-Terrorist Law: Past, Present and Future," in Ramraj, V.V., Hor, M., Roach, K. and Williams, G. (eds.), *Global Anti-Terrorism Law and Policy*, Cambridge University Press, 2012.

Barak-Erez, D., and Waxman, M.C., "Secret Evidence: The Due Process of Administrative Detentions in the Israeli Supreme Court," 48 *Columbia Journal of Transnational Law* 3, 2009.

Barrett, R., *Beyond the Caliphate: Foreign Fighters and the Threat of Returnees*, The Soufan Group, October 2017.

Barrett, R., "ISIS Foreign Fighters after the Fall of the Caliphate," 6(1) *Armed Conflict Survey*, 2020.

Ben-Naftali, O., and Michaeli, K., "Public Committee against Torture in Israel v. Government of Israel, Case No. HCJ 769/02," 101(2) *American Journal of International Law* 459, April 2007.

Benton, M., and Banulescu-Bogdan, N., *Foreign Fighters: Will Revoking Citizenship Mitigate the Threat?*, Migration Policy Institute, April 2019.

Bergengruen, V., and Hennigan, W.J., "'We Are Being Eaten From Within.' Why America Is Losing the Battle against White Nationalist Terrorism," *Time Magazine*, August 8, 2019.

Bergman, R., *Rise and Kill First*, Random House, 2018.

Bertelsen, P., *Danish Preventive Measures and De-Radicalization Strategies: The Aarhus Model*, Panorama Insights into Asian and European Affairs, January 2015.

Blackbourn, J., Kayis, D., and McGarrity, N., *Anti-Terrorism Law and Foreign Terrorist Fighters*, Routledge, 2018.

Blakeley, R., and Raphael, S., "Accountability, Denial and Future-Proofing of British Torture," 96(3) *International Affairs* 691, 2020.

Blakeley, R., and Raphael, S., "British Torture in the 'War on Terror'," 23(2) *European Journal of International Relations* 243, 2017.

Blank, L., and Noone, G.P., *International Law and Armed Conflict: Fundamental Principles and Contemporary Challenges in the Law of War*, Wolters Kluwer, 2018.

Bolhuis, M.P., and Wijk, J. van, "Citizen Deprivation as a Counterterrorism Measure in Europe: Possible Follow-Up Scenarios, Human Rights Infringements and the Effect on Counterterrorism," 22 *European Journal of Migration and Law* 338, 2020.

Bolick, C., "The Role of the Judiciary," 16(2) *Cato's Letter, Cato Institute*, Spring 2018.

Braun, K., "'Home Sweet Home': Managing Foreign Terrorist Fighters in Germany, the United Kingdom and Australia," 20 *International Community Law Review* 311, 2018.

Braun, K., "Prospects and Challenges of Prosecuting: Foreign Fighters in Australia," in Kfir, I. and Coyne, J. (eds.), *Counterterrorism Yearbook 2020*, Australian Strategic Policy Handbook, March 1, 2020.

Brookman-Byrne, M., "Drone Use 'Outside Areas of Active Hostilities': An Examination of Legal Paradigms Governing US Covert Remote Strikes," 64(3) *Netherlands International Law Review* 3, 2017.

Brooks, R., "Drones and the International Rule of Law," 28(1) *Ethics and International Affairs* 69, 2014.

B'tselem, *The Occupation's Fig Leaf: Israel's Military Law Enforcement System as a Whitewash Mechanism*, May 2016.

Bures, O., and Hawkins, A.J., "Israeli Targeted Killing Operations before and during the Second Intifada," 31(3) *Small Wars and Insurgencies* 569, 2020.

Byman, D., "Will Afghanistan Become a Terrorist Safe Haven Again?," *Foreign Affairs*, August 18, 2021.

Callimard, A., "The Targeted Killing of General Soleimani: Its Lawfulness and Why It Matters," *Just Security*, January 8, 2020.

Casey-Maslen, S., "Introduction," in Casey-Maslen, S., Homayounnejad, M., Stauffer, H. and Weizmann, N. (eds.), *Drones and Other Unmanned Weapons Under International Law*, Brill Nijhoff, 2018.

Casey-Maslen, S., "Unmanned Weapons Systems and the Right to Life," in Casey-Maslen, S., Homayounnejad, M., Stauffer, H. and Weizmann, N. (eds.), *Drones and Other Unmanned Weapons Under International Law*, Brill Nijhoff, 2018.

Ceccoli, S., and Bing, J., "Taking the Lead? Transatlantic Attitudes towards Lethal Drone Strikes," 16(3) *Journal of Transatlantic Studies* 247, 2018.

Center for Civilians in Conflict, *Exception(s) to the Rule(s): Civilian Harm, Oversight and Accountability in the Shadow Wars*, Stimson Center and Security Assistance Monitor, November 2020.

Chachko, E., "Administrative National Security," 108 *Georgetown Law Journal* 1063, 2020.

Chesney, R.M., "Beyond Conspiracy? Anticipatory Prosecution and the Challenge of Unaffiliated Terrorism," 80 *South California Law Review* 425, 2007.

Chesney, R.M., "Military Intelligence Convergence and the Law of the Title 10/Title 50 Debate," 5 *Journal of National Security Law and Policy* 539, 2012.

Chilcot, J., *The Report of the Iraq Inquiry, Executive Summary*, HC 264, July 6, 2016.

Cochran, D.Q., "Material Witness Detention in a Post 9/11 World: Mission Creep or Fresh Start?" 18 *George Mason Law Review* 1, 2010.

Cohen, A., and Cohen, S., "Israel and International Humanitarian Law: Between the Neo-Realism of State Security and the 'Soft Power' of Legal Acceptability," 16 *Israel Studies* 1, 2011.

Cohen, A., and Cohen, S., *Israel's National Security Law: Political Dynamics and Historical Development*, Routledge, 2011.

Cole, D., "Out of the Shadows: Preventive Detention, Suspected Terrorists and War," 97 *California Law Review* 693, 2009.

Cole, D., *The Torture Memos*, The New Press, 2009.

Cominetti, V., *The Italian Approach to De-Radicalization*, International Institute for Counter-Terrorism, IDC Herzliya, December 2018.

Coolsaet, R., and Renard, T., *The Homecoming of Foreign Fighters in the Netherlands, Germany and Belgium: Policies and Challenges*, Egmont Institute, April 12, 2018.

Cooper-Blum, S., *The Necessary Evil of Preventive Detention in the War on Terror*, Cambria Press, 2009.

Corsi, J.L., "Drone Deaths Violate Human Rights: The Applicability of the ICCR to Civilian Deaths Caused By Drones," 6(2) *International Human Rights Law Review* 205, December 2017.

Coyne, J., and Kfir, I., *Australia's Citizenship-Stripping Legislation May Be Doing More Harm Than Good*, The Strategist, Australian Strategic Policy Institute, August 8, 2019.

Crijns, J., Leeuw, B., and Wermink, H., *Pre-Trial Detention in the Netherlands: Legal Principles versus Practical Reality*, University of Leiden, March 2016.

Davis, L.E., McNerney, M., and Greenberg, M.D., *Clarifying the Rules for Targeted Killing*, Rand Corporation, 2016.

Dick, S., and Stohl, R., *U.S. Drone Policy: Transparency and Oversight*, Stimson, February 11, 2020.

Dickinson, L., *Extraterritorial Counterterrorism: Policymaking v. Law*, Just Security, July 15, 2021.

Dinstein, Y., *The Conduct of Hostilities under the Law of Armed Conflict*, Cambridge University Press, 2016.

Doolan, B., *Lawless v. Ireland (1957–1961): The First Case before the European Court of Human Rights*, Routledge, 2001.

Duffy, H., *Detention of Terror Suspects*, Hart Publishing, 2018.

Dworkin, A., *Beyond Good and Evil: Why Europe Should Bring ISIS Foreign Fighters Home*, European Council on Foreign Relations, October 25, 2019.

Dworkin, A., *Israel's High Court on Targeted Killing: A Model for the War on Terror?*, Crimes of War Project, December 15, 2006.

Emmerson, B., "New Counter-Terrorism Measures: New Challenges for Human Rights," in Nowak, M. and Chabord, A. (eds.), *Using Human Rights to Counter Terrorism*, Edward Elgar, 2018.

Europol, *European Union Terrorism Situation and Trend Report*, 2020.

Falk, O., *Targeted Killings, Law and Counter-Terrorism Effectiveness: Does Fair Play Pay Off?*, Routledge, 2021.

Falk, O., and Hefetz, A., "Minimizing Unintended Deaths Enhanced the Effectiveness of Targeted Killing in the Israel-Palestinian Conflict," 42(6) *Studies in Conflict and Terrorism* 600, 2019.

FIDH (International Federation for Human Rights), *Shielded From Accountability: Israel's Unwillingness to Investigate and Prosecute International Crimes*, September 2011.

Frew, J., *In the Frame*, Drone Wars, January 2020.

Frisso, G.M., "The Duty to Investigate Violations of the Right to Life in Armed Conflicts in the Jurisprudence of the Inter-American Court of Human Rights," 51(2) *Israel Law Review* 169, July 2018.

Fuller, C.J., *See It/ Shoot It: The Secret History of the CIA's Lethal Drone Program*, Yale University Press, 2017.

Gartenstein-Ross, D., Chace-Donahue, E., and Clark, C.P., *The Enduring Legacy of French and Belgian Islamic State Foreign Fighters*, Foreign Policy Research Institute, February 5, 2020.

Gartenstein-Ross, D., Chace-Donahue, E., and Clark, C.P., *The Threat of Jihadist Terrorism in Germany*, International Center for Counter-Terrorism – The Hague, May 22, 2020.

Ginkel, B. Van, and Minks, S., *Addressing the Challenge of Returnees: Threat Perceptions, Policies and Practices in the Netherlands*, Egmont Institute, 2018.

Ginsborg, L., "One Step Forward, Two Steps Back: The Security Council, 'Foreign Fighters' and Human Rights," in Nowak, M. and Chabord, A. (eds.), *Using Human Rights to Counter Terrorism*, Edward Elgar, 2018.

Goodman, R., *Legal Questions (and some Answers) Concerning the U.S. Military Strike in Syria*, Just Security, March 1, 2021.

Government of Canada, Public Safety Canada, *Canadian Extremist Travelers*, September 10, 2020.

Gray, C., "Targeted Killing Outside Armed Conflict: A New Departure for the U.K.?," 3(2) *Journal on the Use of Force and International Law*, December 21, 2016.

Gross, E., *The Struggle of Democracy against Terrorism*, University of Virginia Press, 2006.

Gross, O., "'Once More Unto the Breach': The Systemic Failure of Applying the European Convention on Human Rights to Entrenched Emergencies," 23 *Yale Journal of International Law* 437, 1998.

Gunneflo, M., *Targeted Killing: A Legal and Political History*, Cambridge University Press, 2016.

Gurski, P., *The Foreign Terrorist Fighter Repatriation Challenge: The View from Canada*, International Centre for Counter-Terrorism – The Hague, February 21, 2019.

Gussarova, A., *Repatriating Foreign Fighters: The Case of Kazakhstan*, European Eye on Radicalization, April 17, 2020.

Hall, J., *The Terrorism Acts in 2018, Report of Independent Reviewer of the Terrorism Legislation on the Operation of the Terrorism Acts 2000 and 2006*, Home Office, March 2020.

Hall, J., *The Terrorism Acts in 2019, Report of Independent Reviewer of the Terrorism Legislation on the Operation of the Terrorism Acts 2000 and 2006*, Home Office, March 2021.

Haque, A.A., *Biden's First Strike and the International Law of Self-Defense*, Just Security, February 26, 2021.

Hassan, A.S.R., "Denmark's Deradicalisation Programme for Returning Foreign Terrorist Fighters," 11(3) *Counter Terrorist Trends and Analyses* 13, International Centre for Political Violence and Terrorism Research, March 2019.

Hathaway, O., "The Soleimani Strike Defied the Constitution," *The Atlantic*, January 4, 2020.

Heinke, D.H., and Raudszus, J., "Germany's Returning Foreign Fighters and What to Do About Them," in Renard, T. and Coolsaet, R. (eds.), *Returnees: Who Are They, Why Are They (Not) Coming Back and How Should We Deal with Them?* Egmont Institute, February 2018.

Henkaerts, J.M., and Doswald-Beck, L., *Customary International Humanitarian Law*, Volume 1, Cambridge University Press, 2009.

H.M. Government, *Pursue, Prevent, Protect, Prepare: The United Kingdom's Strategy for Countering International Terrorism*, CM 7547, March 2009.

H.M. Government, *CONTEST: The United Kingdom's Strategy for Countering International Terrorism*, CM 9608, June 2018.

H.M. Government, *Factsheet: Desistence and Disengagement Program*, November 5, 2019.

H.M. Government, Home Office, *Operation of Police Powers under the Terrorism Act 2000 and Subsequent Legislation: Arrests, Outcomes, and Stop and Search. Great Britain, Year Ending September 2020*, December 10, 2020.

H.M. Government, Iraq Historic Allegations Team, *Allegations Under Investigation*, March 31, 2016.

H.M. Government, *Review of Counter-Terrorism and Security Powers, Review Findings and Recommendations*, CM 8004, January 2011.

H.M. Government, *Transparency Report 2018: Disruptive and Investigatory Powers*, July 2018.

H.M. Government, *Transparency Report: Disruptive Powers 2019/19*, March 2020.

Heyns, C., Akande, D., Hill-Cawthorne, L., and Chengeta, T., "The International Law Framework Regulating the Use of Armed Drones," 65(4) *International and Comparative Law Quarterly* 791, 2016.

Hill-Cawthorne, L., *Detention in Non-International Armed Conflict*, Oxford University Press, 2016.

Hofstee, G., *The Debate around Returning Foreign Fighters in the Netherlands*, Italian Institute for International Political Studies, January 9, 2020.

House of Lords, House of Commons, Joint Committee on Human Rights (JCHR), *The Government's Policy on the Use of Drones for Targeted Killing*, HL Article 141, HC 574, 2016.

Hughes, E., "Entrenched Emergencies and the 'War on Terror': Time to Reform the Derogation Procedure in International Law?," 20 *New York International Law Review* 1, 2007.

Human Rights First, *Jails and Jumpsuits, Transforming the U.S. Immigration Detention System – A Two Year Review*, 2011.

Human Rights Watch, *The Road to Abu Ghraib*, June 8, 2004.

Human Rights Watch, *Between a Drone and Al-Qaeda: The Civilian Cost of U.S. Targeted Killings in Yemen*, October 22, 2013.

Human Rights Watch, *No More Excuses: A Roadmap to Justice for CIA Torture*, December 1, 2015.

Human Rights Watch, *Q&A: Guantanamo Bay, US Detentions, And the Trump Administration*, June 27, 2018.

Human Rights Watch, *Bring Me Back to Canada*, June 29, 2020.

Independent National Security Monitor (Australia), *Annual Report 2019–2020*, February 11, 2021.

Institute for Economics and Peace and National Consortium for the Study of Terrorism and Responses to Terrorism, *Global Terrorism Index 2020.*

International Bar Association Human Rights Institute, *The Legality of Armed Drones under International Law*, July 2017.

International Commission of Jurists, *The Arab Court of Human Rights: A Flawed Statute for an Ineffective Court*, 2015.

International Committee of the Red Cross, *Guidelines for Investigating Deaths in Custody*, October 2013.

International Committee of the Red Cross, *International Humanitarian Law and the Challenges of Contemporary Armed Conflicts*, 32 IC/15/11, Geneva, October 2015.

International Committee of the Red Cross, *People on War*, 2016.

International Criminal Court, *Situation in Iraq/UK, Final Report*, December 9, 2020.

International Federation for Human Rights, *The United Nations Counter-Terrorism Complex*, September 2017.

Jacobson, D., and Kaplan, E.H., "Suicide Bombings and Targeted Killings in (Counter)-Terror Games," 51(5) *Journal of Conflict Resolution* 772, October 2007.

Jaffer, J., *The Drone Memos: Targeted Killing, Secrecy and the Law*, The New Press, 2016.

Jones, S.G., and Doxsee, C., *The Escalating Terrorism Problem in the United States*, Center for Strategic and International Studies, June 17, 2020.

Jones, S.G., Doxsee, C., Harrington, N., Hwang, G., and Suber, J., *The War Comes Home: The Evolution of Domestic Terrorism in the United States*, Center for Strategic and International Studies Briefs, October 22, 2020.

Joseph, S., "Extending the Right to Life Under the International Covenant on Civil and Political Rights: General Comment 36," 19(2) *Human Rights Law Review* 347, June 2019.

Kalin, W., and Kunzli, J., *The Law of International Human Rights Protection*, Oxford University Press, 2019.

Kaufman, B.M., and Durkin, A., "United States Targeted Killing Litigation Report," in *Litigating Drone Strikes: Challenging the Global Network of Remote Killing*, European Center for Constitutional and Human Rights, 2017.

Klein, A., and Wittes, B., "Preventive Detention in American Theory and Practice," 2 *Harvard National Security Journal* 85, 2011.

Knuckley, S. (ed.), *Drones, and Targeted Killings: Ethics, Law, Politics*, IDebate Press, 2015.

Krebs, S., "Lifting the Veil of Secrecy: Judicial Review of Administrative Detentions in the Israeli Supreme Court," 25(3) *Vanderbilt Journal of Transnational Law* 639, 2012.

Kreps. S.E., and Wallace, G.R., "International Law, Military Effectiveness and Public Support for Drone Strikes," 53(6) *Journal of Peace Research* 830, 2016.

Kurban, D., "Forsaking Individual Justice: The Implications of the European Court of Human Rights' Pilot Judgment Procedure for Victims of Gross and Systematic Violations," 16(4) *Human Rights Review* 731, December 2016.

Legg, A., *The Margin of Appreciation in International Human Rights Law*, Oxford University Press, 2012.

Levy, I., *Deradicalization Programs in Australia and the Foreign Fighter Phenomenon*, International Institute for Counter-Terrorism, IDC Herzliya, Israel, April 2018.

Levy, I., "Why Are There So Few Islamic State Recruits from Israel?," *Georgetown Public Policy Review*, April 1, 2019.

Lewis, L., and Vavrichek, D., *Rethinking the Drone War: National Security, Legitimacy, and Civilian Casualties in U.S. Counterterrorism Operations*, CNA Corporation, Marine Corps University Press, 2016.

Lillich, R.B., "The Paris Minimum Standards of Human Rights Norms in a State of Emergency," 79 *American Journal of International Law* 1072, 1985.

Luban, D., *Torture Evidence and the Guantanamo Military Commissions*, Just Security, May 26, 2021.

Macken, C., *Counter-Terrorism and the Detention of Suspected Terrorists*, Routledge, 2011.

Maes, E., Jonckheere, A., Deblock, M., and Hovine, M., *DETOUR: Towards Pre-Trial Detention as Ultima Ratio*, National Institute for Criminality and Criminology (Be.), October 2016.

Marone, F., *Tackling the Foreign Fighter Threat in Europe*, Italian Institute for International Political Studies, January 9, 2020.

Marone, F., and Vidino, L., *Destination Jihad: Italy's Foreign Fighters*, International Center for Counter-Terrorism – The Hague, March 2019.

Masferrer, A., "The Fragility of Fundamental Rights in the Origins of Modern Constitutionalism," in Masferrer, A. and Walker, C. (eds.), *Counter-Terrorism, Human Rights and the Rule of Law*, Edward Elgar, 2013.

Masters, M., and Regilme Jr., S.S.F., "Human Rights and British Citizenship: The Case of Shamima Begum as Citizen to Homo Sacer," 12 *Journal of Human Rights Practice* 341, September 2020.

Mate, D., and Hayes, R., "Foreign Fighter Returnees: An Indefinite Threat?" 32(8) *Terrorism and Political Violence* 1617, 2020.

Matthews, K., *Justice for the Victims: How Canada Should Manage Returning "Foreign Fighters"*, Canadian Global Affairs Institute Policy Paper, September 2018.

McGuiness, T., and Gower, M., *Deprivation of British Citizenship and Withdrawal of Passport Facilities*, House of Commons Library Briefing Article No. 06820, June 9, 2017.

Meisels, T., "Targeted Killing With Drones? Old Arguments, New Technologies," 29(1) *Philosophy and Society* 1, 2017.

Meleagrou-Hitchens, A., Hughes, S., and Clifford, B., *The Travelers: American Jihadists in Syria and Iraq*, George Washington University Program on Extremism, February 2018.

Melzer, N., *Targeted Killing in International Law*, Oxford University Press, 2008.

Melzer, N., *Interpretive Guidance on the Notion of Direct Participation in Hostilities Under International Humanitarian Law*, International Committee of the Red Cross, 2009.

Mersel, Y., "On Aharon Barak's Activist Image," 47(2) *Tulsa Law Review* 339, 2011.

Merz, F., *Dealing with Jihadist Returnees: A Tough Challenge*, Center for Security Studies ETH Zurich, CSS Analyses in Security Policy, 2017.

Meshel, T., "A Decade Later and Still on Target: Revisiting the 2006 Targeted Killing Decision," 7 *Journal of International Humanitarian Legal Studies* 88, 2016.

Michaelson, C., "Permanent Legal Emergencies and the Derogation Clause in International Human Rights Treaties," in Masferrer, A. (ed.), *Post 9/11 and the State of Permanent Legal Emergency*, Springer, 2012.

Milanovic, M., "Repatriating the Children of Foreign Terrorist Fighters and the Extraterritorial Application of Human Rights," *European Journal of International Law: Talk!*, November 10, 2020.

Ministry of Foreign Affairs of Denmark, *Appendix A: Response by the Government of Denmark to Questions Two and Three from the United Nations Special Rapporteur on Extrajudicial, Summary or Arbitrary Executions on Foreign Fighters*, 2019.

Mirza, R., *Canadian Women in ISIS: Deradicalization and Reintegration for Returnees*, University of Ottawa, 2018.

Mneimneh, H., *Response to "Al-Hawl Camp: A Potential Incubator of the Next Generation of Extremism*, Fikra Forum, Washington Institute For Near East Policy, October 10, 2019.

Nowak, M., and Chabord, A., "Key Trends in the Fight against Terrorism and Key Aspects of International Human Rights Law," in Nowak, M. and Chabord, A. (eds.), *Using Human Rights to Counter Terrorism*, Edward Elgar, 2018.

Nylen, A., and Carpenter, C., "Questions of Life and Death: (De)constructing Human Rights Norms through US Public Opinion," 4(2) *European Journal of International Security*, June 2019.

Oraa, J., *Human Rights in States of Emergency in International Law*, Clarendon Press Oxford, 1992.

Oswald, B., and Winkler, T., "The Copenhagen Process on the Handling of Detainees in International Military Operations, Oct. 19, 2012," 16(39) *American Society of International Law, Insights*, December 26, 2012.

Park, I., *The Right to Life in Armed Conflict*, Oxford University Press, 2018.

Parliament of Australia, Media Release, *Public Hearing on Counter-Terrorism 'Declared Areas'*, September 22, 2020.

Parliament of Australia, Parliamentary Committee on Intelligence and Security, *Review of 'Declared Areas' Provisions, Sections 119.2 and 119.3 of the Criminal Code*, February 2021.

Parliament of Australia, Parliamentary Joint Committee on Intelligence and Security, *Annual Report of Committee Activities 2019–2020*, October 2020.

Pejic, J., "Procedural Principles and Safeguards for Internment/Administrative Detention in Armed Conflict and Other Situations of Violence," 87 *International Review of the Red Cross* 375, 2005.

Pejic, J., "The European Court of Human Rights' Al-Jedda Judgment: The Oversight of International Humanitarian Law," 90 *International Review of the Red Cross* 837, 2011.

Pejic, J., "Extraterritorial Targeting By Means of Armed Drones: Some Legal Implications," 96 *International Review of the Red Cross* 893, 2014.

Pokalova, E., *Returning Islamist Foreign Fighters*, Palgrave Macmillan, 2020.

Popp, G., Canna, S., and Day, J., *Common Characteristics of "Successful" Deradicalization Programs of the Past*, NSI Reachback Report, February 2020.

Pryce, B.J., *Targeting Top Terrorists: Understanding Leadership Removal in Counterterrorism Strategy*, Columbia University Press, 2019.

Pugliese, M., *France and Foreign Fighters: The Controversial Outsourcing of Prosecution*, Italian Institute for International Political Studies, January 9, 2020.

Ragazzi, F., and Walmsley, J., "Member States' Approach to Tackling the Return of Foreign Fighters," in *The Return of Foreign Fighters to EU Soil*, European Parliamentary Research Service, May 2018.

Ramirez, S.G., "The Inter-American Court of Human Rights' Perspective on Terrorism," in Salindade Frias, A.M., Samuel, K.L.H. and White, N.D. (eds.), *Counter-Terrorism, International Law and Practice*, Oxford University Press, 2012.

Raudszus, J., *The Strategy of Germany for Handling Foreign Fighters*, Italian Institute for International Political Studies, January 9, 2020.

Renard, T., and Coolsaet, R., "From the Kingdom to the Caliphate and Back: Returnees in Belgium," in Renard, T. and Coolsaet, R. (eds.), *Who Are They, Why Are They (Not) Coming Back and How Should We Deal with Them? Assessing Policies on Returning Foreign Terrorist Fighters in Belgium, Germany and the Netherlands.* Egmont, February 2018.

Rigterink, A.S., "The Wane of Command: Evidence on Drone Strikes and Control Within Terrorist Organizations," 115(1) *American Political Science Review* 31, 2021.

Rivoire, H. de, *Returning Foreign Terrorist Fighters in Europe: A Comparative Analysis*, Council of Europe and University of Strasbourg, 2017.

Roach, K., *The 9/11 Effect, Comparative Counter-Terrorism*, Cambridge University Press, 2011.

Rodenhauser, T., "Strengthening IHL Protecting Persons Deprived of Their Liberty: Main Aspects of the Consultations and Discussions since 2011," 98(3) *International Review of the Red Cross* 941, 2018.

Roithmaier, K., *Germany and Its Returning Foreign Fighters: New Loss of Citizenship Law and the Broader German Repatriation Landscape*, International Centre for Counter-Terrorism – The Hague, April 19, 2019.

Rosenblatt, N., *'A Caliphate That Gathered:' Addressing the Challenge of Jihadist Foreign Fighter Hubs*, The Washington Institute for Near East Policy, Policy Notes No. 104, April 2021.

Rowling, C.M., Sheets, P., Pettit, W., and Gilmore, J., "Consensus at Home, Opposition Abroad: Officials, Foreign Sources, and US New Coverage of Drone Warfare," 95(4) *Journalism & Mass Communication Quarterly* 886, 2018.

Saar, D., and Wahlhaus, B., "Preventive Detention for National Security Purposes in Israel," 9 *Journal of National Security Law and Policy* 413, 2018.

Saul, B., *Defining Terrorism in International Law*, Oxford University Press, 2006.

Scheinin, M., "Impact of Post 9/11 Counter-Terrorism Measures on All Human Rights," in Nowak, M. and Chabord, A. (eds.), *Using Human Rights to Counter Terrorism*, Edward Elgar, 2018.

Schmid, A.P., "The Definition of Terrorism," in Schmid, A.P., Jongman, A. and Price, E., (eds.), *The Routledge Handbook of Terrorism Research*, Routledge, 2011.

Schmitt, M.N., and Merriam, J.J., "Tyranny in Context: Israeli Targeting Practices in Legal Perspective," 37 *University of Pennsylvania Journal of International Law* 53, 2015.

Seyhan, E., *Liberté, Egalité, Absurdity*, Amnesty International, November 22, 2018.

Shah, A., "Do U.S. Drone Strikes Cause Blowback? Evidence from Pakistan and Beyond," 42(4) *International Security* 47, Spring 2018.

Shamsi, H., *Trump's Secret Rules for Drone Strikes and Presidents' Unchecked License to Kill*, Just Security, May 3, 2021.

Shiel, A., and Woods, C., *A Legacy of Unrecognized Harm: DoD's 2020 Civilian Casualties Report*, Just Security, June 7, 2021.

Shereshevsky, Y., "Targeting the Targeted Killings Case: International Lawmaking in Domestic Contexts," 39(2) *Michigan Journal of International Law* 242, 2018.

Simcox, R., and Dyer, E., *Al-Qaeda in the United States: A Complete Analysis of Terrorist Offenses*, Henry Jackson Society, 2013.

Solis, G.D., *The Law of Armed Conflict*, 2nd ed., Cambridge University Press, 2016.

Sottiaux, S., *Terrorism and the Limitation of Rights*, Hart Publishing, 2008.

State of Israel, *The 2014 Gaza Conflict: Factual and Legal Aspects, (Gaza Report)*, May 2015.

Stein, Y., "Any Name Illegal and Immoral," 17(1) *Ethics and International Affairs* 127, March 2003.

Stewart, D.P., "Terrorism and Human Rights: The Perspective of International Law," *Middle East Institute*, June 2018.

Stigall, D.E., *Counterterrorism and the Comparative Law of Investigative Detention*, Cambria Press, 2009.

Stohl, R., *An Action Plan on U.S. Drone Policy: Recommendations for the Trump Administration*, Stimson, June 2018.

Stohl, R., *Drones and the Development of International Standards*, Stimson, February 4, 2020.

Trenta, L., "The Obama Administration's Conceptual Change: Imminence and the Legitimation of Targeted Killings," 3(1) *European Journal of International Security* 69, 2017.

Trimbach, D.J., and Reisz, N., *Unmaking Citizens: The Expansion of Citizenship Revocation in Response to Terrorism*, Center for Migration Studies, January 30, 2018.

United States Central Command, *Combined Task Force, Operation Inherent Resolve Monthly Civilian Report, Release No. 19–025*, April 25, 2019.

United States Department of Defense, *Law of War Manual*, June 2015 (updated December 2016).

United States Department of Defense, *Annual Report on Civilian Casualties in Connection with United States Military Operations in 2018*, April 29, 2019.

United States Department of Defense, *Annual Report on Civilian Casualties in Connection with United States Military Operations in 2019*, April 22, 2020.

United States Department of Defense, *Annual Report on Civilian Casualties in Connection with United States Military Operations in 2020*, April 29, 2021.

United States Department of Defense, Office of Inspector General, '*Operation Inherent Resolve:' Lead Inspector General Report to the United States Congress, April 1 2019–June 30 2019*,' July 2019.

United States Department of Defense, Press Release, *Statement by the Department of Defense*, January 2, 2020.

United States Department of Homeland Security, *Homeland Threat Assessment*, October 2020.

United States Department of Justice, Office of the Inspector General, *A Review of the Department's Use of the Material Witness Statute with a Focus on Select National Security Matters, (Redacted)*, September 2014.

United States Department of Justice, White Paper, *Lawfulness of a Lethal Operation Directed against a U.S. Citizen Who Is a Senior Operational Leader of Al-Qaeda or an Associated Force*, Draft, June 8, 2011.

United States Department of State, *Country Reports on Terrorism 2019.*

United States Department of State, *Denmark 2018 Human Rights Report.*

United States Department of State, Bureau of Counterterrorism, *Country Reports on Terrorism 2018*, October 2019.

United States Department of State, Office of the Spokesperson, *Briefing with Acting Special Envoy for the Global Coalition to Defeat ISIS, John Godfrey on U.S. Participation in the Upcoming D-ISIS Ministerial, Special Briefing, via Teleconference*, March 29, 2021.

United States Director of National Intelligence, *Summary of the Reengagement of Detainees Formerly Hels at Guantanamo Bay, Cuba*, 2016.

United States Government, *The National Security Strategy*, September 2002.

United States House of Representatives Committee of Foreign Affairs, Press Release, *Engel Statement on the White House's Latest Justification for Soleimani Killing*, February 14, 2020.

U.S. Department of Justice, Office of Public Affairs, *ISIS Militants Charged with Deaths of Americans in Syria*, October 7, 2020.

Waas, L. van, and Jaghai, S., "All Citizens Are Created Equal, But Some Are More Equal Than Others," 65 *Netherlands International Law Review* 413, 2018.

Wautelet, P., "Deprivation of Citizenship for 'Jihadists:' Analysis of Belgian and French Practice and Policy in the Light of the Principle of Equal Treatment," in Kruiniger, P. (ed.), *Jihad, Islam and the Law: Jihadism and Reactions from the Netherlands and Belgium*, B.J.U., 2017.

Webber, D., "Hassan v. United Kingdom: A New Approach to Security Detention in Armed Conflict?" 19(7) *American Society of International Law Insights*, April 2, 2015.

Webber, D., "Preventive and Administrative Detention," in Binder, C., Nowak, M., Hofbauer, J.A. and Janig, P. (eds.), *Elgar Encyclopedia of Human Rights*, Edward Elgar Publishing, forthcoming 2022.

Webber, D., *Preventive Detention of Terror Suspects: A New Legal Framework*, Routledge, 2016.

Weill, S., "French Foreign Fighters: The Engagement of Administrative and French Criminal Justice in France," 100 *International Review of the Red Cross* 211, 2018.

Weill, S., *Terror in Courts, French Counter-Terrorism: Administrative and Penal Avenues*, Report for the official visit of the U.N. Special Rapporteur on Counter-Terrorism and Human Rights, May 2018.

Weizmann, N., "Armed Drones and the Law of Armed Conflict," in Casey-Maslen, S., Homayounnejad, M., Stauffer, H. and Weizmann, N. (eds.), *Drones and Other Unmanned Weapons Under International Law*, Brill Nijhoff, 2018.

The White House, *National Security Strategy*, May 2010.

The White House, *National Security Strategy of the United States of America*, December 2017.

The White House, *National Strategy for Countering Domestic Terrorism*, June 2021.

The White House, *Notice on the Legal and Policy Frameworks Guiding the United States' Use of Military Force and Related National Security Operations: United States Military Action against Qassem Soleimani*, February 14, 2020.

The White House, *Presidential Policy Guidance, Procedures for Approving Direct Action Against Terrorist Targets Located Outside the United States and Areas of Active Hostilities*, May 22, 2013.

The White House Briefing Room, *Statements and Releases, Interim National Security Strategic Guidance*, March 3, 2021.

Winkler, T., "The Copenhagen Process and the Copenhagen Process Principles and Guidelines on the Handling of Detainees in International Military Operations: Challenges, Criticism and the Way Ahead," 5 *Journal of International Humanitarian Legal Studies* 258, 2014.

Women's International League for Peace and Freedom, *The Humanitarian Impact of Drones*, Women's International League for Peace and Freedom, International Disarmament Institute, Pace University, October 2017.

Wright, R., "Despite Trump's Guantanamo Threats, Americans Who Joined ISIS Are Quietly Returning Home," *The New Yorker*, June 11, 2019.

Yakare-Oule, N., Reventlow, J., and Curling, R., "The Unique Jurisdiction of the African Court on Human and Peoples' Rights: Protection of Human Rights Beyond the African Charter," 333 *Emory International law Review* 203, 2019.

Zedner, L., "Citizenship Deprivation, Security and Human Rights," 18 *European Journal of Migration and Law* 222, 2016.

Zhirukhina, E., *Foreign Fighters from Central Asia: Between Renunciation and Repatriation*, Italian Institute for International Political Studies, October 3, 2019.

Zwanenburg, M., "The 'External Element' of the Obligation to Ensure Respect for the Geneva Conventions," 97 *International Law Studies* 621, 2021.

Index